American Treasure

The Enduring Spirit of the DAR

THE
DONNING COMPANY
PUBLISHERS

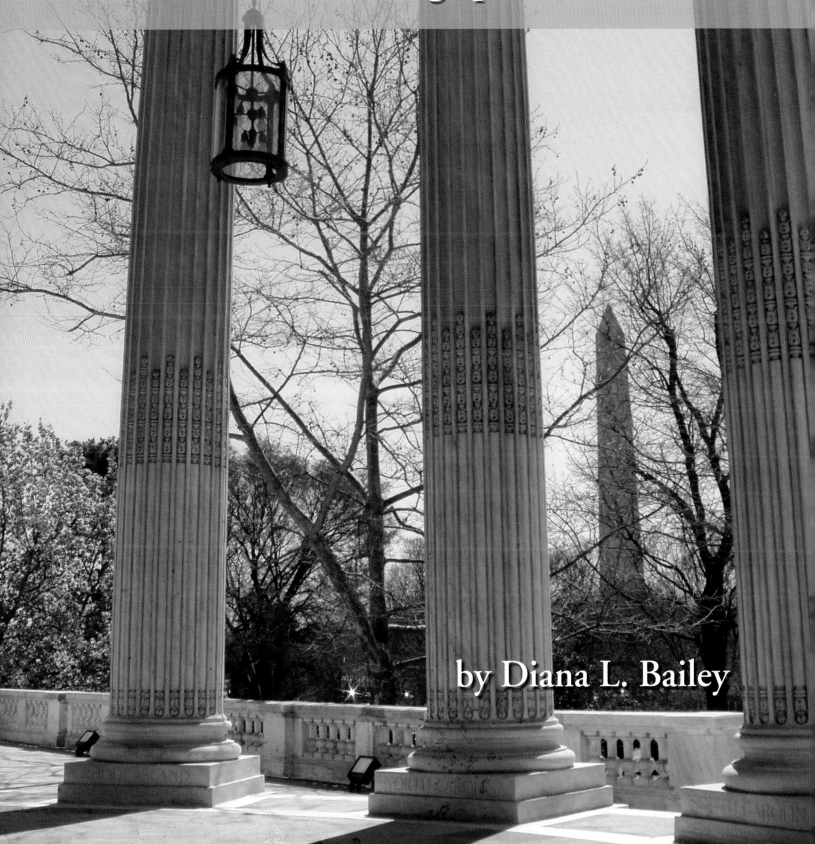

American Treasure
The Enduring Spirit of the DAR

by Diana L. Bailey

Dedication

To my grandmother,
Laura Elizabeth Meadows Lentz Parker,
author, painter, businesswoman, and world traveler,
never a Daughter but ever dazzling.

The Donning Company Publishers
184 Business Park Drive, Suite 206
Virginia Beach, VA 23462

Steve Mull, General Manager
Barbara Buchanan, Office Manager
Pamela Koch, Editor
Amy Thomann, Graphic Designer
Derek Eley, Imaging Artist
Lori Porter, Project Research Coordinator
Scott Rule, Director of Marketing
Tonya Hannink, Marketing Coordinator

Dennis N. Walton, Project Director

Bren Landon, DAR Project Manager

Library of Congress Cataloging-in-Publication Data

Bailey, Diana L., 1950-
  American treasure : the enduring spirit of the DAR / by Diana L. Bailey.
       p. cm.
  Includes bibliographical references and index.
  ISBN 978-1-57864-413-1 (hardcover : alk. paper)
  1. Daughters of the American Revolution--History. 2. Daughters of the American Revolution--History--Pictorial works. I. Title.
  E202.5.A19B35 2007
  369'.135--dc22

                              2007000158

Printed in the United States of America at Walsworth Publishing Company

Endsheet Photos: DAR members in action. Photos courtesy of NSDAR, its chapters and members.

National Society Daughters of the American Revolution
1776 D Street, NW
Washington, DC 20006-5303

The first time I attended Continental Congress at the age of twenty-five was an exciting, eye opening experience . . . and one that changed my life forever. In that brief trip, not only did I marvel at the grandeur of our national headquarters, but I also came to appreciate two fundamental facts about DAR: that the true spirit of DAR is best reflected by those who give of themselves in service to others; and that our focus on historic preservation, education, and patriotism provides an incredibly wide range of opportunities for serving one's community and country.

Since 1890, Daughters have worked tirelessly within their communities to protect the legacy bequeathed to us by our nation's Founding Fathers and all those throughout our history who have labored to preserve our American heritage and way of life for future generations. The founders of our Society were prescient women who created an organization that, for over a century, has influenced the lives of so many individuals in this country and around the world. Their enthusiasm and devotion have inspired hundreds of thousands of women through the years to give of their time, energy, and talents in volunteer efforts locally, nationally, and globally.

While looking back at the organization's fascinating past, *American Treasure* also celebrates the contemporary DAR and the commitment of its members to preserving our nation's history, promoting education, and encouraging a true sense of patriotism and love of country. Through its beautiful photos and text, this book accomplishes all that I had hoped for when the project was conceived. It truly depicts the many facets of our organization and illustrates that there are possibilities for service in DAR for people of diverse backgrounds and interests. We can be proud to be a positive force in our society and the embodiment of the true spirit of America.

Please enjoy this beautiful book.

Presley Merritt Wagoner
President General, 2004–2007

Contents

Acknowledgments

"We may destroy all the men in America, and we shall still have all we can do to defeat the women."

—British General Lord Charles Cornwallis

Those words of General Cornwallis emerged early in the year of research it took to produce this work. Struck initially by what I thought was his wit, I jotted down the quote, thinking to use it somewhere in the text. Over the course of this project, however, I came to know there was less humor and more truth in his pronouncement. General Cornwallis knew first-hand what the British faced in their attempt to quell the American Revolution, having fought in the war from 1776 to his surrender at Yorktown in 1781. He witnessed the bravery of the patriots, men and women of diverse origins who eventually defeated the better trained and outfitted British army through passionate commitment to their cause.

That same passionate commitment lives on in the Daughters of the American Revolution. The letters and records, books, artifacts, and places that continue to be preserved and shared by the Daughters piece together the story of American history as intimate and tangible as the lovely quilts in their incredible collection. With each step in this project, I was reminded again and again, as with the Cornwallis quote, that there is a deeper dimension to history than facts and figures and dates. In telling the story of the Daughters of yesterday and today, I learned so much more about my own American heritage. So, first and foremost, I thank the more than 850,000 Daughters since 1890 who have done so much to capture and preserve the American spirit.

A book of this size and scope is nearly impossible without a team or, in this case, a team of teams. In addition to all the Daughters, certain DAR members and staff had a vision for this project that guided every step. President General Presley Merritt Wagoner believed sincerely that it was time for a new chapter in the DAR story, one that focused on today's DAR. Stephen Nordholt, NSDAR Administrator, was a calming arbiter of the creative process. Merry Ann Wright, Director of Development, became a kindred spirit who shared her wonderful sense of not only the history and values but also the future of the Society. The tireless commitment of Public Relations Manager Bren Landon to both the Society and this project never wavered; I couldn't have told this story without her. Although new to the Public Relations team, Web Content Coordinator Elizabeth Ertner quickly shared the vision and helped immeasurably with insights and support. Eloquent, talented Director of Archives and History Tracy Robinson and her staff, especially Archivist Alisa Johnson (now nicknamed "the research goddess") as well as Sara Cheeseman, Amanda Fulcher, Christina Lehman, and Elizabeth Roscio committed so much of their time, trust, knowledge, and resources to this project. Jennifer Savage, Congress and Special Projects Coordinator, helped to gather information and kept me straight on the workings of Continental Congress. In various interviews, Museum Director and Chief Curator Diane Dunkley and her staff—Geni Ellerbee, Olive Graffam, Alden O'Brien, Anne Ruta, and Patrick Sheary—provided wonderful glimpses into the Museum's priceless collections and period rooms. Library Director Eric Grundset, vanguard of one of the top genealogical resources in the nation, helped me understand the unique nature of the vast collection in the DAR Library. Super sleuth Terry Ward, Genealogy Director and Head Genealogist, shared both the excitement and challenge of genealogical research. Constitution Hall Managing Director and humorist Paul Guilderson shared wonderful stories of what it takes to operate what remains the largest concert hall in Washington. Events and Meetings Manager Peggy Martz quickly became one of this book's most passionate fans, sharing photos, stories, and marketing ideas. Special thanks extend to Edith Rianzares, Printing and Publications Director, who provided unlimited access to the century of history found in the bound volumes of the DAR magazine. Both Edith and Courtney Peter, Publications Coordinator, meticulously reviewed the text. Glenna Acord, Chapter Services Manager, explained the enormous task of providing service to the more than 3,000 DAR chapters worldwide. Security Director Larry Walker and his staff were especially patient and helpful—with both access and parking—during my long hours of research at NSDAR Headquarters. There are countless others behind the scenes whom I never had the pleasure of meeting but who also keep the headquarters facilities and operations running; for all they do, I want to thank them as well.

More than forty individuals shared their time and experiences in personal interviews. Some of those who deserve special thanks include Honorary Presidents General Sarah M. King, Marie H. Yochim, and Dorla Dean E. Kemper; Recording Secretary General Linda Calvin; committee chairmen Joy Cardinal, Char Edson, Carole Farmer, Molly Hawn, Debbie Jamison, Mindy Kammeyer, Laura Kessler, Denise VanBuren, Janet Whittington, and Pamela Wright; members Acquanetta Anderson, Peggy Brookshire, Nancy Daniels, Patricia Dennert, Mary Ned Fotis, Verna Graybill, Gayle Harris, Suzanne Heske, Pazetta Mallette, Patricia Mayer, Mary Ann Philyaw, Dorrie Traficante, Virginia Russell, Anita Speir, and Alice Stratton for their personal stories and photos; and Dr. Allan Keiler and Hugh Price for perspectives on DAR events only they could provide. I also want to thank Daughters Judy Adams, Kiki Dayton, and Sarah Turnbaugh for making me feel so welcome—and somewhat less intimidated—at my first DAR Continental Congress.

There are so many Daughters and others who helped along the way, providing information and photos. Although too many to mention individually, they provided a depth of understanding that I hope allowed me to tell a better story. I wish we could have used everything sent or shared, but that would have required volumes rather than a single book!

The Donning Company Publishers gave me my start in this business more than twenty-five years ago. Their team support has continued with this project, especially Dennis Walton, project manager, always there when I need him; Pamela Koch, patient editor; Amy Thomann, talented designer; Derek Eley, imaging artist; Barbara Buchanan, office manager; and all the other folks at Donning and their parent company, Walsworth. Nancy Allen, my friend and former co-worker, became an awesome editorial assistant who often restored order to the towering stacks of files and notes. Photographers F. T. Eyre and John H. Sheally II, and reporter Phyllis Speidell provided generously of their time and talents as well.

Thanks finally to the home team, my husband Kenneth and all my family and friends who endured my many absences and distractions during the long months when I had to focus solely on the book, and to my muse, who keeps me learning and growing.

As a final note, while every effort was made to verify all information, including reviews by many of the experts listed here, no work such as this is ever perfect. What made this project particularly daunting is the knowledge that nearly every one of the approximately 168,000 current DAR members is also an expert in at least one area. Therefore your feedback is welcome. I hope you find this story of the Daughters as fascinating as I did.

Diana L. Bailey
April 2007

CHAPTER ONE

Today's Daughters
A Proper Introduction

Wᵢₜₕ ITH MORE THAN A CENTURY OF SERVICE, over 850,000 members admitted since its founding, and countless programs serving communities around the world, the portrayal of the National Society Daughters of the American Revolution is so rich that one book can do little justice to its storied accomplishments. In fact, thousands of stories, some of which have never been told, only begin to tell the unique and compelling story of the Daughters and their Society, whose simple mission of preservation, education, and patriotism—the enduring focus of the DAR—remain the timeless, overarching principles that have ensured its perennial strength.

The four founders, the authors of that unwavering mission, were women of substance forced to support their families after devastating losses, women who carved out a life for themselves that echoed those principles even before the Society took shape. The early Daughters were reformers—progressive, creative thinkers who changed the world around them. That same drive persists in today's members. With the current membership at nearly 168,000 and with chapters around the globe, the nonprofit Society awards nearly $1 million a year in scholarships to outstanding scholars; supports six DAR schools; stages hundreds of events for schoolchildren to promote knowledge of our nation's history; recognizes, through ceremonies and medals, thousands of individuals who capture in word and deed the founding spirit of America; and much, much more.

The NSDAR and its chapters both recognize and support American veterans through more than 300,000 hours of volunteer effort annually, including over 60,000 hours at Veterans Affairs hospitals and centers, thereby allowing the critical care professionals to

▶ Cultural Tourism DC, a nonprofit tourism coalition, describes Memorial Continental Hall as "the epicenter of an active DAR," but also a unique D.C. destination. Located two blocks from the White House, directly across from the Ellipse, in the shadow of the Washington Monument and within easy walking distance of the World War II Memorial (built in part with funds contributed by the DAR), it lies in the heart of Washington's most popular tourist attractions. More and more visitors are discovering the treasures at DAR National Headquarters, including its decorative arts museum with its changing exhibits and period rooms, its genealogical library, and its rare manuscript collection, all of which are open to the public.

PHOTO BY BRIANA BAKER

focus on medical and rehabilitative care for returning veterans. DAR members are devoted to supporting active military personnel, both at home and abroad, through shipments of care packages and letter-writing campaigns. Each year, through its chapters, the DAR helps thousands of individuals become citizens. Equally as generous with their funding as they are with their time, individual members, chapters, and state societies have raised millions of dollars to mark and preserve those places both big and small—from battlefields, buildings, and monuments to unmarked graves—where American history was made.

The first DAR Headquarters, Memorial Continental Hall, dedicated in 1905, remains one of the most beautiful and historic buildings in downtown Washington, D.C. Constitution Hall, completed in 1929, continues that tradition as a stage for world events and a cultural hub for the Washington community. Both are Registered National Historic Landmarks. Unique tourism destinations, the DAR Museum and Americana Room—open to the public free of charge—house, preserve, and display thousands of artifacts and documents from the nation's rich past. The DAR Library—also open to the public—is one of the country's most renowned resources

▲ Students attending the 2005 DAR Quilt Camp examine one of the approximately 400 antique quilts and other textiles stored in the DAR Museum's climate-controlled Landes-Luyben Quilt Repository, one of the finest in the country. After a bit of "hands-on" time (with gloves!) under the supervision of Curator of Education Kelli Scott (left), who explains the details and workmanship of one of the quilts in the collection, campers get pointers and the opportunity to make their own quilt squares. "Now I know how to hand-stitch," said Emma Kelly, an eleven-year-old camper. The camp, which began in 1996, includes field trips to such places as the Department of the Interior to learn about Native American quilts and the Smithsonian National Museum of American History where they learn about the conservation of the "Star-Spangled Banner." The DAR sponsors the camp as part of its mission of education, showcasing such aspects of day-to-day life in Colonial America as the history and tradition of quilting and how the Society preserves and exhibits the antique quilts in its collection. The quilt repository was dedicated in December 2001 using funds donated to honor Daughters Helen Louise Landes and Beatrice Delphine Landes Luyben. In addition to keeping both temperature and humidity at a constant level, the repository maximizes storage of the Museum's entire collection of quilts and coverlets with room for more.

▲ Members of the Nelly Custis Chapter of the Virginia Daughters of the American Revolution walk June 1, 2002, in the Susan G. Komen Race for the Cure, the annual five-kilometer march for breast cancer research, in downtown Washington, D.C. Pictured are (left-right) Mary Beth Brookshire (in hat), Donna Porcaro (in rear, partially obscured), Melissa Mitchell, Peggy Brookshire, Julie Doyle, Sharon McMahon, Jacqui McMahon, and Amy Cook.

▲ Visitors take in one of the displays at the opening of Forgotten Patriots: African American and American Indian Service in the Revolutionary War 1775–1783. Opening October 18, 2002, and extended through August 30, 2003, the popular exhibit illuminated, in many cases for the first time, the roles that these patriots played in the battle for American independence. It featured such revolutionaries as James Armistead Lafayette, a slave from New Kent County, Virginia, who served the Marquis de Lafayette near Portsmouth and Yorktown, Virginia, as well as Agrippa Hull, a free black who served as an orderly for General Tadeusz Kościuszko, General George Washington's chief engineer. General Washington was especially interested in seeing that the Penobscot Indians joined the patriotic cause, and included in the exhibit was a portrait of John Neptune, one of the many Penobscot men who fought for the Americans.

◀ Chapter Regent Eunice Merrill, of the John Kendrick Chapter of Wenatchee, Washington, places a wreath at a Memorial Day service at Evergreen Memorial Cemetery. Each year, Daughters organize and participate in hundreds of activities to commemorate important events in American history, celebrating milestones such as the Lewis and Clark Expedition and the Victory at Yorktown, and national holidays like Veterans Day and Independence Day.

◄ Although now the permanent home of the Library, renovations to the Daughters' first home preserved the exquisite features of Memorial Continental Hall, from the richly embellished clock, a gift of the Baltimore Chapter in 1907, to the intricate railing on the balconies. Twenty-five skylights shed light on researchers some sixty feet below. This unique setting provides researchers with one of the most extensive genealogical libraries in the country.

▲ Major Ladda "Tammy" Duckworth shakes hands with Staff Sergeant Heath T. Calhoun at a reception prior to the National Defense Night program of the 2005 114th Continental Congress. Pictured in the center is President General Presley Merritt Wagoner. Staff Sergeant Calhoun, who lost both his legs in Iraq, received both the DAR Medal of Honor and the Outstanding Veteran-Patient of the Year Award. The awards recognized his courageous service and sacrifice overseas, as well as his determination to assist and inspire other wounded soldiers returning from the war. The Levisa River Chapter, of the small town of Grundy, Virginia, raised more than $36,000 to buy a specially equipped vehicle for Staff Sergeant Calhoun, a native of their county. Major Duckworth, who lost her legs as a result of injuries she received when the helicopter she was piloting was shot down outside Baghdad, received the Margaret Cochran Corbin Award for Distinguished Women in Military Service. The award is named for the patriot who rose to fire her husband's cannon after he was mortally wounded during the American Revolution; Corbin became the first woman to receive a pension from the United States government.

for genealogical research, where staff and volunteer genealogists assist both members and citizens alike in uncovering and understanding their own pasts. The complex represents one of the most valuable pieces of property owned by women anywhere in the world.

While their impressive NSDAR headquarters complex is one of the most visible aspects of DAR in the nation's capital, Daughters across the country and the world remain the organization's real ambassadors in local communities. As members of nearly 3,000 chapters, they are the backbone of the Society. Each year, the Daughters gather at their headquarters in Washington at one singular event, Continental Congress, to reaffirm their founding principles, honor the nation's heroes and outstanding youth, and celebrate accomplishments and friendships. They come from all walks of life and, while their interests vary, every member is committed to furthering the organization's founding principles of historic preservation, education, and patriotism.

A variety of programs are drawn from each of the three objectives, which are not mutually exclusive. The Daughters under-

PHOTO COURTESY OF GENERAL FRANCIS NASH CHAPTER

▲ In 1955, the Daughters urged Congress to set aside September 17–23 annually to be dedicated to the observance of Constitution Week. The weeklong commemoration of this precious document—the supreme law of the United States of America—emphasizes citizens' responsibilities for protecting and defending the Constitution and preserving it for posterity; reinforces that the Constitution is the basis for America's great heritage and the foundation for our way of life; and encourages the study of the historical events that led to the framing of the Constitution in September 1787. Dwight D. Eisenhower approved the national holiday in 1956, and over half a century later Daughters are still as actively involved as ever in the tradition of celebrating the Constitution. Pictured here, members Jill Adkins, Andrea D. Lawrence, and Alice K. Ross fill the halls of Hume-Fogg Academic High School in Nashville, Tennessee, handing out Constitution Week flyers and brochures.

PHOTO BY MEGAN WOLLERHAN

◄ At a multichapter event in the summer of 2005, DAR members gather toiletries, DVDs, magazines, and other personal items to be shipped to wounded troops at Landstuhl Regional Medical Center, Germany, as part of DAR Project Patriot. Daughters from the following New York chapters participated: Brooklyn, Knickerbocker, Mary Washington Colonial, New York City, and Peter Minuit. Pictured in the foreground (l-r) are Caroline Hensel Contiguglia, Molly Ker Hawn, and Lisa Wood Shapiro. Formed following the events of September 11, 2001, the DAR Project Patriot Committee worked with the Department of the Navy to sponsor the crew of an aircraft carrier as a show of support for Operation Enduring Freedom. In the first phase of DAR Project Patriot, the Department of Defense assigned the aircraft carrier USS *John C. Stennis* to the DAR for sponsorship. Support to the crew included more than 5,000 prepaid phone cards, 3,200 exercise mats for the crew, and more than 10,000 holiday greeting and thank-you cards, as well as 5,200 "patriot packages" filled with personal items.

▲ The combined collections of the DAR Library and Americana Room, coupled with the enormous, unique holdings of the DAR Museum, offer a treasure trove of more than half a million rare artifacts, documents, historical imprints, manuscripts, records, and genealogies, all of which are available to the public through exhibits and displays or a visit to the Library. Pictured here is just a small sample. From "how-to" books for the beginner to writing your family history and even step-by-step guides for becoming a recognized genealogical expert, the Library offers valuable tools to verify lineage. This sampler (top left) from the Museum collection highlights an incredible example of schoolgirl art that captures family history. Hundreds of precious family Bibles in both the Library and Americana collections cover the period from the seventeenth to the early twentieth century. Intricate family trees, such as those pictured at bottom from the Library collection, reflect centuries of lineage. And in the bucolic watercolor family record at right, completed in 1846 by fifteen-year-old Emeline Newcomb of the Quincy South School in Massachusetts, intersecting rings link the names and birth dates of her extended family.

◄ From the small stone marking the grave of a forgotten patriot to the grandest national monument, such as the Statue of Liberty, the DAR has devoted millions of dollars to preserving these symbols of American history.

stand and teach that preservation and education are both essential components to patriotism, and that an understanding of our history and the sacrifices of our ancestors is essential to comprehending the meaning of freedom. The same is true of the Society itself: to understand what it means to be a Daughter requires an appreciation of how the organization evolved, changing with the times yet remaining true to its mission.

American Treasure: The Enduring Spirit of the DAR, in pictures more than words, looks at today's DAR against the backdrop of the past, with a glimpse of its future. Through hundreds of illustrations demonstrating the work provided through thousands of chapters, the succeeding pages explore the many programs and contributions of the DAR, a Society still vibrant and relevant in its second century of service.

PHOTO COURTESY SALLIE M. GROW

▶ State DAR organizations and many individual chapters preserve, maintain, and furnish historic homes throughout the country, such as the luxurious 1860 Italianate Richards DAR House Museum in Mobile, Alabama. The six DAR chapters in Mobile furnish the house and administer it as a museum. The Daughters not only open such homes to the public but also use them for various DAR meetings and functions.

PHOTO COURTESY HILLSIDE SCHOOL

◀ Hillside School teacher Dan Roy instructs three eager students during a tutorial session. "All of us here at Hillside know how much the DAR does for us, but it is especially nice to receive personal recognition at the end of the year . . . to be reminded of past successes," wrote student Roderick Caruso, a rising senior, in a recent letter to one of the chapters. Hillside is just one of six schools funded annually by more than $1 million from the Daughters to provide a variety of special needs programs that address problems such as attention deficit disorder, dyslexia, adult literacy, and children in family crisis. Stated one grateful fourteen-year-old student of Tamassee, another DAR school, "If there wasn't a [Tamassee] DAR School, then I would be on the streets with my brother begging for food. Tamassee has given me a chance to make something of myself." DAR schools represent an enormous commitment that began with a handful of Daughters at the beginning of the twentieth century. Each of these schools is given assistance by DAR members, including scholarships, material donations, and genuine personal interest. Through its American Indians Committee, the DAR also assists in the education of Indian youth through scholarships and support of two schools with special programs serving Native Americans.

CHAPTER TWO

Daughters Unite
The Legacy Begins

J UST AS AN UNDERSTANDING OF OUR NATION'S PAST is essential to its future, so a prologue of the Daughters' past is necessary to understand the strength and determination that will ensure their continued success.

The Daughters of the American Revolution, among other organizations, grew out of the late-nineteenth-century fervor of the Colonial Revival. One event helped concentrate this passion for the past. On May 10, 1876, the world joined the nation in the opening of one of the grandest birthday parties ever thrown—the Centennial Exposition in Philadelphia. Some ten million people attended the nation's first international exposition, and one exhibit in particular seemed to capture the longings of American hearts after so many battles on so many fronts: "A reconstruction of a 'colonial kitchen' replete with spinning wheel and cos-tumed presenters sparked an era of 'Colonial Revival' in American architecture and house furnishings," as described in more than one reference.

In the first one hundred years after its fight for independence, America, more concerned with its future than its brief past, was absorbed alternately with forming and refining its own unique democracy, exploring and expanding the continent, fighting another war with England in 1812, and reuniting the nation after the bitter battles of the Civil War. At the end of that war, the country was free again to pursue what it considered its "Manifest

▶ The first resolution passed by the new National Society Daughters of the American Revolution, at its first meeting October 11, 1890, was a pledge "that we make it our first work to aid in the completion of the monument to the mother of Washington." From the very beginning, the Daughters proved their generosity by raising nearly three-fourths of the $11,500 needed for the project. Mary Ball Washington, mother of George Washington, was buried in 1789 in Fredericksburg, Virginia, beside "Meditation Rock," an outcropping near her daughter Betty Washington Lewis's house, where Mary had "prayed for the safety of her son and country during the dark days of the Revolution." Gravestones, such as that pictured in the foreground, marked the burial sites of subsequent owners of the homestead beginning in 1819. However, at the time, there was no marker suitable to set apart the grave of the mother of America's first president. The DAR joined forces with the National Mary Washington Memorial Association, and at last, President Grover Cleveland dedicated the present monument on May 10, 1894. The simple obelisk bears only two inscriptions. One side reads, "Mary the Mother of Washington." The opposite side states simply, "Erected by her country-women."

▲ Only months after founding, questions abounded as to the Society's purpose and intended membership, so organizers hosted a grand reception attended by scores of guests. The reception was a huge success, and while the reception apparently put the questions to rest, that event and others (such as this reenactment of a colonial tea by one of the chapters) have at times eclipsed the service of one of the largest philanthropic service organizations in the world. In this circa 1930 photo, President General Edith Irwin Hobart (standing at left) attends a special event staged by one of the chapters, most likely in celebration of the fortieth anniversary of the Society. Some of those pictured are dressed to portray various characters in either DAR or American history. The woman standing third from left, dressed in an early nurse uniform, represents the role the DAR played in founding the Army Nurse Corps, while the figure sixth from the left portrays a Native American woman, possibly Sacagawea. Surely that is Martha Washington reincarnated seated at far left, and the woman next to her wears the somber colors of a suffragist, so many of whom, such as Susan B. Anthony, were among the first to join the Society. A Puritan woman seated second from right personifies those early settlers seeking freedom from religious persecution. The woman standing at far right is wearing a dress in the style of that worn by Caroline Scott Harrison, the first NSDAR President General.

Destiny" to occupy the continent from "sea to shining sea." But following the Centennial Exposition, suddenly the art and architecture, personal possessions, and histories of the founding fathers and mothers became American treasures to be preserved.

Initially, the Daughters thought to join the Sons of the American Revolution, organized in 1889, in what seemed a common mission: to perpetuate the memory and spirit of the Revolutionary patriots. But at a meeting of the Sons in Louisville, Kentucky, on April 30, 1890, the Sons voted to exclude women, galvanizing a force as determined as that which fought for American independence. As Letitia Green Stevenson would later write in her 1913 account of the Society's founding: "It became apparent that if women were to accomplish any distinctive patriotic work, it must be within their own circle, and under their own leadership. The ardor and zeal of a few undaunted women never flagged, and their determination to organize a distinct woman's society became a fixed purpose."

The morning after the Sons' fateful vote, "American women throughout the country read the account in the newspapers and were stirred with indignation," a sentiment documented for posterity in the first annual report to Congress of the newly organized National Society Daughters of the American Revolution. One of those women, Mary Smith Lockwood, widow of a Union soldier, noted author and women's rights advocate, channeled her reaction in a stirring letter to the *Washington Post* printed July 13, 1890. In it, she recounted the thrilling story of the heroic Hannah Arnett, who courageously challenged a meeting of men hosted by her husband in their home, shaming them into supporting the cause of revolution. Mary Lockwood ended her letter with these questions: "Were there no mothers of the Revolution? Where will the Sons and Daughters of the Revolution place Hannah Arnett?" Her questions would be answered swiftly and by hundreds.

The first to respond was William O. McDowell of New York, who had assisted in organizing the Sons of the American Revolution in that city. He also happened to be the great-grandson of Hannah Arnett and, from the first, had voted against the exclusion of women. McDowell immediately joined the debate. In his own letter that appeared in the *Post* only days later, on July 21, he offered to assist any women descended from Revolutionary heroes in forming their own society. Six women responded to this call, including Mary Desha, to whom McDowell forwarded the names and addresses of those who had replied.

Not even Washington's sultry summer heat, which normally transformed the nation's capital into a sleepy ghost town, could tamp the fires of debate that suddenly burned so brightly. A

▲ Ellen Hardin Walworth was staying at Langham Hall, located at the corner of 14th and H streets, NW, in Washington, D.C., when she hosted a meeting August 9, 1890, to propose a society such as DAR. Because of a severe Washington thunderstorm that evening, only three of the four intended guests attended: Eugenia Washington, Mary Desha, and their hostess, Ellen Hardin Walworth. Mary Smith Lockwood, whose letter in the *Post* had set such events in motion, was kept away by the storm. Courtesy of the Historical Society of Washington, D.C.

▶ As Daughter Ann Arnold Hunter wrote in *A Century of Service*, of those first women who organized the NSDAR: "Inevitably, there would be misunderstandings. Women of strong personality, laboring to found an enduring society, competed for control." One of those strong personalities was Flora Adams Darling, who was also corresponding with William O. McDowell. She was not present for the first meeting at Mrs. Walworth's when the constitution was adopted and the officers and board of management had been proposed. A date and place had also already been set for the first organizing meeting, but Mrs. Darling apparently wanted desperately to be credited as founder, even though she had not been in town all summer. Aware of the meeting, and in a transparent attempt at takeover, Mrs. Darling also sent letters of invitation, oddly enough to the same meeting October 11 at Mrs. Lockwood's residence at the Strathmore Arms, emphasizing that she was bringing Mr. McDowell. In fact, she even chaired the meeting, albeit at Mrs. Lockwood's home. While she would resign from the Society on August 7, 1891, less than one year after its founding, in protest over its refusal, among other things, to allow a chapter to be named for a living member (including her), she is credited with the NSDAR's motto. It was at her suggestion during the first year that the original, "Amor Patriae" be amended to "Home and Country." The motto became "God, Home and Country" during the administration of Jeannette O. Baylies, 1977–1980. Immediately after leaving the DAR, Darling founded the Daughters of the Revolution in New York and later the U.S. Daughters of 1812.

A Mark of Distinction

Like the National Society's mission, the DAR insignia also remains virtually unaltered from its original design, adopted on May 26, 1891. A member of the NSDAR Advisory Board, Dr. George Brown Goode—who was also on the staff of the Smithsonian and whose wife was chairman of the Committee on Insignia—recommended a design suggested by his grandmother's spinning wheel, the same one that now resides in the DAR Museum collection.

European colonists brought the spinning wheel when they came to North America, and the early Daughters agreed that both its origin and its symbolism—a machine employing "revolution" and one so closely identified with "women's work"—was the perfect symbol for their new society. The design for the wheel included thirteen spokes and thirteen stars for each of the thirteen original colonies, and a distaff filled with flax resting beneath the wheel.

J. E. Caldwell & Company, long-established jewelers in Philadelphia, was one of those companies submitting a proposal to manufacture the insignia. Although their design was not accepted, they offered not only to pay the cost of registering the patent but also to assume the expense of making the dies, a substantial sum even then. As was noted in the 1906 *Story of the Records*, "For that liberal offer in the days of a somewhat depleted treasury, Caldwell & Co. became the official jewelers of the Daughters of the American Revolution."

Daughters today proudly wear their individually numbered, 14-carat gold and enamel insignia with platinum flax on their ribbon, the distinctive borders of blue and white inspired by George Washington's staff. Each carefully chosen component carries special meaning, as one unidentified Daughter would write for the DAR magazine long ago:

> **The Hub**—A Daughter's loyal heart
> **Each Spoke**—A thought of those who part
> **The Rim/Wheel**—A noble life's bright round
> **Each Star**—A deed in Heaven's profound
> **The Distaff**—A guide that points above
> **Each Flaxen Thread**—A cord of love

PHOTO BY SCOTT BRAMAN

▲ A Daughter's pins are her pride and joy, for each one reflects a step on the ladder of her journey with the DAR. Worn with her insignia pin only for official DAR events, the sash of miniature eagles and sailing ships, quill pins and scrolls, flowers and bells, laurel wreaths and trees, and crosses and scepters symbolize memberships and offices held, great events in American history, and singular accomplishments by the Daughter who wears them. Together they tell the story of her service to the DAR and her country.

series of gatherings throughout the summer of 1890 culminated on October 11, when Mary Smith Lockwood hosted the first organizational meeting of the new National Society Daughters of the American Revolution. The date chosen for the meeting was no accident: as stated in the 1908 pamphlet by the National Board of Management, "October 11 had been selected . . . because it was the date of Columbus' discovery of America . . . ." October 12, the traditional observance of Columbus's discovery, fell on a Sunday in 1890. Most likely, the Daughters chose for their meeting date the Saturday before as being closest to it. Eighteen women attended, as well as four of the six Sons of the American Revolution who would serve as the advisory board to the NSDAR in its first few years of existence. By the end of the meeting, eleven members had paid their dues, and the DAR opened for business with $33 in the bank.

Only months after its founding, however, rumors and questions swirled: "What is it for?" "Who is eligible?" "Is it intended to build up an aristocracy?" According to early records, the first officers and board of the Daughters quickly realized "that something must speedily be done, to bring this organization before the public in such a way as to make it clear there was a vitality and enthusiasm in it based upon American ideas of patriotism." So they "thought and planned for a grand reception" as the proper introduction.

The success of this grand reception, held on February 22, 1891, just four months after the founding of the DAR, was "excitedly" recorded by the Society: "Washington is noted for the magnificence with which such occasions are surrounded, but none had surpassed this one—in its personnel or in the beauty of its appointments." Guests at the gala, held in the home of the Society's first Vice President General, Mary Virginia Ellet Cabell, were greeted by the First Lady of the land, Caroline Scott Harrison, wife of President Benjamin Harrison, who had been unanimously elected as the first NSDAR President General. As the Society's records relate, minutemen dressed in Continental uniforms of buff and blue formed a double line through which the guests passed to the receiving party, adding greatly to the scenic effect produced by flags and bunting, flowers and palms. Rousing speeches and patriotic music filled the elegantly appointed supper rooms adorned with flowers and decorations in the newly chosen light-blue-and-white colors of the new Society, and everything was done to arouse pride in heroic, national ancestry. The Society's records tell the story of a reception marked by the spirit of patriotism in speech and song that reached to the far ends of the country, as newspapers took up the cry and sent news of the event over the land. Success was assured.

▲ William O. McDowell, one of the founders of the Sons of the American Revolution, reacted quickly and strongly when the Sons voted against allowing women to join the SAR, as did Mary Smith Lockwood, one of the four founders of the DAR. Lockwood's letter in the *Washington Post* on July 12, 1890, retold the story of Hannah Arnett, one of the first woman patriots of the Revolution. McDowell was the great-grandson of Hannah Arnett, and immediately after reading Lockwood's letter in the *Post*, he penned his own response, published on July 21, 1890, stating, " . . . in the hands of the women of America patriotic undertakings have never failed. Why not, therefore, invite the formation of the National Society of the 'Daughters of the American Revolution' . . . ." His letter concluded with the invitation to "every woman in America who has the blood of the heroes of the revolution in her veins" to send her name and address to him. McDowell would attend the first organizational meeting and long serve as one of the advisors. He was also one of the first to apply for membership in the Daughters of the American Revolution. They respectfully declined his application.

The Founders

Decidedly not ladies of leisure, the four founders of the DAR were anything but traditional. Two were single and two were widowed, and all four were working women who supported either children or extended family. **Mary Smith Lockwood** (1831–1922) (top left), widow of a Union soldier, author, suffragist, and hostess at the Strathmore Arms where one of the first DAR meetings was held, started it all with her impassioned letter in the *Washington Post* following the vote of the Sons of the American Revolution to exclude women. While passionate about the DAR, she was equally committed to other women's endeavors, serving as president of the Women's Press Club and Lady Manager-at-Large of the World's Columbian Exposition in 1893. She would also serve the DAR the longest of any of the founders—from 1890, when she penned her historic letter, until her death in 1922 at age 92. Her positions within the organization included Historian General, Vice President General, Chaplain General, and Editor of the *American Monthly Magazine*. She was both Honorary Chaplain General and Honorary Vice President at the time of her death and is the only founder buried in Washington.

Eugenia Washington (1840–1900) (bottom left), after the death of her mother at age nineteen, had to support her disabled father, taking her with him to Washington after the Civil War, when she was offered a position with the Post Office Department. She never married and spent every spare moment outside her Post Office position laboring for the organization of the society. Assigned DAR National Member Number 1, she became the first Registrar General, speaking out often regarding her concern for accurate records to ensure their historical value. She would also hold the positions of Vice President General, Recording Secretary General, and later Honorary Vice President General.

Mary Desha (1850–1911) (top right) studied at what is now the University of Kentucky. Impoverished by the Civil War, she and her mother began a private school. Somewhat the adventurer, she took a brief stint teaching in Alaska in 1888 but later also became a federal employee in Washington. Designer of the Society's seal, she would hold five different offices of the NSDAR: Vice President General, Surgeon General, Corresponding Secretary General, Recording Secretary General, and Honorary Vice President General. Mary Desha worked tirelessly as Assistant Director of the DAR Hospital Corps during the Spanish-American War and died suddenly on January 29, 1911, while walking home from work, reportedly clutching DAR paperwork at the time. Her body lay in state at Memorial Continental Hall on January 31 from ten o'clock in the morning until four o'clock in the afternoon, "tenderly guarded by relays of the District Daughters, who, having loved her in life, desired thus to honor her in death," as described in the July 1911 issue of *American Monthly Magazine*. "All day long a silent procession, in twos and threes, of official and social friends passed through the Hall to pay their tribute of honor to Miss Desha." Hers was the only funeral ever held in Memorial Continental Hall. She is buried in Lexington, Kentucky, where she was born.

Following the death of her husband in 1873, **Ellen Hardin Walworth** (1832–1915) (bottom right) ran a boarding and day school from her home in New York. She would eventually earn her law degree and licenses to practice law in both New York and the District of Columbia. She became the founding editor of the DAR *American Monthly Magazine* and would also serve as Vice President General, Corresponding Secretary General, and Honorary Vice President General.

At the Walworth Museum in Saratoga Springs, New York, there was at one time on display a picture of her standing beside a spinning wheel, the inspiration of the DAR insignia. The caption bears her quote: "I am determined not only to hold my own, but to make myself felt in the community to which I belong . . . and I know I will succeed."

FIRST CONTINENTAL CONGRESS, FEBRUARY 22, 1892, OF THE
DAUGHTERS OF THE AMERICAN REVOLUTION.
President General: MRS. BENJAMIN HARRISON.   Vice President General Presiding, MRS. WILLIAM D. CABELL.

◄ The Daughters' first Continental Congress was held February 22, 1892, in the Church of Our Father on 13th and L streets, NW, Washington, D.C. Before they could adjourn, Mathew B. Brady, one of the most renowned photographers of his day, asked for "the privilege of making a photographic group of the Society, to be added to my historical collection of the most eminent people of the world." His image would capture not only the four founders but also the first President General, Caroline Scott Harrison (center), as well as the only member ever to hold the title of Vice President Presiding, Mary Virginia Ellet Cabell (to Mrs. Harrison's right). On Mrs. Harrison's left are founders Eugenia Washington and Mary Desha. Standing between Mrs. Harrison and Miss Washington are founders Ellen Hardin Walworth and Mary S. Lockwood.

Membership applications poured in. Within months, the Society was busy raising money to erect its first monument, an obelisk in Fredericksburg, Virginia, to mark the birthplace of Mary Washington, the mother of George Washington. After only one year, members numbered 1,200, and as the Society noted:

> *The American women were awakened . . . and now "What is it for?" was answered—"It is not for an aristocracy but to honor the men who carried the muskets, and the boys who beat the drums and fifed Yankee Doodle for liberty; to honor the women who served the country in their homes, while the men were away fighting the battles for freedom and that their names should be rescued from the musty annals of the Revolution, and for the first time inscribed on the pages of history, as factors in making the Nation."*

▶ Decidedly nontraditional women were some of the first to join the new NSDAR. Included in the approximately 850,000 application papers maintained by the DAR is that from women's rights pioneer Susan B. Anthony (1820–1906). In a letter to the Kentucky DAR in 1897, she wrote: "I hope . . . you will be exceedingly careful to distinguish those actions in which our revolutionary mothers took part." She became a member of the Irondequoit Chapter, Rochester, New York, in 1898. Anthony was a descendant of Daniel Read, a private in the Continental army and a composer who later became only the second American composer to publish a collection of his own music.

To Whom Much Is Owed

The first members of the DAR were quick to realize and recognize that "there is a woman to whom we owe more than to any other woman . . . ." At the urging of Mary Desha, Mary Virginia Ellet Cabell (1839–1930) attended the first organizing meeting of the National Society on October 11, 1890, and it was she who led it. Mary Cabell agreed that the new Society "should be presided over by a lady prominent in the United States," so that same day, she and William O. McDowell paid a visit to Caroline Scott Harrison, following up on the letter sent by Mary Desha two months prior. The First Lady accepted but only upon the promise that Mrs. Cabell would perform the bulk of those responsibilities, including not only presiding at most meetings but also handling the daily details of the office, forging policy, solving problems, and ensuring the success of the new organization. So she was appointed Vice President Presiding and later President Presiding, singular offices that only Mrs. Cabell ever held.

Her home became the headquarters of the Society for its first year. Daughter of Charles Ellet Jr., a prominent civil engineer who built the first suspension bridge in the United States, it was Mary Virginia Cabell who proposed "the building of a House Beautiful, . . . the finest building ever owned by women . . . ," one that would serve "as an outward and visible sign of an inward and spiritual grace." She would live to see not only the realization of her vision in Memorial Continental Hall but also the Administration Building and Constitution Hall. She died July 4, 1930, at the age of ninety-one, the same date in history marked by American independence as well as the passing of signers of the Declaration of Independence, John Adams and Thomas Jefferson.

During the centennial celebration of the National Society in 1990, under the administration of President General Marie H. Yochim, the Daughters placed a tablet honoring Mary Virginia Ellet Cabell near the Founders Memorial Monument.

PHOTO BY C. M. BELL

▲ These elegantly appointed rooms, at the home of Mary Virginia Ellet Cabell (inset) and her husband, William D. Cabell, served as the first home of the NSDAR for more than a year, during which the Society held several meetings a month to chart the course of the new organization.

While that first reception was certainly the catalyst for communicating the new Society's mission, perhaps the event itself was too successful. Ironically, what seems to have endured most in the public's mind is not the message the Daughters hoped to communicate but rather a snapshot of the social swirl surrounding that evening. What quickly became and remains one of the largest philanthropic volunteer organizations in the nation, if not the world, the National Society Daughters of the American Revolution, also remains one of the least understood.

Yet, as founder Ellen Hardin Walworth would write in the February 1893 *American Monthly Magazine*, "it is not a social organization . . . , it is an order patriotic, historical and genealogical, and holds itself closely to these objects." Created in a time when women "were also reaching for something beyond the household," when "the idea of doing something unrelated to their families was an enormous breakthrough for many," as described by Gail Collins in *America's Women*, this new society of women would harness a desire for service that was the defining feature of their Progressive Era. The next chapters provide a closer look at this legacy of service, in the hope that by their deeds, you shall know them.

▲ Representatives of the Sons of the American Revolution join their hostesses, the Daughters, for this photo taken July 6, 1896. The Daughters and Sons commemorated the Battle of Saratoga, the decisive month-long 1777 battle that resulted in one of the most stunning defeats of the British by the new "Americans." Scholars and strategists also study it as one of the great decisive victories in world history. In 1883, Ellen Hardin Walworth arranged the placement of seven granite monuments at significant locations on the battlefield. Three of the four founders were present for the photograph: in the white blouse in the center is Eugenia Washington; seated next to her at right is Ellen Walworth; and the petite white-haired woman in the second row, second from right, is Mary S. Lockwood. Although the Sons of the American Revolution respectfully declined to allow women as members, they were and remain staunch supporters of the Daughters. A select group of six Sons served as advisors to the DAR for several years after its formation. One of the first Daughters, Belinda Olney Hatheway Wilbour, who was appointed by President General Caroline Scott Harrison to be the first Rhode Island State Regent, even proposed that "Continental Hall . . . be built large enough to include the Sons." This close association remains. Each year, either the SAR President General or his representative delivers remarks at Continental Congress. The DAR President General usually returns the favor at the Sons' annual gatherings. The two organizations also frequently sponsor joint ceremonies to mark or commemorate historic sites and events. Local chapters of the SAR often provide the color guard for various local DAR commemorative events as well.

CHAPTER THREE

A Room of Her Own
"A House Beautiful"

L OCATED IN THE HEART OF WASHINGTON'S most popular tourist attractions, the exquisite buildings of the DAR National Headquarters were prominent structures in downtown D.C. even before some of its better-known neighbors, such as the Jefferson, Vietnam, and World War II memorials. The headquarters buildings are not only home to the Daughters but also feature the DAR Museum, a frequent tourist destination and educational resource; the DAR Library, one of the top genealogical research centers in the nation; the Americana Collection, a unique archive of rare historical documents compiled by members of the Society over the past one hundred years; and DAR Constitution Hall, a premier performance venue. The complex houses the administrative offices for the Society and staff of some 150 NSDAR employees, and serves as a popular place for many private weddings, filmings, and receptions. Thousands of people regularly pass by the DAR Headquarters and, while its immense size can seem intimidating, the Daughters welcome the public to come inside to explore the beautiful interior and take advantage of the outstanding resources offered there.

In the early part of the twentieth century, the phenomenal growth of the Society's permanent home would mirror the growth of their membership. Construction on Memorial Continental Hall, the first building of the headquarters, began in 1904. Constitution Hall, built in 1929, anchors the opposite end of the complex. The Administration Building, originally built in 1920, was expanded in 1950 to completely unite all three buildings and consume an entire city block. While subsequent chapters will provide a more intimate look at the outstanding holdings of the headquarters and the historic events that have taken place within them, they cannot be examined without first reflecting on the determination of the early Daughters to create their very own home, the grandeur of which today not even they could have envisioned.

▶ As a tribute to the thirteen original states, thirteen columns support the Portico on the south side of Memorial Continental Hall. With its spectacular view of the Washington Monument and the Ellipse, it remains one of the most photogenic features of the DAR Headquarters complex.

THE SOCIETY NEEDS A HOME

From their very first informal meeting that summer of 1890, the Daughters found themselves amidst a firestorm of interest in their new patriotic society. Meetings bounced from one noted Washington address to another into the fall and winter, and potential members swarmed in greater numbers with each successive gathering. The founders realized almost immediately that they needed a place of their own.

Mary Smith Lockwood, at the second meeting on October 18, 1890, became the first to propose that the Society build a "fireproof building" to safeguard the relics and papers that the members proposed to preserve. The term and the need would be oft repeated at every meeting of the new Society. But it was the speech by Mary Virginia Ellet Cabell, Vice President Presiding, that articulated the dream at the Conference of State and Chapter Regents held at her home October 6 and 7, 1891: "What the Society needs most and first is a home." In her report to the first Continental Congress in 1892, she was particularly precise in her description of that home:

> *This house should be builded* [sic] *on a hill, that all may see and know it. It should be located in or near the beautiful Capital City named for Washington, the immortal. It should be the fin-*

▲ Memorial Continental Hall would be the first building of its size erected by women anywhere in the world. Architect Edward Pearce Casey's design was in the classical revival style of the Beaux Arts or "fine arts." Pictured here is a watercolor done by Casey of his proposed building. The style drew its inspiration from a variety of sources including ancient Greece and Rome, eighteenth-century England, France, and colonial America. The building, clad in Vermont marble, is filled both inside and out with classical motifs. Because of this detailing, Memorial Continental Hall fit in well with the Colonial Revival, a movement that celebrated America's colonial past.

> *est building ever owned by women . . . . Purely American should this structure be; every fluted column, every gorgeous capital should owe its loveliness to the hand of an American artist.*

Her vision was one of form and function, blended with the business of the Society—a spacious hall, a secure repository for the Society's collections, and a place for conducting business.

Mrs. Cabell's eloquence was probably as much pragmatic as prescient. For more than a year following the founding, starting with that second organizational meeting, her residence at

1407 Massachusetts Avenue became the official address of the Society. She and her husband hosted the grand reception on February 22, 1891, where Mrs. Harrison, the first President General, received hundreds of guests. The Society held monthly meetings of the NSDAR and twice-monthly meetings of the Board of Management in Mrs. Cabell's spacious apartments, where they also kept many of the Society's records. The Cabell home was filled again on October 6, 1891, when Mrs. Harrison presided at the first conference of national officers, state and chapter regents. Never mind the flurry of preparations and the expense of refreshments for each meeting. In addition to her enormous duties as Vice President Presiding, surely by now Mrs. Cabell must have wanted her home back.

MEMORIAL CONTINENTAL HALL

On December 14, 1891, Ellen Hardin Walworth proposed a resolution to appoint a committee to "consider ways and means of erecting a fireproof building and founding a home for the society, which shall also be the Memorial Hall of the Daughters of the American Revolution . . . ." During that same meeting, the Daughters voted to set aside all fees from life memberships and chapter charters as a permanent building fund. In what appears to have been a unanimous decision, the funds "were not to be touched until a sum has been accumulated sufficient to begin the erection of a fireproof building large enough to accommodate the records, the relics, and the meetings of the society," as recorded in the first report to the U.S. Congress. By the time of the first Continental Congress in 1892, the fledgling society had collected $650 in the building fund.

Funds would build, but in the meantime, the Daughters needed a site for their permanent home. Already there was a growing sense of urgency, for they were paying $20 a month

▲ Pictured here are the Riggs National Bank and W. W. Corcoran office buildings on the 1500 block of Pennsylvania Avenue, NW, Washington, D.C., where the DAR rented its first office space. Though small, the location was perfect, for it was diagonally across the street from the White House, a short enough distance so that President General Harrison could preside at monthly meetings. After the sad loss of their beloved first President General, the Society leased two rooms in the Kellogg Building at 1416 F Street, NW, from 1893 to 1894. Six rooms in the "fireproof" Washington Loan and Trust Building just down the street at 902 F Street, NW, would serve as their headquarters until 1910, when they could move into Memorial Continental Hall.

◄ The vast stretches of still undeveloped, marshy land stand out in this circa 1870s photo taken from the top of the Washington Monument. Constitution Avenue runs diagonally along the lower left. Yet it was in this same area where the visionary Daughters of the American Revolution would build their magnificent headquarters, a site described in a June 7, 1902, *Evening Star* article as one that "has been left behind in the march of modern improvements or thrust to one side, and it seemed that a restoration was impossible." The site they chose—on 17th Street just one block south of the Corcoran Gallery of Art, which had opened in 1874—would become one of the choicest pieces of real estate in downtown D.C. *Photo courtesy of Library of Congress Georgetown University Special Collections.*

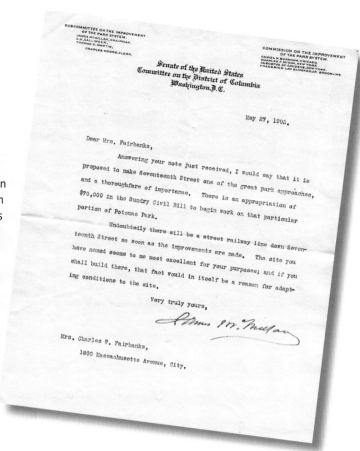

▶ This 1902 letter from Senator James McMillan, chairman of the Senate commission to explore and plan the design of Washington, to President General Cornelia Fairbanks described the lot the Society was considering for Memorial Continental Hall as a prime location. "The site you have named seems to me most excellent for your purposes," he wrote, for "it is proposed to make Seventeenth Street one of the great park approaches, and a thoroughfare of importance." McMillan even gave a hint of a promise that there would be transportation improvements to accommodate the new building, urging, "if you shall build there, that fact would in itself be a reason for adapting conditions to the site." The Daughters purchased the land one month later.

for office space. Kate Kearney Henry chaired the subcommittee to obtain from the Congress of the United States a site for the building, and in 1897, a bill passed both houses of the 54th Congress granting permanent use of a 200-square-foot plot of land. Unfortunately, after much review, that particular site turned out to be a portion of the grounds of the Washington Monument and therefore unavailable. A February 21, 1904, *Washington Times* article observed: "Finally the Daughters saw that they must rely chiefly upon their own exertions and not upon a well meaning but dilatory national legislative body for that important item." Once again men had let the Daughters down, so once again they forged off on their own.

At a meeting on June 4, 1902, at the home of President General Cornelia C. Fairbanks (wife of U.S. Senator and later Vice President Charles Warren Fairbanks), the Memorial Continental Hall Committee agreed that, with $82,190 set aside in the Hall fund, they would purchase the land needed for a home for the Daughters. The subcommittee on investigation of a site had considered various tracts and eventually narrowed their selection to Square 173, located on 17th Street between C and D streets.

There were both positive and negative features of the plot the Daughters had in mind. The land was of questionable composition, reclaimed from the marshy lands of the Potomac River basin, which attributed to the lower price. However, the com-

mittee was warned in a 1902 letter from the Assistant to the Engineer Commissioner that any basement below the street level would be liable to flooding. On the other hand, they were reassured by a letter from Senator James McMillan—author of the McMillan Plan to revive Pierre L'Enfant's dream of Washington as a city beautiful—that outlined a proposal to make 17th Street "one of the great park approaches, and a thoroughfare of importance." No doubt Senator McMillan's assurance carried much weight. But sheer obstinacy likely sealed the deal, after Dr. Anita Newcomb McGee, a member of the site subcommittee, received a letter from Mr. Edward L. Morse stating that "erection of a public hall in the locality of the Corcoran Art Gallery would not meet the public needs of Washington . . . ."

In June 1902, for $50,285.41, or $1.42 per square foot, the Daughters purchased "a most beautiful and suitable site for the purpose, on Seventeenth Street, extending from D to C streets, with a frontage of the entire block 210 feet in length, facing the public reservation, known as the White House Lot," as described in a committee pamphlet. Eventually, the Daughters would outgrow this parcel, but for now it was enough. They would purchase the entire city block by 1912.

As early as 1899, the Continental Congress had approved a competition for design of a "monument to the heroic men and women of the Revolution, as well as an administrative building for the Society," classic in design, with an auditorium as

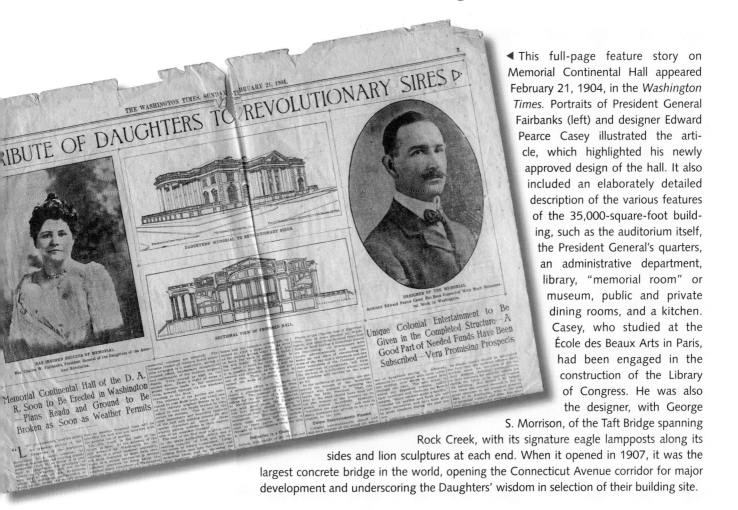

▶ This full-page feature story on Memorial Continental Hall appeared February 21, 1904, in the *Washington Times.* Portraits of President General Fairbanks (left) and designer Edward Pearce Casey illustrated the article, which highlighted his newly approved design of the hall. It also included an elaborately detailed description of the various features of the 35,000-square-foot building, such as the auditorium itself, the President General's quarters, an administrative department, library, "memorial room" or museum, public and private dining rooms, and a kitchen. Casey, who studied at the École des Beaux Arts in Paris, had been engaged in the construction of the Library of Congress. He was also the designer, with George S. Morrison, of the Taft Bridge spanning Rock Creek, with its signature eagle lampposts along its sides and lion sculptures at each end. When it opened in 1907, it was the largest concrete bridge in the world, opening the Connecticut Avenue corridor for major development and underscoring the Daughters' wisdom in selection of their building site.

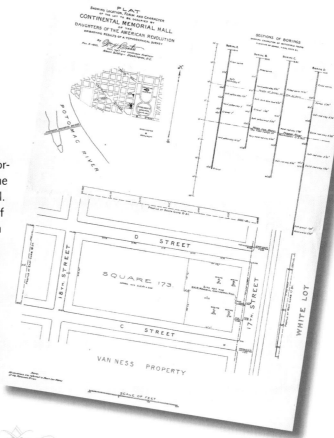

▶ This 1902 plat reports the topographic survey and borings done to investigate the suitability of Square 173, the site the Daughters chose for construction of their great hall. The lettering at right denotes the "White Lot," the plot of land reserved for the White House, Ellipse, and Washington Monument, which can be seen in the detail on the upper left. The Administration Building would emerge in the center of the lot, adjacent to Memorial Continental Hall, in the 1920s, and ultimately Constitution Hall ten years later, on the 18th Street side. Note the name "Continental Memorial Hall." However, the surveyor may be forgiven, for even today the name is sometimes incorrectly referenced.

◄ Initially, the Daughters paid for their new home on a "pay-as-you-go" basis. Perhaps buoyed by the air of excitement and celebration during that 14th Congress, their first in the new headquarters, and based on their phenomenal fundraising efforts thus far, delegates soundly defeated a motion to proceed with a mortgage to fund the rest of the construction. They remained united in their decision to continue to pay for their new home as construction progressed, despite estimates of between $300,000 and $400,000. However, by 1908, the large sums required for each new phase of construction depleted their funds and began to delay construction. The Society still had to rent offices because the building was not habitable year-round. President General Emily R. McLean strongly recommended they finance funds to finish the project using their real estate holdings as collateral. On April 23, a motion was passed that the National Board of Management be authorized to negotiate a $200,000 bank loan. The Daughters' optimism held true, though, and by the next administration, certificates such as the one pictured here honoring those contributing to the building fund and signed by President General Julia G. Scott would signify the liquidation of the debt.

◄ The Daughters raised money for their permanent home through every kind of fundraising event: subscriptions, concerts, luncheons, bazaars, and even something called "penny boxes." At the suggestion of the building committee, each chapter would save a penny a day for a year and place them in a specially labeled cardboard box to be opened on George and Martha Washington's wedding day (January 17). They also sold souvenir coffee and teaspoons. The handle of the spoon, designed by J. E. Caldwell & Co., official jewelers for the Society since its founding, featured the DAR symbol of a colonial dame at her spinning wheel.

the main feature of the building with a seating capacity not to exceed 2,000. Their inspiration for the design came from the 1893 World's Columbian Exposition in Chicago, in which many DAR members were involved.

The architects of the Exposition envisioned a "white city," with all of the buildings in various shades of white and inspired by classical Beaux Arts architecture. Many of the same architects who designed the Exposition were later also part of the McMillan Commission. They brought the ideal of the White City—the "City Beautiful"—to Washington, and Memorial Continental Hall was destined to be a model of this ideal. Plans proposed by Edward Pearce Casey of New York City for "a building of classical style, kept pure throughout, a three-story Parthenon with basement," were accepted on January 8, 1904. Casey's design also closely resembled the White House, only a block away.

Once the architectural plan was in place, parts of the building could be "subscribed" and funded for naming rights. The larger, more populous state societies paid for entire rooms while smaller states funded windows, stair rails, or doors. Indiana, home state of the first President General, First

A Firm Foundation

As crowds gathered under cloudy skies, President General Cornelia Fairbanks—wife of Charles Warren Fairbanks, U.S. Senator and later Vice President under President Theodore Roosevelt—presided at the laying of the cornerstone for Memorial Continental Hall on April 19, 1904, as part of the 13th Continental Congress. To consecrate the event, the ceremony followed Masonic rites, and the Mason's Grand Master, James A. Mason, was on hand for the occasion.

The gavel used at the ceremony was the same one George Washington used during the events surrounding the laying of the cornerstone of the National Capitol on September 18, 1793. The Masonic Grand Master, President General Fairbanks, and the three living founders present—Mrs. Walworth, Miss Desha, and Mrs. Lockwood—each spread a trowel full of cement on the foundation.

The remarks delivered by President General Fairbanks that day would prove to be prophecy as well as pronouncement:

> *The spacious marble hall which here will soon rear its beautiful proportions is an expression from this great society of its broad and comprehensive view of those characters in the past to whom gratitude is due. It is not erected alone to the mighty statesmen of the revolutionary epoch . . . not alone to the immortal generals who organized the patriots into armies . . . not alone to the heroic captains of the infant navy . . . not alone to the inspiring sacrifices of a Rebecca Mott, who so loved the cause of liberty that she burned her own house . . . not alone [to] brave Molly Pitcher to carry out the work which sudden death took from her husband, but to all the men of the line and all the women at the spinning wheel.*

▲ President General Fairbanks officiates at the ceremony. In front of her on the lectern is the actual cornerstone. The more than fifty items placed within it included a Bible belonging to a Revolutionary soldier, a copy of the Declaration of Independence, the American flag, the Daughters' insignia, portraits of the founders, and the current issue of the daily newspapers. The woman to the far left is founder Mary Lockwood. The other two living founders—Ellen Hardin Walworth and Mary Desha—were also present. To the left of Mrs. Fairbanks is Edward Everett Hale, chaplain of the United States Senate, who delivered the invocation. In the bottom foreground of the photo, the Marine Band performs spirited musical selections to fit the occasion. From this day forward, their performance at every Continental Congress would become a tradition.

▼ Hundreds of spectators gathered to witness the cornerstone laying, as shown in this photo that appeared the following day in a local newspaper. The Corcoran Gallery of Art is in the background in center. To the right is the Old Executive Office Building, now the office of the Vice President of the United States.

▶ Fourteen years after committing to the erection of a fireproof building to hold the artifacts and archives of Revolution and Society, this full-color, beribboned program commemorated the Memorial Continental Hall cornerstone laying ceremony.

CEREMONIES OF THE LAYING OF THE CORNER STONE

APRIL 19 1904

13TH CONGRESS

D A R

MEMORIAL CONTINENTAL HALL WASHINGTON ·D·C·

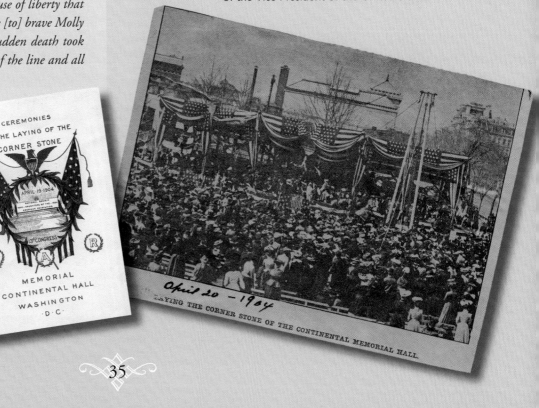

April 20 - 1904

LAYING THE CORNER STONE OF THE CONTINENTAL MEMORIAL HALL.

▲ The lovely Portico with its covered rotunda remains one of the most elegant features of the DAR complex.

▲ Twenty-eight workers and officials pause for this circa 1907 photograph with one of the 43-ton marble monoliths bound for the mill where they would be turned, fluted, and further embellished with elaborately detailed Ionic capitals. The huge stone slab of Vermont marble would become one of the thirteen columns representing the thirteen original states that now surround and support the Memorial Portico on the south side of Memorial Continental Hall.

Lady Caroline Scott Harrison, had the honor of funding the President General's Office, while Vermont paid for stair rails, and Pennsylvania presented the grand entrance foyer.

On April 19, 1904, the 129th anniversary of the Battle of Lexington as well as the second day of the NSDAR 13th Continental Congress, the Daughters placed the cornerstone for their new home. Work proceeded rapidly, and on April 17, 1905, just short of one year later, the eager Daughters dedicated their new, albeit unfinished, home during the 14th Continental Congress. A canvas roof covered the auditorium, both the furnace and seats in the auditorium were temporary, and the elegant porches and pillars would come much later. The building would not be completed until 1910.

In 1921, the Hall would host an event that would alter the course of world events: the first Arms Limitation Conference, more formally known as the International Conference on Naval Limitation. The formal opening of the conference occurred on November 12, 1921, one day after Armistice Day. It brought together the major naval powers of Britain, France, Italy, Japan, and the United States, as well as other nations with concerns about territories in the Pacific, such as Belgium, the Netherlands, Portugal, and China. Envisioned as a meeting to stem the hugely expensive naval construction rivalry between Britain, Japan, and the United States, the nine historic pacts and treaties reached during the three-month conference would be landmark agreements that became models for arms restraint. The conference would also forever elevate Memorial Continental Hall as the stage for that historic meeting. In 1972, it would be designated a National Historic Landmark.

ADMINISTRATION BUILDING

Only ten years after its completion, it had become apparent that Memorial Continental Hall's use as offices for the Society was somewhat in conflict with its role as memorial and repository. In September 1920, Sarah Elizabeth Guernsey, Honorary President General, wrote in an article for the DAR *American Monthly Magazine* that, although "every precaution has been taken to safeguard the priceless historic relics, and valuable furnishings and fittings given by the Daughters throughout the country, using Memorial Continental Hall as a place for daily business was only resulting in wear and tear of the valuable relics inside." In April 1920, to more adequately serve its now 110,000 members, the DAR National Board authorized the construction of a new administration building to be located behind Memorial Continental Hall. President General Sarah E. Guernsey's vision of the structure was "to make of our office building a model of comfort, convenience, and efficiency, just as our Hall has been a model of beauty and dignity."

▲ As bricklayers unload their materials, the Daughters' new home begins to take shape with the beginning of the new year in this photo taken on New Year's Day 1905. Only four months later, with a tarp for a roof and birds in the rafters singing in accompaniment, the Society would celebrate its first Continental Congress in the still-unfinished structure.

▼ Construction debris surrounds Memorial Continental Hall in the exterior view taken from 17th Street on February 22, 1907, before the addition of the columns and porticos. With cobblestones still visible lining the street, the view also shows just how relatively undeveloped the area remained at the time.

This time, while states, chapters, and members were welcome to make gifts of money and furnishings, the Daughters took out a loan to be paid back from regular income. In another elaborate ceremony, the Daughters broke ground for their two-story "room" addition on June 3, 1921, to be erected directly behind Memorial Continental Hall at a cost of $385,126. On October 19, 1921, the 140th anniversary of the surrender at Yorktown, they laid the cornerstone. The address for the new offices would eventually become 1776 D Street, a fitting reminder of their heritage. Two glass-enclosed corridors separated by a garden connected the new building to Memorial Continental Hall. On February 5, 1923, the new Administration Building was occupied and functioning as the business center, and the emptied rooms in Memorial Continental Hall were offered back to the states that originally paid for them. "State of Things" features these state period rooms as they have evolved.

Like any well-run business, this internationally renowned organization kept growing and expanding. By 1948, the Daughters were again raising the roof, this time adding a third floor to the Administration Building and removing the glass corridors to create more office space on the small stretch of land that separated the building from Memorial Continental Hall. This major renovation also included sweeping internal modifications to the Hall that would create one of the most beautiful and important libraries in the nation. They dedicated this addition on April 18, 1950, during the 59th Continental Congress.

▲ On November 12, 1921, one day after Armistice Day, the five principal naval powers of the world at that time—the United States, Great Britain, Italy, France, and Japan—as well as Belgium, the Netherlands, Portugal, China, and the British colonies—convened at Memorial Continental Hall to discuss disarmament as well as issues in the Pacific and Far East. The agreements they reached became the first arms limitation treaty ever signed. Based on this historic occasion, the U.S. Department of the Interior designated Memorial Continental Hall a National Historic Landmark with a plaque presented to Eleanor Washington Spicer, President General, at opening night of the 82nd Continental Congress, April 16, 1973. The plaque stands permanently affixed on the north corner of Memorial Continental Hall on 17th Street.

◄ One of the noted furnishings original to the Memorial Continental Hall stage is this beautiful bronze eagle lectern, donated by the now disbanded Flintlock and Powder Horn Chapter of Rhode Island in 1905. On January 20, 2005, President George W. Bush used the 100-year-old lectern at his inaugural luncheon. The lectern now resides in the President General's Assembly Room.

◀ Although the Daughters held their first Continental Congress in Memorial Continental Hall in 1905, it remained incomplete in 1908, as can be seen in this photo of the opening session of the 17th Continental Congress. As President General Emily R. McLean delivers her welcoming remarks on Easter Monday morning, April 20, temporary wiring supports fixtures to illuminate the hall, and bunting covers the walls and the box seating that would soon feature elaborate wrought iron railings that would cap the balconies and the spread eagles that would adorn them. The life-sized portrait of Martha Washington by Eliphalet Andrews was a gift of the artist's daughter and is a version of the same portrait featured in the White House. The DAR-owned painting still hangs in what is now the DAR Library.

▲ The auditorium of Memorial Continental Hall was the most elaborate room in the building, echoing the monumental character of the exterior. Deeply coffered arched ceilings span each of the original seating galleries that flank the large stage. Box seats overlook the stage and are capped by majestic outstretched American eagles clasping elaborate cartouches. The entire space was illuminated and ventilated by a glass and steel ceiling. Four gilt bronze electric chandeliers provided further lighting. The stage was furnished with seven specially carved mammoth armchairs in the Jacobean and Colonial Revival styles. ▶

◄ Celebrating its centennial anniversary in 2005, Memorial Continental Hall looks virtually the same as it did when it was finally completed in 1910, yet a number of changes have taken place in the interior of the building, a progressive reuse that not only preserved the magnificent interior while retaining the functional office space, but also enhanced the tourism experience within. Memorial Continental Hall now houses one of the most extensive genealogical libraries in the nation. For a small fee, the public is welcome to take advantage of the specialized collection of genealogical and historical manuscripts and publications totaling over half a million items in hard copy and microform. Docents provide free tours of the thirty-one state-sponsored period rooms that reflect a wide range of time and place, from Revolutionary times to the early 1900s and from a humble hearth to an elaborate parlor.

◄ ▲ Located on the third floor of Memorial Continental Hall, the Banquet Hall seats up to 150 people, often hosting luncheons for the National Board of Management. Additionally, the Banquet Hall is a popular rental venue for many noted Washington events. The room features antique furniture, oriental rugs, and Czechoslovakian crystal chandeliers. A balcony just off the hall provides guests with a breathtaking view of the Washington Monument (as seen through the far right window), as well as the Jefferson Memorial and the Smithsonian Castle. Today, the balcony is used for private events and to host the headquarters staff Fourth of July party with front row seats to the amazing fireworks display in the capital city.

◀ Collections for both the Museum and Library began at the very conception of the Society itself, and both found homes in the early Memorial Continental Hall by 1910. The Museum occupied the south gallery, seen here (top) circa 1930, where themed collections of porcelain, textiles, documents, and other articles in the collection already filled the space. It is now the O'Byrne Gallery, used for special events. Meantime, the Library already filled the north gallery in this 1920 photo (bottom), which proclaimed that the Library's collection of "nine thousand volumes, almost entirely relating to Americana, make this one of the finest genealogical and reference libraries in the United States." The galleries were generous in proportion for their time, featuring heavily carved woodwork and molded plaster-arched ceilings. These rooms were also beamed with natural light from double French doors with arched windows above. Naturally lighted public spaces were popular architectural conventions of the day, and many public libraries as well as museum galleries were lighted in this manner. Both the Museum and Library quickly outgrew their respective spaces and moved to larger areas as the headquarters building expanded.

By this time the Museum, after forty years, had also outgrown its home in Memorial Continental Hall. Taking advantage of the Administration Building expansion, in 1950 the Museum moved its collections to the first floor of the newer building, where they remain today. The Museum Gallery would permanently occupy the center of the building.

In 1980, a third expansion of the Administration Building added eight new offices and an atrium, a sunlit oasis that bridges the suite of rooms on the second floor occupied by the President General and her staff. Today, the facilities on this floor also include the Americana Room (added in the early 1950 expansion), as well as the President General's Assembly Room. Along the outside walls are offices of the NSDAR Executive Officers and their staffs. The Betty Newkirk Seimes Technology Center in the Administration Building offers some 53,000 items in its microform, CD-ROM, and online records. The chapter "America's Treasures" provides a more intimate look at the architecture, artifacts, and historic collections of the DAR Museum, DAR Library, and Americana Room.

▲ At one time, the balcony off the Banquet Hall on top of the Memorial Portico on C Street was known as the President General's Balcony. In this 1920 photo, it was being used as a Tea Room for some of the delegates to the 29th Continental Congress.

CONSTITUTION HALL

The Society's membership grew at a phenomenal rate, and it seemed they no sooner finished construction on one new

Dedicated to the Cause

Volunteer Daughters provided the majority of administrative support during the Society's early years, but the operation grew so quickly that paid staff became a necessity. The officers and board found themselves writing hundreds of letters a month in the conduct of Society business. In 1891, they hired Mary Ball as clerk, to be paid $25 a month. She was the first of three sisters who would serve successively in that position. In 1893, the NSDAR hired Nellie Stone for typewriting and stenography.

Today, close to 150 employees help run the administrative affairs of the Society, such as the booking of Constitution Hall and other NSDAR facilities for special events, security services, researchers, genealogists, office automation and mail room support, chapter services, accounting, the DAR magazine, and printing and publications, as well as specialized staff to oversee the vast holdings in the Americana Collection, Museum, and Library. Most are not members of the Society, but their devotion to its mission is evident in the significant number of employees who have worked for the NSDAR for twenty-five, thirty, and in many cases even forty or more years.

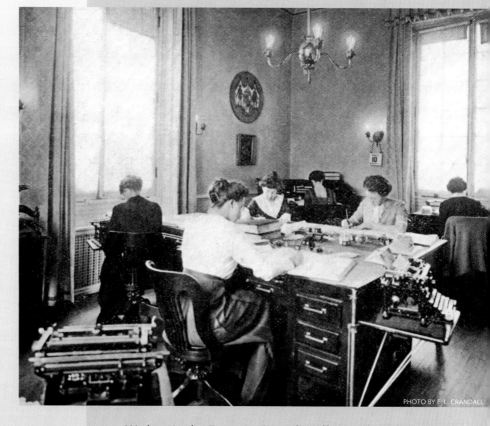

PHOTO BY E. L. CRANDALL

▲ Workers in the Treasurer General's Office worked elbow to elbow amidst artifacts placed throughout Memorial Continental Hall. As staff continued to grow, a building separate from the Hall for running the Society was sorely needed.

PHOTO BY BREN LANDON

▲ NSDAR employees gather in the National Officers Club Assembly Room in Constitution Hall in 2005 for the recognition service held each year to honor their dedicated service.

PHOTO BY UNDERWOOD & UNDERWOOD

▲ While sparse by today's standards, the card catalogue room in the center of the new Administration Building shown in this later photo was clearly more spacious and efficient. The caption accompanying the circa 1930 photo reads: "This beautifully lighted room is part of the Organizing Secretary's department and renders access to the official files easy and efficient."

facility before more space was needed. By April 1923, just two months after occupying the new Administration Building, the Daughters met for their 32nd Continental Congress under a new administration in a Memorial Continental Hall they had totally outgrown. Under the newly elected administration of President General Lora H. Cook, the Daughters began what would be their most ambitious fundraising effort to date: $1 million in cash to match the sale of $1 million in bonds, the total of which would cover the cost of the proposed facility. The sum would also require another amendment to the enabling act of the United States Congress, which limited the Daughters' real and personal estate holdings to $1 million. Congress raised this to $5 million. (In 1951, the limit would double to allow major modifications to the Administration Building, and in 1976, Congress removed specific figures from its 1896 Act of Incorporation for the DAR.)

With the matter of funding addressed, the 33rd Continental Congress in 1924 then appointed a committee to oversee "plans, specifications, and methods of financing a building . . . contain[ing] an auditorium adequate for the future proper seating of our ever-increasing membership." Anna Scott Block sent out a plan to finance the proposed new construction and Mary Virginia Ellet Cabell, Honorary Vice President Presiding, sent the first donation of $1 on March 21, 1924, with a pledge for a total of $5.

PHOTO BY SCOTT BRAMAN

▲ Building and furnishing Memorial Continental Hall became a labor of love for the entire Society. DAR state organizations paid for specified rooms in the building, and either paid for or donated the furnishings, many of which were also relics. Pictured here is the Connecticut Board Room where the National Board of Management held their meetings. One of the most lavish rooms in Memorial Continental Hall, it was also one of the most expensive to furnish, with elaborate woodwork and plaster moldings, custom-carved mahogany furniture, specially woven velvet carpet, and three elaborate gilt bronze electric chandeliers costing $6,000, the gift of Mrs. John T. Manson of New Haven, Connecticut, as a memorial to her ancestors. Eventually, the National Board of Management outgrew the room and moved to the National Officers Club Assembly Room in upper Constitution Hall. The Connecticut room still boasts a spectacular view of the White House Ellipse.

▶ The grand entrance to Memorial Continental Hall led immediately into the elegant foyer furnished by the Pennsylvania Daughters at an original cost of $6,500 to the Pennsylvania State Society. Furnishings and paintings were either made in Pennsylvania or have a Pennsylvania connection. In niches around the lobby pose ten busts of Revolutionary figures done by George Attilio and Furio Piccirilli, renowned carvers of some of the most significant marble sculptures in the United States, including Daniel Chester French's colossal *Lincoln* in the Lincoln Memorial. The room is classically clad in Vermont marble. The terrazzo and marble floors feature a central bronze medallion of the Pennsylvania state seal, while the ornamental ceiling is made of plaster of Paris in a design of swags, floral bouquets, and acanthus leaves. On the wall in the hallway to the left is a facsimile of the Declaration of Independence done in solid silver, nine feet high by five feet wide, including, in low relief, John Trumbull's depiction of the scene in Independence Hall on July 4, 1776. No longer used as a daily public entrance, the foyer is now used for receptions and weddings, as well as the Society's popular Christmas Open House.

PHOTO BY ARTHUR VITOLS

▲ Internationally famed artist and DAR member Gertrude Vanderbilt Whitney designed and sculpted the Founders Memorial Monument dedicated on April 17, 1929, to Mary Smith Lockwood, Eugenia Washington, Mary Desha, and Ellen Hardin Walworth. Flanking the figure, cut from Tennessee marble, are four panels, each bearing a replica of the Founders' Medals, as well as their names and dates of birth and death. One of the signature events of the Continental Congress each year is a memorial ceremony and wreath laying at the monument, nestled on the C Street side of the DAR complex, on the inset of land in front of the Administration Building.

▲ The design of the new Administration Building, by Eggers & Higgins, successor to Constitution Hall designer John Russell Pope, remains an elegant architectural complement to the two historic halls it connects. The design absorbed the open space that formerly separated the building from Memorial Continental Hall, and the entrance shown here at left would become the main access to the two buildings, boasting the almost predestined address of 1776 D Street, NW. Virtually the backbone of the Society's complex housing the dedicated staff of the NSDAR, it bridges Memorial Continental Hall and Constitution Hall in a manner so seamless, it is difficult to see now where one ends and the other begins.

▲ (Left to right) Immediate past President General Sarah E. Guernsey, Mary S. Lockwood, and President General Anne R. Minor officiate at the groundbreaking for the Administration Building, June 3, 1921.

At the 34th Continental Congress in April 1925, Mrs. Cook, who was Chairman of the Committee on Plans for an Auditorium, reported that renowned architect John Russell Pope had provided drawings for a "splendid structure seating four thousand persons in its auditorium," estimated to cost $1 per cubic foot, including removable seats so the auditorium could be converted to a ballroom or banquet hall. Several days of debate followed, for not all the Daughters supported yet another bold move. They hadn't yet finished paying for the new Administration Building; however, as one Oregon Daughter noted at the crowded Congress, "We came for the inspiration of this meeting . . . [but] we who live on the rim of the United States feel that we can't bring with us as many as we should like to bring for lack of space." She then pledged her state's support to raise the money and "build that new auditorium."

Once again, it was the opposition of men that likely spurred the Daughters to proceed. It was intended that the new auditorium would be rented for events in Washington as a source of revenue for the organization. As Agnes Holton Banks, New Jersey State Regent, pointed out: "It seems to me that one of the best arguments in favor of this proposed building is that businessmen of the City of Washington are opposing it. Men

▲ The Office of the President General, located on the second floor of the Administration Building, blends form as well as function, featuring richly appointed furnishings while tastefully incorporating today's technology. The President General travels extensively but she also spends a great deal of time in the office meeting with staff, reviewing reports and documents requiring her signature, and handling the affairs of her position.

▲ Recognizing the critical need for more office space and major modifications to Memorial Continental Hall, in 1948, the 57th Continental Congress directed construction of an extensive expansion to the Administration Building. Under the administration of President General Estella O'Byrne, the Daughters would embrace bold plans not only to expand the walls of the original Administration Building and add a third floor but also to convert their beloved Memorial Continental Hall auditorium into a genealogical library that would rival all others. On April 21, 1949, thousands filled the lawn to witness the laying of the cornerstone by Mrs. O'Byrne, shown here holding the metal box containing mementoes of the day to be placed underneath the stone. Her corsage is made of dollar bills, just one of the ways the Daughters raised money for the building. In testament to President General O'Byrne's firm but gentle leadership, under the Georgane Ferguson Love administration (1998–2001), the Daughters would name the lavishly appointed space that once held the old Museum the O'Byrne Gallery. The O'Byrne Room, a large room on the lower floor or basement of the Administration Building, is also named in her honor. It is used for meetings and seminars, and is action central for check-in, badges, information packets, and other logistics during Continental Congress.

▲ With the Washington Monument as watchman, the last, largest building of the NSDAR Headquarters begins to rise in this October 30, 1928, photo.

▲ On February 2, 1929, Daughters "step inside" for a tour of what will be their new auditorium in Constitution Hall.

don't offer a project or oppose other people's projects unless it is a source of revenue. This is a business investment." The recommendation to proceed was approved by a vote of 444 to 292.

Fundraising proved difficult, though, and stretched into the next administration. Members, chapters, and states pledged to purchase inscribed seats, boxes, and even cubic feet of dirt, but it would take three years and the bold near-postponement of the cornerstone-laying by President General Grace Brosseau before the Daughters reached their goal of $1 million. The 37th Continental Congress in 1928 resembled a telethon as rousing speeches from Finance Chairman Edith Scott Magna, who would later become President General, whipped the Daughters into a frenzy of giving. On the final night of the Congress, at the closing banquet on April 21, 1928, pledges finally hit $1 million.

On October 30, 1928, with as much pomp as previous ceremonies, and assisted by special guest First Lady Grace Anna Goodhue Coolidge, President General Brosseau spread the mortar and tapped in the cornerstone using the same trowel and historic gavel loaned for Memorial Continental Hall. Construction raced forward on the Daughters' largest undertaking to date. Barely six months later, another First Lady would join the Daughters in welcoming their newest addition. On April 19, 1929, with First Lady Lou Henry Hoover as guest speaker, Mrs. Brosseau, during her final Congress as President General, would again preside at the dedication of Constitution Hall, the only building built as a "Memorial to that Immortal Document The Constitution of the United States," reads the inscription carved on the cornerstone of the building. The Daughters held their very next Continental Congress, the 39th, in the new, spacious Constitution Hall. Like its predecessor Memorial Continental Hall, Constitution Hall would also be designated a National Historic Landmark in 1985 for its significance in commemorating the history of the United States of America.

▲ Dedicated April 19, 1929, Constitution Hall remains the largest concert hall in Washington, D.C., with a seating capacity of 3,700. (Originally designed to seat as many as 4,000, a stage enlargement in later years eliminated approximately 300 seats.) In its lifetime spanning almost three-quarters of a century, it has served as the stage for the world's most celebrated artists and historic events.

▼ At the entrance to Constitution Hall, the watchful eyes of a majestic carved eagle, flanked by the dates of the Revolutionary War from 1776 to 1783, observe those entering the main entrance of the hall. Each year, approximately 600,000 people attend a variety of events at Constitution Hall, one of the most popular venues in the capital city for public as well as private functions.

▲ The beautifully appointed President General's Reception Room, located in the northeast corner of Constitution Hall, is used by the President General to receive members and honored guests. Originally known as the Caroline Scott Harrison Room in honor of the first President General, it prominently features a portrait of Mrs. Harrison, a copy by Mathilde Leisenring made in 1931. The original, by Daniel Huntington, was commissioned and presented by NSDAR to the White House in 1894. The circa 1850s gilt mirror over the mantel came from the Price Mansion, Jefferson City, Missouri, a gift of the Missouri State Society in 1958. The plaster ceiling and other architectural details reflect the work of John Russell Pope, who designed the Hall. The first major refurbishing of the room occurred in 1958 with consultation by Franco Scalamandre, who donated a portion of the silk from his world-renowned company for the draperies and upholstery. Through the generosity of a major gift, the room underwent major renovation and restoration again in 2006, as captured in the contemporary photo seen here. This upgrade employed new fabric color schemes and a specially commissioned handwoven rug by Edward Fields of New York, especially fitting for this room, since it is the same company that provides carpet for the White House.

▲ This contemporary aerial perspective of the DAR complex captures how completely it fills one city block in downtown D.C. and tells the story of its evolution more vividly than any description. The newer Constitution Hall in the lower center dwarfs Memorial Continental Hall at the other end, highlighting just how much the Society had outgrown its original home. A close look at the Administration Building in the center shows the original structure outlined by the slanted roof and the later additions that would envelop it.

AGING BEAUTIFULLY

Over its many years of existence, the complex has seen many changes. As with any home, the NSDAR headquarters needs constant tending and upgrading, including electrical and plumbing maintenance, installation of air conditioning, expansions, renovations, and exacting repairs to crumbling marble to maintain these historic properties. Practically every President General has served as both CEO and chief engineer, overseeing million-dollar contracts for new construction, restoration, and renovations. Despite these modernizations, the buildings remain strikingly true to their original form and beauty. While the vibrancy of Daughters thrives in their local communities and cannot be contained behind marble walls, their spirit, determination, and giving nature are reflected in the headquarters they built from their hearts with their own funds. Like the Society itself, the DAR National Headquarters has an incredible history, the hub reflected in the DAR insignia where it all began. Succeeding chapters will show how this "old house" continues to provide vibrancy and diversity in its holdings and events, truly something for everyone today and for future patrons.

▲ Visitors to Constitution Hall often think of it as occupying the whole block between 17th and 18th streets when, in fact, there are three connected yet separate buildings that comprise the Headquarters of the National Society Daughters of the American Revolution, as this 1932 photo captures clearly. At right, the exquisite Beaux Arts architecture of Memorial Continental Hall, the original "house beautiful," clearly sets it apart as a historic D.C. landmark. At left, Constitution Hall, completed in 1929, and still Washington's largest concert hall, provides a venue for almost daily public events and concerts. In the center, the Administration Building houses the NSDAR Museum Gallery and Americana Room. At the completion of Memorial Continental Hall in 1905, a reporter for the *Washington Evening Star* wrote: "This Valhalla is unique. It is the costliest and most impressive monument of its kind ever built by women in this country or any other. Many other halls of fame have been erected and other grand monuments consecrated to the memory of some individual heroic figure in the history of our nation, but this is the first building dedicated to all the recognized heroes of the American Revolution: men and women alike. From the artistic standpoint it is one of the finest buildings which the beautiful Capital contains, and from the utilitarian it is destined to become one of the most useful." One hundred years later, the buildings occupying the Washington city block circumscribed by 17th, 18th, C, and D streets offer far more "usefulness" today—to its members and the general public.

CHAPTER FOUR

Work of the Chapters
Grassroots as Cornerstones

"I F THE NATIONAL SOCIETY OF THE DAUGHTERS of the American Revolution may be said to be the body of the organization, much more might its Chapters be recognized as its soul," wrote Mary Smith Lockwood and Emily Lee Sherwood in the *Story of the Records, D.A.R.* in 1906. That sentiment has been evident throughout the history of the DAR, from its first chapters formed just months after the organization's founding, to today with new chapters forming nearly every month.

The monumental work of the Society is carried out daily in local communities through the various chapters, where the "heart is at the grassroots level," emphasizes President General Presley Wagoner. As the citizens of this nation are key to its prosperity and security, the chapters and members of the DAR remain the heart and soul, the bedrock of the organization, where 168,000 members of nearly 3,000 chapters in the United States and abroad raise funds for scholarships and conservation, rescue and preserve historic sites, volunteer at veterans' hospitals, work with neighborhood schools to promote literacy and understanding of our democracy, provide wheelchairs for veterans, and donate funds and "womanpower" to support shelters for the homeless or victims of domestic violence. Members also have a long history in providing critical support to two DAR Schools, four DAR-approved schools, and two American Indian Schools.

A look at examples from the past shows the timeless and openhearted nature of the DAR mission. In 1918, one year after the end of World War I, the General Lafayette Chapter, Atlantic City, New Jersey, reported they had 127 members and had held twelve board and four chapter meetings. Their "patriotic work" included "two sustaining memberships to the

▶ DAR Members are a regular presence in schools throughout the country. Daughters Gary Cox (center at left) and Rita Horton of the Hunts Spring Chapter in Madison, Alabama, are pictured here during a visit with students at the Kate Duncan Smith DAR School. As part of the Adopt-A-Classroom project, DAR chapters are matched with classrooms at the school, and members correspond with the students, donate supplies, and visit the class to read stories and spend time with the children. "Through donations to a DAR school or by spending time mentoring a child, we are changing the world for the better, one child at a time," says Gary Cox, who is also Chairman of the Board of Trustees for the KDS School.

Red Cross, $20; Y.M.C.A. War Fund, $153.25; Soldiers Xmas fund, $10; Soldiers' Club at Camp Dix, N.J., $12; Memorial Continental Hall, $10; Scholarship for Berry School, Rome, Ga., $60; Child Federation, $10; and four $50 Liberty Bonds." The report also described several historic Revolutionary artifacts forwarded to the museum in Memorial Continental Hall in the name of the chapter. Certainly, the General Lafayette Chapter through its endeavors showed its commitment to the mission of the DAR—education, preservation, and patriotism.

It is the last entry from that 1918 chapter summary—"67 knitted goods sent to the Battleship *New Jersey*"—and a letter appended to the end that captures the chapter's full-hearted commitment to supporting the nation. In a letter enclosed with her handiwork, one chapter member wrote:

Dear Soldier Man,

If you are in your early twenties I am old enough to be your mother—and I have no sons to fight for me, so I try to do something for the sons of other mothers.

My daughters and I have eliminated waste in our household, conserved food by canning, preserving, etc., and we sew or knit for soldiers and sailors, besides which we have bought some Liberty Bonds, so you see, we are doing our bit here at home.

▲ They're off and running! Members of the newly formed Knickerbocker Chapter of the DAR in New York City applaud at the closing of the New York Stock Exchange July 5, 2005. Vice Regent Suzy Chase Osborne (center, at microphone) rang the official closing bell for fifteen seconds, and Laura Engelhardt (standing behind Osborne to the left), Chapter Treasurer, struck the gavel to close the market. Recalls Osborne of the experience, "It was such a great day at the Stock Exchange and was very fitting because it was the day after Independence Day, so we filled the NYSE with patriotism!" Also pictured (l-r) are chapter members Sandy Toth, Elizabeth Cohan, Karen McLaughlin, Lauren Kinelski, a representative of the NYSE, Blair Fox, Megan Von Behren, Judy Schuddeboom, Lisa Cosman (in hat), Virginia Syron, and Raegan Lambert. Members of the chapter thought this would be a great way to get a first-hand look at events that affect history every day and spread the word about the DAR and Knickerbocker Chapter, formed only eight months before. After the closing ceremony, chapter members enjoyed a reception and tour of Stock Exchange Headquarters.

When you return to this country, if you land in New York I wonder if your heart will beat faster and your throat ache as you see Liberty (the gift of the French to our nation) illuminating our harbor.

When we sew or knit we often offer a silent little prayer for the man who will wear the work of our hands (and you needn't think we sew or knit badly either!).

So, soldier man, I close my letter with a prayer for you personally. May God keep you and bring you in safety back to your own—victorious over wrong and oppression.

Very sincerely yours,
Emily G. Shinn

With her letter, Mrs. Shinn also enclosed a package of newspaper clippings, editorials, jokes, and cartoons she thought would interest and amuse the soldiers.

While the specific chapter events and amount of money raised for various causes have changed over the years to reflect the times, generosity and dedication to the enduring DAR mission have been visible in chapters since 1890. The strong foundation set for DAR chapters, a network of vibrant units all linked under a central, democratic leadership, would ensure its overwhelming success. It also set a precedent of chapters governed by a national society, which set the DAR apart from other societies.

The prevailing concept for many patriotic and fraternal societies founded around the turn of the century was that of inde-

PHOTO BY COOKI THIER

▲ Daughters Bea Seebohm, left, and Jackie Flannery of the John Reily Chapter, Hamilton, Ohio, portray Christian Waldschmidt and his wife at the Waldschmidt Homestead Barn in this May 2003 photo. Waldschmidt was a pioneer papermaker and businessman who played a significant role in the early history of Columbia, Ohio. The Ohio DAR restored the historic buildings that make up the museum complex, and in 1989, they completed construction of the memorial barn where they hold meetings and host educational programs.

▶ In remembrance of those who died both recently and long ago, members of the Huntsville Chapter in Alabama chose September 11, 2005, to unveil the marker on the grave of Revolutionary War soldier John Peyton Powell. With members from the Tennessee Valley and John Henry Lentz chapters of the Sons of the American Revolution in period costumes as color guard, C.A.R. members Caleb Knapp and Duncan Blair assist with the unveiling of the marker. Chapter members and guests include (left to right) color guard members Otha H. Vaughan, James Smith, Hoyt O. Smith, and James Maples; Daughters Elizabeth Blair and Marjorie Markham; guests Bob Knapp and John Peyton Powell; Alabama State Regent Jean Vaughan; and chapter members Nancy Adair and Martha Miller. Chapter Regent Davie Ann Thomas Williams, at the podium, presided at the event.

PHOTO COURTESY OF HUNTSVILLE CHAPTER

pendent parts or divisions loosely held together by common missions or interests, instead of functioning under one over-arching national-level entity. For example, the Sons of the Revolution began with one society in New York in 1875 that was not linked to other separate units, including Pennsylvania and Washington, D.C., until the founding of the General Society in 1890. The Sons of the American Revolution started out in similar fashion in 1876. They, too, would find it necessary to form a National Society in 1889.

The six Sons who served as advisors to the new Daughters of the American Revolution, and in particular William O. McDowell, recommended that they not follow the Sons' initial example. Rather, they recommended that, from the outset, there be "one National Society pervading the whole union of States and Territories, each member being responsible to the National Society," wrote Organizing Secretary General Marie H. Yochim (later President General) in 1982. Each member would be represented by her vote for delegates to the Continental Congress, much the same as individual voters today elect their senators and congressmen. Founding members "wished to have a Society that would embody and illustrate a profound principle of their country—the responsibility of the individual to the whole," described Mrs. Yochim.

This concept proved so successful that Mary L. Shields, Recording Secretary General, would write in her 1893 annual report: "We have had an unusually prosperous year, for to-day, although but a little over two years old, we have nearly twice as many members as the Sons of the Revolution, . . . and three-fourths as many as the Sons of the American Revolution . . . .

▲ In this 1941 photo, Eula Gill Corbett serves tea to a group of Colorado Daughters, a scene in sharp contrast to the various events and community efforts across the nation sponsored by today's Daughters. Based on the huge success of that first grand reception hosted by the Daughters in Washington, D.C., to properly introduce the new society, chapters often used teas, luncheons, and other social events to raise money for their service work. However, such events have often eclipsed the real work of the DAR, one of the largest philanthropic service organizations in the world.

◄ The notion of period rooms to reflect Colonial history swept the nation following the Philadelphia Centennial. In only its third annual report, the Mary Wooster Chapter, Danbury, Connecticut, included this circa 1900 photo of its "chapter home and historical rooms" in which a spinning wheel, the DAR symbol, is featured prominently. An issue of *American Monthly Magazine* from 1897 gives this account of the chapter's efforts: "The Mary Wooster Chapter, of Danbury, . . . which has the distinction of being the only Chapter in the State with a home of its own, has many cases of choice relics lining the sides of the pleasant rooms it occupies. These rooms are thrown open to the general public one day each week, and it is probable that the enterprise will eventually lead to the establishment in the city of Danbury, of a historical museum, of which the present collection will be the nucleus."

Ladies of the Board

Not unlike the government of the nation with its three branches, the NSDAR bylaws divide the Society's governing body into three units: the President General, the Executive Officers, and the Board of Management. The President General serves as the Society's chief executive officer. Much like the federal elected officials who serve U.S. citizens in Washington, in addition to the President General, the NSDAR bylaws provide for the following Executive Officers: First Vice President General, Chaplain General, Recording Secretary General, Corresponding Secretary General, Organizing Secretary General, Treasurer General, Registrar General, Historian General, Librarian General, Curator General, and Reporter General. As a whole, they serve in an administration for a three-year term elected by the delegates to DAR Continental Congress. The members of the National Board of Management include the twelve Executive Officers, twenty-one Vice Presidents General, and fifty-three State Regents (including those of the District of Columbia and two overseas "state" societies).

▲ This 1996 photo of the Executive Committee captures four current or future Presidents General. Pictured are, front row (left to right): Chaplain General Mary Jo Paisley Mordhorst, President General Dorla Dean E. Kemper, First Vice President General Georgane Ferguson Love, and Recording Secretary General Merry Ann Wright; second row (left to right): Historian General Jane Haymaker Rehl, Curator General Rebecca Jackson Graves, Registrar General Linda Tinker Watkins, Corresponding Secretary General Mary Lu Saavedra, Organizing Secretary General Presley Merritt Wagoner, Treasurer General Bettie Phillips Tracy, Librarian General Barbara Bennett Ulrich, and Reporter General Hilda Brock Dobrzanski. In addition to Mrs. Kemper, subsequent NSDAR Presidents General would include Mrs. Love, Mrs. Watkins, and Mrs. Wagoner. Merry Ann Wright became the first to hold the staff position of NSDAR Director of Development, created in April 1998.

▲ The 1904 National Board of Management assembled for this photo during the 13th Continental Congress. The thirty-eight members pictured here include founder Mary S. Lockwood, seated in the ornate chair third from right in the second row, and President General Cornelia C. Fairbanks, to the left of Mrs. Lockwood wearing the white shirtwaist with her arm draped affectionately over the arm of Mary Lockwood's chair. Mrs. Fairbanks was the wife of Charles Warren Fairbanks, Vice President under Theodore Roosevelt. In the very center, in the striped bodice, is Julia G. Scott, who would serve as President General from 1909 to 1913.

What's in a Name?

"The naming of a chapter should be chosen with care," wrote Marie Yochim in 1982. Since the founding of the first chapter in Chicago, names have varied from people, places, and things to Native American tribes and historic trails, from Declaration signers and their wives to Revolutionary drummer boys and women patriots.

Obviously there is a lot of latitude, but there are some rules for names set out in the bylaws. No two chapters may have the same name (although there are two Martha Washington Chapters—in the District of Columbia and Iowa—that likely were named before rules were set). What's more, chapters may not bear the name of anyone living. Chapters in states admitted to the Union before 1825 should choose names of events, sites, or individuals relating to the American Revolution. Chapter names in states admitted after 1825 may be named for historic territorial events, sites, or names of prominent early pioneers. The National Board of Management must approve all names.

The list of DAR chapter names from around the country and overseas provides an itemized history lesson of countless men, women, and, in some cases, children who played a role in American independence. These names honor such known patriots as Paul Revere, Betsy Ross, and Samuel Adams in Massachusetts, Nathan Hale in Connecticut, and Samuel Bacon in Virginia. The District of Columbia chose names like Dolley Madison and Mary and Martha Washington, capturing the spirit of the rousing article on "Women Worthy of Honor" by Mary Lockwood that first galvanized the Daughters. Chapters in no less than four states incorporated Washington— the Father of His Country—into their name, such as General Washington, Washington Crossing, and Washington-Lewis. However, a chapter in Texas boldly claimed his given name—George Washington—to designate their chapter.

Some, like Chicago (Illinois) and Cedar Falls (Iowa) simply take their names from the cities they represent. Others evoke pastoral scenes, such as the Prairie Grass Chapter in North Dakota, the Black Hills Chapter in South Dakota, and the Shining Mountain Chapter in Billings, Montana. Still others pay tribute to state flowers or animals, like the Blue Bell Chapter in Texas, the Beaver Chapter in Oregon, and the Manatee Chapter in Florida. In tribute to foreign patriots, chapters may choose to name themselves after those from other

▶ Letitia Green Stevenson, wife of Adlai E. Stevenson Sr. and second NSDAR President General, was likely one of only two women who had a chapter named after her while still living. Flora Adams Darling, who insisted she was one of the NSDAR founders, resigned when the National Society protested at the naming of a New York chapter after her. In November 1891, the Darling Chapter of the DAR in New York City followed her in reorganizing as the Daughters of the Revolution. To avoid future conflicts, in October 1894 the Board approved a resolution stating, "Chapters must not be named for living persons; and unless there is good and sufficient reason[,] they should not be named for persons who belong to a later historical period than the one ending in 1820."

▲ Executive officers of the EE-DAH-HOW Chapter in Nampa, Idaho, meet to plan for upcoming chapter activities and initiatives. The chapter takes its name from the Shoshone phrase the tribe used to describe their beautiful home in Idaho. "EE-DAH-HOW" means "the sun comes down the mountain," or "it is morning." As idyllic as their name may be, it takes hard work at the local level to manage the philanthropic, business, and social aspects of the chapters.

HAYMARKET THEATRE
161 WEST MADISON ST.
CHICAGO.

▲ Members, individual chapters, and states continue to be the main source of the thousands of priceless articles in the DAR Museum, Library, and Americana collections. Christine Gentry of the Los Cerritos Chapter, California, presents an 1888–1889 Benjamin Harrison political campaign bandana to Linda Wetzel, Curator General, during the 2005 Continental Congress. The bandana was the gift of member Nellie Gould Young.

countries who aided in the Revolution, such as General Bernardo de Gálvez and, of course, Rochambeau (a chapter in France) and Lafayette.

The Sleeping Lady Chapter in Alaska begs a story. The Princess Timpanogos in Salt Lake City, Utah, and the Oconomowoc and Nay Osh Ing chapters in Wisconsin are almost lyrical. Connecticut seems to favor three-word chapter names, such as Willard-Welles-Stanley, Agnes Dickinson Lee, and Freelove Baldwin Stow. One chapter in Washington, D.C., Descendants of 76, seems all-encompassing, while the Dodge City and Cimarron chapters in Kansas evoke images of the Wild West. At least two chapter names, the Loyalty Chapter in Louisiana and Contentment Chapter in Massachusetts, reflect both virtue and history: "Contentment" was the original name of the town of Dedham, Massachusetts. A revolutionary invention sets apart the Cotton Gin Port Chapter in Mississippi, but the Shuk-Ho-Ta Tom-A-Ha Chapter (also Mississippi) and the Elizabeth Ludington Hagans-Colonel John Evan Chapter (West Virginia) may be tied for the longest.

There are on our rolls 2,760 members." She predicted that the Society would likely double its membership by the following year. Little did she know that, by 1898, the Society would swell to eight times that number, or 23,000 members.

The Chicago Chapter, with Effie Beulah Reeme Osborn as Regent, formed first, in March 1891, just five months after the Society's founding. The Atlanta and New York City chapters seemed almost in competition for which one would be second: Atlanta became an official chapter on April 15, 1891, and New York City just four days later, on April 19. By 1893, there were fifty-one chapters in twenty states, two alone in the District of Columbia. Illinois might boast the first chapter, but it was the Daughters in Connecticut, under State Regent Jane Sumner Owen Keim, who forged ahead with seven new chapters by the time of the Second Continental Congress. By 1897, Hawaii, not yet a state, chartered the first overseas chapter, and by 1928, membership swelled to 170,395 members in 2,341 chapters. As of June 1965, the active DAR membership stood at "183,182 in 2,880 chapters in the United States, Canal Zone, England, France, Mexico, and Puerto Rico," according to the 1965 handbook, *What the Daughters Do*, published on the Society's seventy-fifth anniversary.

▲ This map of the United States hangs in the Chapter Services Office of the Organizing Secretary General at NSDAR Headquarters in Washington, D.C. Each of the nearly 3,000 orange pins indicates a DAR chapter location.

▲ During a 2003 visit, Oregon State Registrar Nedra Brill, also a member of the Portland Chapter in Oregon, uses the map behind her to explain the westward expansion of the United States to the first grade class at Tucker-Maxon Oral School. The private school for hearing-impaired children is a recipient of yearly donations from the chapter.

At first, the Daughters of the American Revolution "in this new broad West, especially in South Dakota, found the work of forming chapters slow and difficult," wrote Margaret Chambers Kellar, State Regent of South Dakota in her annual report for August 1899. Undaunted in her efforts to found a chapter there, she asserted that, while "the West has no such historic spots, ancestral homes, or graves; the absence of these object lessons must be met by other forces; we must be taught that our patriotic order can extend across the plains and mountains and join in the great work of those 'at home,' and that doing this will inspire us to discover local work in frontier fields." Today there are some 450 chapters in what Mrs. Kellar called the "broad West," including 120 in California. She would be proud to know that South Dakota now boasts six chapters in what were once those "frontier fields."

Initially, the head or "regent" of each chapter reported directly to the National Society. Soon chapters mushroomed so quickly that before the Society could celebrate its first anniversary, leaders realized there needed to be another layer to manage the very active chapters. By April 1891, just six months after founding, they made the first amendment to the DAR Constitution, creating the office of "state regent." They appointed five at that April meeting, one each for the states of Pennsylvania, Rhode

▶ Instead of exchanging gifts at Christmas, members of the Aloha Chapter gave fifty-eight books, plus puzzles and pencils, to the Family Library of the Mayor Wright Homes public housing community in Honolulu on January 29, 2005. In addition, the chapter's Daughters presented a $482 check to Katy Chen (seated at left), Executive Director of Hawaii Literacy, Inc. "I had heard wonderful things about the program and felt our contribution could help in their efforts," elaborated Jeanie Bouthillier, Aloha Chapter DAR Literacy Challenge chairman (pictured in the Hawaii DAR t-shirt). Sales of the t-shirts also helped raise funds for the gifts. Some of the children who use the library also joined Hawaii State Regent Diane Hom (seated in back second from right) and Lani Almanza, Family Literacy Program Manager. Founded in 1897, before Hawaii's statehood, the chapter chose the name "Aloha" as a symbol of relations between the United States and Hawaii at that time. Eleven of its thirteen charter members were missionaries. The early days of the Aloha Chapter focused on patriotic activities: celebrating Revolutionary anniversaries; ministering to the needs of soldiers on their way to the Philippines; proper use and respect for the flag; and patriotic essays in the public schools. Today, the chapter remains an active participant in community activities, and because of its geographic location, the chapter is particularly active in promoting Americanism and assisting those interested in becoming citizens. Since its founding, the chapter has provided $400,000 in scholarships and loans through its Hawaii Student Loan Fund.

◀ On August 14, 2002, President General Linda Tinker Watkins tours Fort Ticonderoga in New York, the site of America's first victory in the American Revolution. Sarah Pell and her husband, Stephen, restored Fort Ticonderoga and opened it to the public in 1909.

▲ Daughters of the Trumbull-Porter Chapter, Waterbury, Connecticut, provide elbow grease, as well as financial support, to help clean up and restore what is locally called the "Old Burying Ground" in Watertown (formerly Westbury), Connecticut. The cemetery, which predates the Revolution, is the final resting place of some of the area's early settlers and is maintained by the Trumbull-Porter Chapter as one of its most important projects.

Island, New York, Connecticut, and Virginia. Each State Regent would be a member of the Board of Management, the governing body of the NSDAR, joining the Executive Officers and Vice Presidents General in the oversight of the Society's property, business, activities, and policies as provided by the bylaws.

There is no doubt among NSDAR leaders, though, that the vast work of the Society is done through the chapters. Merry Ann Wright, Director of Development, Honorary State Regent of New York and past Recording Secretary General, explains that the work of the DAR "is propagated at the chapter level." The chapters, she continues, "are a very powerful mechanism for change, to make a difference in the community."

Today, work at the chapter level is as varied as the backgrounds and talents of its members, who balance support of national projects with local work unique to their communities. At the national level, the money from their penny boxes built Memorial Continental Hall, while their collective donations contributed $500,000 to the National World War II Memorial in Washington. Through the Genealogy Preservation Project, financial support from the chapters is also helping to digitize and preserve the

Friends in Far Places

The phenomenon of overseas chapters began when the first one was organized in 1897 in Honolulu, Hawaii, before it even became a state. Yet even before that first overseas chapter, members-at-large represented Switzerland, then Paris, Naples, Samoa, China, and South Africa. The newest overseas chapter, Francis Duclos Chapter, Montreal, Quebec, was confirmed on April 9, 2005. Today, twenty-one chapters are engaged in the work of the National Society in eleven countries, including Australia, the Bahamas, Bermuda, Canada, France, Germany, Italy, Japan, Mexico, Spain, and the United Kingdom. "This is the most we've ever had at one time," emphasizes Joy Cardinal, National Chairman of the Units Overseas Committee and a member of the John Edwards Chapter, Mexico City.

The Units Overseas Committee was formed in 1950 to form a link between the National Society and those members living outside the United States. Some of the members overseas are U.S. citizens. Some are native-born but have ancestors who aided in the American Revolution. For instance, most of the members in the Paris Chapter are French-speaking and trace their roots to Rochambeau and Lafayette.

Cardinal credits the current surge in overseas interest in the renewed sense of patriotism. "Patriotism and genealogy have become such a big hobby. And when you live overseas you want some bond with your roots," she explains. But she also cites technology as a factor, since the Internet allows constant contact. Cardinal is currently working with potential members to establish chapters in Nova Scotia and Switzerland.

Alissa Mendes de Leon, a prospective DAR member in Switzerland, sent this e-mail capturing her urge to join: "I may have made Switzerland my home but am afraid of neglecting my American heritage in the process! I find that my ancestry has become more important to me as time and distance separate me from 'home' and I want my children to feel that they are Americans too."

What do Daughters do overseas? "They stay in touch with the embassy or consulate. They work with Girl Scouts, the American Legion, international women's groups. Some of them have their own scholarships, independent of NSDAR scholarships. For the past two years, our Mexico City Chapter has been helping one Mexican

Members of the Bahamas Chapter gather before a luncheon at the Café Matisse, Nassau, on January 21, 2006, on the occasion of the first President General's visit there since the chapter was formed in 2001. Seated (left-right) are Chapter Regent Jayne Holland, Ruth Mytty, President General Presley Merritt Wagoner, and Joy Cardinal, National Chairman of Units Overseas. Members standing include (left-right) Patty Roker, Donna Baucom, Faye Sands, Melinda Rockwell, Karen Richford, Anne Highly, Kathy Feingold, Erin Mytty, Sally Alshouse, Victoria Thomas, and Nancy LeBlanc. The President General also visited the Somers Isles Chapter, Bermuda, in early 2006 and paid a courtesy call on its mayor, E. Michael Jones. Her visits to both chapters included tours of many of the historic sites with ties to the United States.

girl who is in her second year at the University of Guadalajara. A chapter in Canada gives twelve $500 scholarships a year to students through the American History essay contest. Mexico's John Edwards Chapter even had a national essay contest winner in 2000," said Cardinal.

Many of the overseas chapters focus their efforts on DAR missions unique to where they live. The Somers Isles Chapter in Hamilton, Bermuda, chartered in 2001, is working on a 1600s cemetery. In Colonial times, many Americans would go to Bermuda to recuperate from various 'fevers,' so there are a surprising number of Americans buried there, she elaborates. "They found six graves they're restoring. One is of a woman whose husband was a member of the Continental Congress. Another is of a Midshipman Dale, who fought in the War of 1812 and whose father was a commodore who served with John Paul Jones."

The chapter in Germany is working with Landstuhl Regional Medical Center, a critical way station for military personnel wounded in Iraq and Afghanistan. Some of them arrive at the hospital with only the clothing or uniforms they had on their backs when they were wounded. Daughters there provide personal care and entertainment items (CDs, DVDs, books), tennis shoes, backpacks, jackets, lap robes, and phone cards—anything they can think of that the military members may need.

Members of the now-disbanded Shanghai Chapter show their allegiance with a flag with forty-eight stars at their organizing meeting June 27, 1923. Since the DAR founding, in addition to Shanghai, China, there have been chapters or members in other unlikely locales, such as Cuba, Australia, South Africa, Samoa, and Venezuela.

Becoming a Daughter

Any woman may join the DAR, regardless of race, creed, or religious affiliation, so long as she is at least eighteen years of age and able to document her lineage to an ancestor, either male or female, who materially aided in the cause of American independence through military, civil, or patriotic service. However, while membership is straightforward, sometimes tracing lineage proves more challenging. Chapters welcome new Daughters, and most have members skilled in genealogy who love the research. What's more, the vast DAR Library provides almost one-stop shopping for tracing elusive ancestors. Their records, matched with recorded family histories, such as Bibles and deeds, birth certificates and wills, can usually help shake an ancestor out of a family tree. The prospective member then submits her documented application papers to the National Society through the chapter.

After verification by one of the genealogy experts on staff at Headquarters, the applicant becomes a member upon admittance by the National Board of Management and receives her unique NSDAR member number, a sequential number begun with the founding of the Society. Founder Eugenia Washington held National Number 1. Mary Lockwood, who had difficulty documenting her lineage, received National Number 27. The first year after founding, the NSDAR had issued 140,000 member numbers. Today, National Numbers total more than 850,000.

◄ ▲ The DAR appeals to the young and young at heart, including Alice Bruce Menzel (left), pictured here receiving her DAR pin on her 105th birthday party in March of 2003. "It's never too late to join the DAR," asserts Barbara Regling Jordanger, Wisconsin Society Corresponding Secretary and Stevens Point Chapter Vice Regent, who presented the pin. Others, like Gretchen E. Gailey (above) of the Kushkushkee Trail Chapter in Pittsburgh, Pennsylvania, join as soon as they are eligible at age 18.

▲ Representatives from chapters across California gathered in 1946 for their thirty-eighth annual state conference at the Mission Inn, now a National Historic Landmark in Riverside, California. State conferences such as this serve a dual purpose by bringing attention to historic sites. Often states and chapters work together to place historic markers at such sites during their annual gatherings.

▲ Members of the Cincinnati Chapter celebrate their sixtieth anniversary in this 1953 photo. Edith Irwin Hobart, seated at right, served as President General 1929–1932.

Society's vast genealogical records, not just for members but also for others interested in learning about their ancestors.

On any given week, the Clara Barton Chapter in California may be collecting soda pull-tabs to raise money for Ronald McDonald House, setting up a display at the local library, awarding nursing scholarships to a nearby nursing school, collecting personal items for veterans at a local Veterans Affairs hospital or funds for DAR Project Patriot, or participating in a parade. Meanwhile, the Trumbull-Porter Chapter in Connecticut could be hosting a genealogy workshop and presenting DAR Good Citizen Awards and savings bonds to deserving high school students. In addition to their work in the local community, the Caroline Scott Harrison Chapter in Indiana sponsored HarvestFest, raising $5,352 as their 2005 contribution to the national project to digitize the hundreds of thousands of records in the DAR Library.

◄ In a gesture symbolizing former slave Peter Green's journey across the Atlantic in a slave ship to his ultimate freedom in America, Maya Brewington pours water on the flowers beside the marker commemorating the patriot who earned his freedom by joining the Revolutionary Army and serving in a New York Unit. The marker was placed next to Green's son's grave since the patriot's final resting place is unknown. The ceremony took place June 12, 2005, in Colrain, Massachusetts. The Mary Mattoon Chapter had not only arranged the event but also located the grave of Peter Green's descendant and paid for extra engraving and placement of the Veterans Administration marker. Members of the Betty Allen and Margery Morton chapters joined the Mary Mattoon Chapter that day. It culminated a four-year journey begun with a phone call from Hazel Kreinheder, a minority and ethnic research specialist at DAR headquarters who, after noticing his name on the pension rolls, asked Chapter Regent Joanne Garland to look for Green's grave. While this African American patriot's final resting place remains a mystery, his name has been added to Colrain's list of Revolutionary War veterans. James Sheppard, of Portland, Maine, a member of the original Tuskegee Airmen and special guest at the event, stated in an interview with the Greenfield, Massachusetts, *Recorder*, "I'm so happy that the DAR is doing this. DAR's history with blacks hasn't always been a good one, but that has happily reversed and this chapter is proving that today."

◄ Members of the Ruth Wyllys Chapter, Hartford, Connecticut, funded the restoration of an entire area known as Gold Street in a historic area of Hartford. Originally, the city block was used as a combination grazing area and cemetery as early as the 1600s, but several structures—including a church, a school, and retail establishments—were built atop portions of the property, including some of the burial plots. By the 1890s, the cemetery (named the Ancient Burying Ground) had become neglected, and south Gold Street was a sixteen-foot-wide alley of slums. According to information from researcher Karen O'Maxfield, Emily Seymour Goodwin Holcombe, an early regent of the chapter, spearheaded a major effort in 1896 to clean up the area and widen the street. The Daughters not only saw to the restoration of the street and the cemetery, but also funded construction of an iron fence and memorial gate, pictured here, on Gold Street. Nicknamed "the Gold Street Lady," Emily Holcombe, her husband, and her daughter were ultimately laid to rest in the Ancient Burying Ground, a rare honor. The Ruth Wyllys Chapter continues its support for the Ancient Burying Ground to this day.

▲ Patriotic parades are a popular DAR event. Members of the Prairie Grass Chapter in Grand Forks, North Dakota, participated in their sister city's Heritage Days in East Grand Forks, Minnesota. Members of the chapter decorated the float the night before, just in time for the big parade, August 20, 2005. Pictured on the float are (left to right) Prairie Grass members Donna Trosen, who is also North Dakota State Vice Regent; Laurie McHenry, Chapter Regent; Virginia Tupa, North Dakota State Regent; Beverly Jensen, past Historian General; and Peggy Vanyo, Chapter Chaplain. The young man at the extreme left is Hunter McHenry, grandson of Laurie McHenry.

▲ The Molly Stark Chapter in Manchester, New Hampshire, makes historic preservation a key priority of their chapter's work. The chapter owns and maintains the boyhood home of General John Stark, built in 1736. Molly Stark, daughter of the first postmaster of New Hampshire, married John Stark in 1758. Molly was both nurse and doctor to her husband's troops during a smallpox epidemic. This historic home acts not only as the chapter house but is also a certified museum. Chapter member Anne Landini is shown here at Molly Stark's very own kitchen table polishing the museum's silver service.

The same commitment of Mrs. Shinn and her fellow New Jersey General Lafayette Daughters in 1918 fuels the chapters today. A common message emerges in scores of interviews with chapter members across the country, such as Denise Doring VanBuren, a member of the Melzingah Chapter, founded in 1895 and one of the oldest in New York. A former newscaster and currently vice president for a regional electric utility, VanBuren elaborates, "From coast to coast, there are thousands of women doing what the four founders envisioned, celebrating places of historic importance, preserving sites of local history, documenting their genealogy, thereby honoring the history of their local community." She continues, "We sponsor naturalization ceremonies, comfort veteran patients, recognize outstanding citizens and support a strong national defense. There are literally thousands of ways that our members today are living out what the founders dreamed of more than a century ago."

► The five new members inducted into the Hollywood Chapter, California, at their October 15, 2005, meeting included Dr. Essie Mae Washington-Williams (left), daughter of the late Senator Strom Thurmond, and her daughter, Wanda Williams Terry (center). Also pictured are Nancy Daniels (second from left), Chapter Regent; chapter member Dr. Nelle Becker-Slaton (second from right), who played a key role in helping Dr. Washington-Williams and her daughter with their membership; and Jan Gordon, DAR District IX Director who, noted Daniels, "has been instrumental in supporting our revitalization." Countless chapters have altered their meeting dates and times and expanded the variety of events and activities to accommodate the needs of women today. Alice Magner, Ashley Atkinson, and Lauren Azeltine joined the chapter that day as well.

PHOTO COURTESY HOLLYWOOD CHAPTER

WOMANS BUILDING.

COLUMBIAN EXPOSITION LIBRARY OF CONGRESS PHOTO BY WINTERS ART LITHOGRAPHING COMPANY

LADY MANAGERS OF THE WHITE CITY

Effie Beulah Reeme Osborn, the State Regent for Illinois, called the first meeting of the first chapter of the NSDAR in Chicago, March 16, 1891, in the commissioner's room of the World's Columbian Exposition that would take place in 1893. As reported in the January 1893 issue of *American Monthly Magazine*, "The first work planned by the Chicago Chapter was the Colonial Exhibit, to be placed in the Woman's Building at the World's Fair," pictured here. The meeting proved portentous, for it was the architecture of that fabled "White City" that became the inspiration for the design for Memorial Continental Hall. Under the Act of Congress providing for the appointment of a Woman's Board to promote the interests and work of women at the Columbian Exposition, Frances Wells Shepard (pictured in inset), who succeeded Mrs. Osborn as chapter regent, was appointed one of the two "Lady Managers" for the state of Illinois. Founder Mary Smith Lockwood was also a member of the Board of Lady Managers for the Exposition, cited at the time as "the most powerful organization that has ever existed among women."

Fans of Flight

Every President General logs thousands of miles and hours of travel crisscrossing the country to participate in the events sponsored each year by the DAR state societies and overseas chapters. However, as President General Edith Scott Magna wrote in an article titled "Happy Landings," in the 1934 issue of the DAR magazine, "Fate has decreed that I am the first President General to use flying as a method of transportation to facilitate the demands of my office and to save time."

She flew so often in those early days of flight that she noted she had "long since ceased to treat it as an adventure, or as a courageous feat." In this 1933 photo, Pilot Bowen (first name unknown) prepares her for yet another plane ride, this time in an open cockpit two-seater to attend the New Mexico state conference October 20 of that year. Just a few months before, following the address of keynote speaker Amelia Earhart at Continental Congress, President General Magna had confessed to those assembled: "Daughters, I am telling Miss Earhart your President General is air-minded also."

Earhart's remarks would also challenge the Daughters to blaze new trails. "I am going to make two prophecies," she pronounced. "One is that many in this audience will be in their plane in the next two years. Further, that many of you will have a chance to fly over regular scheduled Atlantic service. That will come in our lifetime," she predicted. "I hope that you will think of aviation possibly not as a means of defense in the army and navy, but through the development of its industrial side and the use to which it can be put in those peaceful occupations," she concluded.

▶ As with all DAR Presidents General, Mrs. Magna was also highly regarded. Alabama Poet Laureate Samuel Minturn Peck wrote the personally signed poem pictured here in her honor, on the occasion of her visit to that state.

To Edith Scott Magna
President-General of the Daughters of the American Revolution

Alabama greets you,
The Leader of a band
Of patriotic women
Who love their native land,
Chosen Daughter of the Heroes
Who fought a gallant fight
And won a Nation's freedom,
We welcome you tonight.

In that welcome there is woven
The breath of Southern flowers,
The incense of all blossoms
That grace our Southland bowers;
Beloved and gracious Herald,
With message glad and bright,
With words we cannot tell you
That our hearts are yours tonight.

Samuel Minturn Peck.

CHAPTER FIVE

A Life of Service
Educating America

EORGE WASHINGTON BELIEVED FERVENTLY that the greatest asset to and necessity of a free government was an enlightened public. In his farewell address to the nation, printed in the *American Daily Advertiser* in Philadelphia on September 19, 1796, he urged his fellow citizens to "promote, then, as an object of primary importance, institutions for the general diffusion of knowledge." In 1890, almost a century later, the Daughters of the American Revolution would take the Father of our Nation's injunction to their heart, making it an intrinsic element of their three-fold mission of preservation, education, and patriotism, for it is education that often facilitates the other two. An understanding of the history and fight for democracy fosters a sense of patriotism and the need to preserve the art, artifacts, and architecture of that history.

Patricia W. Shelby, 1980–1983 President General, asserted in 1982, "If there were no other reasons for the DAR (and there are many), our work with youth justifies our existence." Through its many education programs for youth and adults, the DAR provides training in literacy, leadership, American history and citizenship, and a deeper appreciation for the history of the United States and the freedoms it secured. At least twenty-eight of the forty-two DAR national and special committees focus, in whole or in part, on education.

SCHOLARSHIPS

Partly through donations and endowments from its members, each year the NSDAR awards more than $1 million in scholarships and financial aid to high school and college students

▶ Shiloh Wersen (left) and Andrew Bratten, both of Salisbury, Maryland, and both sponsored by the Samuel Chase Chapter, show off the certificates noting their selection as DAR national scholarship winners. Shiloh, who is pursuing a major in vocal performance, was the first winner of the new Nellie Love Butcher Scholarship, a $5,000 award given to a student pursuing an education in piano or voice. Andrew won the Lillian and Arthur Dunn Scholarship, reserved for deserving sons and daughters of members of the NSDAR. He will receive $2,000 for up to four years and beyond. Nearly all DAR scholarships bear the names of Daughters or donors whose generosity has funded endowments that allow the NSDAR to award some $1 million in scholarships annually for academic excellence, students with special learning challenges, as well as those with financial need.

PHOTO COURTESY DONNA BOTTINI

through at least four separate committees—the DAR School, Good Citizens, Scholarship, and American Indians committees—and on the local level. Individual chapters hold bake sales, raffles, auctions, special events, and other functions to generate funds. One Daughter raised $500 by auctioning herself off to make and serve dinner for ten.

▲ Colorado State Regent Donna Bottini hands out flags and certificates of accomplishment to a local preschooler in this 2005 photo. Bottini's goal during her tenure as State Regent is to hand out flags and certificates to every kindergarten student in Colorado who learns the Pledge of Allegiance.

The DAR Scholarship Committee, which determines most DAR scholarships, awards a total of approximately $840,000 each year at the national, state, and chapter levels combined, all based on bequests or outright gifts by Daughters or interested donors. The scholarship categories under the Scholarship Committee include nursing and medicine, occupational and physical therapy, music, clinical science, history, government, economics, dentistry, business, law, medicine, and chemistry. There are 800 applications annually for medical scholarships alone, which provide for up to a total of $20,000 for four years of medical school. Applications for all DAR scholarships average more than 1,600 each year.

"You never know how many lives you're going to touch," emphasizes Carole Farmer, DAR Scholarship Committee National Chairman. One year, after a Scholarship Committee meeting at the NSDAR headquarters in Washington, D.C., she came back with "some sort of bug," as she described it. "I went to the doctor, and he asked what I was doing in Washington. I explained, and he replied, 'I got a DAR medical scholarship.'" That doctor got her well, but it was the 2005 medical scholarship winner from California who brought tears

to Farmer's eyes when the student asserted, "You don't know how much this will help me."

DAR SCHOOLS

The DAR schools are funded by more than $1 million annually from the Daughters. The six schools provide a variety of special needs programs that address problems such as attention deficit disorder, dyslexia, adult literacy, and children in family crisis. It is an enormous commitment that began with a handful of Daughters at the turn of the twentieth century, which remains a labor of love.

Prior to 1919, various chapters had annually contributed funds for scholarships and other financial support to numerous schools across the country under church, corporation, or individual ownership and control, according to a circa 1924 pamphlet published by the New York State Organization. They had embraced the cause of the South Carolina Daughters, who recognized the plight of mountain children. The South Carolina Society had voted at its 1914 conference to establish a school in a remote area where the need was greatest, for "those girls of the Southern Mountains who seek learning at Tamassee," South Carolina, named for the area the Cherokees called "the Place of the Sunlight of God."

The "sunlight of God" lit such a fire in the hearts of the Daughters that by 1919, the 29th Continental Congress voted to adopt Tamassee as a National Society project, making it the first DAR school. Here was a labor of love so close to the heart of the Daughters' mission of education that the National Society would adopt a second mountain school—Kate Duncan Smith School, in Grant, Alabama—less than ten years later, in 1928. Amanda A. Thomas, National Chairman of the DAR School Committee in 1973, referred to Tamassee and KDS as "DAR Jewels" in an article published in the DAR magazine that year: "These schools have given thousands of mountain boys and girls the opportunity to obtain an education. Buildings and maintenance costs represent an expenditure of millions of dollars, and the thousands of capable, well-adjusted alumni are living proof of the validity of DAR's educational effort." John Willard, Tamassee class of 1947, a retired educator and alumni board member, is just one example. Asserts Willard, "All I am or ever hope to be is due to the divine guidance I received at Tamassee." The youngsters there also know Tamassee is about

▲ Sarah Cutler, a Virginia Daughter and volunteer docent at the DAR Museum, reads to a young visitor in the "Touch of Independence" children's play area at DAR Headquarters while another young lady enjoys the pleasures of an afternoon tea with some of the items provided for children to learn about early American daily life.

◀ ▲ Boys and girls dressed as young patriots show off their crafts—gumdrop trees and ribbon medallions—during Colonial Camp 2005, sponsored by the DAR Museum as part of its summer program for youngsters. The two-week camp allows youngsters, aged eight to twelve, to step back in time to experience life in the early days of this country through hands-on activities from colonial and Revolutionary times. Campers wear historically accurate costumes, participate in an all-day field trip to an area site, play colonial games, sample colonial food, and learn period dances.

PHOTO COURTESY OF HILLSIDE SCHOOL

▲ Located in a rural section of Marlborough, Massachusetts, Hillside School for boys serves traditional learners who want a more personalized education as well as those with learning differences or attention problems. It also remains a working farm where many of the boys, who are primarily from urban areas, delight in their first exposure to farming and tending livestock. The young man pictured feeds the school's herd of alpacas, which are raised for their wool. The school's interesting menagerie of livestock also includes a llama.

more than education. As one ten-year-old put it, "People say that this is just a boarding school, but this is much more to me . . . this is my home." Another classmate adds, "Tamassee is a beautiful place to live and it is safe. I found out what it felt like to be loved."

Support for these two DAR schools is the major focus of DAR Junior members, those Daughters from eighteen through thirty-five years of age. Juniors hold full membership in the national and state societies as well as their chapters and serve as officers and chairmen at all levels. Established in 1937, the National Junior Membership Committee projects include the Helen Pouch Memorial Fund authorized in 1938. The fund is named in memory of the daughter of Helena R. Pouch, the first National Chairman of the Junior Membership Committee and later President General, 1941–1944. The fund provides scholarships, medical aid, and general financial assistance to Kate Duncan Smith and Tamassee. Each year, the Juniors and their chapters alone raise more than $100,000 for the schools.

While Tamassee and KDS receive a substantial portion of their funding from the DAR, the Daughters are equally proud of the other four DAR schools they assist—Crossnore School, Hillside School, Hindman Settlement School, and Berry College. Founded in 1902 by Martha Berry, a DAR member, as a boys' industrial school with five students, Berry School (now College) was the first to receive DAR assistance. Martha Berry's devotion to youth and her appeal to the Daughters for support at the 13th Continental Congress assured the school's success. In 1904, it became the first to be placed on the DAR list of approved schools. Helena R. Pouch, whose family had interests in the Birmingham, Alabama, steel mills, personally contributed the steel for their Roy Richards Memorial Gymnasium. Berry College, located in Mount Berry, Georgia, is now an independent, coeducational college with fully accredited arts, sciences, and professional programs serving some 2,000 students, and in 2005 was ranked the No. 2 undergraduate comprehensive college in the South by *U.S. News & World Report*.

Another Daughter, Dr. Mary Martin Sloop, and her sister, Dr. Eustace Sloop, founded Crossnore School in 1913 in the

PHOTO COURTESY OF HILLSIDE SCHOOL

◄ In May 2006, Hillside School hosted a DAR Day celebration to express thanks for the support the school receives from Daughters across the country. As part of the celebration, students performed the first act of their spring musical, *1776*. Faculty and students, such as the three young men pictured here, also hosted a luncheon for visiting DAR officials, pictured in the background.

◄ ▲ Berry College, a DAR-supported facility in Mount Berry, Georgia, was founded by Martha Berry (pictured in inset), a DAR member committed to providing industrial school training for boys in the area. Since then, the school has become a coeducational, fully accredited college providing degrees in arts, sciences, and professional programs serving some two thousand students.

◄ Students admire photos taken as part of a school project at Hindman Settlement School, in Hindman, Kentucky, a DAR-supported school with a special curriculum for students with dyslexia.

▲ Barbara (left), resident counselor of Belk Cottage at Crossnore School, assists the special "chef for the day" while making popcorn balls.

remote mountains of the Blue Ridge in Crossnore, North Carolina, believing that "education is the best way for a child to rise above his circumstances." Relates the school's official history of its first few years, "The Sloops trudged on foot and rode horseback on steep dirt trails in isolated mountain valleys to bring medicine to the people and convince farmers to let their children come to school." Initially, because of poverty and distance, the school took in boarders and built dormitories to accommodate them. Crossnore became the fourth DAR Approved School in 1921. By 1973, the school had housed, fed, and clothed more than four thousand deprived youngsters. Referred to today as the "Miracle in the Mountains," Crossnore School is a private, nonprofit children's home and school in the western North Carolina mountains, serving children who, for circumstances beyond their control, can no longer live at home, whether permanently or temporarily.

Hillside School, an independent boarding and day school for middle school boys in grades five through nine, was founded in 1901 by two sisters who wanted to educate needy boys in Massachusetts. The 200-acre independent boarding and day school is located in a rural section of

C.A.R.: Young Patriots

On February 22, 1895, at the 4th Continental Congress, Harriet M. Lothrop, the Regent of the Old Concord Chapter, Massachusetts, believing that "good citizens cannot be made suddenly" but must grow, offered a resolution to organize the National Society Children of the American Revolution. Congress quickly passed the resolution and only five months later, by July, the new children's organization had grown rapidly. Perhaps it was inevitable that the state boasting the first NSDAR Chapter, Illinois, would also be one of the first to form a C.A.R. society, the Zeally Moss Society, named for the only Revolutionary soldier buried among the 78,000 citizens in the historic Springdale Cemetery in Peoria, Illinois.

Almost immediately after the society's founding, with the outbreak of the Spanish-American War, C.A.R. members exhibited what has remained a priority—support of military personnel and veterans. In 1898, C.A.R. members raised money for the Spanish-American War Relief Fund. They donated clothing, yarn, knitting needles, and gauze for bandages to the Red Cross for use by women and children in Belgium during World War I. Their "Peck O' Pennies Fund" supported the "Children of the Frontier" in France. During World War II, they raised funds for a bed for the Children's Hospital in Washington, D.C., an ambulance for Red Cross use on Staten Island, a Jeep and ambulance for the War Department, adoption of six children in war-torn countries, purchase of war bonds and stamps, and sponsorship of the crew of an amphibious ship.

The nation's oldest, largest, patriotic youth organization, C.A.R. mirrors DAR on many levels, with local and state societies under the umbrella of a National Society. The ten thousand current C.A.R. members represent more than one thousand individual societies in forty-eight states, the District of Columbia, England, France, Mexico, and Canada. The NSDAR shares a portion of their headquarters building in Washington with the N.S.C.A.R. offices and museum.

C.A.R. trains good citizens, develops leaders, and promotes commitment to the United States of America and its heritage among young people. Much like the DAR, C.A.R. members serve on local, state, and national levels as officers and chairmen. Each C.A.R. society has a corresponding "senior," one of approximately two thousand DAR and SAR members who play active roles as advisors

▲ Members of New York's Highland Pass Society, C.A.R., join Daughters of the Melzingah Chapter at the rededication in 2000 of the DAR Mount Beacon Monument overlooking the Hudson Valley in Beacon, New York. The city was named in honor of the famous signal fires that had burned atop the Fishkill Mountain. Revolutionary soldiers used the beacon fires to warn General George Washington, stationed across the Hudson River at Newburgh, of British ships and troop movements during the war. The Melzingah Chapter erected the monument and unveiled it July 4, 1900, when more than one hundred participants climbed the mountain on foot and in carriages to attend the impressive ceremony, according to accounts of the event. Made of native stone in the shape of a pyramid patterned after the original pyres, which were built of logs, fourteen feet square at the base and twenty-five feet high, the monument has been maintained by Melzingah for more than a century. C.A.R. member Colleen Hollowood, age twelve, wrote of a 2005 Memorial Day pilgrimage by members of Melzingah and the Highland Pass Society to Mount Beacon during the 230th anniversary of the signal fires and the monument's 105th anniversary: "We reached the top of the mountain after about one hour. We could see the City of Beacon and the Hudson River below us. It was a beautiful day, and we could see for many miles. It's no wonder they wanted to put the beacon fire there so that it could be seen by all the people below. It was a great hike that gave me a better appreciation for what our soldiers did to win our independence."

and mentors. All children under the age of twenty-one are eligible for membership, so long as they are lineally descended from a person who directly aided in the cause of the American Revolution. At age eighteen, girls and boys become eligible for dual membership in the DAR or SAR, respectively.

C.A.R. activities are as varied as their members' young imaginations. They write skits, dress in period costumes, march in parades, present musical programs, participate in wreath-layings and other patriotic observances, place flags on graves of veterans, visit VA hospitals, tutor children, support children in Special Olympics, clean cemeteries, pick up trash along streams and rivers, plant trees, and more. Through various fundraising projects, they provide financial and material aid to children in the DAR Schools, Tamassee and Kate Duncan Smith.

▲ Members of the Lt. Isaiah Fuller Society of C.A.R., in Romeo, Michigan, adopted a dog named Kipper and raised funds through their "Kids 'N' Coins" program to send him to school to be a Leader Dog for the blind and visually impaired. Pictured in the front row are (l-r) Chelsea Linders, Erin Tepatti, and Caleb Kozen; back row (l-r) Ian Krause, Peter Krause, and Timmy Tepatti.

▲ A young art enthusiast inspects the painting, *The Signing of the Constitution,* by renowned artist Louis S. Glanzman, a gift commissioned by several DAR state societies commemorating the celebration of the Bicentennial of the U.S. Constitution in 1987. DAR members and national officers, including President General Ann D. Fleck, assembled in Philadelphia, Pennsylvania, to present the painting and to participate in a variety of special events that year. The painting hangs in Independence Hall in Philadelphia.

▲ A young Crossnore resident shares a hug with her cottage pet, Ginger, part of the pet nurturing program at the school.

Marlborough, Massachusetts, approximately forty miles west of downtown Boston, and includes a working farm. "Initially it was a farm, and to get their education, they had to work on the farm," explains Mindy Kammeyer, National Chairman of the DAR School Committee. What they raised not only fed the students but also was one of its main sources of income until the 1980s. While these days the focus is a bit different for the boys, the farm program is still part of their education. Kammeyer continues, "The boys are all from urban areas now, and they love to go over to the farm and see animals born and rake out the barn." Hillside offers schooling for both traditional learners who want a more personalized education and those boys with learning differences and attention problems. "Hillside has had a tremendous impact on my life over the past two years and I am proud to be a student here," wrote Hillside graduate James German in his note thanking the Daughters for their support.

▲ ▶ Especially in the first few decades of the DAR, one way local chapter members brought public attention to historic dates was to act them out or dress in period costume. On the 200th anniversary of George Washington's 1732 birth, Teresa Stevens Kane (right), Regent of the Seneca Chapter, Geneva, New York, and her daughter Judith dressed as they would have in the eighteenth century for this February 22, 1932, photo. Judith Kane Connors later became Regent for the Lynnhaven Parish Chapter, Virginia Beach, Virginia. Dressing up in period costumes is still a popular way to celebrate history, as evidenced in this circa 2001 photo of California Junior American Citizens and Children of the American Revolution members marching in a parade.

▶ The collaborative efforts of the first DAR schools proved so successful that at one time the National Society supported as many as thirty-five schools, such as the Missionary School for Girls whose 1919 graduating class is pictured here. Other DAR-supported schools included Saint Mary's and the Commonwealth School for Boys. As public schooling became more accessible, the Daughters shifted their support to other aspects of their substantial mission of preservation and patriotism as well as education. By 1934, the Continental Congress voted to limit the number of approved schools to seventeen, and, in 1940, they resolved that as vacancies occurred, no new schools would be added.

Tamassee: The Place of the Sunlight of God

▲ The five Barnes children at left all attended Tamassee in the early 1930s. They are pictured here in front of their home with their mother, Mrs. Barnes, and "Granpa Barnes" at far right standing in the garden. Like the Barnes children, many students traveled quite a distance to attend the school.

"In 1914, the future was bleak for children living in the isolated mountain areas of northwestern South Carolina," wrote Marilyn R. Creedon, National Chairman of the DAR School Committee in 1995. "With no schools near their homes, many were faced with the probability of a life of poverty and illiteracy."

To address this issue, the South Carolina DAR secured a commitment of support from the National Society, which voted to establish a school for mountain girls. The South Carolina Daughters, in turn, worked with the local Tamassee community, which ultimately donated $1,000 and 110 acres of land, along with pledges of labor and materials. Tamassee opened its doors as a day school in February 1919, the same year the school was adopted by the National Society. However, each day young girls came as much as forty miles or more and crossed several mountaintops each way on foot and by horseback to reach the school, so within months it began accepting its first boarding pupils. "During the Depression days," relates Mindy Kammeyer, DAR School Committee National Chairman, "their families couldn't even feed them, so they brought them to Tamassee where they would be placed in the cottages."

From those one hundred acres and one building, Tamassee grew to a campus that now encompasses more than eight hundred acres and thirty buildings, many of which bear the names of prominent Daughters or DAR state societies that funded their construction, such as the Edla Stannard Gibson Memorial Chapel, New York Cottage, and Ohio Hall. Tamassee serves the community by providing a boarding school and home-like atmosphere for as many as sixty-five needy children seeking a chance to succeed in life, putting behind them histories of abuse, neglect, or misunderstanding. In a unique partnership between the DAR and the School District of Oconee County, Tamassee provides formal education for grades K–5 at Tamassee Elementary School, while Tamassee-Salem Middle and Senior High Schools serve grades 6–12.

DAR members provide nearly 100 percent of the needs, in-kind gifts, and necessary funding to care for the children at the school. Many of the more than thirty buildings and cottages on the 800-acre main campus were built by funds from DAR state societies, including New York, Florida, and Missouri, whose Daughters, "really take a positive role" in supporting their cottages, providing everything from linens, clothes, shoes, and socks, to Christmas presents for the children, said Mindy Kammeyer. Campbell's Soup labels collected by hundreds of chapters earn vans and recreational and educational materials, while college scholarships funded by the Daughters provide opportunities for higher education.

What started almost a century ago as a tiny school planted on fertile ground to feed the bodies and souls of girls hungry for an education has evolved into an educational facility with thirty-four full-time staff that includes childcare, administration, maintenance, and nutrition. As thousands of former at-risk girls and boys can attest, Tamassee has never wavered from its focus on every child's fullest growth and development.

Tamassee student Sean Saunders—whose father, facing cancer treatments, was forced to place Sean there—credits the school with changing his life:

> I came to Tamassee as a last resort. . . . I was very undisciplined in many areas and lacked both the knowledge and maturity that someone my age should have already had. I began to see dramatic changes in my life. The depressions that accumulated over my childhood were filled with the caring attitudes and temperance of the teaching parents and staff. Without a great place like Tamassee DAR School, I wouldn't be . . . the changed person I am now. My life has been turned around by the will of God through Tamassee DAR School and is heading for the first time . . . in the right direction.

This page from a 1924 Tamassee pamphlet provides a snapshot of its growth during the years since its establishment in 1914, as well as "opportunities" for both the girls—"a chance"—and the Daughters—"to help in citizen building." One of the main assets listed in the pamphlet was the cottage built by the New York Daughters and dedicated in 1923. Tamassee student Janie Nicholson, one of the first Tamassee students, wrote of the school: "In the summer of 1919 the Keowee *Courier* published a notice of the new Industrial School to be opened by the D.A.R. My mother and I rode horseback from our home in Mountain Rest, across Station Mountain to Tamassee to see about the school. As financial assistance could be gotten for only one of us, my sister, Mary, entered school in November. She was the first boarding pupil. The next winter we both came. I had to begin in the fifth grade because our home terms had always been too short for us to get far in our books. I live in the beautiful New York Cottage and the Belvidere Chapter of the Mississippi [Daughters] gives me a scholarship. When I remember how we students used to bring water from a distant spring, scour the floor every week, and do so much work, I can scarcely imagine I am in the same place. Now I turn a water spigot in a bath room, mop an oiled floor, and have more time for classes."

TAMASSEE INDUSTRIAL SCHOOL

Main Building

ESTABLISHED
OWNED
CONTROLLED
BY
DAUGHTERS
OF THE
**AMERICAN
REVOLUTION**

First Tamassee District School

MILESTONES

Nov. 1914. Establishment voted by South Carolina Conference.
Nov. 1916, Present site accepted.
1918, Main Building erected.
Feb. 1919, First Day School.
1919-1920, First Boarding Pupils.
April 1923, New York Cottage dedicated.
1924, Must Have Administration Building.

ASSETS

1. Endowment
2. Permanent Scholarships ____ $50,000
3. Land—110 acres ____ 3,200
4. Buildings:
   Main Building ____ 12,000
   N. Y. Cottage ____ 14,000
   Farmers Cottage ____ 1,000
   Cheese Factory ____ 2,000
5. Stock, farm equip., etc. ____ 500
6. Opportunity, the greatest asset:
   To the girls—a "chance".
   To you—to help in citizen building.

Through Endowment. $100 enrolls the donor as a Patron of Arts and Crafts.
Scholarships, $50 per year. Permanent Scholarship, $1000. Contingent. Any amount acceptable.
Administration Building. Bonds for General Fund $50. Rooms and features $300—$5000.

General Building Fund

200 Bonds at $50 Each
Rooms and Features:
Auditorium
*Library ____ $5,000
4 School rooms, each ____ 3,000
2 Offices, each ____ 500
Domestic Science ____ 500
Weaving Room ____ 300
Heating Plant ____ 1,000
Lighting System ____ 600
*Taken by Illinois D. A. R ____ 1,200

Administration Building

▼ Life at Tamassee is not all work. Here, students pit their strength against one another in a good-natured tug of war, while Executive Director Dean Bare helps them "keep their cool."

Hindman Settlement School, founded in 1902 on the Forks of Troublesome Creek in Hindman, Kentucky, also serves children with special needs such as dyslexia. DAR funds go toward scholarships for those children who cannot afford to attend. Kammeyer sings the praises of Hindman: "In the summer they board as many as fifty kids for a six-week program. They can catch children up as much as two grade levels," some of whom, like Angel, could not read before attending summer school there. Hindman "flipped her life around," according to her aunt. Announces Angel proudly, "Education is knowledge so you can go to college!" The adult education program at Hindman also allows adult students to attain their GED and go on to take college courses. In recent years, Hindman's mission has spread to celebrate the surrounding unique culture. Their Appalachian Family Folk Week, describes Kammeyer, "highlights the crafts and folklore to keep the old traditions alive, from dulcimer playing to hand carving, art, and pottery."

INDIAN SCHOOLS

Two DAR-supported schools fill a special niche in the NSDAR educational mission, for they primarily serve America's first people, the Native American Indians. The schools are a major mission of the DAR American Indians Committee established in 1936. The National Society's philosophy is that these first

CONVENTION PHOTOGRAPHY SERVICES PHOTO

▲ Madeline Iles, of Natchez, Mississippi, sponsored by the William Dunbar Chapter, holds the certificate presented to her at the 114th Continental Congress as fifth-grade winner of the National American History Essay Contest. In her acceptance speech, she particularly thanked her history teacher: "She spent many hours outside of class this year working to inspire her students to love and understand the importance of history."

PHOTO COURTESY OF IDAHO STATESMAN

◀ Every year since 1982, the National Society has honored teachers of American History and related fields for their service. Gail K. Chumbley, sponsored by the Pioneer Chapter in Idaho, was honored at the 114th Continental Congress as the DAR National Outstanding Teacher of American History. In addition to initiating a program in her eleventh grade classes to record the oral histories of World War II soldiers and Navy pilots as part of the Library of Congress Oral History Project, in 1999 she and her students raised $25,000 for the World War II Memorial in Washington, more than any other school in the country. She and two of her students attended the 2000 groundbreaking. In Chumbley's remarks to the Daughters at Congress, she noted: "You and I are on the same path. Strength in science, math, and even in literature has its place, but if our students are unaware of who they are as Americans, [do not] understand the glue that holds our nation together, the other disciplines are moot. We cease to be a distinct people without a shared past."

PHOTO COURTESY OF BACONE COLLEGE

PHOTO COURTESY OF BACONE COLLEGE

▲ ▶ Students from Bacone College show their team spirit at a sporting event. A DAR Indian school located in Muskogee, Oklahoma, Bacone College is an accredited four-year liberal arts facility that includes a nursing school. Chartered in 1880, it is the oldest college in Oklahoma. Over 40 percent of Bacone students are Native Americans, and the college remains faithful to its historic mission of providing an education to American Indians while creating a diverse curriculum to serve students from all regions, nations, and walks of life.

▶ Theopholus William Krug wrote this award-winning essay, "Trials and Triumphs of America," for the first DAR American History contest in 1898. As his reward, Krug received $5 from the New York Daughters. The original copy of the essay is part of a display in the Americana Room that also highlights other previous local winners prior to the mid-1950s, when individual DAR chapters and state organizations presented their own unique awards to students for writing on American history topics. Today, through a nationally coordinated program that encourages youngsters to learn about history in a new light, more than 4,000 schools participate in this annual contest for students in grades 5–8, with nearly 66,000 essays submitted yearly.

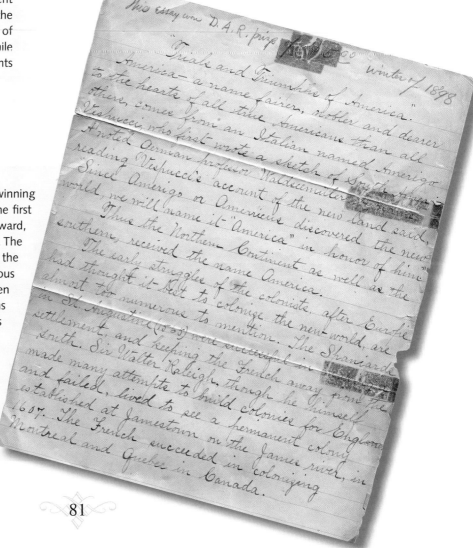

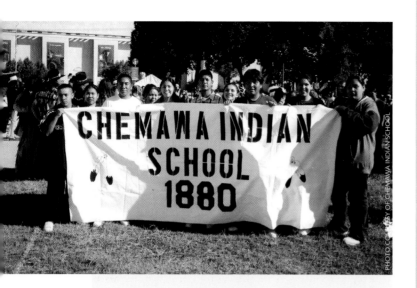

▲ Although officially established in 1880, the history of Chemawa Indian School dates back to the 1870s when the U.S. government authorized a school for Indian children in the Northwest. Chemawa celebrated its 125th anniversary in 2005 and is the oldest continuously operating boarding school in the United States. Its four hundred students represent more than seventy different Indian tribes, including Alaskan Natives. DAR funding provides scholarships, general operating expenses, and donations for the students' personal needs.

Americans "shaped our nation through their cultural, religious, social, and political contributions"; therefore, "it is up to us, as Daughters, to contribute back to them through the many programs of the American Indians Committee." With that mission in mind, the NSDAR supports Bacone College in Muskogee, Oklahoma, and Chemawa Indian Preparatory Academy in Salem, Oregon, with scholarships, general operating expenses, and donations for the personal needs of the students. The DAR American Indians Committee also promotes "American Indian Minutes" at chapter meetings and participation in community celebrations of National American Indian Heritage Month in November.

GOOD CITIZENS

There is one aspect of the DAR commitment to young Americans—the DAR Good Citizens Program—where students need not apply. Instead, faculty members in either public or private schools nominate three seniors who display qualities of good citizenship, such as leadership, service, loyalty, and unselfish commitment to family, school, community, and country. United States citizenship is not a requirement. From these three students, the

Citizenship: A Welcoming Hand

In 1920, President General Anne R. Minor would state to the 29th Continental Congress: "There is this one concrete work which your President General desires to recommend—this is the financing of a manual of information in several languages for free distribution to the immigrant on landing on these shores, . . . what he needs to know in order to lead the life of a law-abiding American citizen." According to early proceedings of the Continental Congress, Connecticut Daughters had already been engaged "for twenty years at least . . . teaching American ideals of life, government and citizenship to the immigrant." They had also published their own *Guide to the United States for Immigrants* in Italian. The 29th Congress wholeheartedly supported Mrs. Minor's recommendation and directed that a national manual patterned after the Connecticut model be produced.

By the next Continental Congress in 1921, the *Manual of the United States for the Information of Immigrants* was ready for the press and for translation. That first edition contained welcoming comments by Mrs. Minor and a list of thirty topics beginning with "The American's Creed" (penned just three years before by William Tyler Page), and addressing such topics as "Finding Work," "How to

▲ Graduates of DAR citizenship classes pose for a group portrait on the steps of a California courthouse in this 1940 photo. The new citizens display flags presented to them by the Santa Ana Chapter, which sponsored the classes and served as tutors. Under the direction of the Americanism Committee, hundreds of local DAR chapters provide citizenship training and promote the study of American government.

THE LIBERTY BELL

The Liberty Bell was originally hung in the tower of the State House (later Independence Hall) June 7, 1753. The inscription is from the Bible, Leviticus 25:10, in incribed on the bell "Proclaim Liberty throughout all the land unto all the inhabitants thereof." On September 18, 1777, it was taken to Allentown to prevent its capture by the British. It was stored back to Philadelphia. It was rung out on the anniversary of Independence and tolled when the Country died. The bell cracked sometime 1846.

DAR
MANUAL for
CITIZENSHIP

Published as a public service by
Daughters of the American Revolution National Society

◄ More than twelve million *DAR Manual for Citizenship* booklets have helped those preparing for the naturalization process. DAR chapters throughout the country continue to attend naturalization ceremonies, with flags of the United States of America, to welcome those taking the oath of citizenship.

Learn English," "Are You a Farmer?" "Buying a Farm," "Duties of a Good Citizen," "Naturalization Law," "The American Flag," "United States History and Government," and ending with "The Constitution of the United States." Only one year later, in 1922, nearly 35,000 copies had been distributed in English, Spanish, and Italian. In 1923, distribution had tripled and translations had doubled: forty-five states, the District of Columbia, and even Cuba had distributed 102,860 copies of the manual in English, Spanish, Italian, Hungarian, Polish, and Yiddish.

The New York State Organization sent out the largest number of manuals by far that year—41,617, or more than five times the amount of any other state. As DAR Historian Mollie Somerville wrote in her history of the manual in 1983, "Ellis Island, the tiny speck of land in Upper New York Harbor in the shadow of the Statue of Liberty, housed the largest immigration station in the United States. This became the center of immigrant activities for the New York Daughters." California's Angel Island, the largest island in San Francisco Bay, also served as a gateway for immigrants seeking a better life. (Please see chapter 9 for a look at the significant role the DAR would play in the work and history of both islands.)

Annual distribution of the citizenship manuals reached its peak—nearly half a million—in 1928. In 1952, the NSDAR ceased publishing the manual in foreign languages, at the request of what was then the Immigration and Naturalization Service. Future distribution was to be in English only. As the number of immigrants to the United States declined, so did distribution of the manual, yet it remained in demand, and the Society handed out approximately 50,000 per year through 1982. The year 1983 would prove pivotal for the DAR and its bestseller, whose title had evolved to the *DAR Manual for Citizenship*. Under the administration of President General Patricia W. Shelby, the Society celebrated the free distribution of ten million copies of its popular booklet.

Distribution would remain fairly steady for the next two decades, and by 2000, it had topped twelve million copies. In 2004, Americanism and DAR Manual for Citizenship Committee Chairman Lynn F. Young would report that, recognizing the efforts of DAR, the Bureau of Citizenship and Immigration Services (formerly INS) had requested DAR participation in the restructuring of the official citizenship ceremony. The BCIS also announced plans to publish new study materials for citizenship using the *DAR Manual for Citizenship* as a guide. While the NSDAR no longer prints its manual, it launched the first online version in 2004. It remains available for download from the DAR public and member Web site and is still being used. As reported in the April 9, 2006, Virginia Beach, Virginia, *Beacon*, Dennis Borgerding, a history teacher selected as Outstanding Teacher of American History by Virginia's Lynnhaven Parish Chapter, uses the *DAR Manual for Citizenship* to quiz his students on their knowledge of their country. In fact, the DAR manual Borgerding uses is personal to him and his family. His wife, Olivia, formerly a British citizen, used the book to study for her citizenship exam.

▲ Joan Zumwalt of the Major Jacob Gray Chapter in Jacksonville, Arkansas, presents a flag to new citizen Stacy Gaddy of Canada during naturalization ceremonies in Little Rock, Arkansas, in August 2006. Zumwalt is a past NSDAR Vice President General, as well as Honorary State Regent of Arkansas.

▲ President General Patricia W. Shelby presents awards to outstanding Junior American Citizens in her office during the 1983 Continental Congress.

senior class selects one. Some schools use other methods of selection, but only one student from each school may be so honored. According to National Chairman of the DAR Good Citizens Committee Laura Kessler, thanks to the hard work by the chapters who work with schools to promote the program, 6,940 seniors across the country and overseas were recognized as their school's Good Citizens in 2005.

Individual school selection is only the beginning, though. From there, three non-DAR judges select deserving students at the chapter, state, district, and national level, based on essays, transcripts, and letters of recommendation. Students selected at the school level also become eligible to apply for the DAR Good Citizen Scholarship Contest. "The generosity of Daughters at the chapter, state, district, and national levels made it possible to award over $201,000 in scholarships and gifts in 2005," points out Kessler. An endowment from Daughter Patricia Houck Holvick in California also helps fund scholarships at the national level.

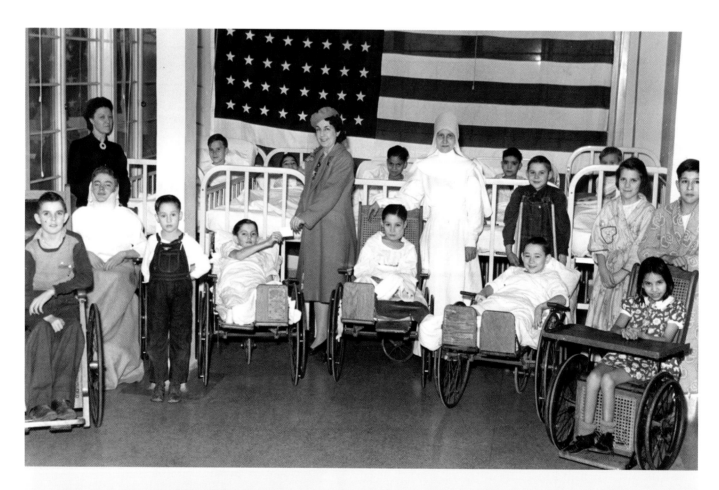

▲ DAR Junior American Citizen Clubs are open to every child in every environment. In this 1940s photo, members of the Eddie Rickenbacker Club of Junior American Citizens at the Crippled Children's Pediatric Ward at St. Mary's Hospital pose with the oversized flag donated to them by the Pueblo Chapter of the DAR. Alice Finlay Hughes, pictured in the center in hat and coat, was chapter JAC chairman. The woman at left is the children's teacher, Mrs. Powell; Sister Gertrude Marion was ward supervisor.

Besides the selection process, there is another unique aspect of the DAR Good Citizens Program—the topic of the essay. As part of her will that endowed the DAR Good Citizens Program in 1979, Daughter Gertrude O. Richards stipulated that students must write on one specific topic that, each year, remains a closely held secret. In the presence of faculty or a DAR member, students have two hours, without any resources or computers, to capture their thoughts on a topic only revealed to them with the opening of a sealed envelope.

It has been said that good citizens are not born, but made, through an appreciation instilled in childhood of community service, the value of a good education, and the history and price of freedom. There are other committees besides DAR Good Citizens with a student focus. In addition to promoting American history by honoring significant historical people, places, dates, and events, each year the American History Committee works through chapters to conduct the American History Essay contest. All students in grades five through eight, whether in a public, private, or parochial school, or homeschooled, are eligible. As with the DAR Good Citizens program, the American History Essay process often starts students on their own quest, about history and about themselves. Wrote Mary Ann Becca Haller, the 2005 national sixth grade winner, "Between 1804 and 1806, Meriwether Lewis and William Clark led an expedition across this continent. This past year, I wrote an essay about that voyage . . . and started on my own journey filled with many amazing experiences."

▲ Area Junior American Citizens participate as part of an interactive display on the Bill of Rights at the Rapides Parish Library in Louisiana (top). JACs also take special pride in saluting and supporting American veterans, such as the JACs who teamed with local Boy Scouts in this Phoenix Academy Magnet School float as part of a Veterans Day Parade (center). Meanwhile, some very young JACs show off one of the valentines they made for the veterans at a nearby Veterans Administration Medical Center (right). The JAC program is the largest youth program of the National Society, with hundreds of JAC clubs in schools across the country, some of whose members are the entire school enrollment. JACs across the country also collect food for homeless shelters, participate in the "Just Say 'No'" program against drugs, put on skits about the Revolution, and support conservation through participation in tree plantings and other beautification projects. Teachers find the programs and clubs so much fun for the students that one teacher in Texas uses participation as a reward for their behavior during the week, noted JAC National Chairman Janet Whittington. *Photos courtesy of Loyalty Chapter* ▶

Linda Gist Calvin, Recording Secretary General, is certain that DAR Good Citizens inspire students long after the award. "Just having the Good Citizen program has put a goal in the minds of many students, and they strive to attain these goals," to become active and patriotic citizens throughout their life. There was just such a student at Maine Township High School in Park Ridge, Illinois, which opened in the fall of 1964. In 1965, the Park Ridge Chapter (now Twenty-First Star Chapter) presented the first DAR Good Citizen medal to a senior student voted by the

▲ Keri Sims, of the Navy JROTC at La Vega High School in Bellmead, Texas, accepts the 2003 NSDAR Reserve Officer Training Corps medal and certificate from Linda Wyllie Totten, National Defense chairman of the Elizabeth Gordon Bradley Chapter in Waco, Texas. Presented by the NSDAR National Defense Committee, the ROTC medals recognize graduating cadets in secondary schools, junior colleges, and universities who fulfill the qualities of honor, service, courage, leadership, and patriotism.

school to receive the award. That young woman became Senator Hillary Rodham Clinton.

Another DAR essay contest holds special meaning for the Society, for as a 1908 pamphlet published by the Board of Management stated, "October 11 had been selected as the day on which to celebrate . . . organization of the society, because it was closest to the date of Columbus' discovery of America, and because that discovery was made possible by the generosity of Queen Isabella." In 1996, four years after the 500th anniversary of Christopher Columbus' arrival in the western hemisphere, the DAR joined with the National Italian American Foundation in sponsoring an annual essay contest focusing on the explorer. The contest, administered by the DAR and open to students in grades nine through twelve, attracted over 1,700 entries in its first year. In addition to national recognition, the first-place winner each year receives $1,200 and a trip financed by the National Italian American Foundation to the Columbus Memorial in Washington, D.C., to participate in annual Columbus Day activities there.

A Pledge of Allegiance

The only resolution adopted at the first Continental Congress in 1892 focused on paying homage to the U.S. flag and the musical tribute to it, the "Star-Spangled Banner." From that moment on, one overarching objective of the Society has been to keep the flag flying, protect it continuously under all conditions, and educate citizens regarding its correct usage. As early as 1897, the Society had begun lobbying for a bill to be passed by the U.S. Congress that would prevent misuse, mutilation, or improper use of the flag, but despite the Daughters' continuous crusading, it would not be until June 22, 1942, in the heat of World War II, that Public Law No. 623, the Flag Code, would be enacted.

In the meantime, in 1909, the Daughters formalized their own pledge of allegiance to their nation's ensign and established the Flag of the United States of America Committee to promote and encourage a strong patriotic feeling and respect for this national symbol. The DAR booklet, "Flag Code of the United States of America," is distributed free to schools and organizations to foster an appreciation for the flag and what it represents, as well as its correct use and display. Hundreds of chapters also teach flag etiquette and general flag knowledge to students in their community.

Part of their special commitment to keep the flag flying includes the presentation of flags for special occasions. In 1907, the Daughters of the American Revolution presented a silk flag to the U.S. Navy to drape the remains of naval hero John Paul Jones when they were returned from France for burial. The silk flag planted by Robert Peary at the North Pole in 1909 was the one presented to him by the Daughters on July 6, 1908.

The Daughters' devotion also inevitably led to one of their most enduring, popular, and generous gestures. For nearly a century now, every year, particularly on Flag Day and Independence Day, Daughters from hundreds of chapters across the country donate thousands of flags to schoolchildren, governmental bodies, military establishments, and civic organizations throughout the country, and place flags on the graves of countless Revolutionary War patriots. During the Centennial Administration from 1989 to 1992, the DAR distributed 500,000 American flags. In addition, since 1901, the NSDAR has provided U.S. flags as needed to both houses of the U.S. Congress; this gift of the Daughters hangs on the wall behind the Speaker of the House.

PHOTO COURTESY MRS. HAROLD N. WOOD JR.

▲ In this 1981 photo, Flag of the United States of America Chairman Bland H. MacGillivray (right) and Americanism Chairman Josephine Baddeley Sumon Troth of the Williamsburg Chapter, Virginia, present a Braille flag to Ernest E. James, a blind student.

Joy D. Hagg, National Chairman of the Flag of the United States of America Committee from 2001 to 2004, wrote in the May/June 2004 issue of the *Daughters* newsletter: "This term has been marked by world-changing events—September 11, the war in Afghanistan, and the war in Iraq. A renewed sense of patriotism has evolved and DAR has been visibly present to support our men and women in uniform and to encourage a grieving nation."

▶ The work of the Society begins in the chapter where Daughters carry out the DAR mission of patriotism, education, and preservation at the grassroots level. For instance, as part of a special program on flag etiquette, Oklahoma's Ardmore Chapter Regent Patricia Hyde Jurey uses "Betsy," the Society's patriotic bear, to teach kindergartners how to show respect for the flag. The program, "Five Things to Do When You See Our Flag," is designed to help children show respect for the flag, including teaching them to stand still, remove their caps, look at the flag, put their right hands over their hearts, and keep their left hands at their sides. They have a number of flag programs that so far have reached approximately two thousand children from kindergarten to eighth grade. In addition, the chapter used more than $7,000 in grant funds to purchase American history books and flags for schools and to send cards and monetary gifts to patients at the Ardmore Veterans Center.

PHOTO COURTESY ARDMORE CHAPTER

▲ Top, a kindergartner from a local school received a small sum to tutor these equally young immigrant children while their mothers, in the photo below, were taught sewing and English. Members of the now disbanded Sierra Chapter of California worked with the adults four afternoons a week. ▼

JUNIOR AMERICAN CITIZENS

The Junior American Citizens (JAC) Committee, officially established in 1906, is one of the Society's oldest youth-oriented committees. The DAR program itself, though, is even older—a chapter in Illinois formed the first Junior American Citizen club in October 1901. With the primary mission of teaching and promoting Americanism and good citizenship, the program reaches out to students from kindergarten through grade twelve, teaching to tens of thousands of young people, many for the first time, the American's Creed, the Pledge of Allegiance, and the National Anthem. Notes Janet Whittington, JAC National Chairman, "So often, kids don't learn patriotic values. The JAC program is designed to promote patriotism in every child . . . , whether gifted, regular, or disabled, regardless of whether they attend public or private school or are home schooled."

Through the efforts of the chapters to promote the program in their community schools, Daughters at the local, state, and national levels recognize thousands of outstanding students each year with certificates, pins, and monetary awards for their art, photography, community service, and writing abilities, all centered on topics specific to American heritage. What may be the committee's most popular program are the contests it offers in art, creative expression, and community service for grades 1–12. Preschoolers may also participate in the art category. Of the nearly 29,000 students involved in JAC programs, more than 12,000 of them participated in at least one of the various contests in 2005, some with special judging categories. One particular winner stands out in Whittington's memory. "I got a call one day from a mother whose child is a special needs child," she remembers. The boy won first place in the nation with his art entry. The mother told Whittington, "My son has never had a chance to succeed at anything. Today, he said to me, 'Mama, I'm a good artist.'"

LITERACY

As many as 44 million adults in this country cannot read at levels necessary to succeed in today's society. In response to this critical issue, the Society established one of its newest Special Committees, the DAR Literacy Challenge Committee, in 1989 to meet the needs of the increasing number of illiterate individuals. Daughters across the country tutor reading, teach English as a second language, educate the public about literary levels, encourage parents to instill in their children a love of reading, donate books, help students prepare for their GED, mentor at-risk students, read to the blind, record books on tape, partner with literacy organizations, and raise funds for literacy initiatives. More than 6,500 Daughters in 1,332 chapters accumulated 186,105 hours of volunteer service in the promotion of literacy among adults and children in 2003 alone.

PHOTO COURTESY OF LOYALTY CHAPTER

▲ A Junior American Citizen tutors younger children as part of the DAR Literacy Challenge.

PHOTO COURTESY OF BETTY ENZ

▲ In response to the critical issue of millions of those who cannot read at a level necessary to succeed in today's society, the DAR established the Literacy Challenge Committee. One of the committee's missions is to instill in youngsters a love of reading. Betty Enz, Honorary State Regent of Arizona, reads to students at the Cook Indian School in Tempe, Arizona.

Even without George Washington's challenge to "promote institutions for the general diffusion of knowledge," it was inevitable that the Daughters would embrace and perpetuate education as their overarching mission. Starting with the founders and continuing through today, some of the most prominent leaders of the NSDAR have been educators. Mary Desha operated a private school and later worked in public schools. After the death of her husband, Ellen Walworth supported her family for a time by accepting pupils for private instruction. Mary Virginia Ellet Cabell, the Society's only Vice President Presiding, oversaw an exclusive school for her own six children as well as many other children of prominent Washington families. Since then, the list of Daughters who have been teachers, professors, and educators throughout the century-plus history of the Society would likely number in the thousands. That same tradition continues with today's Daughters, many of whom are professional educators.

In the end, what continues to fuel the fire of the Daughters' commitment to their mission of education is the students, such as Jonathan Scott Sheller, 2005 National Winner of the DAR Good Citizens Award and Scholarship, who, in accepting his award, remarked:

I have been continually amazed by your history, by your accomplishments, by how quietly you have done all this for over 100 years, and most importantly by the women of your organization. As we continue to accelerate into the 21st century and our liberties are assailed at every side, it truly will be the duty of each and every American to preserve and protect the freedoms, liberties, and way of life so generously bestowed upon America as our veterans, ancestors, and women like you have unfailingly done for us.

Kate Duncan Smith: Changing Lives

The Alabama Society of the DAR founded the Kate Duncan Smith School in Grant, Alabama, as a unique educational experiment to serve children in what was then a remote mountain community with little opportunity or means to educate their children. They named it for the Honorary State Regent of Alabama, Honorary Vice President General, and charismatic leader of the Alabama Society for more than twenty-one years.

Classes began at Kate Duncan Smith DAR School in February 1924 with one four-room building, only two teachers, and fewer than one hundred students. The report from the Special Chairman, DAR Schools, Lucille S. Earle would describe later life at KDS during World War II:

> *Greetings from six hundred little cotton pickers of the Kate Duncan Smith Daughters of the American Revolution School. Classes have just been resumed after a vacation of six weeks, made necessary by labor shortage, when all ages were called to help gather the crop, even the small 'first graders' minding the babies while their mothers were in the field. . . .*

> *Of course the war has come to Gunter Mountain and many of the older boys are now in the service but we are made proud by the good reports that come back to us.*

The report also highlighted the many facilities funded by Daughters that year, such as a service wing by the Pennsylvania State Society; a potato storage house, the gift of California; a lighting system from the National Officers Club; and a model classroom furnished by Connecticut. President General Edith S. Magna sent replacements for worn, battered double desks that had endured eighteen years of hard use.

What began as one building with two teachers is now a sprawling campus on 240 acres with more than sixty teachers, three principals, and an administrator. Today, more than 1,200 children attend this privately owned public facility—fondly known to Daughters by its initials, KDS—serving students in the Appalachian Mountain area with schooling, extracurricular activities, clothing, health care, daily nutrition through a free breakfast and lunch program, and training in life skills through a home economics practice cottage. Salaries for teachers, textbooks, student transportation, and the nutrition program are some of the services now paid for with local, state, and federal funds through the Marshall County Board of Education.

"KDS really could stand as a model throughout the nation," asserts DAR School Chairman Mindy Kammeyer. "Shared with the county, it's an example of the private and public sectors working together. We pay for the nurse there, for the art program, life science classes, extra computers, and books. We

▲ At the Kate Duncan Smith DAR School, Junior American Citizens dressed as George Washington, Benjamin Franklin, and other delegates to the Continental Congress confer over "revolutionary" decisions. Reenactments, such as this one in October 2004, are one of the ways students learn about and share American history.

even furnish the library because the county and state just don't have the money."

Its greatest legacy, though, is the role KDS has played in shaping the lives of students and the community. The school's newest executive director, Charles H. Edmonds Jr., is himself a 1986 KDS graduate and has lived at the school for twenty-two years as student, teacher, coach, and administrator. His grandmothers, his father, all six of his brothers and sisters, and his wife all attended KDS where his children also now attend.

"My ties to the school run deep within the tremendous heritage and tradition that exists for this wonderful DAR School," writes Edmonds. "I firmly believe that we have one of the finest schools that the educational system has to offer. The dedication and commitment of time, love, effort and financial assistance are what the very foundation of this school is based upon. We are so fortunate that the DAR has aspired to provide us with our 'Gem on Gunter Mountain,' our blessed KDS DAR School."

▲ This 1930s photo shows the early buildings and remote mountaintop location of Kate Duncan Smith DAR School. Mules and wagons, one of which can be seen between the two buildings at left, provided the only means of transportation for most in the area. Now referred to fondly as the "Gem of Gunter Mountain," KDS is now home to more than 1,200 children on its 240-acre campus. The number of buildings has grown from the few seen here to forty.

▼ Students at KDS take the lead in a play titled, "Becker Hall: Restoring a Historic Landmark One Log at a Time!" The play, written by the sixth-grade teachers at KDS, celebrated the rededication of Becker Hall and featured students portraying the roles of the founders who built Kate Duncan Smith DAR School and Becker Hall. The performance took place inside the hall immediately following the rededication October 24, 2005.

CHAPTER SIX

Citizen Soldiers
An Army of Volunteers

THE DEDICATION OF THE $22 MILLION WOMEN in Military Service for America Memorial at Arlington National Cemetery on October 18, 1997, was a proud day for the DAR, but not just because of the Daughters' substantial partnership in helping to fund it. The memorial recognizes all women who have served in or with the United States Armed Forces. Documented so far are the records of some 350,000, which include the names of hundreds of members of Daughters of the American Revolution who served in the Spanish-American War all the way up to and including the conflict in Iraq. The memorial also realized a decade-long dream of NSDAR member Brigadier General Wilma Vaught, U.S. Air Force (Retired), who was the driving force behind construction of the memorial and who remains president of the board of directors of the nonprofit Women in Military Service for America Memorial Foundation. General Vaught says the goal of the foundation is to register every woman who served either in or with the military—no small task since she estimates that to be about 1.8 million women.

In a special way, the memorial pays tribute to such Daughters as Red Cross founder Clara Barton, Civil War surgeon Dr. Mary Walker, Secretary of the American Red Cross Mabel T. Boardman, as well as Red Cross Nursing Service founder Jane Delano and Dr. Anita Newcomb McGee, DAR Surgeon General in 1894 and 1895, who organized the Daughters of the American Revolution Hospital Corps, which would later become the Army Nurse

▶ With the assistance of Army Chaplain Major Wieslaw Dynek (center) and Mark Tillery, a local volunteer, Captain Bridget E. Ward, a member of the U.S. Air Force Reserve as well as Vice Regent of the Stone Bridge Chapter, in Sterling, Virginia, delivers clothing and other items to the Wounded Warrior Ministry Center in Landstuhl, Germany, where wounded servicemembers from Iraq and Afghanistan are brought to the Regional Medical Center for treatment. "The women and men who arrive from the battlefield do so with no personal possessions," notes Captain Ward, who also serves as the chief of Mobility and Readiness for the 16th Air Force War Fighting Headquarters at Ramstein Air Base, Germany. "They are lucky to have more than a hospital gown on their backs," she continues. "This center is a lifeline to these heroes. Without the generous support of the public, this facility would not be possible. DAR Project Patriot is an outstanding committee of women whose work touches so many lives. I am proud to serve as a member of the armed forces, but I am honored to be a part of this Society." Twyla Jackino, Stone Bridge Chapter Project Patriot Chairman and an employee of the Genealogy Department at NSDAR, oversaw collections that included new sweatsuits, underwear, duffle bags, athletic shoes, toiletries, sundries, winter coats, phone cards, and other helpful items that Captain Ward delivered to the service personnel.

Corps. Ollie Josephine Prescott Baird Bennett, of the Mary Washington Chapter in the District of Columbia, a contract surgeon and first lieutenant in the U.S. Army, was one of the first women to serve in the U.S. Army Medical Corps and is credited with helping design an early version of the women's uniform. They are just a few of the incredible DAR members who have made and continue to make equally significant contributions in service to their country.

DAR records are filled with a myriad of reports from each chapter relating their members' faithful efforts during World War I. Daughters rolled bandages, knitted garments for the soldiers, collected clothing, baked thousands of cookies for the USO, and raised funds through rummage sales, luncheons, and other events. They assembled kits with personal items for the soldiers in the hospitals who were sent back home to recover from their serious wounds, often wearing only hospital garments. Typical of other chapters across the nation, the San Bernardino Chapter, California, purchased and cut 50,000 yards of surgical dressings and donated bathrobes, personal bags, and flannel pajamas for the war effort.

During the First World War, the Daughters also chose as one of their projects the adoption of French war orphans. Through the work of the chapters, War Relief Committee Chairman Julia G. Scott, who would later become President General, collected $36.50 for each of 5,000 children, or $182,500, a staggering sum, especially for the time. The Treasurer General presented the contributions to Madame Jusserand, the wife of Jean Jules Jusserand, the Ambassador of France to the United States.

▲ Conceived by DAR member and retired Air Force Brigadier General Wilma Vaught and funded in part by contributions from the DAR, the Women in Military Service for America (WIMSA) Memorial honors all women who have served both in or with the United States Armed Forces. Located on the 4.2-acre site that is the ceremonial entrance to Arlington National Cemetery, it is the only major national memorial honoring the women who have defended the United States from the Revolutionary War to the present. Dedicated on October 18, 1997, the names of those registered at the memorial include thousands of Daughters who have served. The Daughters wholeheartedly embraced support of this important memorial for, in a special way, it symbolizes the mission of the Daughters themselves, who have given support in every American conflict since the founding of the Society.

Many Daughters became American Red Cross volunteers. In addition, the financial support given to the Red Cross by the DAR at all levels totaled approximately $300,000. At the national level, throughout the duration of World War I, the NSDAR loaned two-thirds of its property adjacent to Memorial Continental Hall to the War Department for construction of buildings needed for support of the war effort, when every lot of available space was needed to house the enormous influx of workers to Washington, D.C. Chapters across the country prepared 331,686 surgical supplies, such as bandages, knitted 296,268 garments, sent Christmas gifts, drove ambulances, and purchased bonds. They met troop trains, providing lunches and lemonade.

NATIONAL ARCHIVES PHOTO

▶ A National Archives brochure promoting the 1987 exhibition, The American Experiment: Living with the Constitution, featured this photo showing members of the Cincinnati DAR knitting for the troops. The caption says, "An important factor in the passage of the 19th amendment, giving women the vote, was the work women had done in the war effort during World War I." As Susan Zeiger related in her book, *In Uncle Sam's Service*, "Thousands of American men died in those campaigns, and thousands of American women streamed to France to back their efforts," including those from the DAR Hospital Corps. In a speech he made to the U.S. Senate on September 30, 1918, President Woodrow Wilson urged passage of the women's suffrage amendment, stating that women had been the "partners" of men in the war. He argued: "This war could not have been fought . . . if it had not been for the services of the women. Democracy means that women shall play their part in affairs alongside men and upon an equal footing with them." The Daughters of those patriots who had won American independence had become patriots themselves in the battle for women's independence.

LIBRARY OF CONGRESS PHOTO BY HARRIS & EWING

◀ DAR member Jane Arminda Delano was a pioneer of the modern nursing profession who almost single-handedly created American Red Cross nursing when she united the work of the American Nurses Association, the Army Nurse Corps, and the American Red Cross. In 1898, during the Spanish-American War, she became a member of the New York Chapter of the American Red Cross and served as the secretary for the enrollment of nurses. In 1909, she became superintendent of the United States Army Nurse Corps. Through her efforts, emergency response teams were organized for disaster relief, and over 8,000 registered nurses were trained and ready for duty by the time the United States entered World War I. Jane Delano died in France while on a Red Cross mission in 1919 and was buried in the American military cemetery at Savenay, France. Awarded the Distinguished Service Medal posthumously, her remains were brought home one year later by the Army Quartermaster Corps and re-interred in Arlington National Cemetery on April 15, 1920. Her last words were, "I must get back to my work." She was a member of the Judge Lynn Chapter in the District of Columbia.

▲ This pilot's-eye-view of Memorial Continental Hall, seen just below the landing gear of this Martin bomber biplane, captures the Hall as it looked shortly after the turn of the twentieth century, before construction would begin on the Administration Building and later Constitution Hall. The lower half of the Washington Monument rises next to the plane's tail. Such a photo would be impossible today, for the presidential helicopter would likely be the only aircraft allowed to fly so close to the White House. During World War I, the Daughters loaned the land they owned (seen to the right of Memorial Continental Hall in the photo just below the plan's wheels) for construction of the temporary office buildings used by the Council of National Defense. These were removed just in time for construction of the Administration Building.

▲ During the Spanish-American War, the DAR purchased a steam launch and presented it to the hospital ship *Missouri*, to be used for ferrying crew back and forth to shore. On each side of the bow, it bore the letters *"DAR."*

After the attack on Pearl Harbor on December 7, 1941, DAR Headquarters became a center of wartime activity. The corridors of Constitution Hall, along with every room that could be spared, were given to the American Red Cross. The Prisoner of War Office of the American Red Cross occupied twenty-three rooms. The day nursery in the basement of Constitution Hall for the children of enlisted men whose wives were working added the cheerful notes of youthful laughter to the otherwise somber business of war. In Memorial Continental Hall, a War Service Center entertained servicemen six times a week. War Relief shows were held in Constitution Hall. Forty rooms in all were given to the war effort.

DAR chapters and individual members once again also did their part. DAR member contributions supported the important Red Cross Blood Plasma Fund and helped to buy ambulances, trucks, and mobile canteens. Members also devoted hours of service to civil defense and served on Rationing and Draft Boards and other home projects. In 1943 and 1944 alone, the Daughters purchased a total of $69 million in war

◄ Many state DAR societies and local chapters provided humanitarian support in America's 1898 conflict with Spain, including New Jersey Daughters who nursed the sick in the hospital at Sea Girt, New Jersey.

bonds and stamps. Some 112,000 DAR members volunteered over 26 million hours for the Red Cross. For example, the Bend Chapter in Oregon reported 2,042 hours of service from 1945 to 1946. And at least 637 DAR members "signed up," serving in all branches of service both in the United States and overseas, including the Women's Army Corps (WACs), Women Accepted for Volunteer Emergency Service (WAVES), the American Red Cross, as entertainers in recreational centers, and as plane spotters. Just months after war was declared, as the February 1942 DAR *National Historical Magazine* reported, "The two-thousand five hundred sixty chapters of the Daughters of the American Revolution are geared into the national program for all-out defense. Numbers are in training for First Aid, Nurses Aides, Motor Corps, Home Services, and being drilled as wardens in precautions to be taken in case of air raids."

While the collective support of Daughters nationwide was substantial, some of their efforts took on a far more personal touch. In their annual reports, chapters often reported that every single chapter member had entertained servicemen in her home. And, as they did in the previous war, DAR chapters in every state prepared "buddy bags" that were delivered to nearby camps or forts. As reported in the August 1942 *National Historical Magazine*, specific instructions to each state indicated that the bags should include personal articles, such as shaving cream, razor blades, toothbrush, washcloth, writing paper, soap, chewing gum, hard candy, sewing articles to include khaki thread, detective stories, and a New Testament or small Bible.

DAR work did not end with World War II. As with soldiers returning from World War I, Daughters continued their monetary and volunteer efforts to help soldiers coming home

▲ The DAR screened thousands of women for the DAR Hospital Corps before it became the Army Nurse Corps headed by Dr. Anita Newcomb McGee. DAR chapters "adopted" some of those nurse volunteers, providing monetary aid and supplies. The Mary Wooster Chapter, Connecticut, adopted Esther V. Hasson, who sent several moving letters back home to the chapter describing her life as a shipboard nurse. In 1908, she became the first supervisor of Navy nurses. Nurse Hasson is likely pictured here circa 1898 standing in the center onboard the U.S. Hospital Ship *Relief*, according to an article written one hundred years later by Heidi Campbell-Shoaf in the October 1998 DAR magazine on the centennial of the founding of the Nurse Corps.

Dr. McGee:
First Army Nurse

In the days of peace, between the Civil War and the Spanish wars, nursing in the Army was done entirely by men. At the end of March 1898, there was a body of 520 Hospital Corps men in all degrees of training as nurses for Army work, as well as 100 Hospital Stewards and 103 Acting Stewards. . . . This number, barely adequate for an army of 25,000 men in time of peace, was, of course, wholly inadequate in time of war for an army of ten times that size.

Those words, delivered by Dr. Anita Newcomb McGee in September 1899 in Kansas City, Missouri, at the Eighth Annual Meeting of the Association of Military Surgeons, reveal precisely the clear-eyed insight, leadership, and understanding of national defense issues that would propel her to the forefront of military medical care during her time. Dr. McGee received her medical degree from Columbian College (now George Washington University) in 1892 and was one of a select few woman doctors practicing in Washington, D.C.

Congress declared a state of war beginning April 20, 1898. Realizing the enormity of what this country faced in treating casualties as a result of the conflict with Spain over the colonies in the Caribbean and Pacific, and knowing that the limited force of the Surgeon General's Office could never screen the hundreds of applications from women who had already applied to be nurses, Dr. McGee suggested to the NSDAR (of which she was a Vice President General) that they should act as an examining board for women nurses for the government. The National Board of Management immediately approved, and Dr. McGee was appointed head of the committee. Dr. McGee submitted the committee's "practical and immediately available" plan to the Surgeons General of both the Army and Navy. In personally signed letters addressed to Dr. McGee, both responded quickly and on the same day—April 28, 1898—heartily approving the plan and leaving the details of competency standards "entirely to the discretion of your committee," placing "the same reliance on your judgment as it does on your patriotism," wrote W. K. Van Reypen, Surgeon General of the U.S. Navy.

The newly established DAR Hospital Corps immediately began screening thousands of applications of women, both trained and untrained, who wanted to serve. One of the DAR Hospital Corps officers, Mary Desha, worked almost around the clock screening applications and certifying nurses for duty. By the tenth of May, less than three weeks after getting the go-ahead from the Surgeons General, the first nurses were appointed and on their way to Key West, Florida.

Army Surgeon General George M. Sternberg had stated in his letter, "I expect to depend principally upon our trained men of the Hospital Corps for service as nurses in the wards" but added, "I am quite willing to turn this whole matter [of screening] over to your committee . . . to select proper persons for the service required in case I have occasion to call for the assistance of trained female nurses." He also stated, "It is not my intention to send any female nurses with troops to Cuba." By the fifteenth of July, he was begging for nurses, and, as Dr. McGee would relate the following year in her speech, "47 had been asked for by surgeons at different General Hospitals and had been selected by the Daughters for appointment by the Surgeon General."

▲ At the outbreak of the Spanish-American War in 1898, Dr. Anita Newcomb McGee became director of the DAR Hospital Corps. Her proposal for a permanent nurse corps became a part of the Army Recognition Act of 1901, which by law established the Army Nurse Corps on February 2, 1901.

▲ Recent winners of the NSDAR Dr. Anita Newcomb McGee award pause for a photo with other Army Medical Service Personnel during the 2005 Continental Congress. Pictured, left to right, are Lieutenant Colonel Ann Hussa, Colonel Janet Harris (2000 award winner), Colonel Norma Garrett (2005 award winner), Colonel Patricia Patrician (2004 award winner), Lieutenant Colonel Bruce Schoneboom, and Lieutenant Colonel Thomas Ceremuga, who would receive the award in 2006.

The volunteer efforts of the Daughters in screening and coordinating nursing support were straining the DAR organization to its limits, and by the end of August 1898, the need to establish an Army Nurse Corps Division was undeniable. The once-skeptical Army Surgeon General appointed Dr. McGee as an Acting Assistant Surgeon in charge of the Army Nurse Corps. However, they would not become a part of the Army Medical Department until 1901.

Hostilities ceased on August 12, 1898, and the peace treaty was signed in Paris on December 10, 1898. Before it was over, the number of women who served as nurses certified by the DAR Hospital Corps would total 1,563; the number of applications, nearly 6,000. Nurses would serve not only at both general and field hospitals and camps in the United States but also Puerto Rico, Cuba, Honolulu, the Philippine Islands, China, Japan, and on the hospital ship *Relief*. Fourteen of them died, primarily from infectious diseases such as typhoid. Reubena Walworth, daughter of founder Ellen Walworth, was one of those who died while serving in 1898.

Despite their heroic service, some of the nurses would not qualify for government pensions. As a result, the Daughters took up this cause as well, by providing funding for those denied pensions. Myrtle Lamb, who died in Towanda, Pennsylvania, in 1955 at age 82, was the last of those receiving a DAR pension. She received $45 per month.

In her remarks in September 1899, Dr. McGee related that her "work of 1899 has been to organize the 'Army Nurse Corps' and to perfect the nursing records of the war." By then, the Surgeon General had issued rules governing the corps, which were approved by the Secretary of War. While many of those who served would not be eligible retroactively, the rules finally included specifics regarding compensation as well as travel orders, paid leave of absence, and, at last, uniforms and badges designating this new service of the Armed Forces of the United States.

In 1900, Dr. McGee left her position with the Army but continued leading the Society of Spanish-American War Nurses, a group she had founded in 1898. With the threat of war between Russia and Japan looming, she led a group of nine volunteer nurses to Japan in 1904. She returned the following year as an official U.S. Army observer and later lectured and wrote on her experiences in the war. Dr. McGee died in 1940 and is buried in Arlington National Cemetery. Her life and the lives of those who served the DAR Hospital Corps would fulfill in full measure the trust articulated by the Navy Surgeon General in that April 1898 letter: "The Bureau . . . rests assured that a manifestation of the same loyalty and the same zeal in good works will be shown in the labors of your committee as was shown by your ancestors, whose never-failing support and devotion sustained the courage of their husbands and brothers in the struggle of the Nation for independence."

▲ Taking their namesake to heart, the Daughters of the Mercy Warren Chapter of Springfield, Massachusetts, did indeed show true mercy in their early chapter work. In this 1919 photo, dozens of members and volunteers are attending an all-day meeting and training session of their War Relief Service Committee for Red Cross work. Members of the chapter also staffed a victory bread shop, hosted first aid classes, bought war bonds and stamps, made a donation of $301.50 to help rebuild the entire water system in the city of Tilloloy in France, made 17,700 articles of clothing, held clothing drives for Belgian relief, and adopted twelve French orphans.

▼ Lined up under the welcoming arms of the Founders Monument are some of the little ones who attended the American Red Cross nursery in the NSDAR building during World War II.

from World War II. The DAR record of support continued during the Korean Conflict. During the controversial war in Vietnam, despite personal risk, President General Adele E. Sullivan traveled to Vietnam to personally assure troops serving there that the Daughters of the American Revolution appreciated their service.

Following September 11, 2001, the DAR worked with the Department of the Navy to sponsor the crew of the aircraft carrier USS *John C. Stennis*. Project Patriot became the official DAR effort in support of the USS *Stennis* and the service men and women fighting the war against terrorism. Through the generous monetary donations and volunteer efforts of DAR members, from 2002 to 2005, several shipments of care packages containing thousands of letters of appreciation, holiday greeting cards, prepaid phone cards, exercise mats, books, DVDs, personal care products, and other useful items were sent to the 3,000 men and women who serve aboard the USS *Stennis*.

With the return of the *Stennis* to Bremerton, Washington, the Daughters' support shifted to the Landstuhl Regional Medical Center, the military facility in Landstuhl, Germany, which cares for wounded military personnel. Member Merry Ann Wright, Director of Development, recalls a flight from Texas when she was seated in the row against the bulkhead of the airplane where there happens to be more legroom. She noticed the young couple next to her, especially the young man, who

◀ The DAR building safeguarded more than Revolutionary treasures during World War II, as this picture of a Red Cross volunteer and her rapt audience taken on the lawn in front of the Administration Building captures so intimately. On November 2, 1942, the American Red Cross opened a day nursery for fifteen children in three rooms in the basement of Constitution Hall. The nursery, headed by Mary Perrine Patterson Davidson of the Red Cross, who was also a DAR member, was the first day nursery of the American Red Cross in the District of Columbia. The nursery provided care to the children of servicemen whose wives had taken employment.

▶ In the summer of 1941, in response to the American Red Cross "expanding its activities as the war clouds gathered, the DAR turned over the spacious corridors of Constitution Hall to office workers," as related in the Society's records. In this newspaper photo taken during that time, President General Helena R. Pouch, far right, gets a closer look at the signs posted on the lawn of Memorial Continental Hall proudly proclaiming the loan of space in its headquarters to the American Red Cross. Even before the United States entered the war, the Daughters rallied their support in the war effort, as reported in monthly issues of the DAR *National Historical Magazine* throughout 1942. The north Museum was dismantled and became the War Service Room used by "a great number of Daughters for work for the American Red Cross such as knitting, sewing, etc." Two large conference rooms as well as the Banquet Hall provided additional space for "classes in Orientation and Military and Naval Welfare Training to train Red Cross staff for work in the hospitals and recreational centers." The rooms held as many as one hundred workers each.

▲ DAR support continued after World War I as troops returned home. Here, members of the Daughters of the American Revolution conduct mending day at Camp Custer in 1919. Camp Custer, near Battle Creek, Michigan, was a training facility during World War I. As the war came to a close, many chapters redirected their efforts to national defense. For instance, the Dewalt Mechlin Chapter, Illinois, put together a play performed on April 6, 1918, at the Cosmopolitan Theatre to make the public aware of the need for preparedness. Prior to war's end, this busy chapter, typical of hundreds of DAR chapters across the country, operated a Red Cross shop; adopted three French orphans; subscribed to the $1 million DAR Liberty Loan Fund; and gave the American Red Cross 468 knitted garments, 280 hospital garments, and 23 suits for children.

◄ ▲ The Daughters offer continuous support to war veterans. In the circa 1960s photo above at a VA hospital, members dance and clap along with veterans to the big band sounds of a live ensemble. Daughters bring that same lively spirit to the Veterans Health Care Center in Orlando, Florida, in this 2006 photo at left, where members of the Orlando Chapter provide the music while patients and guests jitterbug to one of their favorites.

was wearing a baseball cap with a Purple Heart symbol. She thought, "Oh, it must be from his dad." But she also noticed that the jeans on his right leg looked funny. Just then, excusing his actions, the young man raised his pant leg and unhooked his prosthesis for the long flight. Wright realized he was a veteran who had lost his leg in Iraq. It was then that Wright shared she was with the DAR. "You're with the DAR?" he replied. "The DAR was so supportive. They were the ones who provided a razor at Landstuhl. They were at the hospital every day. They helped me write letters. They helped my wife." As they did when she and the young couple parted, tears again filled Wright's eyes as she related the story. "I felt so bad for that young man," she remembers, "but I also feel so wonderful about the work the DAR is doing to support our troops."

Member Mindy Kammeyer accompanied the President General, National Units Overseas Chairman Joy Cardinal, and eight others on a trip to Landstuhl in 2006 to present a check for $25,000, phone cards, blankets, special breakaway clothing, and stamps to help meet the needs of the soldiers the hospital staff calls "Wounded Warriors." She relates of the experience in her journal: "I stood trembling in the cold as one by one our wounded soldiers from Iraq were ever so gently lifted off the medivac bus and brought into the hospital after a very long flight. The first Wounded Warrior I visited held up his DAR phone card and thanked me! He had already used it to call home and assure his parents he was all right! Today my pride in being a Daughter of the American Revolution brought me to tears."

▲ In this circa 1944 photo, President General Mary E. Talmadge, right, buys the first bond at the War Bond booth set up in the foyer of Memorial Continental Hall. In 1943 and 1944 alone, the Daughters purchased a total of $69 million in war bonds and stamps. By war's end, the grand total purchased reached $206,619,715.

▶ As captured in this exhibit, in addition to donating blood, the DAR helped support the Red Cross Blood Donor Project by contributing $148,582 for the equipment pictured: "38 mobile units, 15 station wagons and cars, 20 centers equipped . . . thousands saved with plasma." At both the national and chapter levels, support provided by the DAR during World War II was probably one of the most concentrated efforts of service ever undertaken by the Daughters. Chapters and state societies funded ambulances and Red Cross blood donor mobile units such as those pictured here, while the DAR Headquarters became a center of wartime activity, giving up forty rooms for the war effort.

▲ During World War II, at least 637 DAR members served in all branches of service both here and overseas, including the Women's Army Corps (WACs), Women Accepted for Volunteer Emergency Service (WAVES), American Red Cross, entertainers in recreational centers, air raid wardens, and plane spotters. Dozens are pictured here on the steps of Constitution Hall in this 1986 photo that also included those serving in the Army, Navy, Air Force, Marines, and Coast Guard at the time.

◄ Members of the Mary Shirley McGuire Chapter, in Plano, Texas, show off their handiwork with the "Sew Much Comfort" program. The group provides clothing adapted for severely injured military men and women who often must wear external rehabilitative devices such as braces that require special openings in their clothing. Velcro closures replace some seams. Ginger Dosedel co-founded "Sew Much Comfort" based on her own experience with her young son, a muscular-cancer survivor. The chapter, in partnership with a local senior center, also knits or crochets helmet caps for service members in Iraq to wear under their helmets at night for extra warmth from cold desert temperatures. So far, the chapter has provided more than 75 t-shirts and undergarments and 1,450 helmet caps.

DAR members continue to devote their time and resources to veterans in both Veterans Affairs hospitals and non-VA facilities. The over 60,000 hours of volunteer effort they provide annually frees up critical medical staff for more essential care to patients. They donate holiday gifts and cards, decorate the facilities for various occasions, deliver a homemade slice of pie or birthday cake, organize special meals, and provide "canteen" spending money. Often chapters or state societies sponsor rooms at veterans facilities that need remodeling or donate funds for special hospital projects, such as construction of lounges or swimming pools for rehabilitation. They often furnish the rooms as well. These DAR gifts to service men and women totaled over $1 million in 2005 alone.

The DAR encourages many volunteers who are not DAR members. "There are people who sign up at VA hospitals who donate their time through the DAR program," explains Service to Veterans Committee National Chairman Debra S. Jamison. "We had 14,337 volunteers who worked 297,299 hours in 2005. Of that total, 3,587 were youth volunteers, who worked 14,000 hours." Each year, on National Defense Night at the NSDAR Continental Congress in Washington, D.C., the Daughters recognize the national outstanding youth volunteer and DAR member chosen as the Service for Veterans Award Winner, based on nominations from chapters. A special presentation also goes to an outstanding veteran-patient who

▲ Members of the DAR Project Patriot Committee (top) paid a visit to the USS *John C. Stennis* in January 2005, as part of the "Happy New Year, Happy New Home" phase of Project Patriot to welcome them to their new homeport in Bremerton, Washington. During this phase, in addition to the 6,600 holiday greeting cards sent by the Daughters in time for Christmas, at the captain's reception in January 2005, the committee presented 3,200 phone cards. Pictured with Captain David H. Buss (right), commanding officer of the *Stennis*, are DAR Project Patriot National Chairman Virginia Sebastian Storage and her daughter McGowan (second and third from right), DAR Registrar General Shirley Wagers (back row beside Storage), and other members of the committee.

PHOTO BY BREN LANDON

▲ Students at the Kate Duncan Smith DAR School in Alabama created dozens of cards and signs to show their support for the crew of the aircraft carrier USS *John C. Stennis* during its deployment overseas in 2002. The letters and cards were sent as part of the DAR Project Patriot Committee established following the events of September 11, 2001, to organize and coordinate DAR support for the service men and women fighting the war against terrorism. As their contribution to Project Patriot, children at Crossnore School wrote letters to the sailors aboard the *Stennis*, "to help adopt our troops," wrote Phyllis H. Crain, Crossnore Executive Director.

PHOTO COURTESY OF SAM HOUSTON CHAPTER

▲ The Sam Houston Chapter, Houston, Texas, provides toiletries, books, and other comforts to patients at local VA facilities. Pictured with some of the appreciative veterans for whom she crocheted colorful lap robes is Valeria Hansen.

has demonstrated both personal and professional courage and determination in readjusting following a disability.

The National Society DAR also serves as one of the largest groups on the Veterans Affairs Voluntary Service (VAVS) National Advisory Board and Executive Committee. Founded in 1946 to provide for the nation's veterans at VA health care facilities, they assist veteran patients by augmenting staff hospice care programs, foster care, community-based volunteer programs, hospital wards, nursing homes, and veteran outreach centers. DAR volunteers like Barbara Dale, a member of the Topeka Chapter of the DAR in Kansas, were among the thousands of VAVS volunteers who contributed more than 13 million hours of service to veterans in 2005. Dale, the 2004 Outstanding Veterans Affairs Volunteer, logged more than 3,200 hours at the Colmery-O'Neil VA Medical Center, including helping to coordinate about 650 volunteers who work at the hospital.

As one of the founding members of the Library of Congress Veterans History Project, the Daughters' support to veterans also provides the perfect setting for capturing and recording their stories. Established by Congress in 2000, the project's goal is to record "The extraordinary wartime stories of ordinary people . . . not a formal history of war, but a treasure trove of individual feeling and personal recollections . . . ." The Veterans History Project relies on volunteers to collect and preserve stories of wartime service. The Sacramento, California, Chapter alone conducted seventy-one oral interviews in 2005. Since the project began in 2001, Daughters nationwide have contributed more than 700 oral histories, some of which include videotapes, old photos, letters, and other memorabilia. The history of World War II veteran Lynwood Clark of Frederick, Maryland, not only recounted his war service but also uncovered a grave oversight. Thanks to Daughter Pati Redmond, a member of the Frederick Chapter who conducted the oral history interview, Clark at last received his second Bronze Star, sixty-two years late. She also helped World War II veteran Robert Roberson receive his first Bronze Star. "It's wonderful to be able to hear their stories," Redmond told reporter Alison Walker-Baird in an interview for an article in the *Frederick News-Post* that ran August 27, 2006. "To help them if they haven't gotten the award they deserve is very rewarding."

Some of the approximately 2,000 veterans buried every day sadly come to the end of their lives far away from family members and friends. To honor veterans, Valerie K. Price, of the Grand Canyon Chapter in Mesa, Arizona, founded a program that has spread throughout Arizona, Texas, Ohio, Virginia,

▲ Cherished veterans and re-enactors representing those from both World Wars were the guests of honor at the dedication of the $50,000 Escalante-Boulder Veterans' Memorial on July 24, 2004, at the City Park in Escalante, Utah. The dedication fulfilled a dream held for years by local citizens and members of the Bald Eagle Chapter of the DAR, who spearheaded the fundraising drive and placement of the bronze sculpture honoring more than 450 area veterans of all wars. Community partners in the effort included the Lions Club, Sons of the Utah Pioneers, American Legion, the City of Escalante, and elected officials from nearby Boulder. ▶

and even Mexico. Chapters like Grand Canyon and Yuma have a specially trained cadre of members—modeled after the Arlington Ladies at Arlington National Cemetery—who attend veteran funerals to ensure that no veteran is buried without appropriate respect and recognition for their service to their country. They also provide emotional support to grieving family members. These Cemetery Memorial Ladies have attended more than 5,000 veteran services since 2002.

As the Women in Military Service Memorial salutes women exclusively, so did the Isabella Weldin Chapter in Augusta, Kansas. As part of the NSDAR "adopt a woman veteran" program, they ran newspaper ads for six months and contacted every American Legion and Veterans of Foreign Wars office in the area to identify female veterans. They located twenty-five women who had served in various branches of the armed services from World War II to the present. On December 17, 2005, they hosted all the women veterans of the area at a reception and program highlighting the contributions of women from the Revolution to today. Men are not the only tellers of war stories. In spirited discussions, the veterans shared personal experiences both moving and humorous. They even chatted about the challenges of their uniforms, especially those from earlier conflicts, when shoes were too big or too small, hems too long or too short, and wool uniforms were required even in hot areas. The program was such a rousing success, the chapter plans to make it an annual event.

The mission of the Women in Military Service for America Memorial Foundation echoes many of the century-old tenets of

▲ Jean Ribault Chapter member Alice M. Stratton, of Florida, interviews two more veterans for the Library of Congress Veterans History Project. The DAR is a partner in this effort to capture and preserve stories of wartime service. Stratton has interviewed fifteen veterans so far, whose experiences are now on file in the national project's database. In the photo above, she interviews Desert Storm veteran Col. Judith Calcagni, U.S. Army (Retired). The photo at right, however, captures a more intimate interview with her husband, Richard A. Stratton, a U.S. Navy retiree, who spent six years at the infamous Hanoi Hilton as a prisoner of war in Vietnam, 1967–1973. On the table in front of them are photos of him taken while he was a prisoner, including the cover of *Life* magazine. Stratton also captured the service of her two sons and daughter-in-law, all Marines who served in the Gulf War. Alice Stratton's POW-MIA support led to her appointment as Deputy Assistant Secretary of the Navy for Personnel and Family Matters from 1985 to 1989 under the Reagan administration. ▶

▲ Sarah Uribe, center, a D.C. DAR member, assists World War II veterans Alyce Dixon, right, and Robert Harkins in selecting reading materials from the dozens of books and magazines she delivers regularly to the Comprehensive Nursing and Rehabilitative Center, part of the Washington, D.C., VA Medical Center.

the National Society Daughters of the American Revolution: to document the experiences of all those who fought for freedom and tell their stories of service, sacrifice, and achievement; to make their contributions a visible part of our history; and serve as an inspiration for others. In many ways, the Daughters themselves are the living embodiment of the citizen soldiers who won the battle for American independence, volunteers who fought for what they believed in while still carving out a life for themselves as citizens. This feminine force of nearly 168,000 current members of the DAR—more than 850,000 since its founding—performs a vital range of services in support of the military. From volunteer support in both world wars to financial contributions to the American Red Cross, from pensions for early members of the Nurse Corps to thousands of hours of volunteer effort each year on behalf of veterans, the Daughters of the American Revolution have continued to honor the appeal of Abraham Lincoln "To care for him who shall have borne the battle and for his widow and his orphan . . . ."

▲ The Los Cerritos Chapter hosted a Las Vegas–themed Valentine's Day party for veterans at the Long Beach VA Hospital, California. Member Chris Gentry, standing, takes a moment at one of the gaming tables with these veterans who, from their smiles, were all winners.

CHAPTER SEVEN

A Nation's Past
America's Treasures

WITHIN THE SHADOW OF THE WHITE HOUSE, the DAR complex is easily recognizable for its remarkable and historic edifice. What might be overlooked, however, is what resides within the beautiful buildings. Arts and artifacts, manuscripts and mementos, fabrics and furnishings, and personal possessions of patriots and their descendants all combine to form a rich collection of treasures that is available to the public for viewing. Here are housed some of America's most compelling tales and valued treasures, most lovingly preserved and often donated by Daughters around the world.

AMERICANA COLLECTION

Author Andrew Carroll found a gold mine of stories in the NSDAR Americana Collection while doing research for his bestselling book, *Behind the Lines*, published in 2005, which features hundreds of letters and emails from U.S. soldiers and their loved ones, from the Revolutionary War to the war in Iraq and Afghanistan. The opening page features a letter in the Americana Collection from Private John Eggleston to his fianceé, written on October 27, 1776, "while he and thousands of other American soldiers awaited an imminent British invasion of White Plains, New York," wrote Carroll. Despite the danger, young Eggleston daydreamed of his young lover, writing "I got your letter at York Island—telling me I was a saucy fellow to kiss you before all the folks—Ah My Darling—I wish the World Knew you are to marry me . . . . The thoughts of your dear promise has nerved my arm so far & will

▶ The collections of the DAR Museum, Library, and Americana Room offer a unique resource for researchers, genealogists, historians, and other visitors to the DAR complex. The sampling of articles from each collection pictured here (clockwise) include pension books (upper left), pictures and a letter documenting "Real Daughters" (first-generation descendants of Revolutionary patriots), the diary of a soldier who served with General Washington at Valley Forge (center), an order authorizing the long-delayed payment of $200,000 to General Lafayette for his "services and sacrifices in the War of the Revolution" dated January 8, 1825 (lower right), and a 1780 muster roll for the Second Regiment of New Jersey (lower left). The 1777 powder horn (left) bears the inscription "J. McKee" with the symbol of the Free Masons as well as the poetic warning: "The Red Coat Who Steals The Horn Will Go To Hell From Whence He's Born." Marches played on the fife eased the monotony and provided cadence for the movement of the foot soldiers.

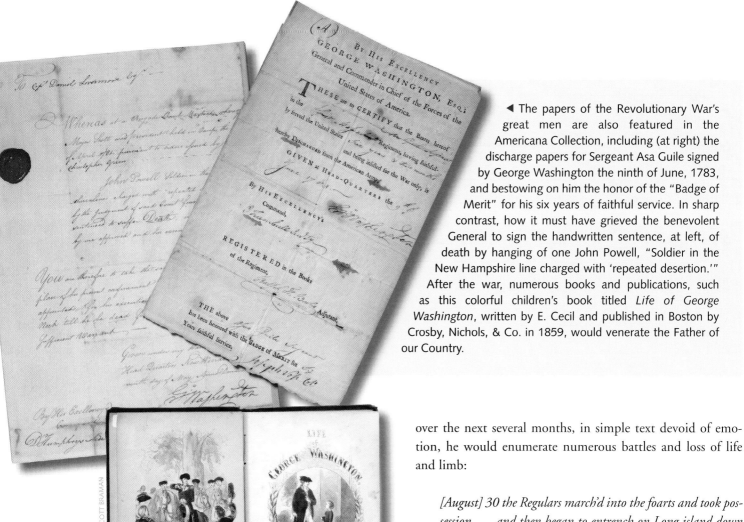

PHOTO BY SCOTT BRAMAN

◀ The papers of the Revolutionary War's great men are also featured in the Americana Collection, including (at right) the discharge papers for Sergeant Asa Guile signed by George Washington the ninth of June, 1783, and bestowing on him the honor of the "Badge of Merit" for his six years of faithful service. In sharp contrast, how it must have grieved the benevolent General to sign the handwritten sentence, at left, of death by hanging of one John Powell, "Soldier in the New Hampshire line charged with 'repeated desertion.'" After the war, numerous books and publications, such as this colorful children's book titled *Life of George Washington*, written by E. Cecil and published in Boston by Crosby, Nichols, & Co. in 1859, would venerate the Father of our Country.

over the next several months, in simple text devoid of emotion, he would enumerate numerous battles and loss of life and limb:

> [August] 30 the Regulars march'd into the foarts and took possession . . . and then began to entrench on Long island down by the water . . . and they fired on us from all quarters but through gods goodness their was but one man hurt and he had his arm shot off

> The 13 Day the Regulars Shot a four pound bawl over to York and kil'd one man and wounded five more one of the five Died about noon. The others air slightly wounded In the afternoon four ships Came up the East river and Droped anchor against our lines.

again." He gives her assurance he will be safe, a promise that would hold true, for he survived the battle and the war.

A different fate met another young man. Jesse Story of Ipswich, Massachusetts, upon learning that his son, his namesake, had been lost at Bunker Hill, penned a polite but poignant letter on March 16, 1776, asking that Captain Abraham Dodge be obliged to send him his son's meager possessions and whatever pay Jesse Junior was due. The reserved tone, the absence of any recrimination or request for details of his son's death, speak volumes of the resignation, the sacrifice yet determination in the face of terrible loss by such humble patriots.

John Fisher of Connecticut began a diary "maid by him in the year 1776 when he Inlested in to the army under Col'n Comfort Sage into Capt Stephen Crosbeys Company the 14 day of July." He would sail from Norwich to New York where,

John Fisher also survived the war. Later entries in his journal shifted from momentous events to the unremarkable, day-to-day accounting of life in 1780: a loan of four dollars to Mrs. Buck, the hiring of William Warrin, a list of supplies—a bushel of rye, one pair of stockings, a pound of flour.

The papers of renowned patriots and Colonial leaders also fill the files of the Americana Collection, including a significant number of documents such as dispatches and orders signed by General George Washington. A document of payment dated January 8, 1825, signed by Secretary of the Treasury William H. Crawford, authorizes the payment of $200,000 to General Lafayette, "being the amount allowed him in consideration of his services and sacrifices in the War of the Revolution." A

▲ Early American imprints in the American Collection include newspapers that provide in rich detail the accounts of historic events as they occurred. The *Boston Gazette and Country Journal* from March 12, 1770, (at right) describes in detail events associated with the March 5 Boston Massacre: "The Town of Boston affords a recent and melancholy Demonstration of the definitive Consequences of quartering Troops among Citizens in a Time of Peace, under a Pretence of supporting the Laws and aiding Civil Authority . . . but in Reality to inforce oppressive Measures . . . and to quell a Spirit of Liberty." On June 17, 1875, the one-hundred-year anniversary of the Battle of Bunker Hill, the *Bunker Hill Centennial* devoted its entire edition to reprints of the stories reporting accounts of the battle, including woodcut prints of officers who fought or died in battle, as well as a panoramic engraving originally printed and sold by Paul Revere titled "A View of the Town of Boston in New England and Brittish [*sic*] Ships of War Landing Their Troops."

▶ Items in the Americana Collection include some of the most compelling, historic, yet heretofore unpublished accountings of the Revolutionary War by everyday men and women. In the letter at right, dated March 1776, at Ipswich (Massachusetts), a grieving but stoic Jesse Story, upon learning of the death of his son Jesse Junior at Bunker Hill, requests that Captain Abraham Dodge return his son's possessions—his knapsack, britches, shirt, stockings, shoes, hat, gun, and powder—and any monies due. In the journal of John Fisher at lower left, for several months throughout the summer and into the harsh winter of 1776, he kept a day-by-day account of the battles fought and lives lost, beginning with July 14, the day he reported for duty in Captain Stephen Crosbey's Company, which sailed from Norwich, Connecticut, to New York. After the war, he used the precious journal for his business accounts.

yellowed, fragile *Boston Gazette* dated March 12, 1770, gives an incensed account of escalating acts of British aggression at the Boston Massacre, while a British broadside that same year orders a general day of fasting to repent of sins and offer prayers for the health of King George.

A tattered Bible printed in England in the late sixteenth century includes handwritten notations of new life and death in the New World, while an elaborately engraved and colored 1836 marriage certificate reflects the images and solemn oaths of John Trenton and Margaret McKee as they began their life together. Oversized deeds bearing great seals grant hundreds of acres of land to the survivors of those who gave their lives in the battle for freedom. Intricate, entwined, hand-colored circles drawn by a gifted young daughter tell the story of brothers and sisters who came before and after, some whose short lives spanned mere hours or days.

These rare, diverse, precious documents recount the story of the Revolution and the early days of the new nation through not only the eyes of great leaders whose stories are epic but also the simple folk who settled it and later fought for its freedom. As NSDAR Vice President Presiding Mary Virginia Ellet Cabell stated in her address to the First Continental Congress: "It is in old letters and journals and documents handed down through the generations that some of the most inspiring truths and incidents must be found." Casting light upon an array of figures who shaped our past, from George Washington and John Hancock to the common citizen going about the business of daily life, they are among more than four thousand priceless documents in the Americana Collection accumulated and

▲ Broadsides and other orders, such as these issued on behalf of King George, are also an important part of the Americana Collection. The document at left, dated May 3, 1770, and signed by John Wentworth, Esq., Captain-General and Governor in Chief over His Majesty's Province of New-Hampshire, appoints James Gilmore as lieutenant and leader of the Seventh Company, Eighth Regiment of Militia. Pictured at center, the unusual proclamation by the Massachusetts Province Lieutenant-Governor Thomas Hutchinson orders "a General Fast" to be observed the fifth day of April, 1770, in honor of "our absolute Dependance [sic] upon Almighty GOD," for the "humble penitent confession of sins," and "more especially—that the Life and Health of our Sovereign Lord the KING [George] may be long preserved." The document at right dated December 20, 1775, likely spurred the citizens of the Massachusetts Bay Colony to add their voices to the increasing crescendo of calls for revolt against England. It ordered the payment of one hundred six pounds and some change, their assessed portion of "Forty six Thousand Pounds" in taxes "for defraying the public Charges, and for the Support of Government." The "Constable or Collector" of this egregious sum bore the unfortunate name of Fortunatus Eager, neither moniker likely aiding the execution of his duties.

preserved by the DAR over the past 110-plus years. Created in 1940, as part of the fiftieth anniversary celebration of the DAR, the Americana Collection brought together rare manuscripts and imprints previously scattered among the holdings of the DAR Museum and DAR Library. Many, if not most, of the items have never been published nor thoroughly researched

▲ Guests enjoy carolers in the Americana Room. Created in 1940 as part of the fiftieth anniversary celebration of the Society, the Americana Collection brought together early American manuscripts and imprints that had been scattered among the holdings of the Library and Museum. This special climate-controlled room now houses the irreplaceable collection that has grown to more than four thousand items, with a focus on Colonial America, the Revolutionary War era, and the Early Republic.

▼ In the spring of 2002, the NSDAR thought it had acquired the final autograph—that of Button Gwinnett (left)—needed to complete its collection of the original autographs of all the signers of the Declaration of Independence. Known, verifiable signatures of Gwinnett, a representative from Georgia, are rare because he died in a duel at age 42. But on March 27, 2002, a Button Gwinnett signature came up for auction at Christie's as part of the Malcolm Forbes Collection. Joseph Rubinfine served as the Society's agent at the auction and made the successful bid of $250,000, thanks largely to the generous contributions of the Georgia State Society, the state Gwinnett represented. The acquisition made it one of only approximately thirty-five complete sets in existence. But another signature turned out to be more elusive. A document signed by one George Ross, also one of the original signers, was given to the NSDAR in 1973. It was described as an "appointment signed by George Ross as Vice-President of the Supreme Executive Council of the Commonwealth of Pennsylvania to Ephraim Douglass, Philadelphia, 31st July 1790." What was not noted at the time of the gift was the fact that the Declaration signer George Ross had died in 1779, eleven years before the date of the document in the collection. It seems the autograph was that of the signer's son, also named George Ross. A generous gift from Joseph Rubinfine, the earlier agent for the Society at the Christie's auction, would correct the mistake. In January 2003, he presented the Society with a document (at left) signed by the real George Ross, dated July 2, 1764, and signed in Lancaster County, Pennsylvania.

A Matter of Records

On March 3, 1897, the report of the second NSDAR Librarian General, Gertrude Bascom Darwin, to the officers and National Board would prove prescient: "Years hence, when the beginnings of our Society have so far receded into the past as to gain something of the dignity of antiquity, . . . even our letter heads will have for them something of interest with which we now gaze at the cups and saucers from which the dames of revolutionary times once drank their tea." Her prediction was proved through the looking glass of history, for in the archives of the NSDAR—an accumulation of information and artifacts separate from the Americana, Museum and Library collections—reside documents and correspondence that reflect a historical perspective all their own.

THE WHITE HOUSE
WASHINGTON

April 7, 1943

Dear Mrs. Pouch:

I am delighted to have an opportunity once again to send my greetings to the Daughters of the American Revolution. This war involves the fate of every one of us, but in a profound sense it is a woman's war. It is indeed fitting that women's organizations consider how they may best contribute to victory.

It is a woman's war first because we have never before faced an enemy whose pronounced policy has been the degradation of womanhood, whose ultimate design is to build a world where women everywhere will be slaves.

It is a woman's war also because no other war has so completely engaged the skill and strength of women. In shops and in offices, in factories and on farms, women are doing men's jobs, that men may be free to do the supreme job of beating the Axis.

If we are to send arms across the seas in an ever increasing flow, women must take an ever greater part in the task of production. I am confident that organizations like the Daughters of the American Revolution will take the lead in helping mobilize the womanpower of America in defense of their democratic heritage. Women have played heroic roles in every crisis of our history, but no other crisis has so deeply threatened their freedom, or so urgently demanded their strength.

Very sincerely yours,

Franklin D. Roosevelt

Mrs. William H. Pouch,
President General,
National Society of the Daughters
of the American Revolution,
Memorial Continental Hall,
Washington, D. C.

PHOTO BY SCOTT BRAMAN

The NSDAR Archives includes items such as this 1943 letter from President Franklin D. Roosevelt to President General Helena R. Pouch, in response to her invitation to the 52nd Continental Congress. Prevented from attending by the urgent matters of World War II, the President sent his greetings and commended the Daughters for their war efforts. His letter provides a special insight into his view of the role of women in society, for he writes: "It is a woman's war first because we have never before faced an enemy whose pronounced policy has been the degradation of womanhood, whose ultimate design is to build a world where women everywhere will be slaves. It is a woman's war also because no other war has so completely engaged the skill and strength of women." Clearly, he was among the first to recognize the dramatic impact the Second World War would have on American society and a woman's place in it. In his closing sentence, he states, "Women have played heroic roles in every crisis of our history, but no other crisis has so deeply threatened their freedom, or so urgently demanded their strength."

The Roosevelt letter is just one example of the scores of correspondence from nearly every U.S. president and first lady holding those titles since the Society's founding in 1890. There are also letters and references to other national and international figures over the span of the Society's more than 100–year history.

The thousands of letters written by NSDAR officers since 1890, as well as documents and ledgers, chronicle not only the historical record of the Society, but also provide a timeline of the evolution of societal issues and concerns not limited to the NSDAR or women in general. From the last days of the Gilded Age to the War on Terror, there are commentaries on social reform, prohibition, conservatism and the threat of Communism, education, preservation, conservation, and national defense, an uncommon dialogue with a special perspective on issues and events that have shaped the nation over the past century.

While not showcased for the public as much as other DAR collections, this archive has nonetheless been tended carefully and with gratitude for the wisdom of Librarian General Darwin a century before. This valued collection includes many of the photos and news clippings used as illustrations for this book. Like the relics, artifacts, furnishings, fabrics, and historical papers of America itself, this collection will also continue to take on more significance among America's treasures.

due to the nature and variety of the collection, yet they provide rare glimpses of occasions both monumental and intimate.

While the focus of the Americana Collection is on Colonial America, the Revolutionary War era, and the Early Republic, the collection spans five centuries. Each item, in its own way, tells a piece of our nation's story. In addition to letters, diaries, deeds, and grants, the DAR treasury of manuscript holdings features ledgers, currency, indentures, wills, maps, sermons, school books, musical scores, business and tax records, and the autographs of famous figures, including a complete collection of the autographs of the signers of the Declaration of Independence as well as the signatures of the Framers of the Constitution. While the breadth of the collection and fragile condition of a majority of the items prohibits large-scale exhibit, visitors to the Americana Room at the DAR complex can view the changing displays that reflect different themes, including schooling in America, women's history, the signers of the Declaration, and the essence of the American Revolution.

DAR MUSEUM

Just as the Americana Collection offers both scholars and citizens a look at the nation's past through its original documents, the DAR Museum gives dimension to that history through its art, personal possessions, furnishings, and other "fabrics" of life. What began with an inventory of thirty-nine "relics" placed on

▲ The often-thematic displays featured in the DAR Museum collection tell stories of the owners as well as the period. Women could not vote but were some of the strongest supporters of the antislavery movement. The larger 1820s silk purses in this collection of articles with an abolitionist theme are two of only five known surviving examples, which declared their feminine owners sympathizers of the movement to abolish slavery. These purses and the silk pin holder centered between them belonged to Elizabeth Margaret Chandler, a Quaker and the first female writer to take on the evils of slavery as her principal theme. Even before she turned 18, her work had appeared in several literary journals. At age 24, two years before her death in 1834, she founded the first antislavery organization in the Michigan Territory, which helped establish the Underground Railroad. In the summer of 1787, Josiah Wedgwood ordered the oval cameo medallions of white jasper made and distributed free of charge to anyone concerned with the issue. They were set as hatpins, bracelets, rings, and buckles. Supporters of the cause even declared their sympathies when they entertained, as can be seen in the two porcelain sugar bowls, made in England, that are also part of the Museum collection. The bowls probably held "free labor" sugar, made without the labor of slaves. Margaret M. Broecker, a member, donated the Chandler pieces, while the other items pictured were Museum purchases.

▲ Quite often, objects in the Museum tell remarkable personal stories. For example, young Joshua Barney, born in Baltimore in 1759, went to sea before he was 16 years old and, by the time he was 17, had risen to the rank of lieutenant based on his gallant conduct in that fateful year of 1776. His valiant deeds over 41 years of public service would span both the Revolution and the War of 1812 and include the rank of captain in the French navy. A hero at the Battle of Bladensburg in August 1814, one of the last battles of the War of 1812, Barney was severely wounded and would carry the bullet until it was removed after his death in 1819. The DAR Museum collection includes not only this circa 1800 miniature portrait of the commodore but also the bullet, mounted in engraved silver.

temporary display at the Smithsonian—including four pieces of Continental script "which were in General Washington's pocketbook at the close of the War of the Revolution"—now numbers more than thirty thousand treasured remembrances of things past. They form a collective memory of life and luxury, the decorative and fine arts in pre-industrial America, as well as the story of the Revolution. It is accredited by the American Association of Museums, founded in 1906, which sets exacting standards for collecting, preserving, and exhibiting objects valuable to art, history, and science, as well as educational institutions, research agencies, and cultural centers.

Items in the period rooms (highlighted in "State of Things") and general collections provide tableaux of daily life for both the wealthy merchant and the simple settler. Homemade dolls and hand-carved dominoes helped to while away spare hours. Mahogany pianos, rosewood and ivory flutes, and handmade harps provided entertainment. Visitors to period rooms can almost picture a fashionably dressed American lady seated on her armchair serving guests on the curved sofa in her parlor from an exquisite tea service of imported and domestic china and hand-crafted silver, offering sugar and cream from cut glass dishes. Quill pens on display seem poised to capture great thoughts or financial accounts at intricate inlaid desks surrounded by gold-embossed, leather-bound books and ledgers. Silks and richly embroidered fabrics cover the windows and walls of parlors and bedchambers, where fine fabric and needlework fashioned into quilts became art almost too exquisite for daily use. Gilt mirrors reflect the stately countenances of ancestors, posed and painted by some of the most famous artists of their times.

At the opposite end of this historical spectrum, scores of cooking implements demonstrate daily life in a colonial kitchen.

◄ Dolley Madison owned these earrings, part of the extensive collection of jewelry in the DAR Museum. Made around 1800 using blue glass stones to imitate sapphires, the earrings were given by Mrs. Madison to Marianne Preble, the daughter of a member of the Jackson administration, and handed down in her family. In addition to the earrings, other items now in the DAR Museum collection that once belonged to her include an ornate carved tortoise-shell comb with an unusual patriotic theme, china cups and saucers, pitchers and teapots, and a letter from her signed "Dolley Payne Madison" that lays to rest the question of the spelling of her first name.

▲ Often the tools used to create works of art take on a patina and beauty all their own in the passage of time. Young Betsy Lewis used the 1803 handmade copy book at left, bound in wallpaper, to practice her penmanship, record verses, draw and paint, or press flowers that might later become the models for her needlework. The initials "N.K" engraved on the brass nameplate of the leather sewing box, circa 1800, mark it as the possession of Nancy Kimball. The contents of the case, including thread, scissors, tape measure, thimble, and needle case, spill out onto the table surface, much as they would have during her use. They are outlined by a nineteenth-century embroidery frame similar to one she would have used to stretch the fabric taut for her hand-stitching.

▶ Instruction in the art of needlework and painting was an important part of a young girl's education, often reflecting family stories of valor, tributes to family and friends, mythology and lessons of morality, and their own views of life's uncertainties. Numbering more than three hundred examples, this "schoolgirl art"—from samplers and allegorical pictures stitched in silk to incredibly detailed and remarkably proportioned paintings—forms a unique part of the DAR collection and was featured in a 1997 exhibit in the DAR Museum Gallery. Eliza Camp, of Connecticut, stitched this silk embroidery with added watercolor in 1810. Her model was the *Emblem of America*, an 1801 English engraving.

▲ As with the DAR Museum gallery, exhibits in the Americana Room rotate to spotlight various aspects of our nation's history and early American way of life. Pictured here, visitors to the Americana Room in the Administration Building at NSDAR Headquarters take in the Dazzling Daughters exhibit at the National Society's Open House in 2004. The exhibit features women—all DAR members—who, in the past century-plus, achieved greatness in the fields of science, the arts, theatre, politics and law, aviation, education, and medicine. The ever-expanding list of more than one hundred "Dazzling Daughters" also includes ten first ladies, one daughter, and one granddaughter of presidents of the United States. Other exhibits mounted by the Americana Collection staff under the direction of the Historian General have included America's Past Through Pen and Press; The 39 Signers of the Constitution; Schooling in America, 1700–1850; and Inauguration of America's Presidents: A Bicentennial Tribute.

Farm implements, saws, washtubs, and ironing boards adorn the humble combination parlor-bedroom-kitchen-nursery of a pioneer home, where simpler quilts, perhaps recycled from clothing and other scraps, provided both warmth and adornment for the room. Segments of everyday life are not the only images reflected in the DAR Museum collection. Revolutionary War artifacts speak of the patriotism of the men and women whose courage and conviction formed the new nation.

The Museum's changing exhibitions often generate rave reviews and extensive media coverage for their variety and unique focus. One example is the 2006 exhibit, Obsolete, Odd and Absolutely Ooky Stuff from the DAR Museum Vaults, which showcased some of the

World Affairs: Circa 1776

Stored in a special area in the climate-controlled Americana Room are some of its rarest and most valuable papers and imprints. One leather-bound volume represents a collection within the collection. Flora A. Walker, who served as Organizing Secretary General of the Society in 1925, would assemble a collection of autographs that, while astounding when she made them a gift to the Society in 1921, today are not only priceless but also staggering now viewed through the telescope of time.

Described as "an autographical record of the American Revolution from a European standpoint" in an article written by Katharine Calvert Goodwin for the October 1925 DAR magazine, in the volume are fifty-nine autographs of kings, queens, princes, emperors and empresses, comtes and comtesses, and even a pope, all of them "foreigners who had some bearing on that period of our history," wrote Goodwin. In most cases, reproductions of finely detailed likenesses of the signatories from old copper and steel engravings accompany the autographs, as well as a brief biographical chronology.

Some of those represented include King Willem V of Holland and King Charles III of Spain, who were sympathizers to the cause. King George III of England most certainly was not. His signature, dated 1776, is affixed with the seal of Great Britain. Still others were rulers of countries that no longer exist, for instance, Frederick the Great, King of Prussia. As Goodwin would write, "Perhaps the most interesting autograph among the European rulers . . . is the signature in Russian of Catherine II, Empress of Russia, one of the greatest women who ever occupied a throne and who played a conspicuous and influential role in European affairs for thirty-five years." Catherine would refuse King George's offer of substantial amounts of money in exchange for Russian troops to supplement the British army.

The autographs were affixed to an assortment of documents, including letters, receipts, military orders, legal papers, and even documents signed by naval officers at sea transporting French troops to the British colonies. In a religious vein, there is a receipt signed by Cardinal Giovanni Braschi who became Pope Pius VI in 1775. There is also the signature of Joseph II, Emperor of the Holy Roman Empire.

While many are the signatures of rulers, others are of famous political advisers and important members of cabinets. The signatures of French officers who came to this country and fought in the cause of the colonies make up the largest group. These include Lafayette, Comte d'Estaing, Comte de Grasse, and Vicomte Jean Marie de Rochambeau, who served as his father's adjutant in America.

Each autograph bears a fascinating story unto itself, but collectively they paint a unique and interesting perspective of the people, places, and times they represent. As with nearly every single item of the more than four thousand in the Americana Collection, they are a gold mine of history and research just waiting to be discovered.

▲ Daughter Flora A. Walker presented her prized collection to the Society in this oversized, elegantly bound, and gold-embossed leather volume. Pictured around it are some of the autographs inside: (clockwise from top left) the infamous King George III of Great Britain; Catherine II, Empress of Russia; the Marquis de Lafayette; Pope Pius VI; and Louis XVI, King of France from 1774 to 1793.

▲ American women were often esteemed as mothers and homemakers because of their attentiveness to both. Perhaps that was not entirely by choice, since many a wife bore a child nearly every two years as long as she was able. Many of the collections in the DAR Museum reflect both the traditional and unusual implements of the time. Building blocks, dolls, and tea sets kept busy little hands occupied. At lower left, the combination bells and rattle made of silver once had a gold wash and was a luxury item prized in early America. While the silver nipple and tube and the pewter nursing bottle were undoubtedly uncomfortable, at least they were more sanitary than alternatives, such as rags soaked in milk. Other inventions, such as the silver pap boat at right made by Harvey Lewis of Philadelphia around 1815, served a dual purpose. Filled with pap—water or milk-soaked bread or meal—it could be used to nourish both little ones and invalids.

▶ This small sampling of English teapots made between 1745 and 1800 represents hundreds in the DAR Museum collection. A 1776 advertisement in a Philadelphia newspaper listed some of the different kinds of teapots for sale to the American consumer and described almost to a "tea" those pictured from the collection: "Egyptian, Etruscan, embossed red china, agate, green, black, colliflower [sic], white, and blue and white stone, enameled, striped, fluted, pierced and plain Queens' ware teapots."

strangest and most intriguing items in the collection. Others exhibits have included Home and Country: American Quilts and Samplers; Something Old, Something New: Inventing the American Wedding; and Degrees of Latitude: Mapping Colonial America.

During the run of the 1992 exhibit, Souvenirs of the Voyage of Life, showing objects saved as mementos of life events, the DAR Museum sponsored its first symposium on the subject. The keynote speaker was Laurel Thatcher Ulrich, Harvard University professor, renowned historian and author, whose book, *A Midwife's Tale: The Life of Martha Ballard Based on Her Diary, 1785–1812*, won the Pulitzer Prize for History in 1991. Her book became the basis of a PBS documentary. Professor Ulrich later did research in the DAR Museum collection and consulted with DAR curators on other projects.

DAR LIBRARY

While items in the Americana and Museum collections are certainly priceless, equally precious are the half a million biographies, family histories, Bible records, genealogies, cemetery transcriptions, and other chronicles in the DAR Library that tell America's story through its people. From its modest 125-book beginning, the DAR has created and nurtured one of the country's premier genealogical research centers. Founded in 1896, the DAR Library has grown into a vast specialized collection of well over half a million genealogical and historical manuscripts and publications that outgrew the lovely gallery the Daughters thought would be its permanent home. The Library

◄ This curious object is a perspective glass, one of a small but important group of scientific instruments in the Museum collection. Special engravings, printed in reverse, appeared in correct "perspective" when viewed through the glass. In the eighteenth century, people were fascinated by science, and optical instruments like this were used for entertainment.

▶ These elegant but functional pieces made quite an impression on guests at lunch, dinner, or tea and represent only a fraction of the silver, ceramics, and glass assortments in the DAR Museum collection. The silver caster set at center and silver saltcellar at right were used to sprinkle condiments. The blown glass covered sugar bowl, made between 1813 and 1835, features glittering "chains" of glass, a costly option for the time. The tea bowl and saucer at left, made of hard paste porcelain, bear the initials of George Washington and are part of a set given to him by the Comte de Custine, owner of the Niderviller Factory in France, where they were made. The only adornment on the creamware sauce bowl, beyond its classic nautilus shape, is the uniquely turned handle.

Volumes to Treasure

"Why would a patriotic society feel the necessity of maintaining so costly an activity as a library of its own within a comparatively short distance of the Library of Congress, where one could anticipate finding a wealth of reading matter concerning the American Revolution?" This was the question that would be asked, and answered, by nationally renowned archaeologist and historian Moreau B. C. Chambers in his 1967 appraisal of the DAR Library as a "special" library.

As former Librarian General Isabel Anderson wrote in tracing the history of the Library from 1896 to 1926, the pressing need for their own inventory of reference books to assist the Registrar General in verifying the application papers was recognized soon after the organization of the Society. As many as 600 applications a month were pouring in, and without ready reference, workers in the Registrar General's office spent countless hours at other libraries trying to verify lineage. The Society's continued existence and growth required a more efficient system.

Acknowledging that need, the 5th Continental Congress in 1896 created the office of Librarian General and unanimously elected Dr. Anita Newcomb McGee as the first to hold this office. Upon assuming her duties in April of that year, Dr. McGee reported a collection of "one hundred and twenty-five books and pamphlets and one wall map," housed in the little room at 902 F Street, in Washington, the administrative offices of the Society.

Almost immediately, Dr. McGee had a chance to double the collection with the offer of 153 books not only of history but also poetry and English literature. She saw right away the need to define the scope and nature of the collection, so she asked an important question of the leadership: What would be the distinguishing qualities of the library? The decision was that "the area covered would be local history in America, embracing state, county, town, and church materials—genealogies, biographies, and vital records," unique holdings not generally found in the libraries in Washington or, in some cases, any library whatsoever.

By the end of Dr. McGee's term in 1897, she was asking for shelves to hold the collection that had swelled from 125 to 857 volumes. By 1910, when both the Library and the Daughters finally had their new home in the long-awaited Memorial Continental Hall, the Library collection had reached 5,000 volumes. Librarian General Mary H. Willis described the move:

> We have removed from our dingy little room at 902 F Street to our spacious chamber in Continental Hall . . . . Before we were so crowded and "stacked" in that it seemed impossible to even breathe freely. Some of them, the pretty ones, were stored in a lumber room; some were behind the shelves; some were on top of the cases, and we have even seen them beneath the desks.

The most valuable sources for the collection were the Daughters themselves. The precious journals of their ancestors, generously donated or shared, shed light on that period of history never before published and almost lost in the passage of time. Each family Bible and family history, each application made the Library more and more unique. In time, with the creation of DAR State and Chapter Librarians, biographies, journals, deeds, and records from churches, counties, towns, and states began filling the shelves to overflowing. As reflected in the pages of the DAR magazine and in Librarian General's reports, chapters and states, in a healthy competition, attempted to outdo one another with the number of books they donated to "their" Library. Local chapters also began searching old cemeteries, many crumbling and overgrown with weeds in remote family plots, for the headstones of forgotten patriots. Their

PHOTO BY CRANDALL

▲ The Library finally moved its growing collection of five thousand volumes to its new home in Memorial Continental Hall in 1910. A decade after the move, the collection had nearly doubled.

transcriptions from these headstones and other local records were added to the swelling stacks of unique information amassed in the Library.

One chapter in particular displayed enormous financial generosity with the first move to Memorial Continental Hall. The Mary Washington Chapter of the District of Columbia—founded by three of the four members who also founded the Society—took on the task of furnishing the new library almost entirely, including stacks, catalog cases, desks, and chairs. The chapter maintained that support until 1930 when, like the Daughters themselves, the Library had outgrown its first "house beautiful" and moved to the second floor of Constitution Hall. The Library returned to that first real home in 1949, after a most creative remodeling of the Memorial Continental Hall auditorium that preserved all the exquisitely beautiful architectural details designed by Edward Pearce Casey.

▲ In this 1930 photo, tables for researchers line the halls leading to the main Library space in the newly built Constitution Hall, the Library's home for twenty years, from 1929 to 1949.

Today, not only is it ranked third in the nation as an important resource for genealogy research, but the DAR Library is also one of the most beautiful. The estimated 20,000 annual visitors from all over the country, both members and the general public, marvel at the vast, valuable information available, where readers have direct access to the stacks housing nearly half a million books, family histories, and other files and imprints. As the collection continues to grow, the DAR Library continually re-evaluates how to take advantage of technology and provide state-of-the-art resources and service to researchers and still maintain the historic beauty of its home. New shelving and reorganization of high priority holdings enhance access, while relocation of the Seimes Technology Center allows more room for microfilm and other research.

As to the question asked in 1967 by historian Moreau Chambers about the need of the Society to maintain so costly a resource as a library amidst other such resources in Washington, in his final report he wrote, "here is a specialized library which provides help as needed by its special clientele," a unique resource available to every visitor on a quest to understand their past, either on a personal or more global level.

◄ From 125 volumes in 1896, the Library has grown into a specialized collection of American genealogical and historical manuscripts and publications totaling over 185,000 volumes, 300,000 files, and 65,000 microforms. In its permanent home in Memorial Continental Hall, twenty-five intricately detailed, opaque glass skylights provide visitors with sunlit space for research, where they have access to one of the most exhaustive genealogical collections in the country, including some types of documents found only in the DAR Library. Renovations to accommodate the Library preserved the exquisite features of Memorial Continental Hall.

would move again, to a spacious expanse that now serves as the meeting place for the National Board of Management before finding its permanent home in 1949 in the auditorium of Memorial Continental Hall where thousands of Daughters once met annually at their Continental Congress.

Established originally to serve the growing research needs of the National Society's staff genealogists, today both professional researchers and family members in pursuit of elusive ancestors take advantage of a wealth of unique materials in the DAR Library. Specialized research guides, online resources and databases, and an exhaustive and ongoing microform program centered in the Seimes Technology Center make the collection one of the most accessible as well as unique. (Chapter 10, "Heroes All," provides more detail on the ongoing work and relevance of the Library and genealogy research.) Although there are a few larger genealogical repositories, in 1998, *America's Best Genealogy Resource Centers* ranked the DAR Library third nationally in importance. With a collection of 25,000 family histories as well as 180,000 typescript volumes and court records from all states, this rich resource provides almost inexhaustible accountings of American lineage. Special collections on women's history, African American research, and American Indian culture provide a unique historical perspective and offer information not as readily available in traditional histories.

Daughters do not confine their contributions to the four walls of the DAR Library, "for through the cooperation of National

▲ This ornate lantern clock is the earliest clock in the extensive DAR collection. Made in England between 1690 and 1715, it sits on a specially made bracket. The practice of creating special cases for clocks like this led to the development of the tall case clock, examples of which are also included in the Museum collection. Notice that this clock, like other early timepieces, has only one hand. Punctuality was not very important until the eighteenth century.

▶ Specially trained volunteer docents like Linda Guest of the Janet Montgomery Chapter, Maryland, provide tours to visitors to the DAR complex, including the thirty-one period rooms. "Correspondent" docents—those not in the Washington, D.C., area—also present "virtual" tours of the Museum collection through slide shows to those across the country unable to visit the Museum.

PHOTO BY MARK GULEZIAN

◀ From homespun fabrics to the finest silks, wedding and night gowns, evening and day dresses, hankies and hats, and even uniforms, costumes in the Museum collection present the many facets of life in America in the seventeenth, eighteenth, and nineteenth centuries. However, none may bear a story more poignant than this one-piece "skeleton suit" (left) Lydia Winslow Briggs of Sumner, Maine, made for her son John in 1822 from linen she spun and wove herself. Little John died that same year, so Lydia lovingly stitched his memory into a "Family Record" that records his birth and death dates, also part of the collection. The yellow silk costume at right also reveals a compelling story. Consisting of coat, waistcoat, and breeches, it was worn approximately 1780–1790 by Edward Lyde Jr., son of Edward Lyde Sr., a wealthy merchant, and Elizabeth Oliver Lyde. Hawaii Daughter Maybell W. McCleery donated it to the Museum in 1971. It needed preservation for a planned exhibit in 1998, so members from the Hawaii State Society raised $1,000 in one month for its restoration.

▶ The DAR Museum collection efforts actually predate the organization date of the Society. As Mollie Somerville would relate in *Washington Landmark*, "On August 17, 1890, a notice appeared in *The Washington Post* which proposed the founding of a society whose purpose would be to 'gather materials for history, to preserve souvenirs of the Revolution, to study the manners and measures of those days, to devise the best methods of perpetuating the memories of our ancestors and celebrating their achievements.'" Their collection quickly outgrew the first rooms rented for their storage. By 1896, the Charter granted to the Society by the U.S. Congress, and signed by President Grover Cleveland in 1896, also addressed their need for space, authorizing the Regents of the Smithsonian Institution "to permit said National Society to deposit its collections, manuscripts, books, pamphlets, and other material for history" in the institution. The

Daughters' by now burgeoning collection is pictured here at the Smithsonian not long before it was moved to Memorial Continental Hall in 1909. The display case in the center holds the spinning wheel, made between 1775 and 1825, that was the inspiration for design of the DAR insignia. It was presented to the Society as one of the first items in its collection, where it remains a treasured piece that not only tells the story of early America but also the Daughters and other pioneering women.

▲ At last, in 1950, with the major addition to the Administration Building, the Museum would gain a gallery for what would feature its very popular and well-attended exhibitions. In this early view of the then-new gallery space, located just past the main entrance to the DAR Headquarters, cabinets with groupings of like items line the walls, while a drawing room area in the rear showcases many furniture pieces owned in the eighteenth century by Americans of prominence. At the far end hangs the larger-than-lifesize portrait of Martha Washington painted by E. F. Andrews, who painted another portrait of the "first" First Lady that hangs in the East Room of the White House. Andrews's daughter presented the painting to the NSDAR in 1909, and it has recently been returned to its original place of honor in Memorial Continental Hall. The cabinet at right appears to hold souvenir postcards and other items that would now be part of the wide variety of educational materials and reproduction items for sale in the DAR Museum Gift Shop, located at the entrance to the gallery. Later modifications would include not only the addition of the gift shop but also spacious, well-lit cases for permanent display of certain segments of the Museum's collection, such as silver, china, glass, and other artifacts.

Vice-Chairmen, State and Chapter librarians, hundreds of books have been given to the various schools in which the Society is interested, where up-to-date reference books, maps, good fiction and children's books are much needed," wrote Librarian General Edith Scott Magna for an article titled "Your Working Library" in the DAR magazine in April 1931. Many public libraries also got a boost from local DAR chapters. The Public Library of Fort Wayne and Allen County in Indiana is considered one of the largest genealogy and family history collections in any public library in the nation, thanks to the early efforts of the Mary Penrose Wayne Chapter.

Access to the Library is not restricted to Daughters. While DAR members support the Library with their member-

Revolution: A Family Matter

The Lukens letters, just a few of which are pictured here, may represent the most prolonged and unique perspective in the Americana Collection of the time leading up to and following the War for Independence. The letters of Charles Lukens, most likely a surveyor posted at York, Pennsylvania, to his father John, a solicitor in Philadelphia, and from James Lukens to his sister Nancy, span the period from 1775 to 1798 and cover a range of topics from "intermitting" fevers and "ague" and the purchase of land away from the city to such soul-searing issues as the dire consequences should they side with the cause to break from England. Charles would include in his letters mention of some of the most famous patriots who inspired the colonies to declare independence.

Writing from York on July 20, 1775, Charles provides his father with a first-hand account of the buildup of troops as hostilities escalated between England and the colonies: "Yesterday came here on their way to Boston, one Comp'y of Virginians Commanded by Capt. Morgan. Of this morning about 9 o'Clock Came a Comp'y of Marylanders Commanded by Capt. Price, which two Comp'ys intend staying until tomorrow . . . . We have Just recv'd acct. that another Comp'y of Virginians will be here this evening or tomorrow. . . ."

As a surveyor traveling the countryside and filing his land surveys, Charles undoubtedly interacted with some of York's most prominent citizens, encounters that surely led to discussions of current events. On November 3, 1776, Charles would write to his father:

> After my last letter we Received one signed, John Dickinson, Tho's McKean, Benj. Rush, Wm. Bradford, & others, signifying a Majority of the Respectable Inhabitants of the City and Liberties had Come to a determination to choose . . . Representatives and Invest them with power to alter and amend the Constitution as formed by the late Convention—Our Town Committee met and Passed a Resolve to the same Effect.

Charles would leave no doubt of his loyalty when he wrote to his father, now dispatched to Washington, regarding apparently unsettling news passed to the senior Lukens by one Captain Godfrey "Perhaps Godfrey may be wrong informed; at any rate it gives me very little uneasiness, for I would rather go to the Plow than serve under a Certain set of men."

The peace following the Revolution was short-lived, for not long after, the new Americans would face terrible conflicts in a battle to wrest the land from those who came before, the Native Americans. This time, it would be another Lukens—James, most likely the brother of Charles—in harm's way upon his posting to Fort St. Clair (later renamed Fort Wayne), Ohio, the site of some of the most devastating, bloody battles between Indians and settlers. In a telling letter penned to John McDowell in Pittsburgh October 13, 1794, James would write: "We have gained a complete Victory with the loss of 120 noncommissioned officers & soldiers . . . we have to lament also the Death of Capt Camparle [sp?] of the Horse Volunt of the Infantry. Capts Slough and Vanransalear, wounded. Lieut C. Smith also wounded."

As with his brother Charles, James also found himself lacking, both in supplies and news from home, for in numerous letters to his dear sister and "best friend" Nancy Lukens, he entreats her to write, for "not one single scrape of a pen has ever arrived to announce your health or that of any of our friends." In February 1794 he penned, "I must beg my Sister to make me some shirts."

While the Army would prevail and James Lukens would survive the battles at Fort St. Clair, undoubtedly the loss of life from the battle so recently fought for American independence still weighed heavily in his own heart as he recounted the deaths of officers and men as well as those of the Indians, who now desperately waged their own losing battle for independence. On July 15, 1794, he would write: "The Indians [are] so numerous as to cut off every hope of Victory . . . . The Indians continued round the Garrison that whole day & night & the next day until 3 oclock in the afternoon. It is conjectured their kill'd & wounded amounts to 60 or 70. Our loss including officers & privates to 24." While certainly unintended, the last line of this letter to sister Nancy is an epitaph to all who would die then: "It is a loss which our country will deplore & at least drove a tear to the memories of Brave Men."

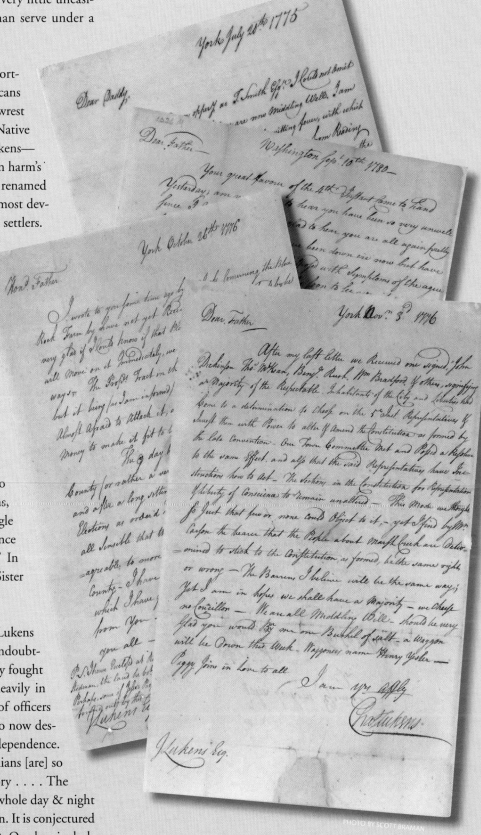

◄ Modifications to the lower level of Memorial Continental Hall in the early 1990s created a gallery where the Museum could feature selections from its collection of furniture and paintings. It was named the Yochim Gallery for President General Marie H. Yochim in honor of contributions during her administration, 1989 to 1992. Displayed in gallery format are such unique items as the rural New England 1820s settee at right. The first version of the hide-a-bed, it opens into a bed by removing the wooden seat (originally upholstered) and pulling the front rail forward. The lovely painting by an unknown artist at the far right colorfully captures the attire of two nineteenth-century children—William Henry Underhill and George Washington Lafayette Underhill. The eighteenth-century Philadelphia reverse-curve sofa is one of only nine known and has a history of ownership by Thomas McKean, a signer of the Declaration of Independence. Cromwell Child ordered the elegant and costly mahogany and chestnut high chest (left) for his daughter Elizabeth as a wedding present in 1776. Near the back of the gallery, between an early Virginia fireback (left), a chair from Virginia's colonial Governor's Palace (along the wall at right), and one of the many tall case clocks in the collection, an open doorway offers a glimpse into one of the Museum's thirty-one period rooms, featured in "State of Things."

The DAR Museum's collection of quilts is not only one of the most popular and widely known, but it is also hailed as one of the nation's most significant, with quilts in the collection recognized both as works of art and important historical markers. Unlike most other quilt collections, over half those in the DAR inventory are pre-1850. They are frequently showcased at NSDAR exhibits. Only small segments of the 300-quilt collection can be displayed at one time. For instance, this small sampling in a 1980s exhibit in the Museum Gallery spotlighted Maryland crafters. Fifty of the DAR Museum quilts even went on the road in 1999 for a thirteen-month tour in several cities in Japan where an estimated 60,000 viewed the traveling exhibit. More than 75 percent of the quilts have verifiable family histories, such as the counterpane quilt created during the 1840s by Mary Tayloe Lloyd Key, wife of Francis Scott Key who wrote "The Star-Spangled Banner." The Museum owns two of the eleven intricate reverse appliqué quilts made by Anna Catherine Hummel Markey Garnhart (1773–1860), considered one of the most highly skilled and prolific quilt-makers of the nineteenth century. The Catherine Parker Custis quilt made in 1820 features block-printed linens made in England between 1760 and 1780. Another unusual quilt was made from the wool military uniforms of British soldiers from the War of 1812, according to the family history that accompanied it. ►

◀ Incredibly detailed documents such as this Thomas Howes family tree and the chart embellished with the wonderfully elaborate Warren coat of arms are not only important for their intrinsic historical value, but also are a rich research resource for genealogists. At the base of the tree on the left, the whimsical artist, F. F. Myrick, labeled the earth "British Soil." Each of the hundreds of branches bears the names of every descendant, starting with the arrival of Howes and his wife Mary in New England in 1637, as "carved" on the rock at right. Other documents trace family lineages centuries before American independence, as illustrated by this beautifully embellished chart tracing Warren family members back to 1215 in Normandy.

PHOTO BY BREN LANDON

ship dues, gifts, and bequests, the Daughters welcome the general public for a small fee that helps to maintain the collections. And few, if any, libraries are more beautifully appointed. Bathed in sunlight from the original skylights and surrounded by the rich architecture of the Beaux Arts design, visitors lose themselves in row upon row of books, biographies, state and local histories, church records, and vital statistics that often reveal the researcher's own history.

HISTORY CONNECTED

While distinctly different, the Museum, Library, and Americana collections provide a network of resources and historical perspective rarely found in one setting. Aside from the Smithsonian, there is probably no other single source for such a rich array of history as that housed in the DAR complex. *Washington Times* reporter Denise Barnes referred to the DAR Headquarters in an October 27, 1997, article as "A treasure trove of American history, a haven for Americana (where) heritage comes alive." Cited by J. Carter Brown, Chairman Emeritus, National Gallery of Art and former Chairman of the

▲ Visitors fill the Museum Gallery during this exhibit featuring vintage wedding dresses, as well as groom's attire and other accoutrements in the Museum's collection. Titled Something Old, Something New: Inventing the American Wedding, the exhibit ran for six months in 2004 and traced the evolution of the American wedding from the eighteenth century to today's elaborate event. The exhibition included a rare collection of dresses worn by three generations—mother, daughter, and granddaughter—of one family, dating from 1885 to 1942. As the exhibit explained, recycling is not unique to today: the lace on the bodice of the 1914 dress was used as part of the headpiece for the 1942 gown.

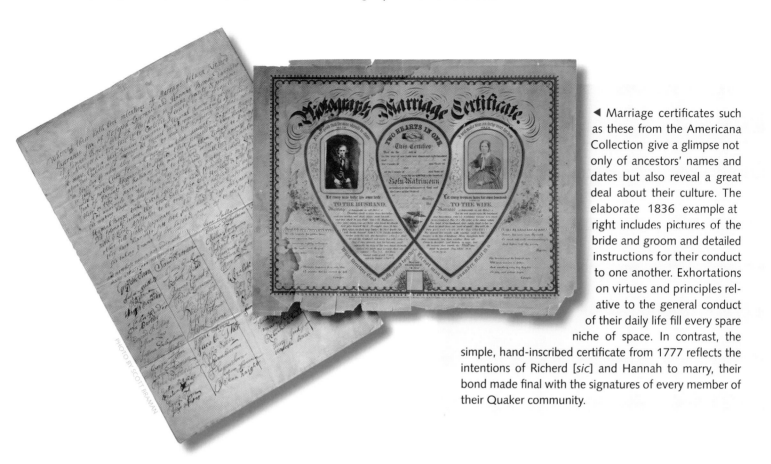

◄ Marriage certificates such as these from the Americana Collection give a glimpse not only of ancestors' names and dates but also reveal a great deal about their culture. The elaborate 1836 example at right includes pictures of the bride and groom and detailed instructions for their conduct to one another. Exhortations on virtues and principles relative to the general conduct of their daily life fill every spare niche of space. In contrast, the simple, hand-inscribed certificate from 1777 reflects the intentions of Richerd [*sic*] and Hannah to marry, their bond made final with the signatures of every member of their Quaker community.

Over 25,000 family histories, many of them one-of-a-kind, comprise a major portion of the Library book collection. Such unique accounts, coupled with the Library's collection of county records and histories, Bible records, cemetery records, birth, marriage, and death records, military rosters, census records, and a variety of other published materials assist researchers in compiling their own family histories. The early motto of "Home and Country" adopted by the Society set the parameters for the collections, so the Daughters immediately set about preserving both artifacts and accounts, those testaments to both great events and small. As Mary Cabell noted in her address to the first Continental Congress, "It is in old letters and journals and documents handed down through the generations that some of the most inspiring truths and incidents must be found . . . The quaint inscriptions in family Bibles, and under her skillful pencil the home-life of the cottage, the diary of some young girl, the love-letters of a forgotten beauty throw their light, soft, warm, human and true, upon the splendid pages of history." ►

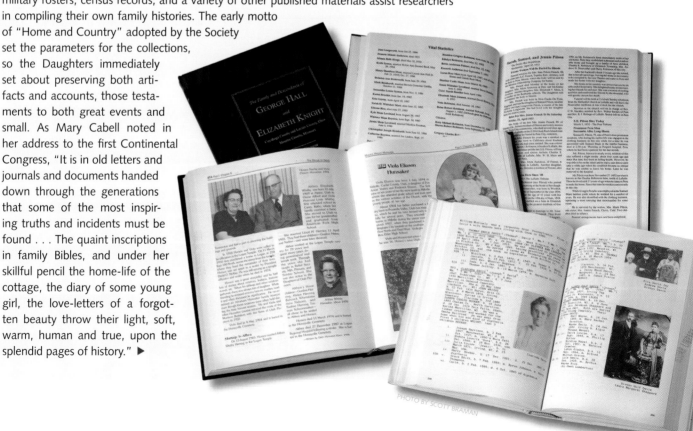

◄ The Library features several collections with a special focus on the role of women in American history, African American research, and American Indian history, culture, and genealogy. As a major women's organization, the DAR has collected women's history materials for many years, and in the late 1980s, the Library began to develop an organized women's history collection using existing holdings and new publications. The assembled materials focus on the role played by women in the development of the United States, the women's rights movement of the nineteenth and early twentieth centuries, and histories of women in general. The American Indian Collection, now numbering some 2,000 volumes, provides historical and genealogical information on America's first peoples. The 2001 DAR publication *African American and American Indian Patriots of the Revolutionary War*, to be republished soon with major additions, represents a major effort to collect materials on this important aspect of American history and independence.

▲ Beginning around 1910, the DAR made a concerted effort to have members transcribe previously unpublished records of genealogical value—including Bible records, cemetery transcriptions, court record abstracts, censuses, military and vital records, and other similar information—to assist both the staff genealogists, potential members, and the public. In 1913, the DAR established the Genealogical Research Committee (subsequently renamed the Genealogical Records Committee) to coordinate this nationwide attempt to save historical records. The result has been nearly 17,000 volumes of records from across the country. These volumes are referred to collectively as the *Genealogical Records Committee Reports*. They represent one of the most important and unique segments of the DAR Library collection. State DAR Societies and local chapters have also donated smaller, state-specific sets of these reports to various libraries.

D.C. Commission on Fine Arts, as "one of Washington D.C.'s undiscovered gems," both the permanent collections and changing exhibits at the DAR Headquarters provide a constant feast for the eye and the mind.

From rare maps to household oddities, from forgotten patriots to feminine images and issues, the thematic exhibits mounted by the DAR every few months combine items from each collection that explore new facets of the face of American history and culture, and elicit rave reviews. As Anne Veigle, another *Washington Times* reporter, noted in a July 1999 article, "Spring and summer are the peak seasons for tourists, who rate the museum as one of their favorite buildings next to the White House . . . ."

The praise most valued by the keepers of these precious collections, though, comes from visitors themselves. As one recent guest to the DAR complex would declare, "Throw out any preconceived notions you may have about the DAR and come here prepared to see some beautiful rooms, a fantastic genealogy library, and a lovely building. I don't know what I thought it would be like, but I was totally unprepared to wish I could join [the DAR]." Tourists and guests, researchers and genealogists, families and children, members and prospective members, the Daughters welcome and encourage all to take advantage of this incredible repository, for they are truly America's treasures.

CHAPTER EIGHT

Trailblazers
Leaving Their Mark

FOLLOWING THE REVOLUTION, AMERICA WOULD TURN its attention to expanding this new country. Today, the National Park Service lists no fewer than thirty-six trails and overland routes used for centuries by Native Americans and later by American settlers. Federal and state agencies as well as nonprofit groups such as American Trails preserve and promote the pathways as both recreational resources and historical reminders of America's early beginnings. But the markers set by the early western Daughters would, for many decades, be the only monuments to the trails that played a prominent role in the settlement of the American West.

In May 2005, the Mississippi Daughters celebrated the realization of a labor of love that had lasted almost a century, with the unveiling of a new marker commemorating the completion of the Natchez Trace Parkway. Spanish explorers, British troops, and Southern frontier settlers would all traverse what began as a trail created by Indians and wild animals almost eight thousand years earlier. During French and British occupation, as well as the subsequent American settlement, the trace provided an important route between the interior highlands and the lower Mississippi River Valley until the advent of the steamboat, when use of the Natchez Trace dropped significantly. While still used for local travel, the importance of the trail began to fade until, in 1905, the Mississippi Society, led by State Regent Elizabeth Howard Jones, spearheaded an effort to place granite markers in every Mississippi county through which the Old Trace ran. They placed the first marker in 1909, but it wasn't until 1935 that legislation was passed to create the Natchez Trace Parkway. It would be another seventy years before the final section was paved in 2005. According to the Natchez Trace Compact, an advocacy group for the trail, the wide variety of historic sites and scenic

▶ The DAR would lead the way in creating an ocean-to-ocean highway called the Old Trails Road, an outgrowth of Missouri State Society efforts to mark and pave the Santa Fe Trail. To commemorate the historic transcontinental road that would stretch through twelve states, the NSDAR funded twelve monuments to be known as the "Madonna of the Trail." Pictured here is the Madonna erected in Lexington, Missouri, on September 17, 1928. The keynote speaker was Judge Harry S. Truman, president of the National Old Trails Association.

MADONNA OF THE TRAIL

N·S·D·A·R· MEMORIAL
TO THE
PIONEER MOTHERS
OF THE
COVERED WAGON DAYS

▲ The Arkansas Daughters may hold the distinction of one of the most unusual locations for a DAR marker. Following the discovery in 1921 of the slash marks on gum trees made by the original surveyors of the Louisiana Purchase in 1815, the L'Anguille Chapter in Marianna, Arkansas, seized the rediscovery as a historical cause. In 1926, they met at a temporarily dry site to dedicate this stone monument erected at the Louisiana Purchase Initial Survey Point. It is from this point that all land in the Louisiana Purchase, 83,000 miles of wilderness, was mapped. A survey of the new land began in 1815 in East Arkansas. The 1921 discovery and subsequent marking focused attention on the site, located in a swamp in the Little Cypress Creek watershed at the corner of Lee, Phillips, and Monroe counties, that had gone unheralded for more than a century. The DAR had also obtained deeds from landowners dedicating enough land for a small park at the site. The Arkansas General Assembly passed legislation in 1961 setting aside the area that ultimately became the Louisiana Purchase Historic State Park, where visitors can walk along a boardwalk through the swamp to see the stone and experience the sites and sounds of the wilderness, as did the original surveyors.

venues makes the parkway one of America's treasures, one long recognized and marked by the Mississippi Daughters.

Beginning in 1843, more than half a million people went west on the 2,000-mile Oregon Trail, which linked eight states: Missouri, Iowa, Kansas, Nebraska, Wyoming, Idaho, Oregon, and Washington. Charlotte "Lottie" Gove Norton, organizing regent of the Fort Kearney Chapter, Nebraska, would almost single-handedly see to the marking of the Oregon Trail. In 1983, the Buffalo County Historical Society newsletter explained, "Lottie and [Fort Kearney] chapter members decided that the historic Oregon Trail should be perpetuated by suitable markings throughout Nebraska. The old trail, so long a narrow ribbon of road forgotten by all but those who traveled it locally, needed to be permanently remembered. The first marble stone erected in Nebraska to mark the Old Oregon Trail was dedicated in Kearney by the Fort Kearney Chapter on February 14, 1910, on Central Avenue at Union Pacific Park." The event marked the beginning of many successive monuments placed throughout Nebraska and several of the other states through which the trail stretched.

Nebraska DAR chapters also placed some of the first markers on the route used by explorers Lewis and Clark. The Bitter Root Chapter in Montana would mark "Travellers Rest," one of the explorers' campsites, long before archaeological investigations in 2002 provided physical proof of the Corps of Discovery's encampment. Chapters in Colorado, Kansas, and Missouri placed hundreds of stone markers on the Santa Fe Trail beginning in 1910, some thirty years after the railroad made the trail obsolete. And thanks to the early efforts of the Texas State Society, at least a portion of the 1,500-mile El Camino Real remains visible. While the trails themselves paved the way for westward expansion, the Daughters of the American Revolution saved many of them from obscurity.

As with the often-unheralded patriots of the Revolution, the Daughters remain champions of the pioneer women who helped to settle the New World. Before today's pop culture, no other word evoked the symbol of motherhood as powerfully as

◄ During a rededication ceremony in September 1999, Ol' Shavano Chapter, Texas, member Doris Froehmer explains the story and importance of a King's Highway marker to students from Northern Hills Elementary School. The marker, at Nacogdoches and Higgens Road, San Antonio, marks a portion of El Camino Real or King's Highway, a route used in the seventeenth century to connect the Spanish settlement of St. Augustine, Florida, to Spanish colonies in Mexico. The route provided a vital trade and cultural link among Spanish-speaking territories, as well as other Europeans, Native Americans, and early American settlers. The Texas Society of the Daughters of the American Revolution undertook a project to resurvey and mark the trail, providing substantial financial support. In 1918, they placed one hundred granite markers in five-mile increments along the Texas section of the road, at a cost to the Society of $10,544, with the state contributing $8,000.

"Madonna." And like the most patient and persistent mothers of the Revolution, in the 1920s, the members of the National Society Daughters of the American Revolution would knit together in an ocean-to-ocean highway nearly every historic trail important to American history, including the Santa Fe Trail, the Oregon Trail, the Natchez Trace, the Braddock Trail, and the Cumberland Route. Twelve towering markers that today symbolize the brave mothers, sisters, and daughters—"Madonnas of the trail"—who rode and walked thousands of miles to help settle this nation would mark these pivotal paths from east to west.

As early as 1903, the Kansas Daughters realized that the Santa Fe Trail needed to be marked. They had placed ninety-five stones by 1909, the same year the Colorado Daughters were busy marking their portion of the trail. Meantime, in 1906, the Missouri Daughters proposed to pave the pathways of the past as modern roads that memorialized the pioneers. This road would become the Missouri State Highway, dedicated on October 28, 1911. Thanks to the Nebraska Daughters, in April 1908, Congress introduced a bill funding $50,000 to mark the route of the Oregon Trail. The Texas Daughters brought emphasis to the Old Spanish Trail, which by some accounts extended some 3,500 miles, from Florida to California. Meantime, the Michigan Society researched the Old Macinac Trail. By 1909, the Tennessee, Alabama, and Mississippi Daughters had united

▲ This marker is also in one of the more interesting locations, for it sits directly on the beach in Fort Lauderdale, Florida. The oceanfront plaque commemorates the location of the third site of the "original Lauderdale fort," originally built to house and protect soldiers and families during the Seminole wars. First placed in 1929 by the Himmarshee Chapter, the plaque was worn down and eventually lost over the years. In an effort to refurbish their historical markers, the Himmarshee Chapter replaced this one. Pictured here during the 2005 ceremony are Chapter Regent Marge McClain, center, and Jim Naugle, Mayor of Fort Lauderdale, to her left.

◄ Daughters also note important lines and boundaries, such as those of the nation's capital. In 1791, after years of controversy and debate over Washington, D.C.'s defining lines, President George Washington issued a proclamation giving the exact boundaries of the "district for the permanent seat of government." The first stone, at the southern corner, was ceremoniously laid at Jones Point on April 15, 1791. The last of the forty original stones defining the ten-mile-square area delineated by Andrew Ellicott (advisor to explorer Meriwether Lewis and most noted surveyor of his time) and his technical assistant, Benjamin Banneker (an astronomer, mathematician, and urban planner considered by many to be the first African American scientist), were laid in 1792. All of the stones bear the inscription "Jurisdiction of the United States" on the side facing the district; the opposite sides bear the inscriptions of either "Virginia" or "Maryland," as appropriate to the state that ceded the land. For over a century, many of the stones languished, forgotten or lost in the mushrooming growth of the Capital City. On April 7, 1915, the District of Columbia DAR adopted the reclaiming of the boundary stones as their project for the year. It was a permanent adoption. Over the years, they have located and cataloged the original stones, improving the sites where possible, and noting exact locations. They continue to preserve the historical monuments and create public awareness of their importance. In this July 11, 1916, photo, the Columbia Chapter and their guests gather to commemorate the Northwest #4 stone. Chaplain General Mary Lockwood joined them for the celebration.

▶ The DAR has also placed markers in foreign lands to honor important chapters in American history. President General Linda Tinker Watkins visited the Dutch Caribbean Island of St. Eustatius on November 16, 2001, to celebrate the 225th anniversary of the "First Salute" Statia-America Day. St. Eustatius was the major supplier of arms and ammunition to the rebellious British colonies in North America. On November 16, 1776, the *Andrew Doria*, the American brig of war, sailed into the harbor, firing a thirteen-gun salute indicating America's long-sought independence. Statia responded with an eleven-gun salute from its cannons at Fort Oranje, becoming the first foreign nation to officially recognize the newly formed United States of America. President General Watkins and the governor of St. Eustatius unveiled a DAR marker commemorating the historic event. Those in attendance included the governors from neighboring islands, the U.S. Consul General to the Netherlands Antilles, and the Chief of Staff of the U.S. Naval Forces Southern Command. The USS *Doyle*, a navy frigate, reenacted the historic salute, which the local militia returned from the parapet of Fort Oranje. Pictured at the anniversary event are David Russell (left), husband of Virginia Russell (second from left), Chairman of the Special Projects and Events committee, and Susan Conger (second from right), National Chairman of Units Overseas.

No Stone Unturned

According to a variety of sources, as many as 250,000 men served as sailors, regulars, or militiamen for the Revolutionary cause in the eight years of the war from 1775 to 1783. An estimated 25,000 American Revolutionaries died during active military service: up to 8,000 in battle and the other 17,000 from disease and deprivation, including between 8,000 and 11,000 who died while prisoners of war. Estimates of the number of Revolutionaries seriously wounded or disabled by the war range from 8,500 to 25,000. Therefore, the total American military casualty figure could have been as high as 50,000, or one man in five who served.

As staggering as the numbers may be, they still cannot provide the true picture of the cost for American Independence, the impact to cities and towns, to fortunes and families who lost husbands and fathers and sons in the only war with a foreign nation fought on American soil. Yet more than a century had passed since the end of the war when the Daughters founded their national society. Already the stories as well as the gravestones of Revolutionary patriots were fading, worn away or lost by time, weather, and even fortune as family graveyards, once lovingly tended, were sold or forgotten as descendants died out or moved on. The ebb and flow of fortune's tide also affects cities and towns, leaving churches empty and abandoned, their structures and their cemeteries left to the elements. Not even the gravesites of those most prominently known and fondly remembered are spared, such as Mary the mother of George Washington, whose grave marker became the Daughters' first project.

But from their founding, these Daughters of the American Revolution passionately embraced the precious memory and legacy of all their ancestors, not just those already recorded in the pages of history. One of their overarching goals remains to find, mark, and record the service and grave of every patriot. Literally leaving no stone unturned, for more than one hundred years, thousands of Daughters in hundreds of chapters have dusted off records and tramped through fields and forests and forgotten cemeteries to locate and resurrect the memory as well as the patriotic spirit of those who secured America's freedom. Through their diligence, they have often given back to families the history they had lost. They have also, at times, rewritten history. While he was never on a pension roll, records uncovered by the Daughters verify that the last surviving American veteran of the conflict, George Fruits, died in 1876 at the

PHOTO COURTESY OF FORT CRAILO CHAPTER

▲ Members of the Fort Crailo Chapter, Rensselaer, New York, participate in the July 2006 rededication and remarking of the grave of Fife Major Ira Hayford, a Revolutionary War patriot who is buried in the Brookside Cemetery in Poestenkill, New York. With the help of members of the Poestenkill VFW post, also pictured, the chapter placed a brass plaque at the grave noting his service. Hayford enlisted in the army when he was only seventeen, becoming a "fife major," a noncommissioned officer who superintends the fifers of a regiment. He "survived the Revolution, received a land grant for his service, and settled down to marry, have a family, and grow old," wrote Chapter Regent Kathy Keenan (pictured at center), noting that "the stone placed on his grave was weathered to practically nothing, but the new, brass plaque seemed to sparkle in the sunshine." Such stories, and the more intimate, striking insights of the Revolution they provide, continue to be captured in the research and records maintained by the DAR. Touched by the service of this patriot and of all veterans who defend American freedom, Keenan recalled, "As I stood by Fife Major Hayford's graveside, I could see them all—generations in their prime, ready to be cut down if necessary, for the perpetuation of freedom. My heart fills with gratitude and love for them all."

age of 114. According to records at the U.S. Department of Veterans Affairs, Daniel F. Bakeman, who died in 1869, was the last survivor of the war. But thanks to the Daughters, the contribution of George Fruits is also now recorded.

The Daughters' legacy continues. With every application for membership, another family connection is made and sometimes a new patriot discovered. In time, and with luck and perseverance, the Daughters of another chapter will find the latest patriot's grave and mark it, perhaps for the first time, with appropriate honor and reverence for the sacrifice it represents. In doing so, they capture the most compelling stories of the American Revolution, those told through the lives of individuals, both those who fought and died and those who lived to hand down their stories to their children and grandchildren. Each discovery adds to the intimate history of the promise of America.

▲ Members of the Cherokee Outlet Chapter in Alva, Oklahoma, stand before the brick wall they erected in 1993 to commemorate a century of Woods County history. In the thirteen panels (only three of which are shown), engraved bricks reflect the names of all those who lived in Woods County from 1892 to 1993. Those names highlighted with an asterisk indicate those who made the September 16, 1893, Cherokee Strip Land Run, which opened nearly seven million acres to settlement.

to record and mark the Natchez Trace. And toward the east, the states of Vermont, New York, Ohio, West Virginia, and Maryland had set about finding and marking historic trails in their states. With so many state societies involved in such important work, in 1911, the National Society Daughters of the American Revolution created the DAR National Old Trails Road Committee whose purpose was to establish the Old Trails Road as a National Memorial Highway.

The need for a national road became more critical as railroads struggled to keep up with transportation needs, and the idea of a transcontinental highway had been proposed as early as the 1890s. The U.S. Department of Agriculture's Office of Road Inquiry (now the Federal Highway Administration) suggested combining existing roads into a network. One of the earliest was the National Old Trails Road established in 1912, an outgrowth of the effort by the Missouri State Society to pave the Santa Fe Trail. The bylaws of the National Old Trails Association stated that "the object of the Association shall be to assist the Daughters of the American Revolution in marking Old Trails and to promote the construction of an Ocean-to-

▲ In 1915, the Lady Stirling Chapter in Seattle, Washington, unveiled a boulder and plaque placed in memory of the sinking of the USS *Maine*, the incident that would launch the Spanish-American War in 1898.

Ocean Highway of modern type worthy of its memorial character." The president of this association was none other than Judge Harry S. Truman (later President), who guaranteed the expense of erecting suitable monuments along the route.

While Congress failed to pass an Old Trails Bill championed by the Daughters in 1911, and the looming war overseas put such sweeping domestic capital investments on hold, by 1921, a continuous ribbon of road stretched from Washington, D.C., to within a few miles of St. Louis, Missouri, thanks in large measure to the initiatives of the DAR state societies. Work also moved forward on roads in Illinois, Kansas, Colorado, New Mexico, Arizona, and California.

The National Society renewed its push for federal legislation of the Old Trails Road even while they raised funds to mark it. In 1924, they appointed Arline B. Nichols Moss to head the DAR

▶ In 1910, the Lexington Chapter dedicated a plaque (top) on the original site of the Old Belfry on Belfry Hill in Lexington, Massachusetts. From there, the bell summoned people to worship, warned them of danger, tolled on their deaths, and sounded the alarm of April 19, 1775. In Lexington later that day would be fired the "shot heard round the world" that began the war for American independence. The plaque was refurbished in 1999. That famous "shot heard round the world" was almost fired in Framingham instead of Lexington. British spies in Buckminster's Tavern observed the minutemen of Framingham drilling on the old training field, and their report back to General Thomas Gage would convince him to take a less direct route in his march to Worcester. In 1910, in honor of the minutemen, the DAR and the Town of Framingham jointly commissioned the minuteman statue known as the *Framingham Blacksmith* that now stands on Buckminster Square, across the street from the site of Buckminster's Tavern. It is estimated that four thousand guests attended the original unveiling. Designed by sculptor Henry Hudson Kitson and sculpted by his wife Theo Alice Ruggles Kitson, the minuteman is one of only three original minuteman statues in existence, two of which were commissioned by the United States Congress. The powerful blacksmith, having left his home, his anvil, and tools of his trade to fight for freedom, shows his grim determination as he pours gunpowder into the pan of his musket. The bronze statue received a much-needed refurbishing and waxing by the Paul King Foundry in 2003, when it was rededicated in a ceremony hosted by the Framingham Chapter (right).

The Way West

After the War for Independence, fully more than half of what would become the United States remained to be explored or claimed. By the time of Kentucky's admission to the Union in 1792, over ten thousand people had passed through the Cumberland Gap, the first great gateway to the west. Trails of exploration, such as the Lewis and Clark Trail, the Santa Fe Trail, El Camino Real or King's Highway, the Natchez Trace, the Oregon Trail, and the Chisholm Trail would provide routes to such territories whose acquisition would eventually link the United States from the east to the west. Almost immediately after its founding, the Society recognized that the sites, stories, and artifacts of not only the Revolution but also America's growth over the preceding century were being lost. Today, thanks to the zeal of those early Daughters, trails such as the Natchez Trace and Santa Fe Trail are some of the most popular routes traveled by tourists out to explore America today.

▲ At Lolo, near Missoula, Montana, on October 9, 1925, members of the Bitter Root Chapter, Montana, unveiled a massive stone and plaque marking the location of a centuries-old Native American campsite used by Meriwether Lewis and William Clark in 1805 and 1806. Other guests that day included Montana State Regent Mary Adelia Kelly Caldwell (second from left) and Anne Margaret Long (second from right), Vice President General. The explorers named the nearby creek "Travellers Rest," the name repeated on the plaque. The DAR plaque also listed every single member of the expedition, including "Sacajawea" and her infant Baptiste, born on the trail. In digs as recent as 2002, archaeologists found physical evidence of the Corps of Discovery's encampment, marking the site as one of the few in the nation with physical confirmation of the expedition's sojourn at the site.

▶ Several Virginia chapters, including the Fort Chiswell Chapter in Bristol, Virginia, donated both time and money to the project of Virginia State Regent Mary Jane Irwin Davis to restore the monument and marker on Daniel Boone's trail west through the Cumberland Gap. Pictured at the rededication in 2004 are Davis, left, and Patricia Hatfield Mayer, who would succeed her as state regent.

RECEIVING FIRST CHECK FOR PAVING OF TRACE
Identification of Historic Photo is Found Below In Box

DIS AN' DAT

Natchez Trace Was First Only A Dream of the DAR

THESE WERE PRESENT WHEN PAVING OKEH WAS RECEIVED

▲ ▶ One of the most traveled National Park Service highways was once only the dream of the Mississippi DAR. The Natchez Trace extends 444 miles in twenty-five counties across three states, from Natchez, Mississippi, through Alabama to Nashville, Tennessee. Such notable figures as Davy Crockett, Meriwether Lewis, and President Andrew Jackson traveled this major trade route used in the eighteenth and nineteenth centuries by the Cherokee, Choctaw, and Chickasaw Indians. In 1909, the Mississippi Daughters blazed a trail of their own in historic preservation when they placed the first of fourteen markers in every Mississippi county through which the Old Trace ran, beginning with one on the Mississippi River bluff in Natchez. Their work would lead to congressional authorization in 1935 to pave the highway. Work began in 1938, but the dream of the Mississippi Daughters, as described in the May 26, 1963, *Clarion Ledger Jackson Daily News* article pictured, would not be realized until May 2005 when representatives of the Mississippi State DAR, U.S. Senators Trent Lott and Thad Cochran, and U.S. Representative Charles Pickering, as well as Mississippi State Regent Sharon Cothern Nettles unveiled a new marker honoring the tireless efforts of the Mississippi Society and the completion of the Natchez Trace Parkway.

► The Kansas State Society alone placed some one hundred markers, monuments, and plaques on the Santa Fe Trail, while on March 2, 1910, the Colorado Daughters dedicated what is believed to be the largest DAR marker on the Santa Fe Trail, pictured here. The monument, with historical facts on the west and east sides and the DAR insignia and the Colorado state seal on the other sides, is located in Kit Carson Park, Trinidad, Colorado, home of the state's newest chapter.

▼ The 800-mile Santa Fe Trail remains probably the mostly widely known of all the trails for exploration and settlement. In 1821, William Becknell, a Missouri trader, became the first to follow the ancient passageway through what would become five states, from Independence, Missouri, to Santa Fe, New Mexico. In 1846, the Army of the West followed the Santa Fe Trail to invade New Mexico. After the war ended, trade resumed on the trail and thousands of stagecoaches, wagon trains, and caravans carrying gold seekers, adventurers, pioneers, fur trappers, and emigrants would be among those settling the American West. By 1880, the railroad reached Santa Fe, and the trail almost faded into history. However, as early as 1910, the DAR societies of Colorado, Kansas, and Missouri began marking the trail, placing hundreds of stone markers, monuments, and plaques along the now-revered route, a National Historic Trail maintained by the National Park Service. Pictured in this 1909 photo is a portion of the trail in Kansas City, Missouri, less than a dozen miles from the northern start of the Santa Fe Trail.

PHOTO COURTESY DONNA BOTTIN

▶ Almost exactly one hundred years after its initial dedication, DAR and Nebraska officials pause for a photo July 31, 2004, at the marker commemorating Lewis and Clark's first council with the Indians. Pictured (l-r) are President General Presley Merritt Wagoner; Nebraska Regent Julie Fancher; First Vice President General Gale Jones Fixmer; Sandra Spicer, Omaha Chapter member and rededication event co-chair; Judy Ekeler, Lewis-Clark Chapter member and event co-chair; Nebraska Congressman Doug Bereuter; and Nebraska Governor Mike Johanns. The boulder was originally unveiled August 3, 1904, at the village of Fort Calhoun, to commemorate the first peace council between the United States government, represented by Lewis and Clark, and the chiefs of the Otoe and other Missouri River Indians. Laura B. Pound, former Nebraska State Regent and head of the committee to raise funds and place the marker, presided at the unveiling and dedication in 1904. According to her reminiscences, the funds were hard to come by because the state legislature "failed to make the desired appropriation." But the four state chapters at the time (there are now thirty-one) rallied to the cause. Wrote Pound, "The Deborah Avery Chapter gave seventy-five dollars, the Omaha chapter one hundred, and the two new chapters organized in 1902, Quivira of Fairbury and Lewis-Clark of Fremont, raised the sum to two hundred, each promising more if it was needed." The simple inscription on the front of the boulder reads: "1804–1904/Lewis & Clark" and bears the NSDAR insignia. The side inscription states: "Dedicated by the/Sons of the American Revolution/Daughters of the American Revolution/State Historical Society."

national committee. Under her leadership, instead of 3,096 cast-iron markers at each mile of the trail, the DAR proposed instead to erect in each of the twelve states through which the Old Trails Road passed "one marker of dignified and pretentious proportions, to cost approximately one thousand dollars" and to "mark an historic spot or commemorate some great act of historical interest of the Revolutionary period . . .."

In 1926, she proposed another amendment, "a monument, not a marker—to be the figure of a pioneer mother, to be known as 'The Madonna of the Trail.'" The Daughters agreed. All twelve statues would feature the same inscriptions on the front and reverse. The front panel would read, "THE MADONNA OF THE TRAIL" and "NSDAR MEMORIAL TO THE PIONEER MOTHERS OF THE COVERED WAGON DAYS," separated by the NSDAR insignia. The reverse would read simply, "THE NATIONAL OLD TRAILS ROAD." The unique features of each statue would be the inscriptions on the two side panels: twenty-five-word descriptions briefly outlining what historic event took place at each location.

The NSDAR paid a total of $12,000 for the creation of the twelve statues, with each DAR member asked to contribute ten cents. The National Old Trails Road Association and local authorities picked up the tab for freight and placement of the five-ton statues, the final estimate between $60,000 and $70,000.

▲ Inspired by the statue of Sacagawea erected in Portland, Oregon, DAR National Committee Chairman Arline B. Nichols Moss worked for five months with her son John Moss Jr., an artist and architect, to develop designs for the Madonna of the Trail monument. In 1927, at the recommendation of the stone manufacturing company who would produce the statues, she presented her ideas to architectural sculptor August Leimbach of St. Louis, even though he had not entered the competition for the design. Within three days, he had created a model and shown it to Arline Moss, who was departing immediately for a DAR meeting in Washington. Within days, she wired back that he was awarded the contract. The design features a pioneer woman of heroic proportions clasping her baby with her left arm while clutching a rifle with her right. Her young son clings to her skirts. Her face captures the beauty of a mother, strong in character but also gentle. Her roughshod boot strides forward on a path toward progress, crushing a thistle symbolizing the obstacles she would overcome. Arline Moss and August Leimbach are pictured here circa 1928 putting the finishing touches on one of the *Madonnas*.

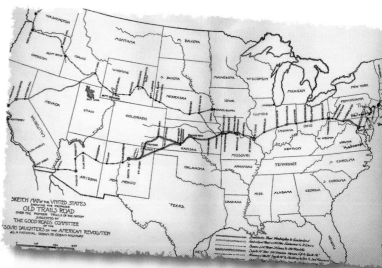

▲ The idea of a transcontinental highway had been proposed as early as the 1890s, with various routes debated, but the Missouri Daughters drove the point home, with their own efforts to mark the Santa Fe Trail in their own state, inspiring the establishment of the National Old Trails Road Association, first headed by then-Judge Harry S. Truman.

▲ Participants at the Washington County, Pennsylvania, *Madonna of the Trail* dedication bundled up for the event held on a cold, blustery day, December 8, 1928. Honored guests included NSDAR President General Grace Brosseau, pictured at center holding the large bouquet. The winter temperature was not as cold as the chilly reception the monument had received a few months earlier in Pennsylvania, when the original plan called for this statue to be placed on the grounds of the Washington County Courthouse. The Pennsylvania State Art Commission ruled in September that the statue could not be erected on public property because "the figure submitted has not sufficient artistic merit to justify its erection . . . ." The Nemacolin Country Club quickly and most generously donated a piece of its property on Route 40, the National Road, so that the *Madonna of the Trail* statue could remain in Washington County. Not to be undone, the Daughters deemed the more visible location a better one than the original site at the local courthouse.

A committee of three—Arline Moss, Judge Truman, and Frank A. Davis, National Old Trails secretary—traveled all over the country to make the final selection of location in each of the twelve states from east to west:

Bethesda, Maryland
Washington County, Pennsylvania
Wheeling, West Virginia
Springfield, Ohio
Richmond, Indiana
Vandalia, Illinois
Lexington, Missouri
Council Grove, Kansas
Lamar, Colorado
Albuquerque, New Mexico
Springerville, Arizona
Upland, California

The first unveiling took place in Springfield, Ohio, on July 4, 1928, and, even with some delays, within nine months, all

[The Washington Post]

METRO

SATURDAY, DECEMBER 11, 2004

Listing Madonna Rescued in Bethesda

Sinkhole Had Statue Tilting to Its Left

By CAMERON W. BARR
Washington Post Staff Writer

Bethesda's Madonna of the Trail strides forward, a baby in one arm and a boy tugging at her skirt, a bonnet on her head and boots on her feet. A stone monument to the women who took part in America's westward expansion, for 75 years she has been a pioneer presence along a stretch of Wisconsin Avenue near a Bethesda post office.

This week, she began to lean, a little forward and a little to her left, in ways that prompted comparisons to a tall building in Italy. It seemed as if the Madonna might topple over—all 17 tons of her.

So the statue's owners, the Maryland State Society of the Daughters of the American Revolution, had her hauled from her sidewalk perch and into storage yesterday, acting in concert with a phalanx of county and state official and numerous representatives of utilities and public agencies.

Montgomery's Fire and Rescue Service set up an "incident command post"—a black-and-red RV with flashing lights—causing bystanders to wonder whether calamity had struck. Police stopped southbound traffic on Wisconsin Avenue for most of the afternoon and early evening to allow a crane to remove the Madonna.

See MADONNA, B4, Col. 1

BY RICKY CARIOTI—THE WASHINGTON POST

Workers saw Bethesda's Madonna of the Trail statue from its base before removing it from a Wisconsin Avenue sidewalk.

◀ The Bethesda, Maryland, Madonna seems to have inherited the wandering spirit of the pioneer woman she represents. In the early 1980s, the great lady had to be moved to make way for the Washington, D.C., red line Metro subway system. She found a new home in 1986 in downtown Bethesda. However, in December 2004, she suddenly began to lean due to a sinkhole, possibly caused by a water main break. Her caretakers, the Maryland State Society, had her hauled away, and placed in protective custody until she was returned to her original spot. But maybe there is a reason for her wanderlust. All her sisters face west, while she alone faced east, a concession to each of her previous two locations so that passersby saw her front, not her backside. But as reporter Cameron W. Barr of the *Washington Post* noted in this 2004 article covering the Madonna's latest dilemma, "as dusk fell and emergency lights illuminated the street . . . workers set her down, gently, gently, on the back of a flatbed. For once, like her sisters across the country, she faced west."

twelve had been dedicated. Mrs. Moss participated in all twelve celebrations; her partner, Judge Truman, in most, including the last. Ironically, the last two unveiled were the eastern and westernmost monuments: the Upland, California, Madonna on February 1, 1929, and finally the Madonna in Bethesda, Maryland, in by far the longest celebration that lasted the entire week of April 19, 1929.

Much of the National Old Trails Road later became U.S. Highways 40 and 66. Despite some moves required by the continued march of progress, such as wider, newer roads and other community developments, more than three-quarters of a century later all twelve Madonnas endure, thanks to a few facelifts and careful moves, and the tender nurturing of the Daughters who see to their care. Exhibiting the same resilience and determination of the pioneer women represented by the Madonna of the Trail, the diligent Daughters charted a course that cemented a paved pathway from east to west, described by Arline Moss as "the autograph of a nation written across the continent."

Some DAR preservation efforts focus on the end of the journey for some weary travelers, like the Taos and Picuric Indians of El

Cuartelejo in Scott County, Kansas. El Cuartelejo, or "distant quarters," predates the settlement of Europeans in Kansas and was built by first the Taos about 1664 and later the Picuric Indians, who arrived in 1696. The pueblo dwellings and irrigation system for crops were abandoned around 1727 until pioneer Herbert L. Steele rediscovered them in the 1890s. The Kansas Daughters accepted the deed from the Steeles for the small tract of land containing the ruins in 1922. The Kansas State Historical Society has maintained the property for the Kansas DAR since 1970. In 2006, the Kansas DAR, the historical society, and the Kansas Department of Wildlife and Parks partnered to build an enclosed interpretive center over the ruins that now protect the northernmost site of pueblo culture in North America. The ruins sit surrounded by Lake Scott, Kansas's first state park.

In affirmation of the timeless truth and elegant simplicity of the NSDAR mission of preservation, education, and patriotism, Daughters across the nation tackle projects with their hands and hearts in keeping with the spirit and intent of the founders. Two long-standing initiatives remain: to mark American history sites that merit special recognition, and to identify and mark the final resting places of patriots who might otherwise have been forgotten. Although the Society has maintained an accurate count of the number of historical and grave markers for approximately the past twenty years, no doubt DAR state societies and chapters have placed thousands throughout the world.

From birthplaces and battlefields, hospitals and hearths to homesteads and headquarters, with each marking or re-marking, they make every effort to retell the story of that place or event in such a way that the history comes alive, both for those who know the tale and for those to whom the story is fresh and new. For example, on April 18, 1895, the Paul Revere Chapter of Massachusetts staged an elaborate Patriots Day celebration during which they dedicated a plaque marking the house where Paul Revere was living when he made his midnight ride. Sarah Watkins wrote in the *American Spirit* magazine in August 2004, "At the time of the plaque's dedication, Paul Revere's former home contained a cigar factory, grocery story and tenement apartments. The DAR intended this memorial to inspire patriotism among the predominantly foreign-born people who lived and worked in the neighborhood." For more than ten years, the chapter repeated its Patriots Day celebration, and local children became more and more involved in the event, to the point that some two hundred neighborhood children were special guests at the 1904 celebration. While no one can say for certain that the awareness raised by the Daughters helped save the historic home, by 1902 the house had been purchased by a Revere descendant, and money was being raised for its restoration. By 1907, the Paul Revere Memorial Association became the official guardian of the site, and the women of the Paul Revere Chapter became life members.

From the DAR chapters that bear patriots' names to the historic sites marked by the DAR that bear witness to patriots' lives, such reminders of affirmation and restoration abound for nearly every famous champion of the Revolution, from John Adams to George Washington, as well as lesser-known people and places that figured in America's development. Ever true to their mission of historic preservation, the Daughters have marked, and in some cases rescued, trees and trails, rivers and roads, battlegrounds and burial grounds, forts and farms, churches and taverns, faithfully following the Bible verse from Proverbs inscribed on a cartouche beside the doorway of their own landmark, Constitution Hall: "Remove not the ancient landmark, which thy fathers have set."

▲ This photo of the Albuquerque, New Mexico, Madonna, taken on her fiftieth anniversary in 1978, features a New Mexico Daughter dressed in period attire with a gentleman who had attended the statue's original dedication on September 27, 1928.

Witnesses to History

As early as 1894, the Daughters embarked on a mission that would create forests all across America, a natural offshoot that sprang from their three-pronged mission of preservation, education, and patriotism. How did the Daughters come to embrace conservation long before the groundswell movement that began some fifty years later? The answer lies in the roots of the Society's mission to preserve and perpetuate the stories and sites that figured in American independence.

On August 14, 1765, the Sons of Liberty gathered in Boston under a large elm tree at the corner of Essex Street and Orange Street near Hanover Square to protest the hated Stamp Act. They concluded their protest by hanging two tax collectors in effigy from the tree. The tree became known as the "Liberty Tree," and assemblies were regularly held to express views and vent emotions. News of the Boston Liberty Tree spread throughout the thirteen colonies, where each of them formed a Sons of Liberty group and identified a large tree to be used as a meeting place, a safe venue since holding an unauthorized assembly carried threats of imprisonment or death. The trees became visible rallying points that inspired the pen of author Thomas Paine, who wrote the poem, "Liberty Tree," in honor of the Boston behemoth. The Sequoia Chapter in San Francisco, California, planted its own Liberty Tree in 1894 in Golden Gate Park, and chapters in the east sent cuttings and seedlings from eastern trees to create an entire grove in California, a physical as well as symbolic link on the western shore to its American birthplace.

▲ DAR celebrated the bicentennial by dedicating a Rose Garden at Independence Hall in Philadelphia. Just over a decade later, the National Park Service called on the DAR to replace a tree that had died in the garden. To raise money for the new oak sapling, Conservation Chairman Gale Fixmer resourcefully asked each state to donate thirteen dollars, representing the thirteen original colonies. On September 16, 1987, the Bicentennial of the Constitution, the Daughters arrived in Philadelphia to plant the tree. Pictured here at the ceremony, Gale Fixmer (left) and President General Ann Fleck water the newly planted tree.

▶ The Texas DAR still owns its very own forest, the DAR State Forest in the deep Piney Woods area of southeastern Texas. In 1928, Texas Daughter Ida Caldwell McFaddin of Beaumont donated one hundred acres of forestland in east Texas. Subsequently, the State Society purchased fifty adjoining acres, increasing their forest by half its original size. Dedicated on October 31, 1929, it was rededicated October 31, 1995, as a part of the Texas DAR Centennial Celebration.

▲ Members of the Independence Hall Chapter, Philadelphia, pause for a group photo after placing a marker on this giant oak in Dilworthtown, Pennsylvania, circa 1922. The marker can be seen just to the left of the woman in the center with a fur boa.

Likely, this intimate appreciation for these living symbols of history created a commitment by Daughters all over the country to mark and celebrate these blessed beeches and oaks, maples and magnolias, elms and poplars. These mighty trees, mute witnesses to two centuries of American history often recorded under their spreading branches, became a cause célèbre for the National Society, which created a Historic Trees Conservation Subcommittee in 1926 and pledged to save one historic tree each year in a partnership with a nationally renowned tree service noted for saving such aging giants. The last original Liberty Tree standing was a 400-year-old tulip poplar on the front lawn of St. John's College in Annapolis, Maryland. More than ninety feet tall, a hurricane felled it in 1999.

The Daughters' conservation commitment went beyond mere history, however. Early Daughter Mary Eno Pinchot, of the Abigail Phelps Chapter in Connecticut, was a conservationist of some importance who helped foster DAR interest in conservation in the first few years of the twentieth century. Her son, Gifford Pinchot, for whom the Pinchot Institute for Conservation is named, became a leading advocate of environmental conservation. In the six years before her death in 1914,

Mary Pinchot would serve as chairman of the new NSDAR National Committee on Conservation formed in 1909. She would undertake the enormously successful DAR "Penny Pines" project, when Daughters financed the planting of hundreds of thousands of pines, part of a nationwide effort at reforestation following heightened awareness that so much of the land across America had been cleared for settlement. Beginning in 1919, at the end of World War I, the Daughters joined a sweeping movement across the country to plant memorial trees, an endeavor described by American Forests board chairman Charles Lathrop Pack at the time of the November 11, 1918, armistice, to honor "the heroic dead of the Great War" with "a new form of monument—the memorial that lives."

Even in the midst of the worst economic period in America's history, the generous Daughters launched a project in 1932 to plant ten million trees across the country to commemorate the 200th anniversary of George Washington's birth. In a letter that

THE DAVEY BULLETIN

Volume XIX, No. 5   "Do It Right or Not At All"   May 15, 1931

Second Historical Tree Selected by D. A. R. Receives Davey Care

Virginia Veteran Is Chosen

By KARL H. GRISMER

FOR two centuries, more or less, a giant tulip tree growing at Falls Church, Virginia, probably has been bragging to near-by younger trees about how well it knew George Washington in the days that used to be. According to tradition, Washington tied his horse to a ring in the tree when he went there to worship before the Revolutionary War, and often rested on hot summer days in the shade cast by the thriving tree.

Long ago christened the Washington Tulip, this famous old tree now has something else to brag about. It has become a favored protege of the National Society of the Daughters of the American Revolution, chosen from scores of rival "candidates" in accordance with the organization's plan to save one historical tree each year.

Not only that, but the tree now can confide to its neighbors all the intimate details of the sensations it experienced while being operated on by Davey Tree Surgeons and also how it felt when it was given an emergency meal of nearly four hundred pounds of Davey Tree Food.

Yes, this stately old monarch now has so much to talk about, and boast about, that it may swell up with pride one of these days, running risk of bursting the bark on its trunk.

But be that as it may, this story should be told from the beginning. And the beginning goes back six years to the saving of another famous Washington tree by Davey men—the Washington Horse-chestnut in Fredericksburg, Virginia.

Away back in 1783, shortly after the close of the conflict that gave America her freedom, Washington returned to Fredericksburg and planted thirteen horse-chestnuts to shade the walk between his mother's cottage and his sister's home, and he named the trees for the thirteen colonies. They grew and prospered. But as the years went by, the trees began to suffer from the ravages of time. Some were probably killed by lightning; others were killed by disease. Finally only one tree remained, and it was badly decayed.

And Then They Started To Save the Tree

After the ceremonies of officially starting the work of preserving the famous Washington Tulip at Falls Church, Va., had been completed by national officers of the Daughters of the American Revolution, Davey men swung into action, as you see, and began to prune and feed the tree. The fellow in the crotch is Foreman H. I. ALBERT. D. R. BRUSH is on the ground while O. U. SPRAKER is strutting his stuff above ALBERT's head.

Realizing the historical importance of the tree, the people of Fredericksburg were anxious that it be saved. They appealed to M. L., who was then in Congress. He saw the need of preserving this living link between our generation and the life of Washington. He knew that if the tree died, Fredericksburg and the entire nation would suffer an irreparable loss, and he immediately made the necessary arrangements.

Late in the summer of 1925, a crew of Davey men in charge of Foreman A. S. ANDERSON, was sent to Fredericksburg. They found that while the tree was badly decayed, its general condition was reasonably healthy and vigorous. So they proceeded with the treatment of the cavities and also fed the tree and pruned it. It responded as expected. The next spring, its foliage was denser and greener than it had been for years.

For over two centuries, a stately tulip poplar had shaded the entrance to the old church in Falls Church, Virginia, where George Washington had served as warden overseeing work to replace the original wooden church structure with the brick building that still stands today. Legend also recounts that Washington tied his horse to a ring in the tree when he went there to worship before the Revolutionary War. But by 1925, portions of the tree were badly decayed. The work of preserving the historic tree, named the Washington Tulip, was considered such an important event that officials of the National Society, then meeting in Washington in 1931, made a pilgrimage to inspect the tree and start the operation. Professionals from the Davey Tree Expert Company did the preservation work; their track record included the treatment of important plantings at the U.S. Capitol and the White House. NSDAR officials immediately began pondering the possibility of saving other such historic trees as the Washington Tulip poplar. The problem was money. But Martin Davey, who co-founded the company with his father, was so honored to be doing such important work that he committed the Davey Company to assume the task and expense of restoring one historic tree per year chosen by the DAR with the help of its chapters. The company, which would later become an internationally renowned forestry resource, featured each restoration on the front page of the company newsletter, such as the one pictured here showing work on the Falls Church poplar. Despite the Depression, the company's philanthropic endeavor lasted throughout the early 1930s. Unfortunately, not even their heroic efforts could save the historic towering timbers forever. ▼

---

year, the Conservation Committee reported that already seven million of these trees had been registered with the American Tree Association. The NSDAR and its chapters raised thousands of dollars to assist in the reforestation project of the U.S. Forestry Service during the 1940s. DAR records indicate it reforested, at minimum, four thousand acres of land across the country, almost five times the size of New York's Central Park.

In some instances, state DAR societies created entire forests. For example, the Iowa State Society hosted a celebration February 17, 1932, to dedicate their George Washington Memorial Forest, part of the National Society project. In 1940, the fiftieth anniversary of the first DAR chapter in the nation established in Chicago, the Illinois Daughters would fund the planting of one million trees—one thousand trees per acre on one thousand acres of public land, called the "Illinois Daughters of the American Revolution Golden Jubilee Forest." Dedicated October 5, 1940, at Pounds Hollow, the forest remains a treasured piece of the Shawnee National Forest in southern Illinois. In 1955, the Vermont Daughters donated most of the ninety-five acres that now make up the popular park and campground that bears their name—D.A.R. State Park in Addison, on the

Page 2   Vol. XIX, No. 5

D. A. R. Officials Inspect Washington Tulip

Work of preserving the historic Washington Tulip at Falls Church, Va., was considered such an important event by officials of the National Society of the D. A. R., then convening in Washington, that they made a pilgrimage to inspect the tree and start the operation. In the group shown above are Mrs. Lowell Fletcher Hobart, President General, members of the National Board of Management, and officials of the Falls Church Chapter of the D. A. R.

The Washington Tulip

For nearly two centuries this stately old tulip tree has shaded the entrance to this historic old church at Falls Church, Va. George Washington is said to have tied his horse to the tree when he went to the church to worship. Scientists say that the tree, which was treated last month for the D. A. R. by Davey men, is 300 years old.

The DAR State Forest in Goshen, Massachusetts, attracts as many as 68,000 people a year. This spectacular state forest was established in 1929 when the Massachusetts State Society donated 1,020 acres to the state. A temple of timber now surrounds the boulder and marker placed in 1929 commemorating the forest's creation. Since then, they have acquired and donated another 750 acres to the preserve, including the Upper and Lower Highland Lakes. Listed by Reserve America in 2004 as one of America's top one hundred family campgrounds, the forest is a popular recreational destination both summer and winter. As described by state forest supervisor Robert Kabat in a January 2006 story for the Associated Press, "They bought the land with the intention of handing it over to the state, and the state has turned it into a huge conservation and recreation area."

southern shore of Lake Champlain. The picturesque park provided the setting for the movie *What Lies Beneath*, with Michelle Pfeiffer and Harrison Ford.

With the advent of a more organized conservation movement, there was less need for the Daughters to shoulder such massive endeavors by themselves. Nevertheless, tree planting remains a continuing gift of the Society. In 1984, the Society presented three hundred dogwoods to France as continuing tribute to that country's critical aid during the Revolution, and the following year, an avenue of fifty elms was planted on a site in France used as a U.S. Army Air Field in World War II. Members of the General John A. Sutter Chapter of Sacramento, California, were part of the Millennium Tree Celebration of the Sacramento Tree Foundation, winner of a National Arbor Day Foundation Annual Award. During this two-day celebration in 2000, Sacramento Daughters partnered with three thousand others who helped plant one million trees in Sacramento County.

In the aftermath of the terrorist attacks in America on September 11, 2001, the tradition of memorial trees has returned. And tree planting has become a popular event with DAR Junior

American Citizens. As the organization American Forests explains, "Americans have for centuries used trees as a symbol. Throughout our history they have marked rebellions, tallied losses, and celebrated triumphs. From the Liberty Trees that rallied American patriots to the national champion 'General Sherman' sequoia, trees have served as a living calendar, leaving for those who know to look for it a picture of our past as clear as any timeline." As with their other missions, the Daughters continue to play an important role in maintaining and honoring these living memorials

CHAPTER NINE

Sacred Trusts
Sacred Sites

ONLY TWENTY-FIVE MILES SEPARATE JAMESTOWN, where the great experiment in America began in 1607, and Yorktown, where in 1781, as the Marquis de Lafayette asserted, "Humanity has won its battle. Liberty now has a country." In between those two small but critically important places in American history would stretch "one hundred and seventy-four years of hope, adventure, discovery, settlement, struggle, suffering, war, frustration, growth, and development that saw the country expand from a lonely settlement of 107 people in the small wilderness area on the banks of the James River into thirteen colonies and three million people of many races and beliefs," as described by the National Park Service. Yet the circuitous journey between the events at Jamestown and Yorktown would reach across oceans and continents and involve thousands of lives and important dates and places, nearly all of them honored, marked, or preserved in some way by the DAR and its chapters around the world. As a Virginia guidebook from the 1907 Jamestown Exposition states: "The Far East has its Mecca, Palestine its Jerusalem, France its Lourdes, and Italy its Loreto, but America's only shrines are her altars of patriotism . . . ." They are a sacred trust, often rescued and lovingly safeguarded by the Daughters of the American Revolution for future generations.

One such site the DAR helped to save remains one of the Revolution's most well known. Each year, more than one million tourists visit Valley Forge National Historical Park, Pennsylvania, where revered landmarks include George Washington's winter headquarters, re-creations of the log cabins where Washington's guards spent the long cold winter, the elegant Washington Memorial Chapel built in 1903 to the memory of George Washington and the historic encampment, and the sixty-foot-tall National Memorial Arch dedicated in 1917. But the tallest, and certainly one of the most striking of the monuments at the park, is the National Memorial Bell Tower that was built entirely from funds donated by

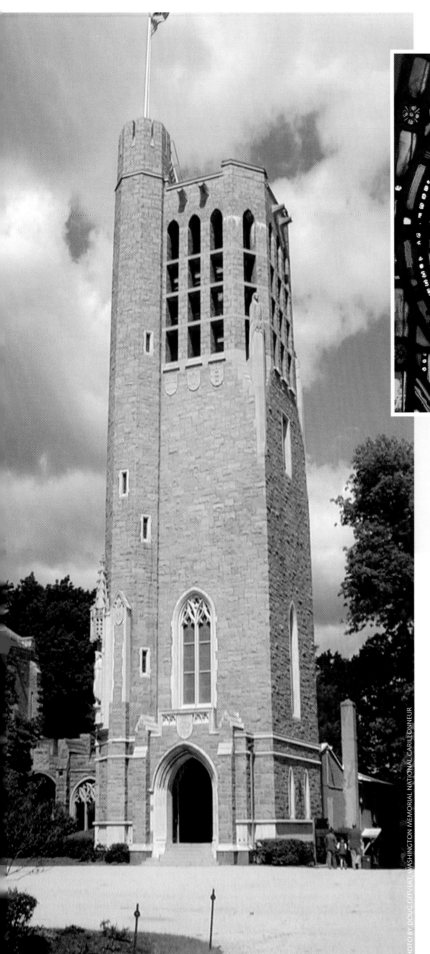

◀ ▲ Built entirely by funds raised by the DAR, the 114-foot Valley Forge Bell Tower holds one of the most unique carillons in the world, with fifty-eight bells and thousands of plaques and inscriptions to honor more than nine thousand veterans of several wars. The tower features fifteen stained-glass windows, such as the one pictured above.

the National Society Daughters of the American Revolution and its chapters. The 114-foot Bell Tower, with its fifty-eight bells varying in size from 13.5 pounds to 4 tons, 26 tons in all, all perfectly tuned, forms a four-and-a-half-octave carillon that still sounds today to mark this historic shrine. Each bell represents one of the fifty states as well as Washington, D.C.; Puerto Rico; Guam; American Samoa; the Virgin Islands; Midway and Wake Islands; and a National Birthday Bell.

Inscribed around the exterior are the names of patriots, generals, and presidents. In the entryway are the names of all the DAR Presidents General. Rich decorative elements cover the inside walls of the Bell Tower, including C. Paul Jennewein's four-panel stone bas relief illustrating the significance of Valley Forge; six bronze gates; bronze memorials; sixty-four patriot stones; honor rolls on the walls and floor naming approximately nine thousand veterans of several wars; and several thousand inscriptions of Daughters and friends who helped to build the tower. Illuminating all this are fifteen stained-glass windows, including the famous Rose Window portraying

▲ The NSDAR actually funded two bell towers commemorating the bravery and determination of George Washington and his men during their winter encampment at Valley Forge. This vintage postcard provides a rare glimpse of the original bell tower, called the Star-Spangled Banner National Peace Chime, and its thirteen bells, one for each of the original colonies, dedicated on July 4, 1926, next to the Washington Memorial Chapel. It would ultimately be torn down in the 1940s to make way for the impressive stone structure that would become such a well-known landmark at Valley Forge.

▶ For more than a century after Washington's famous encampment, the land that was Valley Forge remained in private hands. In 1891, barely one year after its founding, the Society almost found itself the erstwhile owners of this precious property. As reported in this October 11, 1891, edition of the *Philadelphia Inquirer*, "One of the first objects which Mrs. [Caroline Scott] Harrison and the Regents have in view for recommendation to the National Society is an inquiry into the feasibility of the acquisition of Valley Forge as an objective point for the direction of their patriotic efforts." The Society appointed a committee to consider the purchase, but meantime some of the land had already been sold. The Pennsylvania Legislature ultimately purchased some of the land in 1893. Numerous monuments were placed there over the next forty years, but nothing permanent would be erected until the Daughters—despite the nation's sudden involvement in World War II following the bombing of Pearl Harbor—took on the obligation of raising funds to build the Valley Forge Memorial Bell Tower. The project, to include the 114-foot-tall tower, Memorial Room, carillon, and belfry, would stretch over four DAR administrations and eventually cost more than half a million dollars before its dedication on April 18, 1953.

▲ This circa-1950 aerial photo of Ellis Island in its heyday shows the vast network of buildings that housed the thousands of immigrants who arrived through New York Harbor. The facilities later served as a Coast Guard Hospital before it was abandoned for decades. The DAR contributed thousands of dollars to the restoration of the buildings, some of which are now a popular tourist attraction managed by the National Park Service.

George Washington kneeling in prayer, made by the renowned D'Ascenzo Studios in Philadelphia.

The Tower was dedicated on April 18, 1953, but work continued on this magnificent edifice into 1956 when the project was finally completed. In the end, the Daughters expended over $500,000—five times more than originally estimated—to create a testament to those who fought in the American Revolution as well as other U.S. military conflicts. It also remains a fitting tribute to the many Daughters of the American Revolution who sacrificed time and money for the construction of the Bell Tower, as well as those who took an active role with other organizations beginning in 1897 to press for Valley Forge to be made into a National Park and to help ensure that the 3,500 acres on which Valley Forge rests would not be broken apart and sold for private development.

The Daughters would also be instrumental in rescuing the site of another historic event: the surrender of Lord Cornwallis and the British Army at Yorktown, Virginia, in 1781. After 140 years, the original fortifications were being razed, and the land was in danger of being parceled off and sold. In 1921, National

DAR Chairman of Historic Spots and former Vice President General Lucy Leavenworth Wilder Morris presented a resolution at the 30th Continental Congress that the Daughters use their considerable influence with the U.S. President and the Congress to appropriate funds and create a national military park. They succeeded, and the bill became law on March 2, 1922. Lucy Morris would subsequently become the first woman ever appointed as a member of a U.S. government Commission for National Military Parks.

Partly in celebration of their own heroic efforts, the Daughters would play a significant role in the Yorktown Sesquicentennial Celebration just nine years later, in 1931. President General

Edith Irwin Hobart and 283 Daughters sailed on the chartered *Southland* from the Potomac to the York River on a three-day cruise to participate in festivities that included President and Mrs. Herbert Hoover and Marshal Henri Pétain, considered France's greatest hero in World War I. Guns firing, both American and French warships, including the USS *Constitution,* once again guarded the harbor. A huge blimp and bombers from Langley Air Force Base filled the skies. Re-enactors in period costume re-created the historic surrender. On the grounds of the Yorktown Monument, where thousands had assembled to witness the solemn occasion, the Daughters unveiled two bronze plaques on which were inscribed the names, previously unknown, of each of the 103 American soldiers and the 132 Frenchmen who died during the siege of Yorktown. Today, the Yorktown Battlefield endures as an important destination of the National Park Service's Colonial National Historical Park.

Another American monument has been a symbol of freedom for millions around the world. From 1892 to 1954, more than twelve million immigrants streamed through the gates at Ellis Island, in the shadow of the Statue of Liberty, searching for a better life. Unfortunately, approximately 2 percent of the immigrants who came ashore at the feet of Lady Liberty without appropriate documentation or suffering from contagious diseases had to be detained on Ellis Island, often for months, in dormitories separated by gender. Families were also separated

PHOTO FROM PRESS ASSOCIATION, INC.

▲ In 1923, the Daughters began providing occupational therapy, such as needlecrafts, sewing, crochet, and other activities for immigrant detainees on Ellis Island as a means of easing some of the tension while also providing meaningful and productive work. In this undated photo, a young boy learns how to use a sewing machine during a work therapy session.

◄ As the flow of immigrants decreased, the federal government asked the Daughters to once again extend their service, this time to include occupational work with Merchant Marines, U.S. Coast Guard members, and lighthouse keepers treated at the hospital on Ellis Island. Some received tutoring from the staff paid by the Daughters in such areas as math and other subjects that could help them re-enter the workforce. Others became quite skilled in fabric weaving, knitting, painting, leather tooling, woodworking, and other handwork.

and, in many cases, immigrants could converse only in their native tongue. The anxieties of fear, separation, isolation, and idleness contributed to constant tension and frequent fights throughout the Ellis Island complex, including the Women's Detention Room. In 1923, the Daughters of the American Revolution became the only society to sponsor occupational work on Ellis Island. The Daughters provided cloth, yarn, and crochet and embroidery supplies that not only helped the women pass the time but also provided much-needed items for their families.

The calm that prevailed in the women's room was so miraculous that the federal government asked the Daughters to extend their work to the men's living area. As Grace L. H. Brosseau, National Chairman of the Ellis Island Immigrant Aid Committee, 1923–1926, recounted, the men showed "the same avidity for work that the women have displayed," and for both the men and women, "useful activity was the antidote to the mental depression caused by uncertainty and boredom." Daughters taught the men to embroider and bead women's handbags, crochet belts and neckties, hook rugs, and weave woolen scarves using bright colors preferred by the men, to brighten their drab existence. The men also became "seamsters," sewing their own shirts, trousers, underwear, and pajamas. From 1923 to 1940, the Daughters contributed approximately

▲ Pictured here circa 1940 are members of the Ellis Island occupational therapy staff whose salaries were paid for by donations from the DAR.

▶ Beginning in 1896, the Society spearheaded, through its newly formed Fort Greene Chapter in Brooklyn, New York, an effort to raise more than $200,000 for a permanent monument to the thousands of prisoners who died aboard the British prison ships moored in Wallabout Bay during the American Revolution. The British held thousands of captives on eleven prison ships anchored in the East River, including the most notorious *Old Jersey*. As many as 11,500 men and women, representing all thirteen colonies and at least that many nationalities, died of overcrowding, contaminated water, starvation, and disease aboard the ships, and their bodies were hastily buried along the shore by their fellow prisoners. In 1808, the remains of the prison ship martyrs were buried in a tomb near the Brooklyn Navy Yard but with no marker of any consequence. The 149-foot Prison Ship Martyrs Monument, unveiled at Fort Greene Park in Brooklyn on November 14, 1908, at last marked with dignity the final resting place of the prisoners, as depicted on this program for the event.

$230,000 to support the misplaced thousands at Ellis Island as well as Angel Island in San Francisco Bay. Their generosity also included 21,000 boxes of supplies, sewing machines, looms, and carpenter's tools, along with trained workers who provided instruction and distributed the supplies.

Eventually, as quotas began to limit the numbers of immigrants, the hospital on Ellis Island became known as the Marine Hospital run by the Public Health Service to treat American merchant seamen and members of the U.S. Coast Guard. Once again at the request of the U.S. government, in 1934 the Daughters extended their skilled occupational therapy support to these patients, hiring three full-time workers, two therapists, and a crafts teacher. Daughters' contributions funded the salaries as well as supplies needed by this additional staff. Their work with the servicemen continued throughout World War II when the hospital on Ellis Island again became a Marine Hospital for members of the Coast Guard. Before the end of the war, the work of the DAR would spread to a new hospital on Staten Island. While their involvement with Ellis Island immigrants ended when the facility closed in 1951, their support did not. In conjunction with the 1986 centennial restoration of the Statue of Liberty and Ellis Island, under the administrations of Presidents General Sarah M. King, Ann D. Fleck, and Marie H. Yochim, the National Society Daughters of the American Revolution raised $771,000 for the restoration of these symbols of freedom.

▲ A large contingent of DAR members participated in the 1907 Jamestown Exposition held at Sewell's Point in Norfolk, Virginia, to commemorate the 300th anniversary of the founding of the Jamestown Settlement, choosing the Society's seventeenth anniversary on October 11 to attend the ongoing event. President General Emily R. McLean (at center, with boa and bouquet), declared by Exposition President Henry St. George Tucker III as "the most eloquent woman in public in America," delivered a keynote address that day. Also present for the photo were Henrietta Preston Johnston Tucker, wife of Henry St. George Tucker III; Elizabeth Deane Lyons Swanson, first wife of Virginia Governor Claude A. Swanson; Lydia Pleasants Purcell (NSDAR Chairman of the Jamestown Exposition Committee); and Dr. Anita Newcomb McGee. The building behind them was a reproduction of a Swiss chalet, the main structure within the Swiss Alps Village, located in the Exposition's international section. Besides overwhelming moral support and physical presence at the expo, in 1896 the NSDAR dedicated the "small sum of $100" that endorsed the efforts of the Association for the Preservation of Virginia Antiquities (APVA) to construct embankments to protect the site from severe erosion on the James River. The Daughters also funded the $5,500 cost of constructing a "House of Rest," a replica of Malvern Hill on the James, considered at the time one of the "best specimens known of early Colonial architecture," on Jamestown Island itself, for the island was bare and there was no place to shelter the multitudes expected to visit it during the Jamestown Exposition.

On the West Coast, Daughters also worked to assist the thousands of immigrants seeking a new life in America. Numerous references in the DAR records describe their work at Angel Island, the lesser-known counterpart to Ellis Island located in the San Francisco Bay. Individual chapters also supported an immigrant settlement. At one time there were three separate chapters in Berkeley, California—the Sierra, Berkeley Hills, and John Rutledge Chapters. All three contributed funds to build the Berkeley Americanization House, established and maintained by the "Mobilized Women of Berkeley" as a place for easing the transition of the flood of immigrants in the 1930s and 1940s.

In January 1971, under the administration of President General Elizabeth J. Seimes, the Daughters formally presented the Rose Garden in Independence Hall Park to the United States Park Service. Shortly thereafter, and long before America's Bicentennial Celebration reached its feverish climax, the Daughters took on their first bicentennial project: furnishing the Governor's Council Chamber and the Committee of the Assembly's Room on the second floor of Independence Hall, Philadelphia, with authentic eighteenth-century articles at a cost of over $200,000. President General Eleanor W. Spicer and other dignitaries cut the ribbon on July 4, 1972, a day when more than 26,000 visitors viewed the refurbished rooms and the Daughters' "Gift to the Nation."

▲ In 1972, as an early bicentennial birthday gift, the DAR funded the complete furnishing of both the Governor's Council Chamber and the Committee of the Assembly's Room on the second floor of Independence Hall in Philadelphia. The authentic eighteenth-century furnishings in the Governor's Council Chambers, pictured at left, cost a total of $200,000. The funding marked at least the second time the DAR helped to refurbish the great hall. In 1895, at a cost of $6,000, the Philadelphia Chapter received permission to restore the old Banquet Room, at upper right, to its 1776 appearance using Andrew Hamilton's original plans. The first NSDAR report to the Smithsonian in 1897 asserted that "the contagion of their efforts has roused other patriotic citizens to a sense of their own duty in this matter, and the whole building will soon be restored to its original condition."

▲ Following the ribbon cutting July 4, 1972, by President General Eleanor W. Spicer (center) and other dignitaries, 26,023 visitors viewed the restored rooms at Independence Hall, which were re-opened for the first time in twenty-two years.

THE NATION BEHAVES WELL IF IT TREATS
THE NATURAL RESOURCES AS ASSETS
WHICH IT MUST TURN OVER
TO THE NEXT GENERATION
INCREASED AND NOT IMPAIRED IN VALUE
THEODORE ROOSEVELT 1910

Another bicentennial birthday gift from the Daughters to the nation would prove as magnificent as it was munificent. Under the sadly brief administration of President General Sara R. Jones, who died in office on April 7, 1975, the Daughters made plans for sixteen ceiling murals in the East-West Corridor of the House Wing of the United States Capitol. Designed and painted by famed muralist Allyn Cox, the murals would become permanent works of art, each one depicting a turning point in the American experiment. The sixteen murals in the "Great Experiment Hall" commemorate such moments as the Mayflower Compact, 1620; the First Continental Congress, 1774; the Declaration of Independence, 1776; Washington's Inauguration, 1789; the Monroe Doctrine, 1823; Lincoln's Second Inaugural, 1865; the Smithsonian Institution, 1855; Iron Foundry, circa 1850; and the Women's Suffrage Parade, 1917. The NSDAR set aside funds for the project under the tenure of President General Jane F. Smith, but the murals would not be completed until 1982, shortly before the artist's death.

Not all preservation efforts required substantial funding from the Daughters. In 1896, a project was underway to build

▲ The Daughters' ultimate bicentennial birthday gift to the nation was a series of sixteen murals designed and painted by noted artist Allyn Cox in the East-West Corridor of the Capitol, each one capturing a milestone in the American Experiment. Vignettes on either side of each mural highlight a particular aspect of the historic event. The images along the corridor—now known as the "Great Experiment Hall"—include this one of Theodore Roosevelt, our twenty-sixth president, delivering one of his rousing speeches. One of his lasting contributions was the building of the Panama Canal depicted at left. A passionate conservationist, Roosevelt acquired more than 234 million acres of land for the public domain under his administration. He was aided by Gifford Pinchot (pictured at right and in the portrait above the vignette), America's first professional forester as well as the son of Mary Eno Pinchot, first chairman of the NSDAR National Committee on Conservation established in 1909. First Lady Edith Kermit Carow Roosevelt was also a member of the Society. (It is interesting to note that the panel abutting this one depicts a Women's Suffrage Parade in 1912, and the portrait at left is of Clara Barton, not only a staunch women's rights advocate but also Surgeon General for the NSDAR beginning in 1890.)

▲ Unfortunately, the seminal battle of the Revolution would take a terrible toll on the city of Yorktown, Virginia. Few buildings would survive the bombardment of the town by American and French forces in 1781 that drove British General Lord Cornwallis to surrender his army in the Battle of Yorktown. Ironically, one of the buildings that did withstand the assault was the British Custom House (pictured here), which dates from approximately 1720 and occupies a unique place in American history, for it was the storehouse and office of Richard Ambler, the first officially designated collector of customs for the British Crown in Yorktown, at the time one of the largest and busiest ports on the East Coast. Strategically located on Main Street, just a block away from the once-busy waterfront, the Custom House survived again as the Civil War raged through the town during McClellan's Peninsula Campaign in 1862. Although it would undergo several modifications, its character remains, and today it is safeguarded by the stewardship of the Comte de Grasse Chapter of Yorktown, which acquired the property in 1924 and opens it free to the public for tours. Many other states and chapters have restored and own such historic properties. (See "State of Things," page 208.)

▶ The site of the French-American victory over the British during the American Revolution, and where Lord Cornwallis surrendered on October 17, 1781, was in danger of being lost despite the dedication in 1880 of the 96-foot Yorktown Memorial pictured. In 1922, the Daughters of the American Revolution prevailed on Congress and the President to enact a law designating the site as a National Historical Park. In belated celebration, the Daughters played a major role at the Yorktown Sesquicentennial Celebration in 1931, a three-day event attended by President and Mrs. Herbert Hoover, when the Daughters unveiled two plaques listing the American and French patriots who died there.

▲ On Memorial Day weekend, May 29, 2004, President General Linda Tinker Watkins and Honorary President General Dorla Dean Kemper, who served as the NSDAR National Chairman of the World War II Memorial Challenge, represented the Daughters at the dedication of the World War II Memorial in Washington, D.C. Daughters across the nation raised $500,000 for the Memorial building fund. They were recognized at the celebration and also received a commemorative illustration of the Memorial and a letter signed by former U.S. Senator Robert J. Dole, National Chairman of the WWII Memorial Campaign, and Frederick W. Smith, National Co-Chairman.

◀ President General Ann D. Fleck (second from left) pauses for a photo in 1987 with members of the Walter Hines Page Chapter of the DAR in London, after the ribbon cutting of a replica of the United Kingdom-United States Friendship Tablet dedicated at Yorktown in 1984. The tablet, which includes a quote from Benjamin Franklin stating, "We are now friends with England and with all mankind," is located in a small fenced area in front of the house once occupied by John Adams when he served as minister to the Court of St. James from 1785 to 1788. President General Fleck's trip overseas that year included a visit to Sulgrave Manor, the home of George Washington's ancestors, built about 1500 and restored by funds from both the United Kingdom and the United States in 1921 as "a shrine for all Americans who visit the old country and centre from which sentiments of friendship and goodwill between the British and American peoples will forever radiate," the Marquess of Cambridge would declare in remarks at the opening ceremony that year.

▲ President General Dorla Dean E. Kemper chats with a British official in a quiet moment during events in 1995 to commemorate the fiftieth anniversary of the end of the war In Europe. At the recommendation of the Department of Defense World War II Commemorative Committee and the United States Embassy in London, representatives of the Society participated in ceremonies at the United States Military Cemetery at Madingley near Cambridge; a memorial service at St. Paul's Cathedral in London attended by the Queen and other members of the royal family and visiting heads of state, including Vice President Al Gore; and a memorial service, parade, and reception at Weymouth, England, where so many U.S. troops embarked for action on the continent of Europe.

embankments around the Jamestown Settlement to prevent further erosion from the James River. Unfortunately, the project needed further funding, but at the time, the Daughters were pouring every dime into the fund for their first real home, Memorial Continental Hall. Instead, they undertook a campaign to raise awareness and public support for the project that ultimately resulted in a Congressional appropriation that funded the Jamestown floodwall. Archaeologists credit the structure—completed by the U.S. Army Corps of Engineers in 1901 and still standing today—with protecting far more of the site's history than they ever hoped or dreamed at the turn of the last century. In fact, their recent discoveries promise to be the centerpiece of the celebration in 2007. As the first DAR report to the Smithsonian in 1899 stated, "But for this aid the encroaching waters would have washed away the embankments already erected and thus obliterated all traces of the first successful settlement upon this continent."

Sacred sites include not just Jamestown, Yorktown, Valley Forge, and hundreds of other places across the United States, but around the world as well. America won its struggle for independence with the assistance of foreign allies including France, Italy, Germany, the Netherlands, and Scotland, the birthplace of John Paul Jones. Beginning with the his-

toric journey made by Mary F. Manning to Paris in 1900 to unveil the statues of George Washington and Lafayette, nearly every President General has traveled overseas to mark historic sites and pay tribute to the patriots born on these foreign soils. With each visit, they have expressed thanks and shared the story of the success of the American Experiment that would become a beacon of light beckoning millions to her shores in search of freedom, a place where liberty still reigns, and the only sovereigns are its citizens.

Friends in France

France became a pivotal partner in the fight for American independence. Without its leaders, officers, soldiers, and resources, it is doubtful there would be an America as we know it today. The heartfelt bond with, and regard for, this new country felt by the French would especially manifest itself a century after the war ended with their gift of the statue of "Liberty Enlightening the World," dedicated October 28, 1886, on Bedloe's Island in New York Harbor. In return, in 1887, a group of American women formed the Washington Statue Association to decide on an appropriate gesture of gratitude to France, a token of appreciation for both "Lady Liberty" as well as America's liberty itself. But the gesture would require public support.

The Daughters, though newly organized, responded quickly. At only the second meeting of the National Society on October 18, 1890, they adopted a resolution to support the presentation of a bronze equestrian statue of George Washington, upon the recommendation of DAR charter member Harriett L. Coolidge, a descendant of Paul Revere. The members' support was enthusiastic and generous, but because some sent their donations directly to the Washington Statue Association, there remains no final tally. However, the DAR report to the Smithsonian in 1899 stated that "if all sums given by our members directly to the

▲ One day after the unveiling of the statue of George Washington, as the Stars and Stripes flew from the top of the Eiffel Tower, boats in the Seine displayed the French and American flags together, and with the famous Louvre as backdrop, representatives of the Lafayette Memorial Commission and the DAR unveiled the plaster replica of the statue of the Marquis de Lafayette by sculptor Paul Bartlett, which would be replaced later by the final bronze tribute. The replica is shown here shortly after the presentation July 4, 1900.

statue association during the thirteen years could be ascertained, our part in this memorial would probably appear larger by several thousands" more than the $1,141.73 officially collected.

The statue, by American sculptor Daniel C. French, was unveiled on the Place d'Iéna during the Paris Exposition July 3, 1900, the 125th anniversary of the date on which Washington took command of the American Army at Cambridge. By appointment of President William McKinley, President General Mary F. Manning represented the United States government as well as the Daughters of the American Revolution on the speakers' platform that day.

The next day, July 4, the Daughters participated in the unveiling of another statue not far from that of General Washington. This one, of General Lafayette, was funded by the children of America with additional support of almost $2,000 from the NSDAR. By special permission, the Stars and Stripes flew from the top of the Eiffel Tower, and for the first time in the history of France, John Philip Sousa and his band played American national tunes on the Place de l'Opéra. The plaque placed by the Daughters would name Lafayette "The Patriot of Two Countries."

More than eight decades later, from August 30, 1983, to September 4, 1983, a large contingent of Daughters, including President General Sarah M. King, returned to France to celebrate the 200th anniversary of the Treaty of Paris, which formally ended the American Revolutionary War. This five-day French-American celebration and DAR pilgrimage included not only a re-enactment of the treaty signing and return vis-

▼ Five million people attended the Paris Exposition in 1900, during which "The Association of the Women of the United States," which included the DAR, presented a bronze equestrian statue of George Washington to convey "gratitude to France for her generous aid in our struggle for national independence." Thousands line the tree-lined Avenue d'Iéna just moments after the unveiling in this historic photo taken July 3, 1900.

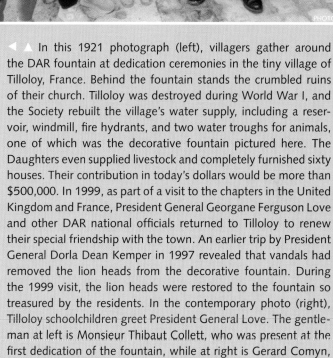

its and wreath-layings at the statues of General Washington and the grave and statue of General Lafayette, but also tributes to Admiral de Grasse, Comte de Rochambeau, and Benjamin Franklin, who was an important emissary to France after the war. In addition to the DAR President General, the contingent included Jean (Mrs. Douglas) MacArthur; Senator John Warner; Virginia Governor and Mrs. Charles Robb, who represented the governors of the thirteen colonies; and Dr. Joan Challinor, Chairman of the U.S. Committee for the celebration of the bicentennial of the Treaty of Paris. One of the French officials who greeted them and participated in the events was then-Mayor of Paris Jacques Chirac, who would become president of France in 1995.

◀ ▲ In this 1921 photograph (left), villagers gather around the DAR fountain at dedication ceremonies in the tiny village of Tilloloy, France. Behind the fountain stands the crumbled ruins of their church. Tilloloy was destroyed during World War I, and the Society rebuilt the village's water supply, including a reservoir, windmill, fire hydrants, and two water troughs for animals, one of which was the decorative fountain pictured here. The Daughters even supplied livestock and completely furnished sixty houses. Their contribution in today's dollars would be more than $500,000. In 1999, as part of a visit to the chapters in the United Kingdom and France, President General Georgane Ferguson Love and other DAR national officials returned to Tilloloy to renew their special friendship with the town. An earlier trip by President General Dorla Dean Kemper in 1997 revealed that vandals had removed the lion heads from the decorative fountain. During the 1999 visit, the lion heads were restored to the fountain so treasured by the residents. In the contemporary photo (right), Tilloloy schoolchildren greet President General Love. The gentleman at left is Monsieur Thibaut Collett, who was present at the first dedication of the fountain, while at right is Gerard Comyn, Mayor of Tilloloy.

◀ President General Sarah M. King (left) pauses for a photo with the Duc de Castries (right) after placing a wreath at the bronze monument by Paul Landowski honoring Admiral de Grasse in Trocadero Garden, Paris. The event, on August 30, 1983, was part of a daylong commemorative pilgrimage to various statues, plaques, and memorials around the city having to do with the American Revolution; a parade down the Champs Élysées where hundreds of Parisians lined the historic avenue; and a banquet in the Hall of Battles (a rare occasion in the revered hall). The President General's bright red suit with the black velvet hat and large plume made her the darling of the French media who thought it was the "uniform" of the leader of the DAR. Also pictured are Mary Ann Long Nixon, holding the wreath, and Susan Barr Hoffman (far right), Sarah King's personal page for the trip and a member of the Liberty Bell Chapter, Pennsylvania.

CHAPTER TEN

Heroes All
A Common Bond

"GENERALS GET MOST OF THE INK WHEN MILITARY HISTORY IS WRITTEN," wrote author Ed Crews in the Autumn 2006 issue of *Colonial Williamsburg* magazine. "We tend to remember the Revolution for its great men, [but] it was a people's revolution, a grassroots movement, the success of which depended upon many individual acts," Crews explained. As many as 250,000 men served in the army or militia. But, emphasized Crews, "individual enlisted men . . . march anonymously across the page in the numbered ranks of armies, battalions, and brigades."

The goal set by the founders of the DAR to honor and preserve the memory of those who served includes not only the signers of the Declaration of Independence or high-ranking military officers but also the everyday soldier or colonist. As described in the Society's first report to the United States Congress in 1897:

> *It was seen very early that the files of application papers contain a mass of more unique material than has hitherto been accessible to the genealogist and historian in any other single place. The deeds of victorious armies and famous commanders have been told over and over again in song and story. But the individual soldiers behind the guns and the patient women in the lonely homes have been quite overlooked in the "famous victory." These papers relate the experiences of many unnoticed heroes and forgotten heroines who composed the rank and file of the nation in 1776. It seemed a sacred duty that these unknown dead, who so freely gave their lives for freedom, should be made realities to their forgetful descendants.*

The battle for independence could not have been won without the help of Elizabeth Coats, who took care of officers quartered at her home, or David Dickinson, who took the oath of allegiance in 1779, or David Taylor, who served as a surgeon in a New Hampshire regi-

▶ Thousands of visitors each year, both DAR members and non-members, take advantage of the incredible resources of the DAR Library. Some of the state flags flying from the cornice were either designed by Daughters or were the result of contests sponsored by them and later adopted by those states.

ment. At the tender age of sixteen, Sarah Rand Carter served as a scout at the Battle of Bunker Hill. Oliver Pollock of New Orleans gave practically his entire considerable fortune to the American cause and was jailed as a debtor because Congress would not reimburse him. Many contributions came from immigrant Germans, Scots-Irish, and other settlers who came just prior to the Revolution.

Often eclipsed in the shadows of more famous patriots are the slaves, free men, and Native Americans who fought for freedom. In the fall of 2002, the DAR opened one of its most celebrated and perhaps most important exhibitions—Forgotten Patriots: African American and American Indian Service in the Revolutionary War, 1775–1783. (See page 178 for a look into the research that led to this exhibit.) One of those featured was Prince Easterbrook, identified in an undated broadside as "A Negro Man" wounded, along with the names of others killed and wounded at the battles of Lexington and Concord in April 1775. Mohican Indian scout Abraham Nimham, who commanded a militia unit stationed at White Plains and the Bronx, New York, died in 1778 in the skirmish with British Colonel John Simcoe's Rangers. John Neptune, who would later become a lieutenant governor of the Penobscots, was one of many Penobscot men who fought for the Americans, helping to defend Maine from British incursions from Canada. The exhibition also featured such revolutionaries as Agrippa Hull, a free black who served as an orderly for General Tadeusz Kościuszko, General George Washington's chief engineer; Peter Harris, a Catawba Indian who fought in the Revolution; and Nero Hawley.

Nero Hawley received his freedom for his service in the Revolution in November 1782 and in 1813 was listed among other Revolutionary pensioners receiving an annual stipend of $40. After the war, Hawley went on to establish himself as a brick maker in Trumbull, Connecticut. Some of the bricks excavated from the site of his brickyard were part of the 2002 Forgotten Patriots display, as well as a 1782 treasury note payable to Hawley loaned by the family of Hugh Price, a Hawley descendant and former president of the National Urban League and now a senior fellow at the Brookings Institution. Proud of his heritage as a direct descendant of the American Revolution, in a February 2006 interview, Price said of the 2002 exhibit: "I think the recognition of the role and contribution of the African American and American Indian in liberation of the country was a very powerful affirmation of the 'American-ness' of the African American population. My ancestors and others fought to liberate all of America."

The ongoing effort to identify African and American Indian patriots also underscores an understanding of why these disparate groups fought for the Revolution. Many men of color

▲ Before leaving America in 1784, the Marquis de Lafayette issued a certificate commending the slave, James Armistead, for his service as a spy. Armistead had secured work as British General Cornwallis's servant and sent information to the Marquis concerning British troop strengths and plans. Armistead pretended to supply Cornwallis with information damaging to the Americans, and his ruse was so effective, the defeated Cornwallis did not discover the truth until he encountered Armistead in Lafayette's headquarters. In homage to the Marquis, James eventually appended Lafayette as his last name. Based on Armistead's service, on January 9, 1786, the Virginia General Assembly granted him his freedom, and he later received a pension of $60. He died in 1830. Armistead is believed to be pictured here with Lafayette in a circa 1780 engraving by the French artist Noel le Mire and dedicated to "his excellency General Washington."

▶ Born in 1754 to the prominent Dana family of Massachusetts, nineteen-year-old Susanna Dana put her costuming skills to work helping her brother Thomas Dana and her fiancé Thomas Williams disguise themselves as Indians for their pivotal part in dunking the tea into Boston Harbor, December 16, 1773. Patriot Susanna is smartly attired in this photograph of an 1823 painting by William Dunlap, one of the founders of the New York Academy of Fine Arts. Susanna Dana Williams died in 1840.

fought because they had a vision that it was the first step to their own emancipation. Others earned their freedom by joining the Army or by serving in place of their masters. One such man, Peter Green, was honored with a grave marker placed by the Mary Mattoon Chapter in Colrain, Massachusetts, in June 2005.

Native Americans had other reasons. While many Indian groups tried to remain neutral, others cast their lot with the colonists once their old allies, the French, joined the American side. Some tribes aligned themselves with the Revolution in support of their colonial neighbors with whom they had formed a long-standing relationship since the landing of the *Mayflower*. Regardless of their allegiance, those who fought, fought furiously, because they knew it was a battle for their own lands and liberty. "The patriotism of members of more than two dozen tribes from Canada to the Gulf Coast, and the Atlantic Ocean to the Mississippi River, can be chronicled," wrote DAR genealogist Hazel Kreinheder in a January/February 2004 article for *American Spirit* magazine titled "Brothers in Arms." "Some served in all-Indian and mixed companies from the outbreak of hostilities until the army was disbanded in 1783. In addition, others participated as guides, spies, intelligence gatherers, messengers, runners, interpreters, translators, and ship builders during the Revolutionary War," Kreinheder elaborated.

Today's Treasure Hunters

Ask any genealogist in the Registrar General's Department what it's like processing eight to ten thousand applications and three thousand supplementals on average every year, and they will likely respond that it is a real treasure hunt. It's not surprising many genealogists prefer mystery novels and shows like *Law & Order* and *CSI*. Only, in the case of the DAR, they are finding patriots not criminals. As the largest department at DAR Headquarters with approximately forty-five employees, its goal is clear: to verify that a prospective member can prove bloodline lineage to someone who aided in the American Revolution, either through military service or as a civilian who provided material aid.

Nearly all applications begin at the chapter level, where there are usually at least one or two members with experience and quite often a passion for helping prospective members complete their paperwork. Applications can include a wide array of supporting documentation to establish descendancy from a patriot, including wills, deeds, marriage and birth certificates, pictures of gravestones, copies of pages from family Bibles, and death certificates. Even old letters, diaries, and other family papers are sometimes accepted so long as the document was made at the time of the event described. DAR staff genealogists use every tool at their disposal to verify applications, starting with the myriad of resources of the DAR Library, general genealogical reference materials, and online databases managed by other reliable genealogy organizations.

▲ The DAR staff provides outreach to others through workshops, conferences, and lectures on genealogy at the headquarters. Some chapters also sponsor discussions. In 2005, the Society began hosting what has become a very popular genealogical conference. Eric Grundset (above), DAR Library Director and conference organizer, welcomes participants to the 2005 event. During this extensive two-day program held in the fall at DAR Headquarters in Washington, D.C., experts from the DAR and the National Archives discuss genealogical research spanning the Colonial period through the pre–Civil War era. Topics included research methods and best practices, Revolutionary War sources, writing your family history, and historical events and military records.

Like the professional investigators portrayed on the genealogists' favorite television shows, these treasure hunters are masters at the search because they know where to look. A properly completed application may only take a short time to verify. Certain quirks call for lengthier investigations, such as a traditionally passive Quaker relative listed as a military man, as explained by DAR genealogist Betsy Wardner in a 2006 *Washington Post Express* interview. In certain cases, though, it's back to the chapter to get additional help if there is not enough supporting documentation to verify the original application.

One of the hardest parts of the genealogist's job is writing to the applicant or member to ask for more documentation. Sometimes the genealogist finds that the lineage is incorrect or that there is no documented service for their ancestor during the Revolution. But the NSDAR genealogists' ultimate goal is to verify the papers. If the applicant's original ancestor cannot be verified, genealogists will attempt to identify an alternate lineage that connects with a different, already-proven patriot.

◄ Terry Ward, Director of the NSDAR Genealogy Department, addresses participants on the use of Revolutionary War pension lists during the October 2005 conference at DAR Headquarters. The genealogy workshops attracted more than three hundred guests, half of whom were from outside the local area, some from as far away as California and Alaska.

In the past, the genealogy staff worked exclusively at headquarters. But in recent years, their service has branched out, both figuratively and literally. They often accept speaking engagements in the community and are encouraged to become members of professional genealogical organizations to share their experience. The Genealogy Department has also teamed with the DAR Library in recent years to conduct genealogical conferences that have proved popular with members and the public alike. They also offer genealogy consultant courses several times each year, both at national headquarters and in the field, at the request of state DAR state societies. This important training process helps broaden the pool of Daughters who can provide invaluable assistance to prospective members who are hoping to tie their lineage back to a patriot of the American Revolution.

Each application promises the possibility of a new treasure hunt for these super sleuths who, like scientists, are constantly seeking new information or reviewing the data they have been provided. "We are transcribing new information sent in all the time," relates Terry Ward, Director of Genealogy. "Each new bit of information, each new line, increases the breadth of knowledge of the patriot ancestors as it renews appreciation for the sacrifices they made for the benefit of Americans today."

▲ While the genealogy office space in the north gallery of Memorial Continental Hall appears very similar to the early photograph shown here, much has changed in the department. Note the lack of typewriters or even telephones on the desks of researchers. In the more recent photo, access to computerized databases and digitized records speeds the process significantly, allowing the staff of genealogists to instantly build on previous patriots' lines and related members without the necessity of paper records.

▲ In this circa 1860s engraving by Frederick Girsch, General George Washington stands with several of the foreign patriots who fought shoulder to shoulder with American patriots during the Revolution. To the right of Washington are (left to right) Johann De Kalb, Baron von Steuben, Kazimierz Pulaski, Tadeusz Kościuszko, the Marquis de Lafayette, John Peter Muhlenberg, and other officers.

Equally as rare as the records are the artifacts and objects of the Revolution specific to African Americans and American Indians. But as interest in genealogy continues to grow, items long forgotten in dusty attics or family archives across the country reveal individual histories of bravery and sacrifice, highlighting their contributions to the Revolution. One of the expressed goals of Forgotten Patriots was to arouse further interest in this topic and inspire descendants of all patriots to safeguard their family heritage and place these treasures in local, state, or national museums, libraries, and archives.

The work of the Society to identify these patriots also has deep meaning for Daughters like Pazetta Mallette, of the Belle Meade Chapter, in Nashville, Tennessee, who joined the DAR in 1996. Mallette is of both Native American and African American descent. While she joined through a white ancestor from her Native American line, she feels sure she is descended from an African American patriot as well, since her mother descended from slaves on George Washington's plantation. "Black patriots were not mentioned in the history books," she explains, "so my perception growing up was that blacks did not fight in that war, that we had no relationship to that war." She emphasized that the search to find details about her ancestors means more than just history. "You're not just doing names and people, you're doing research about what they did. There's a sense of pride that my ancestor played a part in all of this. I

▶ "During the American Revolution, the people of South Carolina were fortunate to have strong allies among the Catawba Nation," wrote DAR ethnic and minority genealogist Elisabeth Schmidt in 1997. "No other southern colony enjoyed the friendship of an entire tribe living within its borders." Peter Harris, of the Catawba Nation, was one of those who fought on the side of independence. Because he was orphaned as a small boy, the Thomas Spratt family in Charlotte, North Carolina, adopted and educated him. In his old age, he petitioned the government of South Carolina for a pension: "I am one of the lingering members of an almost extinguished race . . . the strength of my arm decays, and my feet fail in the chase, the hand which fought for your liberties, is now open for your relief. In my youth, I bled in battle, that you might be independent, let not my heart in my old age, bleed, for want of your Consideration." He was successful in his petition, as evidenced by this 1784 form certifying his enlistment and service. *Telamon Cuyler, Hargrett Rare Book and Manuscript Library, The University of Georgia Libraries, Digital Library of Georgia*

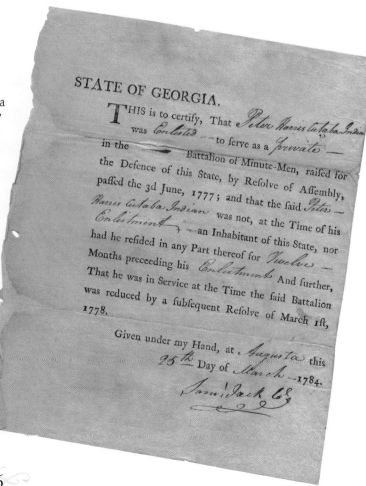

feel that the DAR can play an enormous role in educating the public about the role African Americans and Native Americans played in the Revolutionary War."

Mallette's experience mirrors a growing trend confirmed by a study done in 2000 by Maritz Marketing Research. According to the poll, approximately 60 percent of the U.S. population are interested in family history, up from 45 percent just five years ago. That's close to 180 million people searching for their roots. Some become interested in tracing their family tree after hearing stories from relatives about their family history. Others get hooked talking to a friend, colleague, or family member researching their own genealogy. Still others start their journey after meeting or hearing about long-lost relatives they never met or never knew existed.

That search for "roots" brought one of the most famous ancestry sleuths to the DAR in the 1970s. Alex Haley, whose book *Roots* spurred tremendous interest in genealogy and family history, completed some of his research in the DAR Library. By the late 1990s, the Library was averaging 25,000 researchers a year, both members and the general public. With the increased popularity of the Internet and access to many online databases, the interest continues to increase, as more Americans take advantage of various online tools, many of which are now featured as part of the DAR Library services. To accommodate that interest, for both members and the public, the Library staff continues to incorporate state-of-the-art technology to make the collection even more accessible by both real and "virtual" visitors. Digitization, microfilm and microform, and enhanced database indexing will allow researchers even in remote places to take advantage of all the DAR Library has to offer.

Of course, African American and Native American patriots aren't the only ones often overlooked. Thousands of troops from France made their contribution to the American effort. Sweden, Poland, Germany, Portugal, and the Netherlands also aided the American cause. The French Navy, under the command of Comte de Grasse and Comte D'Estaing, pursued the British fleet along the Atlantic coast. In 1780, fifty-five hundred men arrived with the military leader Comte de Rochambeau providing much-needed supplies. The Marquis de Lafayette, the influential French nobleman who financed his own way, took part in several decisive campaigns, including Williamsburg and Yorktown. Historians credit Louis DuPortail, a Frenchman, and Tadeusz Kościuszko, a Pole, with advancing the art of engineering in the Continental Army. Kazimierz Pulaski, another Pole, was the first to organize a genuine cavalry contingent. Germans Johann de Kalb and especially Friedrich Wilhelm von Steuben made enormous contributions to transforming Washington's troops at Valley Forge into a model army.

▲ Most of the American Indian nations sided with the British because they had formed trade relationships with them and because they feared losing their land to the colonists. Four of the six nations of the Iroquois Confederacy fought on the side of the British, but the Oneidas and the Tuscaroras, and at least half of the Onandagas, fought beside American patriots like General Nicholas Herkimer. General Herkimer was commander of the American forces at the Battle of Oriskany, fought on August 6, 1777, in what is today Rome, New York. General Herkimer continued to give orders from his saddle after his horse was shot from beneath him. The redoubtable Herkimer is captured in bronze sitting astride his saddle in a monument placed in his honor, circa 1905, by the former General Herkimer Chapter, in what was the site of an early village burying ground and is now a quiet park in the small town of Herkimer, New York.

▲ Thomas E. Chavez, PhD, former director of the Palace of the Governors Museum of New Mexico, addresses guests at New Mexico's 85th DAR State Conference at the National Hispanic Cultural Center, in Albuquerque, New Mexico, on April 23, 2005. Also pictured are (left to right) Gene Henley, Deputy Director of the National Hispanic Cultural Center, Roseanne Chadborn, DAR page, President General Presley Merritt Wagoner, and State Regent Lois-Faye Lampson. Dr. Chavez, author of the book *Spain and the Independence of the United States, an Intrinsic Gift,* flew from Argentina that morning to participate in the unveiling of a plaque at the Cultural Center commemorating the importance of Spain's support during the Revolution. The National Hispanic Cultural Center stands on the famous El Camino Real trade and military route to old Mexico. The event was the culmination of more than a decade of research by the DAR Spanish Task Force into Spain's role in American independence. As a result of the research, Eva Torres Aschenbrenner became the first woman to become a Daughter descended from a New Mexico patriot, an accomplishment the New Mexico Daughters hope will inspire other descendants of Spanish patriots to research their lineage.

Perhaps because their initial aid to the American Revolution was given initially in secret, the enormous financial and military support of the Spanish is often overlooked. "From 1776 until declaring war against Great Britain in 1779, Spain covertly—through the merchants Diego de Gardoqui in Bilbao and American Oliver Pollock in New Orleans—sent generous amounts of money, muskets, munitions, medicine, and military supplies to aid America in its unequal war against England, a longtime foe of Spain," wrote historian Robert H. Thornhoff in the March/April 2002 issue of *American Spirit.* Once Spain declared war against Britain in 1779, King Carlos III of Spain ordered General Bernardo de Gálvez, governor of the Spanish-owned Louisiana, to raise an army and navy for a military campaign against the British on the Gulf

Forgotten Patriots

The DAR exhibit Forgotten Patriots: African American and American Indian Service in the Revolutionary War, 1775–1783, which opened October 17, 2002, represented what many consider to be a long-overdue effort to recognize the contributions that African American and American Indian patriots made during the Revolution. The culmination of more than twenty years of DAR research, the popular display had to be extended several months to accommodate the crowds of people who kept streaming in to view the largest such exhibit ever mounted on the subject. President General Linda Tinker Watkins, in her remarks at the opening reception, stated, "This exhibition and subsequent programs acknowledge how far America has come in its unity as one nation of many cultures. During the first fifty years of our organization's existence, our nation suffered under the practice of segregation. America, as well as the DAR, has progressed since those terribly biased times."

Mounted by the DAR Museum, the basis for the exhibit was the DAR publication *African American and American Indian Patriots of the Revolutionary War,* a collaboration between the Library and the DAR Genealogy Department published in 2001. The book covers the eastern states from Georgia to Maine. The book's chapters, written by DAR staff members Elisabeth Schmidt, Hazel Kreinheder, and Rita Souther, and edited by Eric Grundset and Jean Strahan, were originally published as individual booklets beginning in 1988.

Research to document African American and Native American patriots continues. Approximately 4,500 African American and American Indian patriots have been documented for the second edition of the book. "We're adding more names all the time," says Eric Grundset, director of the DAR Library. Unfortunately, there is a scarcity of records for many minority participants, but DAR researchers use every tool available, starting with published lists of soldiers, historical accounts, monographs, journal articles, family genealogies, and other sources in an attempt to document all patriots—men, women, soldiers, citizens, white or minority.

Despite the challenges of the research, the Society remains diligent in expanding the database of names. In the opening pages of the *African American and American Indian Patriots* publication Grundset writes, "Expanding the historical record with such a publication enriches the history

PHOTO BY SCOTT BRAMAN

▲ Members of the Oneida Indian Nation, other honored guests, and re-enactors join President General Linda Tinker Watkins (center) at the table displaying some of the gifts exchanged between the NSDAR and the People of the Oneidas at the Forgotten Patriots exhibit in 2002. To the left of Mrs. Watkins is Oneida Nation representative Ray Halbritter; to the right of the President General is Mark Gresham, president of the Black Revolutionary War Patriots Foundation. Also pictured are Oneida Bear Clan Mother Marilyn John (second from left) and Brian Patterson (third from left), Bear Clan Representative to the Men's Council of the Oneidas. At the opening of the exhibit, Brian Patterson stated, "It's a special feeling for the Oneida People today to be recognized by the DAR for the efforts of our ancestors." The *Washington Times* reported, "For those whose ancestors fought side by side with the Colonists to defeat the British, inclusion in the exhibition touches their hearts and demonstrated the DAR's efforts to recognize the contributions of other nationalities and minorities during the Revolution." Ray Halbritter received a DAR scholarship for his undergraduate studies before earning his law degree from Harvard University.

PHOTO BY SCOTT BRAMAN

▲ A journalist from blackpress.com interviews Hugh B. Price, former president of the National Urban League and now a senior fellow at the Brookings Institution, at the DAR exhibit opening in October 2002 for Forgotten Patriots: African American and American Indian Service in the Revolutionary War. Price, an honored guest at the event, is pictured in front of the portion of the exhibit featuring his ancestor, Nero Hawley. In a 2006 interview, Price emphasized the importance of the DAR in continuing its research into the service of minorities during the Revolution. "Establishing historical records, celebrating contributions, making sure children understand different roles from the very point when this nation was established, is very important."

of the American struggle for independence and illustrates the individual efforts of thousands who helped achieve the goal. By offering a documented listing of names of African Americans and American Indians who supported the cause of the American Revolution, we hope to inspire the interest of descendants in the efforts of their ancestors and in the work of the National Society to understand and preserve this nation's past and honor those who fought for freedom."

▲ DAR member Adeline Robinson Crawford donated this ambrotype of her ancestor, William Hewes (also spelled "Hughes"), to the DAR Museum in 1948. (An ambrotype was an early type of photograph made by imaging a negative on glass backed by a dark surface.) Born in Massachusetts in 1761, William Hewes enlisted as a volunteer private in the Second New Hampshire regiment in 1780. He marched with his regiment to West Point and later Fishkill, New York, where he guarded supplies and prisoners. After the war, he settled into the peace-loving life of a vocal music teacher and farmer in Vermont. In his later years, he moved to live with his son in Illinois, where he died and was buried in 1855.

Coast. Author Thomas Fleming referred to Gálvez as "The Forgotten Revolutionary Conquistador Who Saved Louisiana" in his article of that title published in *American Heritage* magazine in April/May 1982. In the late 1990s, under the Georgane Ferguson Love administration and at the urging of Honorary President General Dorla Dean Kemper, the NSDAR formed the Spanish Task Force to identify Spanish nationals who contributed to the Revolutionary cause. Since that time, members of the task force continue to develop a bibliography of historical events and sources that can prove Revolutionary War service of Spanish nationals.

Revolutionary fervor crossed religious a well as ethnic boundaries. As early as 1654, "Economic opportunity and religious freedom, two powerful pull factors, drew Jews to the New World," wrote Gadi Nevo Ben-Yehuda in his article "Merchants, Soldiers, Spies and Statesmen: Jews in Colonial and Revolutionary America" in the July/August 2003 issue of *American Spirit*. Ambassador John L. Loeb Jr., in the book about his grandmother, DAR member Adeline Moses Loeb, notes that many Jewish colonists fought in the militia, and Jewish merchants provided supplies to the troops. As former President Gerald R. Ford emphasized in his remarks December 10, 1980, at the opening of The Jewish Community in Early America highlighted on page 247 in "DAR Headquarters: A Stage for World Events," "Some of the early Jewish settlers had developed extensive interests in the principal seaport towns of Newport, Philadelphia, New York, Charleston, and Savannah. They were chiefly engaged in inter-colonial and English trade. Their business interest, therefore, lay on the side of England. To support the Revolution meant economic ruin." Despite this certain fate, Jews were among the first volunteers. After the Revolutionary War, George Washington sent letters to the Jewish congregations of New York and Philadelphia, thanking them for their role in the patriots' cause.

And let us not forget the women of the Revolution. In an interview with Cokie Roberts, author of *Founding Mothers: The Women Who Raised Our Nation*, Stacy Evers wrote in the

◄ Despite his apparent stern demeanor, patriot Peter Rogers, a fifer in the Revolution, married three times before his death in 1849 at age ninety-six. Several of his many descendants became Daughters. He enlisted as a fife major in the Fourth Regiment, Connecticut Line, on November 26, 1776, after the Battle of Lexington, and served in Washington's Army in Pennsylvania. He was part of the hostilities in at least three battles, including the defense of Fort Mifflin and the Battle of Monmouth.

A Wealth of Resources

Established in 1896, today the DAR Library is one of the country's premier genealogical research centers, offering a total of more than half a million volumes, files, and records, many of which are unique to the Society's Library. The collection includes nearly 25,000 family histories and genealogies that comprise a major portion of the book collection. The file collection features more than 300,000 records of documentation for some DAR membership applications. Over 20,000 typescript volumes from all states contain previously unpublished genealogical materials such as Bible records, local histories, cemetery transcriptions, court record abstracts, censuses, military records, vital records, and other similar sources. These records, called *Genealogical Records Committee Reports*, or GRC Reports, represent one of the most important and unique segments of the collection.

In 2001, the DAR incorporated the indexing of the GRC Reports to create databases, indexes, and finding aids for many DAR materials. The result of this enormous effort, a collaboration between Library staff and the Genealogical Records Committee, is the creation of the first every-name index of the DAR Library's GRC reports. In this grassroots effort, dozens of volunteer members across the country, using the same software and indexing guidelines, are creating automated databases for every state GRC volume. While it is still a work in progress, the volunteers have completed indexing more than six million records that reference almost twenty-two million names. Type a surname into the search index, and every single reference to that surname in the automated GRC indexes will pop up on the computer screen, giving the specific state index and the page number that the researcher can then order through the DAR Library Search Service.

The past twenty years have seen an explosion of publishing in African American studies including works on African American genealogical research. The DAR Library has developed a strong and growing collection of varied but detailed printed sources on this subject. In addition, the Library offers a basic collection of materials for Jewish research. The Library, Museum, and Genealogy staffs have also amassed a significant repository of information on Native Americans during preparation for the Forgotten Patriots exhibit in 2002–2003, as well as the DAR book, *African American and American Indian Patriots of the Revolutionary War*, and earlier pamphlets. A number of special collections make the DAR Library particularly

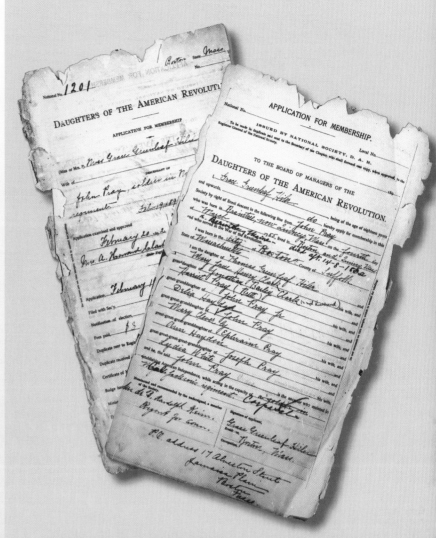

▲ The more than 300,000 files of documentation from DAR membership applications, such as the one pictured here from 1892, also provide an incredible resource for connecting the dots on many family trees, not just those of members.

unique. Now numbering some two thousand volumes, the American Indian Collection provides historical and genealogical information on first peoples across the United States. The DAR Web site features downloadable information for each of these collections, as well as general guides for their use.

Because the DAR is a prominent women's organization, it is not surprising that the Library's American Women's History Collection offers materials that focus on the role played by women in the development of the United States, including the Colonial period and American Revolution as well as the women's rights movement of the nineteenth and early twentieth centuries. There is also a wealth of information relating to women in American history throughout the DAR collections.

To accommodate the rapidly growing interest in genealogy by both members and the public, the Library staff continues to incorporate state-of-the-art technology to make the collection even more accessible by both real and "virtual" visitors.

Continued on next page

▲ Both DAR members and guests on a quest for ancestral information get hands-on experience using the database of records available at the DAR Library. Library staff kept the facility open after hours during genealogy conference days to maximize research opportunities, especially for those from out of town.

Digitization, microfilm and microform, and enhanced database indexing allow researchers to take advantage of all the DAR Library has to offer.

The online catalog provides search options by title, author, and subject, either at terminals in the facility available for public use or online for users far away. For a fee, library staff can help in the search, pull references, and make copies of documents or book pages that quite often provide important pieces of a family puzzle. Workshops at DAR headquarters as well as the assistance provided by chapters teach researchers the ins and outs of tracing family history.

Certainly, the capability of virtual research adds a new dimension to the genealogy quest, but nothing replaces a visit to the DAR Library itself where, on every shelf, tan-

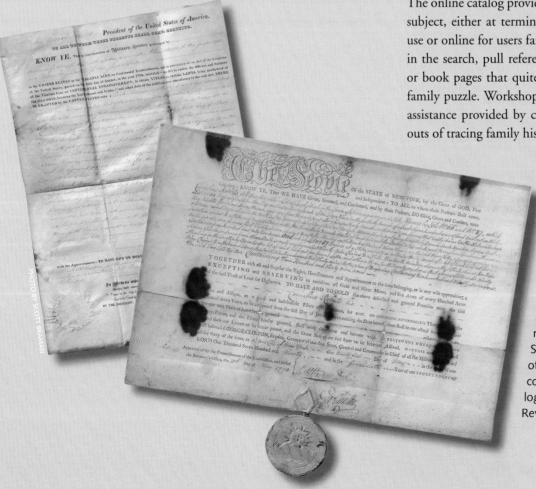

◄ These deeds, dated 1790, bestowed hundreds of acres of land to patriots and their heirs as reward for their sacrifices in the battle for independence. Such documents, as well as grants and other land contracts, provide historical context and offer a rich source of genealogical information, in addition to proving Revolutionary War service.

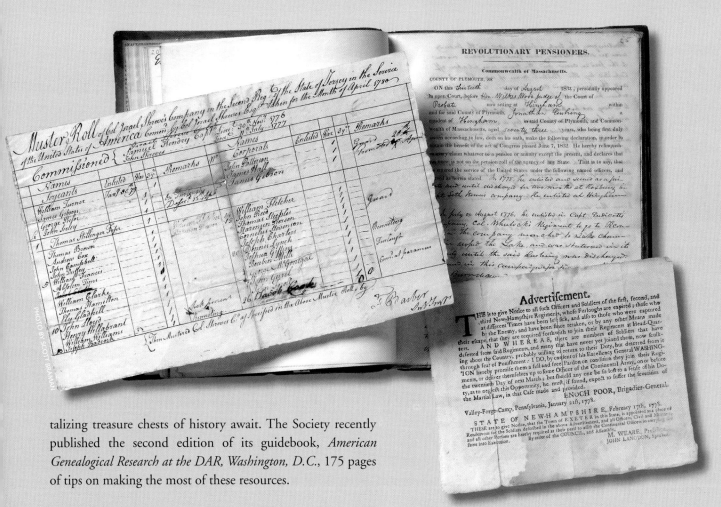

talizing treasure chests of history await. The Society recently published the second edition of its guidebook, *American Genealogical Research at the DAR, Washington, D.C.*, 175 pages of tips on making the most of these resources.

While available only on-site, new electronic resources place hard-to-find data right at the user's fingertips with three powerful and continuously expanding genealogical and historical document databases. Heritage Quest and Ancestry Library Edition are major electronic sources for census data, family records, and local histories. Readex's Early American Newspapers provides access to thousands of full-text articles and images from over two dozen historical U.S. newspapers circa 1690–1876, including New England and New York newspapers such as the *Boston Gazette* and *Federal Gazette*.

Though the Library collections alone are worth the trip, when combined with the resources of the Americana and Museum collections, they become a three-dimensional gold mine of lineal treasure. Both the Library and Americana collections feature substantial collections of family Bibles dating back to the seventeenth century. The Library offers hundreds of pension lists, while priceless muster rolls are part of the Americana Collection, as well as deeds and marriage licenses that often provide missing links in family chains. Even the schoolgirl art in the Museum collection includes samplers that not only taught young ladies the art of needlework but also captured marriages, births, and deaths of family members. A visit to DAR Headquarters often rewards the visitor with not only a glimpse of personal history but also a sense of context and pride in the part their ancestors and others played in the founding of America and its battle for independence.

▲ Some of the imprints in both the Library and Americana collections, like the documents pictured here, provide more than simply a generic recounting of the past. Underscoring the desperate need for troops to match the well-equipped and trained British units, the advertisement or "broadside" at right dated January 21, 1778, and signed by Brigadier General Enoch Poor at Valley Forge, ordered all officers and soldiers of the First, Second, and Third New Hampshire Regiments to rendezvous in the town of Exeter. The broadsides often allow genealogists to pinpoint the movements of patriots assigned to these units, sometimes providing valuable clues to possible descendants. After the war, the muster roll at left documented names and enlistment periods of those men under Colonel Israel Shreve's Company, Second Regiment of the State of New Jersey, to include one player of the fife and drum. The circa-1832 bound journal shown here contains notes, memoranda, official Revolutionary pension documents, and signed personal statements collected by a diligent Solomon Lincoln to justify and "obtain pensions for sundry persons," whom he felt had earned compensation for their service in the Revolutionary War. While certainly important at the time they were issued, documents such as these are perhaps even more valuable today as tangible evidence of patriot service as well as tantalizing puzzle pieces of history for those seeking to fit together the stories of their ancestors.

▲ The life of poet, historical writer, and Colonial playwright Mercy Otis Warren helped to convince newswoman and author Cokie Roberts to write her book, *Founding Mothers*, published in 2004. In an informal survey, Roberts asked several of her friends and associates if they had ever heard of Warren. "I'm talking about PhDs, you know, and hardly anybody outside of women's history expertise had [heard of her]," she revealed. Yet the prolific patriot, dubbed the "conscience of the American Revolution," wrote numerous plays leading up to the Revolution, all thinly disguised attacks on specific public officials. Wife of Massachusetts Representative James Warren, sister to Colonial rights advocate James Otis, and mother of diplomat Winslow Warren, she also hosted political meetings in her home and unhesitatingly urged the taking of risks to achieve American independence. The original of this painting of Warren when she was thirty-five years old, by John Singleton Copley, is part of the collection of the Museum of Fine Arts in Boston, Massachusetts, the patriot's home state for all of her eighty-six years. A *Mayflower* descendant, she died in Plymouth in 1814, just a few years after she wrote *History of the American Revolution*, the first history on the Revolution written by a woman.

May/June 2004 issue of *American Spirit* magazine, "The Founding Mothers were incessantly pregnant; constantly entertaining; taking care of parents and children and in-laws; managing farms, households and businesses; and defending themselves from the British while the important men in their lives were rarely at home. The women also played a vital intelligence role, keeping the men informed of political events and gossip."

Captain Molly

Thanks to the determination of Daughters of the New York State Organization in the early 1920s, the remains of one of the most celebrated women of the American Revolution now rest in a place of honor. Her contributions as a patriot are recalled annually during somber ceremonies at the U.S. Military Academy at West Point and at the DAR Continental Congress. Amelia Campbell Parker, State Historian of New York, and State Regent Mary Francis Tupper Nash rescued the remains. Parker also recorded the story of Captain Molly in the June 1926 issue of the DAR magazine.

Margaret Corbin was one of many women during the Revolution who camped with their husbands. The young wife of John Corbin had endeared herself to the 2,800 troops crowded into Fort Washington, New York, by cooking and mending for them and hauling water 230 feet from the Hudson River far below, wrote Parker. She watched her husband clean and load his cannon, and he likely taught her how to fire it. When he was killed during battle, she sprang forward and asked permission to fire it as he had taught her. She continued to load and fire until enemy grape shot severely wounded her in the shoulder and breast. Recognized for her bravery, she became the only woman on the Corps of Invalids list and was eventually transferred with them to West Point.

Over time, she became known only as "Captain Molly," that name being used even on the official records by the West Point commissary officer who oversaw her care.

◄ On May 2, 2006, the U.S. Military Academy Police Company Honor Guard and others salute Captain Molly after placing a wreath at her grave on the eightieth anniversary of her re-interment in the historic West Point cemetery. Denise Doring VanBuren (pictured at left in front of the wreath), National Chairman of the DAR Magazine Committee, also serves as Chairman of the DAR Margaret Cochran Corbin Day for the New York State Officers Club.

She died in January 1800 and was buried on land some three miles from West Point that, around 1876, had become part of the J. Pierpont Morgan Sr. estate called Cragston. At the time of her burial, a cedar tree was planted at the head of her grave marked with a simple marker bearing only the words, "Captain Molly."

She faded further from memory and was almost lost to history when the grandson of one of the men who helped bury her brought the story his grandfather told him to the attention of state historians. They enlisted the aid of the New York State Daughters, who ultimately linked the records of the service of Margaret Corbin to the records kept at West Point on "Captain Molly," thus convincing West Point officials that she should be buried in a place of honor there.

On March 16, 1926, the West Point Hospital surgeon oversaw the opening of the grave beside the stump of an old cedar tree. Upon examining the remains, the surgeon verified that not only were they those of a woman but that the left shoulder

◄ In this photo taken March 16, 1926, New York State Organization Historian Amelia Campbell Parker (second from right), who led the search to determine Captain Molly's true identity, and New York State Regent Mary Francis Tupper Nash, accompanied by West Point officers Captain George S. Andrew (left) and Lieutenant W. R. Fleming, pall bearers, watch over Margaret Corbin's remains, which had just been reverently placed in the silk-lined casket and wrapped in the U.S. flag. The remains of the cedar stump that helped to verify the site as her original burial place can be seen at the head of the grave.

bones bore evidence of injury. An elaborately appointed hearse bore her casket to a grave in the cemetery beside the West Point cadet chapel.

One month later, the New York State Organization of the DAR unveiled the granite monument that describes her heroic service and marks her final resting place. Each year in May, the New York State Officers Club celebrates Margaret Cochran Corbin Day, where once again Daughters and other officials gather at her gravesite to honor the first woman soldier to receive a pension: a 1779 Act of the Continental Congress granted her half-pay for life and "one compleat suite of cloaths."

In April 2000, at the 109th Continental Congress, President General Georgane Ferguson Love presented the first NSDAR Margaret Cochran Corbin Awards, established during the Kemper Administration to recognize those women who have provided extraordinary military service. The first four recipients were Major General Jeanne M. Holm, U.S. Air Force (Retired), the first woman in the history of the U.S. Armed Forces to achieve that rank; Brigadier General Wilma L. Vaught, U.S. Air Force (Retired), one of the most decorated military women in U.S. history and the driving force behind construction of the Women in Military Service for America Memorial; Colonel Jeanne M. Picariello, a career Army officer with more than twenty-five years of service at the time, who oversaw all Army-wide family support and soldier programs; and Chief Master Sergeant Daisy Jackson, with the U.S. Air Force Band, the most requested vocal soloist in the entire Air Force Band career field.

▲ An artillery wife, Mary Ludwig Hays McCauly (or Mary Ludwig Hays), shared the rigors of Valley Forge with her husband, William Hays. Her actions during the Battle of Monmouth on June 28, 1778, became legendary. She earned her nickname "Molly Pitcher" hauling pitcher after pitcher of cool spring water to the troops as they fought that hot summer day. When her husband fell wounded, Mary McCauly "manned" his cannon, as did the legendary Molly Corbin. Such tales of feminine heroism combined to create the legendary character known as Molly Pitcher, who was the subject of numerous works of art, such as the one pictured here by Percy Moran painted circa 1911.

Catharine Littlefield Greene (young wife of Major General Nathanael Greene) joined her husband during winter encampments, supervising servants, planning meals, and entertaining visiting dignitaries. Deborah Sampson, determined to fight for her country, disguised herself as a man named Robert Shurtleff, fought in numerous battles, and was even wounded more than once before a doctor treating her for a raging fever finally stumbled on her disguise. He kept her secret and arranged for her quiet but honorable discharge. Paul Revere would successfully argue for her back pay with interest.

All of the patriots described here represent different races, different backgrounds, different genders, yet they were in most cases average men and women who found themselves in extraordinary circumstances. It was the choices they made that set them apart and made them heroes and patriots in a common cause.

Elba Rivera, a member of the staff in the NSDAR Chapter Services Office, made such a choice when she came to this country alone from El Salvador thirty years ago when she was only twenty-three years old and seeking opportunities in this country not available in her native land. Like those who came here on the *Mayflower* and those who founded Jamestown in 1607, Rivera came here for a better life. Through a series of coincidences, she came to work for the NSDAR not long after arriving in America. In the past few years, the geneal-

▶ Mary Katharine Goddard "spent most of her life . . . setting type for the first newspapers in the country and editing articles that set the stage for America's rebellion against England and its emergence as a democratic nation," wrote contributing editor Emily McMackin in an article published in the DAR *American Spirit* in March/April 2006. As a printer, journalist, and postmistress, she kept vital information flowing during the precarious years of the Revolution. While the original Declaration was still in Baltimore being ratified, Congress, bolstered by military successes at Trenton and Princeton, ordered the second official printing of the document. The earlier July 4 printing had included only the names of John Hancock and Charles Thomson, and even though the first printing had been promptly circulated to the states, the names of subsequent signers were kept secret for a time, partly because of fear of British reprisals and to obtain each state's endorsement of the document. Congress required that "an authenticated copy of the DECLARATION of INDEPENDENCY, with the Names of the MEMBERS of CONGRESS, subscribing the same, be sent to each of the UNITED STATES, and that they be desired to have the same put upon RECORD." On January 18, 1777, Mary Katherine Goddard duly printed the "authenticated copy," shown here, complete with all signers' names except that of Thomas McKean of Delaware, pending that state's ratification.

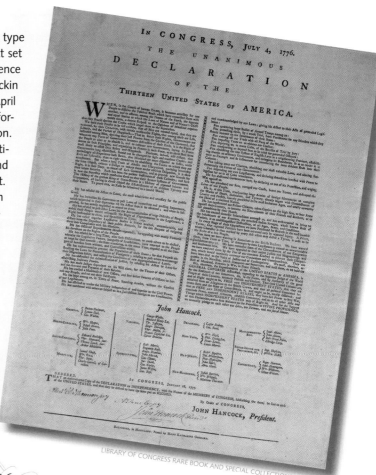

ogy bug has bitten her, too, because of the "connection to so many positive ladies I have met here, working to keep alive their dreams, their heritage." Her quest is for her children as well. "It is important to know the past, to know you have the opportunity to fulfill certain dreams that your ancestors did not have," she emphasizes. Rivera's own quest was not about membership, but rather understanding. However, she recently discovered that one branch of her family tree may include the Spanish patriot General Don Bernardo de Gálvez. If so, Rivera may one day become a member of the organization that sparked her interest in family history.

Sometimes it is the smallest, most fragile scrap of paper that links the lines of lineage to Revolutionary patriots, as Daughter Anita Baxter-Wills learned in researching her ancestry. Her quest led to papers on file at NSDAR, including the faded certification that her ancestor, Charles Lewis, and his brother Ambrose, both African Americans, served in the "Company of Militia from Spotsylvania County," Virginia, with General Horatio Gates at the Battle of Camden in South Carolina.

Meanwhile, member Donna Santistevan Elin's ancestry can be traced back to not one but two of New Mexico's early Spanish mayors, or *alcaldes*. Antonio José Ortiz, mayor of Santa Fe, and José Redondo Campos, mayor of Santa Cruz, are recognized as patriots for the material aid they rendered to the American cause through donations collected from their citizens that allowed Spain to provide muskets, munitions, medicine, and other military supplies.

John Killbuck Jr., chief of the Delaware Indians from 1779 to 1881, also served as captain of scouts and messengers for the Pennsylvania 8th Regiment stationed at Fort Pitt. He led American troops through Indian territory to raid the British, and his reports to Colonel Daniel Brodhead documented the movements of the British and hostile Indian tribes. He was also one of three Delawares to sign the first treaty with the United States in 1778. Encouraged by other DAR members aware of her ancestry, Gloria Jean Marker Fortney, a descendant of the Delaware chief, in 2003 became the first to join the DAR through the Delaware Indian line. She is a member of the Tulsa Chapter in Oklahoma.

Sharod Goings, a freeborn person of color, enlisted in the Revolutionary Army in Albemarle County, Virginia, approximately 1777. A private in the 14th Virginia Regiment and the 2nd Virginia Brigade, he was present at the Battle of Germantown, the Battle of Monmouth, and the Siege of Yorktown. Yvonne Jackson Edwards, a member of the Emily Geiger Chapter in South Carolina, and her daughter, Robin Lynne Edwards, a member of the Descendants of '76 Chapter

▲ This fragile document in the DAR collection certifies the service of Charles and Ambrose Lewis, African American brothers who served in the Revolution.

in Washington, D.C., are descendants of Sharod Goings. Upon learning of her Revolutionary War ancestry, Robin Edwards professed, "I felt a great sense of pride in knowing that there is a representation of African Americans who understood the importance of not only their own rights as freed people but also those rights of a free nation."

Not every genealogy quest leads to a patriot. But more patriots emerge as more and more Americans turn to their roots to examine who they are and where they came from. And not every hero is a "patriot" in the official sense, yet the personal journey into the past often uncovers heroes of a different sort. As President Franklin Delano Roosevelt pointed out when he addressed the 47th Continental Congress in 1938, "Remember that all of us, you and I especially, are descended from immigrants and revolutionists."

As with any treasure hunt, you never know what you will find. It could be a patriot of the Revolution or a hero or heroine of a different sort. Or it could be a villain you may not want to claim but who, in contrast, highlights your own accomplishments in overcoming adversity. In the words of American author John Barth, "Everyone is necessarily the hero of his own life story." One person can make a difference. There are, after all, so many avenues to patriotism and acts of bravery. Regardless of the nature of those acts, each life remains an important thread in the fabric of the American tapestry, and the DAR is eager to help make those discoveries. In a May 2001 article for Genealogy.com, genealogist Rhonda R. McClure wrote of the DAR, "They really have been a moving force in genealogy, and we, present day researchers, owe them a debt of gratitude."

CHAPTER ELEVEN

Dazzling Daughters
Leading Ladies

F ROM ITS OUTSET AND BEGINNING WITH ITS FOUNDERS, the Society's ranks have included uncommon women who achieved uncommon goals. They include First Ladies and firsts in their field, actresses and adventurers, artists and authors, reformers and humanitarians, educators and engineers, doctors and nurses, and even pioneers in space. While their accomplishments are as diverse as their professions, all of them have been brave women who often performed heroic acts and shared a sense of purpose and pride, and an undaunted pursuit of their ideals.

Their success has often been the byproduct of their passionate commitment to succeed despite adversity. Civic activist and businesswoman Frances Osborne Kellogg once lamented, "All my life has been a series of hurdles. I no sooner get over one than there is another ahead . . . with the bars set a little higher." Born in 1876, Kellogg never completed her public school education after losing her vision in one eye from an accident. Yet when her father died suddenly in 1907, she took over his business responsibilities. Her determination and innate business sense led to such accomplishments as becoming president of the Union Fabric Company, vice president of Connecticut Clasp, and treasurer of the F. Kelly Company. She was founding partner of Steels and Busks of Leicester, England, manufacturers of the rigid supports used in corsets.

The persistent myth of the Daughters as idle women sipping tea and reminiscing certainly belies the founders, according to Tracy Robinson, DAR Director of Archives and History, whose recent research reveals a composite of Daughters much removed from the myth. "Three of the founders were born not long before the Seneca Falls convention [on women's

▶ Thousands of Daughters have gone far, but Astronaut Margaret Rhea Seddon, MD, has likely gone the farthest. She carried a DAR insignia during her flight into space aboard the space shuttle *Discovery*, April 12–19, 1985. The insignia is now part of the NSDAR Archives. Dr. Seddon was not the first Daughter into space. In 1934, Jeanette Ridlon Piccard became the first woman in the world to pilot a balloon into the stratosphere. With her husband and scientific partner, Jean Piccard, as passenger, she ascended almost eleven miles beyond the earth's atmosphere, making her the first woman in space, an altitude record for women unchallenged for almost thirty years.

BOBKO ★ WILLIAMS
DISCOVERY
SEDDON ★ GRIGGS ★ HOFFMAN
WALKER ★ GARN

Presented to

The Daughters of the American Revolution

From the National Aeronautics and Space Administration

Rhea Seddon

M. Rhea Seddon
Mission Specialist, STS 51-D

CLARA BARTON
From portrait taken in Civil War and authorized
by her as the one she wished to be remembered by

▲ At the first DAR organizing meeting on October 11,1890, it was Clara Barton (1821–1912) who was appointed Surgeon General, based on her already renowned nursing and relief efforts to soldiers during the Civil War and her founding of the American Red Cross in 1881. However, she pursued a number of different careers before that, including teaching and as a copyist in the U.S. Patent Office. She left the Patent Office to tend to the soldiers when the Civil War erupted and she learned that so many suffered from lack of medical supplies. Known for her compassion and bravery, time and again she crossed enemy lines to assist the wounded. She volunteered again during the Franco-Prussian War. A caption accompanying a Library of Congress Civil War photo by Mathew Brady asserts, "Before the Civil War was over Clara Barton's name had come to mean mercy and help for the wounded in war or peace alike." However, Barton apparently never lost her wish to be viewed as a lady, as this Library of Congress photo attests. It bears this imprint: "From portrait taken in Civil War and authorized by her as the one she wished to be remembered by."

rights], and one founder was born not long after it," she points out. Anything but traditional, they were products of their times, Robinson contends.

Founder Eugenia Washington did not set out to save the world. The death of her mother when she was a teenager left her to care for her disabled father. Her first heroic act was to save her father and herself during the Battle of Fredericksburg, Virginia, in December 1862, when she was only twenty-two. With the battle imminent, she packed up what she could and prepared to leave the city. However, she was delayed by one day when a wounded Federal officer was brought to her door and left in her care while he waited for a surgeon. Forced to flee in the midst of battle, she and her father were caught on the battle-field. With their only shelter a small trench left by a cannon, father and daughter lay trapped there for an entire day where they witnessed the horrible battle. At the close of the Civil War, she was offered a Post Office Department position, and she and her father moved to Washington, D.C. Forever changed by her wartime experience, Eugenia Washington, in helping to found the NSDAR, also found a way to assist and unite women from both the North and South in the common cause of preserving their shared heritage.

The Civil War also altered the course of the life of Mary Desha. Impoverished by the war, Mary and her mother opened a private school where they taught their friends' children. Miss Desha became a skilled teacher, later accepting a position with the Lexington, Kentucky, public schools. The offer of a job as a clerk led her to Washington, but perhaps adventure and the chance to teach again took her clear across the continent, to Sitka, Alaska, in 1888. Her forty pupils included only fourteen Americans; the rest were Russian. She found the living conditions endured by the Alaskan natives deplorable, and her letter of protest to the government in Washington resulted in a federal investigation. She would later work as a copyist in the Office of Indian Affairs upon her return to Washington. In 1898, she was appointed Assistant Director of the DAR Hospital Corps and helped certify the applications of more than 4,500 women who wanted to serve as nurses during the Spanish-American War.

Daughter of one congressman, stepdaughter to another, Ellen Hardin Walworth earned her law degree at New York University and was entitled to practice before the courts of New York and the District of Columbia. She married her stepfather's youngest son, Mansfield Tracy Walworth, but the marriage turned to tragedy. Ellen Walworth may be most admired for defending her son, who killed her abusive husband in one of the first cases involving the successful use of the self-defense claim in domestic abuse cases. After the death of her husband, Mrs. Walworth

◀ Anna Mary Robertson Moses may be the world's most famous "Grandma," but not for doting on her grandchildren (although she undoubtedly did). When arthritis would no longer allow her to embroider, she took up painting in her seventies and would paint for nearly thirty years. A collector noticed her paintings in a Hoosick Falls, New York, drugstore window in 1938, and in 1939, art dealer Otto Kallir exhibited some of her work in his New York City gallery. Her work would be exhibited all over the country, throughout Europe, and even Japan. In 1949, President Harry S. Truman presented her with the Women's National Press Club Award for outstanding accomplishment in art, and in 1951, she appeared on Edward R. Murrow's early television series, *See It Now*. On her one hundredth birthday, September 7, 1960, New York Governor Nelson Rockefeller proclaimed the day "Grandma Moses Day" in her honor, the same month she appeared on the cover of *Life* magazine, pictured here. She died a year later, on December 13, 1961, and her epitaph reads: "Her primitive paintings captured the spirit and preserved the scene of a vanishing countryside." In the inset photo, Gertrude Carraway, President General, holds the painting entitled the *Battle of Bennington*, which Grandma Moses donated to the DAR in 1953. It remains a special part of the Americana Collection.

▶ Born in Miami, Florida, in 1938, DAR member Janet Reno initially majored in chemistry at Cornell University. Her father was a police reporter for the *Miami Herald* for forty-three years; her mother raised their four children and then became an investigative reporter for the *Miami News*. Janet Reno would be one of only sixteen women out of more than five hundred students when she enrolled at Harvard Law School in 1960. Starting with a position as staff director of the Judiciary Committee of the Florida House of Representatives, she held positions of increasing authority in the Miami-Dade County State Attorney's Office. Voters would elect her to the Office of State Attorney in November 1978 and return her four more times. She helped reform the juvenile justice system and established the Miami Drug Court. In 1993, she made history when she was confirmed as the first woman to fill the post of U.S. Attorney General.

First Lady, First President General

Having attended the Oxford Female Institute established by her father, Caroline Lavinia Scott learned at an early age that women were every bit man's equal. According to a White House biography, "With other ladies of progressive views, she helped raise funds for the Johns Hopkins University medical school on condition that it admit women."

In organizing their National Society, the Daughters sought a woman of prominence to lead it. Mary Desha wrote to Caroline Scott Harrison on August 10, 1890, requesting that she agree to become president. The First Lady recognized immediately the importance of the position she was being offered, for she knew if the Society were to be successful, it would need the endorsement of the most prominent women in the nation. However, she also knew that her own fragile health and her duties as First Lady would prevent her from playing as visible and active a role as the position demanded. During the follow-up visit October 19, 1890, by Mary Cabell and William McDowell, she put two conditions on her acceptance: that the vote for her as President General must be unanimous, and that Mary Cabell, as Vice President, perform the bulk of the duties Caroline Harrison could not fulfill. Those conditions met, she immediately submitted her application with her letter of acceptance, becoming a member through the Mary Washington Chapter in the District of Columbia.

Caroline Scott Harrison's opening remarks at the NSDAR 1st Continental Congress on February 22, 1892, became the first public speech by any First Lady. Vice President Mary Virginia Ellet Cabell took over for the Daughters' frail leader and presided through the remainder of the Congress. Meantime, Caroline Harrison's lingering illness "threw a shadow over all the summer and early autumn of 1892," wrote the authors of the first *Report of the Daughters* to the U.S. Congress. She died of tuberculosis in October 1892, almost two years to the day after the founding of the Society.

▲ Caroline Harrison had a deep interest in horticulture, in particular the cultivation of orchids. She was also an accomplished artist, and much of her work featured a variety of orchids. In fond regard of their first President General, the orchid has retained lasting significance to the Society: DAR dignitaries have often worn orchid corsages at DAR Continental Congress, and, in 2003, the DAR introduced a new pin, the NSDAR archives pin, featuring an orchid in its design.

▲ Another Daughter, Frances Benjamin Johnston, took this uncharacteristically informal pose of Daughter Susan Brownwell Anthony circa 1900. A member of the Irondequoit Chapter, Rochester, New York, Susan B. Anthony was a staunch supporter of women's suffrage. Along with Elizabeth Cady Stanton, she formed the National Woman Suffrage Association in 1869 and traveled around the country speaking on behalf of the suffrage cause. Joining the DAR in 1898, she lamented that she could not take a more active role, writing, "I have been and must continue to be busy working to secure for the women of this day the paramount rights for which the Revolutionary War was waged." Sadly, she did not live to see passage of the Nineteenth Amendment in 1920; she died in 1906.

opened her home as a boarding school that became so successful, she had to enlarge the facilities. But ill health and New York's harsh cold pushed her south to winter in Washington. One of her earliest public efforts was her moving plea to fund the renovation of Mount Vernon, George Washington's home in Alexandria, Virginia.

Mary Smith Lockwood was a prolific author whose pen, of course, inspired the birth of the NSDAR. Her books covered such diverse topics as historic homes of Washington, D.C., decorative needlework, and women's accessories. She was also a passionate Progressive and an avid promoter of women's rights and the work of women's clubs, founding the Travel Club and serving for a time as president of the Women's Press Club. A champion for others but not herself, she would later successfully argue that she should not be credited as one of the four founders because the infamous rainstorm prevented her from attending that first meeting in August 1890. The DAR honored her wishes and altered the original medal to honor her for "service" rather than as "founder." The distinction between the two would prove prophetic. As the last surviving "founder," she would also serve the longest and is the only one of the four buried in Washington.

Women's rights advocates Susan B. Anthony, Jane Addams, Madeline Breckinridge, and Sophonisba Breckinridge were among the first to join the Daughters of the American Revolution. Jane Addams founded Hull House, the social settlement in Chicago's West Side, one of the first social welfare agencies designed to develop and improve neighborhoods by providing a "house" where young and old, male and female,

▶ One of the most important American photographers of the early twentieth century, Frances Benjamin Johnston (1864–1952) trained at the Académie Julian in Paris. Upon her return to Washington, D.C., in the mid-1880s, she studied photography and opened a professional studio around 1890. Her family's social prominence provided her access to leading Washington political figures and especially several presidents and their families. "She is probably most known for the photos she did of the Theodore Roosevelt family while they lived in the White House and appears to have been their 'official' photographer," said DAR Museum Curator Diane Dunkley. Dunkley describes her as also "quite the Bohemian," often photographed dressed as a man. In this self-portrait, she is pictured here in 1896 in her studio holding a cigarette in one hand and a beer stein in the other. Johnston's mother, Frances A. Benjamin Johnston, was a DAR member and Corresponding Secretary General in 1897. Both mother and daughter joined the Mary Washington Chapter in 1892. The vast body of her work includes photos taken at the cornerstone laying and dedication of Memorial Continental Hall and various events at more than one Continental Congress.

◀ Actress, singer, and dancer Ginger Rogers had nineteen films to her credit before she teamed up with Fred Astaire and the two took the world by storm. Born in 1911 in Independence, Missouri, Virginia Katherine McMath earned her nickname from her younger cousin Helen, who pronounced her first name as "Ginja." The nickname stuck, translating to "Ginger" in the ears of the theatre men who billed her as such on their marquees. By age ten, she was already appearing at local charity shows, including her stepfather's lodge meetings. It was "Daddy John" Rogers whose last name she permanently "borrowed" as her own. As is typical of so many Dazzling Daughters, Ginger Rogers was a woman of many talents. Both a painter and sculptor, she was once offered a one-woman show in New York. She was also accomplished in such sports as golf, swimming, skeet shooting, and tennis, winning several tennis cups. The actress joined the DAR through the Hollywood Chapter, California, in the 1940s, where members at meetings knew her by her real name. The chapter honored her memory at the unveiling of a special marker at her grave on June 4, 2006. She had no immediate family, so on that day, the Hollywood Chapter was her family, emphasized Chapter Regent Nancy Daniels.

▶ Former presidential candidate and chairman of the National Republican Senatorial Committee, Senator and Daughter Elizabeth Dole frequently addresses Continental Congress, including opening night in 1987 during her tenure as Secretary of Transportation under the Reagan administration. Though her political career has often garnered the most attention, Elizabeth Hanford Dole has long devoted herself to humanitarian causes. From 1991 to 1999, she served as president of the American Red Cross, the DAR National Headquarters' next-door neighbor. She was a frequent visitor to the DAR complex during that time, and she and members of the Board of Governors took advantage of the "beautiful rooms at DAR Headquarters" for some of their meetings, as she shared during one of her many addresses to Continental Congress. Her DAR roots are much deeper, though. Her mother was a member, and young Elizabeth was a member of the C.A.R. before she joined the Elizabeth Maxwell Steele Chapter in North Carolina. "I can remember singing, 'we're children of the C.A.R., a great and mighty band.' I can still remember the song all these years later." She also served as a page at a North Carolina State Convention. During her second address to Congress in 2000, noting that her husband Robert J. Dole would appear some days later, she expressed hope that "maybe some year, Bob and Elizabeth Dole can come together."

rich and poor, American and immigrant could come together to share ideas and learn new skills to better themselves and their communities. Addams's good friend and fellow Hull House resident, Sophonisba Preston Breckinridge, was described by doctoral student Cathy Coghlan in her 1999 dissertation as "a tireless social scientist, social work educator, and advocate for social reform in the Progressive Era [who] left an indelible mark on the profession of social work although few social workers are aware of her name much less her contributions to the discipline."

Quite often, a Daughter excels in an astonishing array of areas. Take, for instance, Julia Ward Howe. A Unitarian best known as the author of "The Battle Hymn of the Republic," she was also, according to the Unitarian Universalist Historical Society, "famous in her lifetime as poet, essayist, lecturer, reformer and biographer, who worked to end slavery, helped to initiate the women's movement in many states, and organized for international peace . . . ." Her three daughters also became noted authors, winning a Pulitzer Prize for the biography of their mother.

Women, many of whom would later join the DAR, made enormous contributions in the medical field during the Civil War and subsequent campaigns. DAR archivist Tracy Robinson wrote, "Dr. Mary Edwards Walker was both a DAR and a physician and surgeon during the Civil War. President Andrew Johnson awarded Dr. Walker the Medal of Honor in recognition of her patriotism, bravery, and untiring services in attending the sick and wounded." American Red Cross Founder Clara Barton, whose given name was Clarissa Harlowe Barton, became DAR Surgeon General at the meeting to organize on

▶ Mary Edwards Walker, the only female in her class at Syracuse Medical College and one of the first licensed women surgeons, volunteered for the Union Army immediately when war broke out. Denied a commission as a medical officer, she eventually was appointed assistant surgeon, the first female surgeon in the U.S. Army. She frequently crossed battle lines, and, on April 10, 1864, she was captured by Confederate troops and arrested as a spy. Imprisoned in Richmond for four months, she was exchanged, with some twenty-four other Union doctors, for seventeen Confederate surgeons, an "in-kind" exchange of which she was particularly proud. President Andrew Johnson awarded Dr. Walker the Medal of Honor—the only woman ever to receive the award—in recognition of her patriotism, bravery, and untiring services in attending the sick and wounded. DAR member Dr. Walker was a staunch advocate for women's rights, including the right to dress comfortably, which for her was in a man's suit and top hat, as pictured here. She died in 1919, one year before passage of the Nineteenth Amendment.

▲ Actress and Daughter Virginia Mayo, whose real name was Virginia Clara Jones, got her start in the St. Louis Municipal Opera chorus as a dancer. Born in 1920, she appeared in more than fifty films, including her last movie, *The Man Next Door*, produced in 1997 when she was seventy-seven. She died in 2005 at the age of eighty-four.

October 11, 1890. Dr. Anita Newcomb McGee formed the DAR Hospital Corps, which later became the Army Nurse Corps, during the Spanish-American War, and was also the first DAR Librarian General.

Benjamin Franklin may have inspired the first American public libraries, but it was Daughter Caroline Maria Hewins who made them accessible to children when, in 1904, she opened one of the first public library children's rooms in the country. Founding the Connecticut Library Association in 1891, she was head of the Hartford Connecticut Public Library for more than fifty years. Best known for her advocacy of children's books and childhood reading, the Connecticut Women's Hall of Fame notes that, "In 1882, she published *Books for the Young*, the first bibliography designed for children; in 1888, she published a history of children's books in the *Atlantic Monthly*." In 1900, she helped found the Children's Section of the American Library Association and became the first woman to speak at the American Library Association conference.

Wives and Daughters

Beginning with Caroline Scott Harrison, First Ladies have figured prominently as both wives and Daughters, ten of whom have been DAR members. They perpetuate the tradition of their pioneer and patriot ancestors who figured large in the settling of America and its fight for freedom, women such as Martha Washington, Dolley Madison, and Abigail Adams. Some shunned the limelight, but, for others, such as Eleanor Roosevelt, the door to the White House opened other doors for making history or effecting social reform.

For Daughter Mamie Geneva Doud Eisenhower, the role of First Lady differed greatly from her predecessor, Eleanor Roosevelt. She preferred to leave the politics to her husband and focused her energies on the social duties required by her position, duties she had perfected to a fine art through the years of her husband's career travels and

ever-increasing positions in the military, especially as commander of North Atlantic Treaty Organization forces, during which time they lived and entertained numerous world leaders at their chateau near Paris. Following Dwight D. Eisenhower's tenure as President, Mamie and her husband retired to their home in Gettysburg, Pennsylvania, the only home they had ever owned and where she was a member of the Gettysburg Chapter of the DAR. Their grandson David married Julie Nixon, another Daughter (as well as the daughter of President and Mrs. Richard M. Nixon) in 1968. Mamie Eisenhower is pictured here (left), circa 1954, in the DAR Library during one of her visits to NSDAR Headquarters.

A crucial member of husband Jimmy's political team, Rosalynn Smith Carter traveled throughout the United States during his presidential bid, campaigning on his behalf. While First Lady, she attended cabinet meetings, served as an advisor regarding Presidential appointees, and was appointed honorary head of the President's Commission on Mental Health. Rosalynn Carter continues her social and humanitarian work with her husband, most especially Habitat for Humanity, and both she and the former President were awarded the Presidential Medal of Freedom in 1999, America's highest honor for civilians.

Though her career began in acting, the most famous role played by Nancy Davis Reagan, wife of Ronald, was that of First Lady. During her eight-year tenure in the White House, 1981–1989, this Daughter launched the "Just Say No" drug awareness campaign and devoted her energy to fighting substance abuse.

In the accompanying photo (above right), Daughter Barbara Pierce Bush chats with President General Patricia W. Shelby in the President General's Reception Room during the 1983 Continental Congress. Wife to one president, George H. W. Bush, and mother to another, George W. Bush, Barbara Bush used her prominent position as First Lady to promote a favorite cause: family literacy. She continues that advocacy today.

Laura Welch Bush (right), a member of the Colonel Theunis Dey Chapter in Texas, speaks publicly and often regarding the plight of women and children worldwide in an effort to raise awareness about the oppression many women face. As First Lady to George W. Bush, and as a former teacher and librarian, she has made education the prime focus of her time in the White House and has worked to promote the teaching profession and initiated the program, "Ready to Read, Ready to Learn."

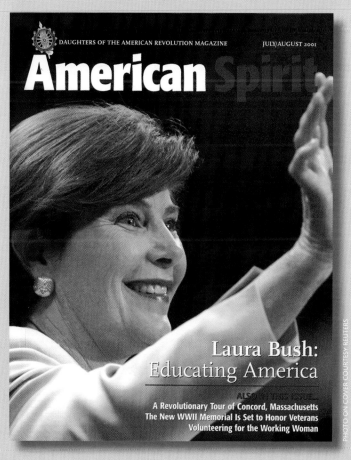

DAUGHTERS OF THE AMERICAN REVOLUTION MAGAZINE   JULY/AUGUST 2001

American Spirit

Laura Bush:
Educating America

ALSO IN THIS ISSUE
A Revolutionary Tour of Concord, Massachusetts
The New WWII Memorial Is Set to Honor Veterans
Volunteering for the Working Woman

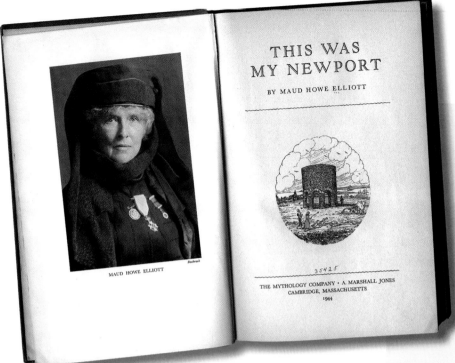

THIS WAS
MY NEWPORT

BY MAUD HOWE ELLIOTT

35425

THE MYTHOLOGY COMPANY · A. MARSHALL JONES
CAMBRIDGE, MASSACHUSETTS
1944

MAUD HOWE ELLIOTT

◄ It was "like mother, like Daughters" in both senses of the word for the Howe family of women. Julia Ward Howe and her daughters, Laura Elizabeth Howe Richards, Maud Howe Elliott, and Florence Howe Hall, all became noted authors as well as DAR members. While best known as the composer of the "Battle Hymn of the Republic," Julia Ward Howe was also a playwright, travel writer, and prolific poet whose "Mother's Day Proclamation" is partially credited with helping to inspire another mother-daughter team, both named Anna Jarvis, to succeed in their push for a national Mother's Day. Later in her life, Julia Howe became a significant force in the women's rights movement. Daughter Laura Elizabeth Howe Richards, children's author, poet, and biographer, is perhaps most noted for her book, *Captain January*, which became an enormously successful movie starring Shirley Temple. Pictured is the book, *This Was My Newport*, by Maude Howe Elliott. But it was the biography of their mother the sisters co-authored that in 1917 earned them the first Pulitzer Prize ever awarded in the biography category.

DAR member Jessie Ann Benton Frémont's literary career sprang from the adventures and eventful life she shared with her husband, officer and explorer John C. Frémont. After her husband's bankruptcy in 1873, her articles, memoirs, travel sketches, and stories appeared in leading magazines. She would write most of the text of her husband's *Memoirs of My Life*, first published in 1873.

American-born DAR member Princess Agnes Elizabeth Winona Leclerq Joy Salm-Salm married her Austrian prince in Washington's St. Patrick's Church and won distinction in both America and Europe when she accompanied her husband into battle. Prince Felix zu Salm-Salm had left Europe to fight in the American Civil War, where he met and married Agnes through their mutual ties to President Abraham Lincoln. Felix

► Lillian Gish, depicted in this MGM movie poster, began her career on the stage in 1902 to help her mother support the family after her father abandoned them. Ten years later, she gained fame as a silent movie star. With her delicate beauty and her ability to project intense emotion, she was the epitome of the silent screen stars. Appearing in more than one hundred movies, both silent and "talkies," including *The Birth of a Nation*, *The Scarlet Letter*, and *Duel in the Sun* for which she won an Academy Award for Best Supporting Actress, she later went on to perform in radio and television. Her last film role was in the acclaimed *The Whales of August* in 1987 at the age of ninety-three. Born in Ohio, she was a Daughter of the Massillon Chapter there.

AMERICAN HERITAGE IMAGE

Lillian Gish

THE SCARLET LETTER
A VICTOR SEASTROM PRODUCTION

was appointed commander of the Eighth New York Regiment and sent to Antietam Creek, where the princess joined him in November 1862 and remained by his side for four years, tending to the sick and wounded. She would also be his constant companion in the years 1866 and 1867 in the Mexican Revolution and between 1868 and 1870 in the French-German wars. Her appeals to President Benito Juárez of Mexico would save the life of her husband, who faced execution. She chronicled these exploits in her book, *Ten Years of My Life,* published in 1875.

Likely the tiniest Dazzling Daughter was actress Lavinia Warren Thumb, better known as Mrs. Tom Thumb. Other well-known stars have included Virginia Mayo, Dina Merrill, Ginger Rogers, and Esther Bell Wheeler. A favorite Daughter remains Lillian Gish, referred to as the first lady of the silent screen and, according to some, the movie industry's first true actor because she was the first to recognize the critical difference between acting for the stage and for the screen. She would remark that she was never interested in money, asserting "I just wanted films I'd be proud of because I felt they were permanent, and I didn't want to apologize for any of them."

Dazzling Daughters are not shy violets, considering there are more than twenty in the category of authors, editors, journalists, and publishers, including founder Mary Smith Lockwood. Mabel Loomis Todd was the first editor of Emily Dickinson's poems. Author Mary Cunningham Logan is credited with much of the success of her husband, Democratic Congressman John Logan of Illinois, including inspiring him to institute the first official recognition of Memorial Day, May 15, 1868, in an order issued by then-General Logan, first commander of the Grand Army of the Republic.

Mother of one author, Nikolai Tolstoy, and wife of another, famed British author Patrick O'Brian, Mary Koutousov Tolstoy translated Leo Tolstoy's *The Law of Love and the Law of Violence.* Her memoir, *The Right Life,* is described by Alibris as "the autobiography of a woman whose valor over the course of two world wars won her, among other awards, the Croix de Guerre, the Military Cross of Montenegro, and the Medal of St. George of Russia."

With more than thirty years of experience in magazine and television journalism, Judsen Ann Culbreth has served as editor-in-chief of *Scholastic Parent & Child* and *Early Childhood Today,* vice president of Scholastic in New York, editor-in-chief of *Working Mother* magazine, executive editor of *Redbook,* and the first work and family contributing editor on the NBC *Today* show. In 2005, she published her timely book, *The Boomers' Guide to Online Dating.*

▲ Of the one hundred statues placed in Statuary Hall in the U.S. Capitol, Frances E. Willard—author, educator, reformer, organizer, and standard-bearer for the rights of women and children—became the first woman so honored when her statue was unveiled in 1905. Despite her other passions, she quickly embraced the DAR mission within its first year of existence, thereby recognized as a charter member. President of both the National Women's Temperance Union and the National Council of Women, she also founded the Women's Christian Temperance Union. The program for the 100th anniversary of the placement of the statue, held February 17, 2005, notes that at the time of her death in 1898, she "was identified by the press as the most famous woman in the world after Queen Victoria." Her good friend and fellow DAR member Susan B. Anthony introduced Willard in 1888 to the United States Senate Committee as a "general with an army of 250,000." The nine-foot marble statue presented by the state of Illinois was the work of another noted woman, sculptor Helen Farnsworth Mears, "the only sculpture of a woman by a woman in the Hall of Statuary," noted Mears biographer Mary Hiles in 2003.

Real Daughters

More than a century had passed following the Revolution, representing three to four generations of patriot descendants, when the DAR was founded. In its first few years, those applying for membership proudly noted that they were granddaughters and even great-granddaughters of the patriots in their lineage. For example, Founder Ellen Hardin Walworth cited her ancestor as her great-grandfather, Colonel John Hardin, who fought in the Battle of Saratoga.

However, in 1893, as more and more applications poured in, chapter registrars like Charlotte O. Randall of Wisconsin began noticing a phenomenon—some of those applying were the actual daughters, the first-generation descendants of patriots who fought for American independence. How could this be, more than a century after the war had ended?

A combination of longevity and very early enlistments held the answer. Patriot Stephen Hassam was ninety years old when he fathered his daughter, Caroline, born September 19, 1849, in Springfield, Vermont. She lived to age ninety-two and died on July 14, 1942. Annie Knight Gregory of Williamsport, Pennsylvania, would become the daughter of a drummer boy who was eleven years old at the time of the war. In 1843, at age seventy-seven, he fathered Annie, who would live to celebrate her one hundredth birthday shortly before her death in 1943, an unbelievable 167 years after the Declaration of Independence.

Realizing the value of these living witnesses to history, they were fondly called "Real Daughters," and chapters across the country worked diligently to locate and honor them and capture their stories for the *American Monthly Magazine.* Mary Anne Hammond Washington, who applied December 5, 1890, just two months after the Society's founding, became the first of 757 Real Daughters to enroll. They were greeted at Continental Congress, and the passing of each one would be duly noted in the DAR magazine.

In 1895, the NSDAR created a special gold spoon featuring the thirteen stars of the original colonies and the motto "Home and Country" above the dame at the spinning wheel. The Daughters also gave material aid to those Real Daughters in need, with the National Society and individual chapters providing food, clothing, household goods, and even pensions where necessary. In Real

▲ Born May 26, 1813, Real Daughter Mary Pettegrew Keyes, of the Princeton Chapter, Illinois, poses for her portrait beside the spinning wheel used by William Cullen Bryant's mother.

Daughter Caroline Randall's last years, the National Society was her sole support.

One story in particular captures what the DAR relationship meant to the Real Daughters. "There is a true and pathetic story of a Real Daughter, who recently lived in the mountains of Georgia, and who was tenderly cared for for several years, by a donation from the Board of Management of the National Society," wrote Lockwood and Sherwood in *Story of the Records.* "Communicated on one occasion by a correspondent, when returning a receipt to the board for this gratuity," the story describes the home of this mountain Daughter, discovered by the Habersham Chapter of Atlanta, Georgia. The ninety-one-year-old woman, daughter of a soldier who fought at Cowpens, Guilford Court House, and King's Mountain, was

▶ The first Real Daughter to join the DAR was Mary Hammond Washington, National DAR Number 81. Her son, Hugh Vernon Washington, contributed the last $1,000 needed to meet the funding goal for construction of Memorial Continental Hall, where this bust of her, by sculptor Fidardo Landi, now stands in an alcove of the Pennsylvania Foyer. She died November 2, 1901.

bowed with age and life. She shared her home, an old log house falling to decay at the end of not more than a cow path against a scarred mountainside, with her daughter, granddaughter, and great-granddaughter, barely subsisting on what they could glean from a small garden, wild roots, and berries. During the visit by the DAR agent, she proudly displayed her gold spoon hidden away in a woolen rag. The visiting Daughter offered to buy the spoon at twice its value, thinking that the five or ten dollars would be of far more service. But the proud Real Daughter demurred, "Yes, we need money for meal, flour and bacon; but I'll hold on to this spoon a while yet. It was give [sic] to me because my father fought for his country. I'll keep it for his sake."

Annie Knight Gregory, the last Real Daughter, sent a message to her fellow Daughters on her one-hundredth birthday in 1943: "I have lived from the days of the Pony Express to the wireless telephone and radio, from the spinning wheel and loom to textile plants and factories. Now in my 100th year the wish, the request, the admonition that I would leave with you . . . is that you inculcate into the minds of our youth the lessons of the hardships and sacrifices which have entered into the making of our country."

▼ Relatives and Daughters gather around Annie Knight Gregory, center, the last living Real Daughter, for the celebration of her century birthday March 23, 1943. The basket in front of her contains one hundred roses. Participants include Mrs. Gregory's son, Forest E. Gregory (standing at left); her nephew, Harry S. Knight (standing, second from right), and his wife (seated, left of woman obscured by flowers), First Vice President General Mary Handley Forney (standing, fourth from left); and state officers from Pennsylvania and New Jersey.

TWO PIECES

Farewell, Summer   Dancing Leaves

FOR SOLO PIANO

by

AMY BEACH

Op. 102

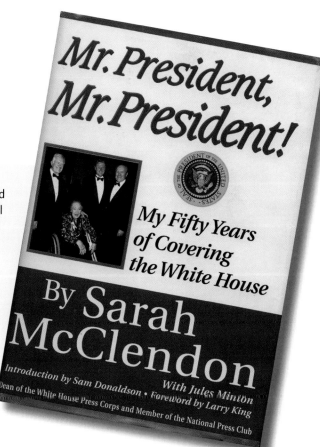

▲ Headlines covering the premiere of composer Amy Marcy Cheney Beach's "Gaelic" Symphony on October 30, 1896, by the Boston Symphony Orchestra, celebrated it as the first symphony by an American woman. A musical prodigy, Amy Beach began composing at age four, gave her first public piano recital at age seven, and debuted with the Boston Symphony Orchestra in 1885 at age eighteen. She married that same year, and, in deference to her husband's wishes, she limited her public appearances and concentrated on composition. Her more than three hundred compositions in a wide variety of musical genres, such as the piano score pictured here, established her as the foremost female composer in America in the early twentieth century. In 1911, after her husband's death, Beach lost no time resuming her public appearances, for many years touring Europe and the United States as a virtuoso pianist performing her own works to critical acclaim. A native of New Hampshire, she was a member of the Eunice Baldwin Chapter of the DAR.

Daughter Emily Warren Roebling would oversee completion of the Brooklyn Bridge when her husband, Washington, became bedridden. The first woman ever to address the American Society of Civil Engineers, she would later serve as a Vice President General of the NSDAR.

Civic leader Lillian H. Coit was quite the character. Nicknamed "Firebelle Lillie," she was the mascot and an honorary member of the Knickerbocker Engine Company Number 5 of the San Francisco Fire Department in the 1850s and 1860s. Her special relationship with firemen began when she was eight and they rescued her from a fire in a vacant house where two playmates died. This spurred little Lillie to chase fire engines, encouraging the then all-volunteer crews to run faster and put out fires quicker. She was regarded as the "patroness" of the city's firemen and always rode the float in local parades. Her passion for the firemen and the city only deepened after the 1906 earthquake fire, and funds from her substantial bequest were used for construction of the landmark art deco Coit Tower at the top of Telegraph Hill. The tower's design captures the nozzle of a fire hose.

More than a dozen politicians fill the list of Dazzling Daughters, many of whom would be the first woman to hold their respective office. When her husband was elected to Congress in 1912, Edith Nourse Rogers became involved in volunteer work in Washington, supporting the American Red Cross, the YMCA, and V.A. hospitals. When her husband

▶ Dazzling Daughter and White House reporter Sarah McClendon covered the administrations of eleven presidents, from Franklin D. Roosevelt to Bill Clinton. A tenacious Texan, known for shouting her questions in press conferences, she often wrote about the treatment of veterans, government secrecy, and other issues. In an AP story published at the time of her death at age ninety-two in January 2003, another famed veteran White House reporter, Helen Thomas, said of McClendon, "She was one of the greatest women Washington ever saw." Author of two books on her fifty years of experience, she once wrote that journalism "offers the best opportunity to serve one's country, the people, and the public interest." At right, the cover of her memoir published in 1996 shows her with Presidents Jimmy Carter, Bill Clinton, and Gerald Ford.

◄ Belva Ann Bennett Lockwood was refused admission to three law schools before being admitted to the new National University Law School in 1871. Inspired by a meeting with Susan B. Anthony, she used her knowledge of the law to draft a bill for equal pay for equal work for women in government employment, a bill that became law in 1872. Denied access once again, this time from admission to the Supreme Court, she successfully lobbied Congress, and in 1879, she became the first woman admitted to practice law before the United States Supreme Court. In this cartoon by artist Frederick Burr Opper published September 17, 1884, in *Puck*, Benjamin F. Butler stands on a stage dressed as a clown, a list of nominations for the 1884 presidential election (including his own) inscribed on pork sausages trailing from his pocket. Next to him Belva Lockwood has emerged through a hole in the stage floor, carrying over her head a scroll announcing the "Nomination for Pres. Womens' Rights Party." She ran for president twice, in 1884 and 1888. In one campaign, she amassed more than four thousand votes—all from men. She died in 1917 at the age of eighty-six, before women got the vote.

died in 1925, she was elected to finish his term, becoming the first congresswoman from New England. She would represent the Fifth District of Massachusetts for thirty-five years, introducing 1,200 bills, half of which concerned veterans and military affairs, including the 1944 Servicemen's Readjustment Act (or "G.I. Bill") and legislation to create what later became the Women's Army Corps.

Margaret Chase Smith's bravery became world renowned in 1950 when she became the first member of the United States Senate to denounce the tactics of her fellow senator, Joseph McCarthy. But her career in politics began inauspiciously, first entering the field as secretary for her husband, Republican Congressman Clyde Smith of Maine. Upon his death in 1940, she succeeded him, subsequently running successfully for the Senate in 1948, becoming the first woman elected to both houses of Congress. In 1945, the same year she cosponsored the Equal Rights Amendment, she introduced legislation granting permanent status for women in the armed forces. She

◄ The founder of the Christian Science Church, Mary Baker Eddy is a figure of prominence in the history of religion in America. After miraculously recovering from a crippling fall, Mary began to teach about the power of Jesus's healing and attracted a large following. In 1908, she founded the *Christian Science Monitor*, winner of seven Pulitzer Prizes now in its ninety-eighth year of publication, with a focus on international and U.S. news and features. In 1995, Eddy was elected to the National Women's Hall of Fame as the only American woman to found a worldwide religion.

▶ In tribute to the four founders, another Dazzling Daughter, renowned sculptor Gertrude Vanderbilt Whitney, would create the Founders Memorial Monument adjacent to Memorial Continental Hall and dedicated April 17, 1929. The elegant form of the nine-foot-high figure, arms outstretched to symbolize the nurturing spirit of womanhood, is draped in a flowing garment that was so well executed, it appears to be floating on a gentle breeze. A member of the prominent Vanderbilt family, during World War I Whitney directed her wealth and her time to various relief efforts, establishing and maintaining a hospital for wounded soldiers in France. She also used her great wealth to serve as a patron of the arts, and she devoted herself to the advancement of women in art. Her works include the Christopher Columbus memorial lighthouse in Palos, Spain; the *Aztec Fountain* and *RMS Titanic Memorial*, Washington, D.C.; the *Victory Arch* in Madison Square, New York City; and the *William F. Cody Memorial*, at the entrance to Yellowstone National Park, Cody, Wyoming. Often striking a regal pose herself, she wears a jeweled gown and tiara and is holding a peacock feather fan in this circa 1916 photo.

◀ Sometimes success is in just showing up. Shown here as a young girl, circa 1880, Janet Elizabeth Hosmer Richards, DAR Charter Member Number 133, certainly did that, attending every one of the fifty Continental Congresses through 1941. However, as with so many other Daughters, she excelled at so much more. Historian, popular lecturer, and advocate for women's rights, she appeared numerous times before Congress during "Woman Suffrage Hearings." A member of the Mary Washington Chapter in D.C. (along with three of the four founders), she would serve as its Historian, Recording Secretary, and Regent, among others. At the 49th Congress, President General Helena R. Pouch presented her with a special pin declaring her Honorary Chairman of the Golden Jubilee, in recognition of her "sound judgment and keenness of vision," noting that "A wise question from her has clarified many a difficult discussion." Sadly, the Golden Jubilee in 1941 was likely the last Congress she would attend. In 1942, the Society made the difficult decision to hold Congress in Chicago because Washington was filled to capacity with visitors all focused on the World War II effort. Unable to attend, as reported in the DAR *National Historical Magazine* in June 1942, she prevailed upon the President General to read a letter to those at Congress: "Greetings from your absent member, Janet Richards, sometimes known as the 'D.A.R. perennial,' who finds it impossible to be present. Her sincere prayers will, however, follow you that you may be guided to the highest achievement in every line of our useful activities, and for ever-increasing service to our beloved Country. Hail and farewell from one whose loyal devotion is dampened with tears."

► Suzanne Bishopric, treasurer of the United Nations and a member of the Walter Hines Page Chapter in London, is one of the thousands of members of the DAR who have achieved national and even international prominence in such fields as government, art, entertainment, science, medicine, literature, engineering, and exploration, including outer space.

▲ Rear Admiral Grace Murray Hopper was a pioneer in the field of computer science. She was the first programmer of the Mark I calculator and developed the first compiler for a computer programming language. A graduate of Vassar College, she received her master's in mathematics and physics at Yale University and later a PhD in mathematics, also at Yale. In 1943, she joined the Naval Reserve. At the end of the war, she separated from active duty, but the Navy would call her back into service time and again. The Navy found it necessary to enforce the mandatory retirement age, so she reluctantly retired in 1986. At the time of her retirement at age seventy-nine, she was the oldest officer in the U.S. Navy aboard the oldest U.S. Navy ship. At a celebration held in Boston on the USS *Constitution* to celebrate her retirement, Hopper was awarded the Defense Distinguished Service Medal. Admiral Hopper was buried at Arlington National Cemetery on January 7, 1992, with full military honors.

would run in several Republican presidential primaries, and, at the Republican National Convention in San Francisco in 1964, Smith became the first woman to have her name placed in nomination for president by any party. She lost the nomination to Arizona Senator Barry Goldwater.

Marie Corinne Morrison Claiborne "Lindy" Boggs first came to Washington as the wife of a newly elected Congress member, but thirty years later, she would find her own political voice. In 1973, her husband, House Majority Leader Hale Boggs, was pronounced presumed dead following the disappearance in remote Alaska of a small airplane in which he was a passenger. In the special election that followed, Lindy Boggs campaigned and won his seat and was re-elected for eight successive terms, serving a total of eighteen years before retiring in 1991. During her time in office, she became the first woman ever to chair a national political convention, the Democratic Party, in 1976, and she helped to organize the Bicentennial Celebration of the Constitution. She came out of retirement in 1997 when President William J. "Bill" Clinton appointed her official U.S. Ambassador to the Vatican, a position she held until 2001. She is the mother of Cokie Roberts, author and noted television news commentator; prominent lobbyist Tommy Boggs; and Barbara Boggs Sigmund, mayor of Princeton, New Jersey, and a 1982 Democratic candidate in the New Jersey senatorial election.

Representing both Democrats and Republicans, radicals and conservatives, homemakers and astronauts, suffragists and prohibitionists, the Dazzling Daughters of the DAR comprise a dizzying list of notable women to rival any compilation of who's who among American women. The disparate list highlights the diversity that has always been the hallmark of the Daughters: strong women with even stronger ideals who found commonality in the timeless DAR mission of education, preservation, and patriotism.

Real Dazzlers

1. **Jane Addams**—prominent American social worker, founder of Hull House, awarded Nobel Prize for Peace

2. **Florence E. Allen**—federal judge, first woman placed on circuit bench

3. **Susan B. Anthony**—suffragist leader

4. **Albion F. Bacon**—social reformer

5. **Irene Temple Bailey**—author, screenwriter

6. **Kate Waller Barrett**—physician, advocate for unwed mothers, cofounder Florence Crittenton Mission

7. **Clara Barton**—teacher, nurse, founder of the American Red Cross

8. **Tryphosa Bates-Batcheller**—singer, lecturer

9. **Amy Marcy Cheney Beach**—composer, pianist

10. **Eunice Bullard Beecher**—author, wife of Henry Ward Beecher

11. **Suzanne Bishopric**—Treasurer of the United Nations

12. **Mabel Thorp Boardman**—American Red Cross leader

13. **Marie Corinne Morrison Claiborne "Lindy" Boggs**—congresswoman, ambassador to the Vatican, mother of journalist and author Cokie Roberts

14. **Madeline Breckinridge**—social reformer, suffragist

15. **Sophonisba Breckinridge**—social reformer, suffragist

16. **Jennie Augusta Brownscombe**—illustrator, painter

17. **Barbara Pierce Bush**—literacy advocate, wife of George H. W. Bush, mother of George W. Bush

18. **Laura Welch Bush**—teacher, education and literacy advocate, women and children's rights advocate, wife of George W. Bush

19. **Julia Cantacuzene-Grant**—princess, granddaughter of Ulysses S. Grant, married into Russian nobility, author whose works depict last days of Tsarist Russia

20. **Rosalynn Smith Carter**—social and humanitarian worker, advocate of mental health, wife of James Earl "Jimmy" Carter

21. **Lillian Hitchcock Coit**—volunteer firefighter, benefactor of San Francisco Fire Department, funded erection of famous Coit Tower

22. **Judsen Ann Culbreth**—publisher, author

23. **Alice Turner Curtis**—author, known for Little Maid and Yankee Girl series

24. **Jane Arminda Delano**—founder of the American Red Cross Nursing Service

25. **Elizabeth Hanford Dole**—U.S. Senator, Secretary of both Transportation and Labor, president of the American Red Cross

26. **Alice Morse Earle**—author, social historian

27. **Mary Baker Eddy**—religious leader, founder of Christian Science Church and Christian Science Monitor

28. **Julie Nixon Eisenhower**—author, editor, lecturer, daughter of Richard Nixon

29. **Mamie Geneva Doud Eisenhower**—wife of Dwight D. Eisenhower

30. **Maud Howe Elliott**—author, daughter of Julia Ward Howe, she and two sisters awarded first Pulitzer Prize in biography

31. **Marsha J. Evans**—U.S. Navy admiral, head of Girl Scouts, past president of American Red Cross

32. **Rebecca Latimer Felton**—first woman U.S. Senator

33. **Penny Sanford Fikes**—porcelain artist

34. **Jessie Ann Benton Frémont**—author, wife of explorer John C. Frémont

35. **Lillian Gish**—real name Lillian Diana de Guiche, actor

36. **Julia Dent Grant**—wife of Ulysses S. Grant

37. **Florence Kling Harding**—women's rights advocate, wife of Warren G. Harding

38. **Caroline Lavinia Scott Harrison**—painter, women's rights advocate, wife of Benjamin Harrison, first NSDAR President General

39. **Caroline Maria Hewins**—author, noted librarian

40. **Ima Hogg**—philanthropist and patron of the arts

41. **Dame Mary Claire Hogg**—British judge, University of Westminster governor

42. **Grace Hopper**—U.S. Navy admiral, computer pioneer, and author of COBOL computer language

43. **Julia Ward Howe**—composer of "Battle Hymn of the Republic," author, and women's rights advocate

44. **Anna Hyatt Huntington**—sculptor

45. **Virginia Ellis Jenckes**—Indiana's first congresswoman

46. **Annie Fellows Johnston**—author, noted for Little Colonel series

47. **Frances Benjamin Johnston**—photographer

48. **Frances Eliza Osborne Kellogg**—businesswoman, entrepreneur

49. **Frances Parkinson Keyes**—author

50. **Madame Albert Lebrun**—wife of President Lebrun of France, christened the SS *Normandie*, honorary DAR

51. **Belva Lockwood**—lawyer, first woman to practice before U.S. Supreme Court

52. **Mary Cuningham Logan**—writer, magazine editor, inspired Memorial Day concept

53. **Rose McConnell Long**—U.S. senator, wife of Huey Long

54. **Harriet Stone Lothrop**—pen name Margaret Sidney, novelist and author of Little Peppers series, founder of C.A.R.

55. **Clare Booth Luce**—ambassador to Italy, also journalist and playwright

56. **Jean Faircloth MacArthur**—wife of Douglas MacArthur, philanthropist, awarded Presidential Medal of Freedom

57. **Virginia Mayo**—real name Virginia Clara Jones, actress, comedienne, dancer

58. **Sarah McClendon**—journalist, historian, author

59. **Dr. Anita Newcomb McGee**—one of first woman doctors, organized DAR Nurse Corps, founder of Army Nurse Corps

60. **Nina McLemore**—fashion designer, businesswoman, founder of Liz Claiborne accessories

61. **Dina Merrill**—real name Nedenia Hutton Robertson, actress

62. **Anna Mary Robertson Moses**—painter known as "Grandma Moses"

63. **Princesse Pauline de Broglie (Comtesse Jean de Pange)**—author, wife of Count Jean de Pange

64. **Alice Paul**—suffragist leader, first author of Equal Rights Amendment, participant in most likely first political protest in front of the White House

65. **Jeanette Ridlon Piccard**—first woman to pilot a balloon into the stratosphere

66. **Frances N. Pillsbury**—pilot and Red Cross worker in World War II, flight instructor, member of the Ninety-Nines international organization of women pilots

67. **Mary Eno Pinchot**—conservationist, first chair of DAR National Committee on Conservation, mother of Gifford Pinchot, leading advocate of conservation

68. **Marjorie Merriweather Post**—businesswoman, philanthropist, patron of the arts

69. **Sara Rice Pryor**—author

70. **Nancy Davis Reagan**—actor, drug awareness advocate, wife of Ronald Reagan

71. **Janet Reno**—lawyer, first woman U.S. Attorney General

72. **Janet Elizabeth Hosmer Richards**—lecturer, historian

73. **Laura Elizabeth Howe Richards**—noted author of children's books including Captain January, poet, Pulitzer Prize–winning biographer, daughter of Julia Ward Howe

74. **Eugenie Ricau Rocherolle**—composer, lyricist, pianist, teacher

75. **Abby Aldrich Rockefeller**—philanthropist, pivotal supporter of New York Museum of Modern Art and Colonial Williamsburg, wife of John D. Rockefeller Jr.

76. **Emily Warren Roebling**—wife of Washington Roebling, oversaw completion of Brooklyn Bridge after her husband's illness

77. **Edith Nourse Rogers**—aviator, U.S. congresswoman, sponsored legislation for GI Bill and Women's Army Corps

78. **Ginger Rogers**—real name Virginia K. McMath, actress, dancer

79. **Ruth Bryan Rohde**—daughter of William Jennings Bryan, U.S. congresswoman, proposed bill to establish Everglades National Park, as Minister to Denmark, first woman to achieve such diplomatic level

80. **Edith Carow Roosevelt**—wife of Theodore Roosevelt, responsible for East Wing of the White House

81. **Eleanor Roosevelt Roosevelt**—humanitarian, author, head of United Nations Human Rights Commission, wife of Franklin D. Roosevelt

82. **Princess Agnes Winona Leclerq Joy Salm-Salm**—author, adventurer, presented Prussian Medal of Honor

83. **Lucy Maynard Salmon**—teacher, historian, school administrator, greatly expanded Vassar library, first woman on American Historical Association executive committee

84. **Phyllis Schlafly**—author, radio host, women's issues advocate

85. **Margaret Rhea Seddon**—surgeon, astronaut

86. **Jane DeForest Shelton**—journalist, historian, author

87. **Margaret Chase Smith**—first woman elected to both House and Senate, first woman named as presidential nominee by major party

88. **Frances Vandegrift Osbourne Stevenson**—wife of Robert Louis Stevenson, co-editor of his work

89. **Olga Samaroff Stowkowski**—pianist and teacher

90. **Lavinia Warren Thumb**—performer, wife of Tom Thumb

91. **Mabel Loomis Todd**—first editor of Emily Dickinson's poems

92. **Mary Koutouzov Tolstoy**—author, translator of Leo Tolstoy's work, awarded the Croix de Guerre, the Military Cross of Montenegro, and the Medal of St. George of Russia

93. **Wilma L. Vaught**—U.S. Army brigadier general, NATO Women in the Allied Forces Committee chairperson, spearheaded campaign for Women in Military Service for America Memorial

94. **Mary Edwards Walker**—Civil War physician, surgeon, awarded Congressional Medal of Honor

95. **Mary Frances Barnett "Frankie" Welch**—fashion designer

96. **Esther Bell Wheeler**—actress

97. **Gertrude Vanderbilt Whitney**—sculptor

98. **Frances E. Willard**—temperance leader, educator, founder of Evanston College incorporated by Northwestern University

99. **Mary Ellen Withrow**—U.S. Treasurer, first woman to serve as treasurer at local, state, and national levels, helped introduce popular state quarters and Sacagawea dollar

100. **Mary Emma Woolley**—president of Mount Holyoke College, presidential appointee to 1932 disarmament conference

CHAPTER TWELVE

State of Things
To Each Her Own

P ERIOD ROOMS, A PHENOMENON OF THE COLONIAL REVIVAL PERIOD, became fixtures in many American art museums by the 1920s. With its first period room installed fully a decade before, the DAR Museum was among the first to embrace the movement. Some of the finest museums in the world would also come to emulate this concept. At the Philadelphia Museum of Art, period rooms became a key component at their building, completed in 1928. The Metropolitan Museum of Art features as many as thirty-five such rooms (twenty-five in the American wing alone), of which museum director Philippe de Montebello wrote: "Period rooms afford the viewer a chance to experience the furnishings as related to each other in time, place, and style in a way that isolating them cannot."

There are now thirty-one period rooms occupying portions of four floors in Memorial Continental Hall, where each year thousands of visitors take the opportunity to "glimpse" history replayed on authentic stages: each room is so lovingly furnished by a different state, so finely and authentically detailed that they lack only the imagination of visitors to populate each scene. The rooms tell the story of life in America, from the humble hearth to the most elegantly appointed parlors. Here, visitors experience the furnishings set in their context of time and space, each room highlighting a different era, lifestyle, level of affluence, or even a moment in time.

The New Jersey Room, installed in 1910 to represent a seventeenth-century style council chamber, was the first period room in Memorial Continental Hall and looks much as it did when it first opened. The parlor of the Massachusetts Room depicts the moment John Hancock and Samuel Adams, guests of a local minister in Maine, had just dashed away

▶ The art of quilting dominates the Vermont parlor in this early nineteenth-century rural setting. The circa 1840 cotton quilt top stretches across a handcrafted quilt frame beside a well-stocked sewing box. Portraits of Samuel and Lydia Dyer Townsend, of Wallingford, Vermont, oversee the room, both captured at age sixty-five in 1832 by Wallingford artist James Whitehorne. Married in 1789, the Townsends had been together forty-three years at the time they posed for the artist. The room also features an impressive collection of Bennington ware, named for the brown-glazed yellow pottery made between 1847 and 1858 at one of two factories in Bennington, Vermont. Three examples of the collection rest on the 1800 maple writing desk at left.

on the morning of April 19, 1775, following the news that the British were coming. In Tondee's Tavern, re-created by the Georgia Daughters, the scene is set for a secret meeting of the "Sons of Liberty." On the floor of the New Hampshire Room—a child's attic playroom filled with dolls and rocking horses, diminutive tea sets, and teddy bears—a fire engine with charging horses is stopped in the middle of time until the little master returns to fight the fires of his imagination. A testament to its maritime heritage, the setting in the Maine Period Room re-creates the elegantly appointed parlor of a wealthy seafaring family enjoying a leisurely afternoon in 1835. In the Oklahoma Room, an oak and pine table sits next to an inviting hearth in a Colonial Revival pioneer-style kitchen.

Rooms funded by states at the DAR complex run the gamut from functional to fabulous. The Arizona Lounge, funded by the Arizona State Society and located on the lower floor of the Administration Building, affords both staff members and guests a welcome spot for lunch and break time. Meanwhile, both the elegant Pennsylvania Foyer and the elaborate Connecticut Board Room, pictured in "A Room of Her Own" (on page 43), serve a variety of Society functions. In the tradition of those early state rooms paid for and furnished by DAR state societies to be used for performing the business of the Daughters, the Colorado Room now serves as a conference room for the office

▲ As many as sixteen of the thirty-one period rooms in Memorial Continental Hall re-create parlors showing the evolution of the American lifestyle from the late 1700s to the 1930s. They range from practical to almost palatial in their furnishings, reflecting the relative wealth of the imagined occupant as well as the availability of both imported and American manufactured goods. The earliest parlor, the Massachusetts Room pictured here, evokes the 1775 multipurpose room from the still-existing Hancock-Clarke House in Lexington, Massachusetts, originally owned by the Reverend John Hancock, minister of the Parish Church in Lexington for fifty-four years. On the morning of April 19, 1775, John Hancock (the reverend's grandson) and Samuel Adams were in one of the parlors when they heard the message that the British were coming. This front parlor served as a dining and work area, as well as a bedchamber, when it was not uncommon for rooms to be used as both a public and private space. Members of the Massachusetts DAR handcrafted the wool reproduction bed hangings. The large oak and pine chest at left was made for the 1716 wedding of Mary Burt, born in 1695 in Northampton, Massachusetts. It bears her name carved across the front, as well as an array of Baroque designs. The smaller chest on top is a lacquered wood and brass Chinese tea chest, circa 1770, reported to be one of those that played a historic role in the Boston Tea Party.

of the Curator General and as a space for teaching and research by the Museum staff. The room also affords a secure space and uncluttered backdrop for photographing and documenting the thousands of items in the Museum collection.

The DAR preservation ideal reaches far beyond the walls of their headquarters. Over the past century, every DAR state society and many individual chapters, including some overseas, have saved historic buildings or sites from the brink of demolition and not only restored and furnished them but in many cases opened them to the public. Many use them as their meeting space, an adaptive re-use that helps to ensure their continued existence. Such undertakings are daunting and always costly. It often costs each chapter thousands of dollars to purchase, preserve, restore, furnish, and operate, as well as insure such important American treasures as Roslyn Heights, the Missouri State DAR Headquarters; the Oliver Ellsworth Homestead museum in Windsor, Connecticut, owned and operated by the Connecticut Daughters; the 1790s John Strong DAR Mansion and Museum run by the Vermont State Society; and the Richards House in Mobile, Alabama, operated by the six Mobile chapters who maintain and furnish it as a period house museum.

Buildings and sites preserved by the DAR are as diverse as the histories they represent, ranging from stately mansions to farmhouses and log cabins, from powder houses to lighthouses, from churches to taverns, and from schoolhouses to stables. In 1979, the NSDAR published the first illustrated inventory of more than 160 historic buildings restored and either still owned or once owned by more than forty state societies or numerous chapters within those states. Even more impressive, the inventory was only a partial list, for it did not include important restorations made by DAR state societies and chap-

PHOTO BY MARK GULEZIAN

▲ In 1906, the Iowa Daughters were the first to furnish a state room in the yet unfinished Memorial Continental Hall. Today, the Iowa Room represents a late 1770s parlor during an afternoon tea party. Here the hostess's young daughter mimics the grownups by serving tea to her wooden doll, one of the earliest in the DAR Museum collection. Summer slipcovers match the red and white copperplate printed curtains; such *en suite* decorations were very popular in the eighteenth and nineteenth centuries.

PHOTO BY MARK GULEZIAN

◄ The District of Columbia Daughters chose Washington City as the inspiration for this Colonial Revival parlor. The painted maple armchair on the right (1790–1800) was part of the original furnishings of Colonel John Tayloe's Washington townhouse, the Octagon, located just a few blocks east of the DAR headquarters. The 1790–1810 painting of George Washington on the left is a copy of Gilbert Stuart's portrait of the president. The mahogany piano at left was made by Carl Christian Stein of Germany, circa 1815. The 1892 painting on the right captures the countryside on the site where Memorial Continental Hall now stands.

◄ In its 1835 parlor of a wealthy seafaring Maine family, the Maine State Society chose to highlight the period just a few years after Maine became a state in 1820. Objects in the room reflect the family's maritime connection: a spyglass and quadrant rest on the merchant's or sea captain's imported mahogany desk. On the Pembroke table is a Chinese porcelain tea service, a costly import. Opposite rests a tape loom used to weave fine threads into hatbands, garters, and purse handles. The expensive sofa, upholstered in silk or horsehair, is covered in fashionable white cotton dimity for summer. A tall mahogany case clock with painted dial and brass workings, made by Frederick Wingate circa 1810, marked the leisure hours. Both the walls and woodwork are painted, another indication of affluence since, prior to the 1860s, paint had to be ground and mixed in oil by hand.

PHOTO BY MARK GULEZIAN

▼ Tennessee native Andrew Jackson figures prominently in the Tennessee Room, for the period represented in this parlor in a wealthy American home are the years 1828 to 1836, the years of Jackson's presidency. Many of the furnishings in the room are linked to one another. For instance, in the 1830–1832 portrait of Jackson, painted by his close friend, painter Ralph E. W. Earl, the president is seated in a gilded armchair that was part of a suite of fifty-three pieces ordered by James Monroe for the White House in 1817 from the Paris firm of Pierre-Antoine Bellangé. The chair under the portrait is from that very set and remains identical to the one in the portrait. The room also features other furniture from the original effort to redecorate the White House, such as the two upholstered armchairs, part of a set of twenty-four chairs and four sofas commissioned in 1818 by President James Monroe from Georgetown cabinetmaker William King, Jr.

PHOTO BY SCOTT BRAWN

▲ As with so many of the period rooms in Memorial Continental Hall, the Alabama Room has served many purposes. In 1911 it was designated as a reception room for the President General, and during World War II, the American Red Cross used it as an office. In 1946, the Alabama DAR redecorated it as a parlor with furnishings in the Empire style of the 1830s and 1840s. The furnishings include the Gothic Revival secretary bookcase originally owned by William Rufus King, vice president during the Franklin Pierce administration. One of the most fashionable items in the room is the center table of finely matched mahogany veneers and carved volute feet reminiscent of Greek and Egyptian revival motifs. The ingrain carpeting features bold designs and contrasting colors in the latest fashion for that time.

▶ The neoclassical theme in the 1830s Maryland parlor incorporates German, French, and English designs. The hand-painted wallpaper, made in France, depicts scenes from the French Revolution of 1830. The Baltimore-made "fancy furniture," such as the card table and chairs, bear painted gilt griffins, cornucopias, and "anthemions." One of the most interesting and rare items in this room is the harmonicon (at right), a unique musical instrument made by Francis Hopkinson Smith of Baltimore. The amateur musician used moistened fingers to rub the rims of blown glasses filled with water to produce various melodies, some of which were specially composed for the harmonicon by Mozart and Beethoven.

◀ The Ohio parlor depicts a wealthy household during the early twentieth century reflecting the Colonial Revival taste. Once again, as with the Missouri's Victorian parlor, an imagined family displays special possessions in this room, such as the matching mid-nineteenth-century French porcelain vases on each side of the fruitwood sofa. The pianoforte, made about 1825 by John Kearsing of New York City in the late neoclassical style, features heavy carving on the legs and highly figured mahogany-veneered surfaces. One of the most interesting articles in this room is the collection of Ohio-produced glass, including items made by Libbey, Imperial, and Heisey. Perhaps the most important piece of glass, seen on the center table, is the pink or "flamingo" colored punch set made by A. H. Heisey in the 1920s in the "Greek key" pattern. Portraits such as those pictured were common in early to mid-nineteenth-century parlors and endured as a popular adornment into the twentieth century.

▼ The Missouri Period Room shifts its representation to the Victorian era, with a parlor setting around 1850. The room's furnishings are in the Rococo Revival style that reflected a newly defined opulence and changing aesthetic tastes of the time. The fashionable gas-lit chandelier, the Aubusson-style carpet, the imported marble fireplace and ornate looking glass, the multitiered display table laden with decorative objects collected from many travels, all suggest a quest for the latest in fashion and a desire to showcase it. The richly detailed Rococo Revival center table, sofa, and chair highlight the ornate style that had come to the United States by 1845 and made popular by furniture maker John Henry Belter of New York.

▲ As with most of the period rooms, the Indiana Room, shown here, served a practical more than decorative purpose in the early days of the Society. Originally the office of the President General, it is the latest period represented by all the parlors. Outfitted as the parlor in a wealthy Indiana home of the 1930s, this room is also arranged in the Colonial Revival style, an era that led to a passion for antique collecting, genealogy, and historic preservation, as well as the founding of heritage organizations like the DAR. By the 1930s, rooms were arranged for comfort and beauty and to show off prized antiques that might date from the Colonial or early Federal periods to the late nineteenth or early twentieth century, such as the Victrola, circa 1910–1925, beside the tall case clock made a century before. One of the oldest items in the room is the circa 1755 tea table, made in coastal Massachusetts, which sits behind the 1780s sofa made in Scotland.

ters on property they only leased. Nor did it include perhaps thousands of historic sites, cemeteries, parks, forests, and monuments that have been owned or maintained by the Society. No formal inventory of buildings and sites has been conducted since 1979, in part because chapters and states remain active in preservation and restoration, so it would be out of date long before it could be published.

A very small sampling from across the country illustrates the diversity of the Daughters' preservation and restoration efforts in their states and local communities. In 1910, the prominent O'Farrell sisters donated their family's pioneer cabin, the first family dwelling in Boise, Idaho, to the Pioneer Chapter of that city, which raised money for its relocation and preservation. The cabin was ultimately added to the National Register of Historic Places and is now maintained by the Boise Parks & Recreation Department. Sitka, Alaska, would host the founding of the first chapter in that state in 1903, with fourteen

◄ Period rooms often feature a particular domestic activity to bring it to life. In this 1830–1840 Kentucky parlor, the imagined occupants have just stepped away from a game of cribbage. Nearby sits a mahogany neoclassical-style sofa, with its imported fabric upholstery made in New York City. Over the mantel, the horizontal mirror of gilded wood provides a broad surface for reflecting the light from the three-piece girandole, whose candlelight and glass prisms provided brilliance to a dim interior. Reinforcing the room's Kentucky roots, in the corner to the right of the tall case clock hangs one of two engravings in the parlor by John James Audubon (1785–1851), who lived in Kentucky for several years.

► While the Maryland Room (pictured on page 213) highlights one special musical instrument, the Rhode Island showcases several. Evening musical recitals often provided the entertainment in early America, where wealthy families placed great value on mastery of an instrument. The wide array of instruments displayed in this room range from the homemade harp with gut strings and the six-octave Oramel Whittlesey piano, both made in America, to the violoncello made in Germany. An accordion made of rosewood, featuring nineteen note keys

inlayed with mother-of-pearl, rests on the right side of the piano. While the musical theme dominates the room, other details add equally interesting notes, like the late eighteenth-century tall case clock in the corner, and the French-made bronze-and-gilt shelf clock featuring the bust of George Washington on the table at left.

▲ Although arranged in the Colonial Revival style, the New York parlor features leisure activities popular in the eighteenth century. Perhaps the most striking feature of the room is the hand-painted Chinese wallpaper. The fascination of all things Chinese became popular after the Revolution, when free trade with China posed a lucrative enterprise. The first American ship to set sail for China, the *Empress of China*, left New York City on February 22, 1784. Other objects of Chinese origin include the porcelain cups and ebony and ivory backgammon game board. Another important object in the room is the elaborately carved and scrolled late neoclassic style sofa made in New York City about 1830. To its right sits a side chair in the Rococo style made by the famous Connecticut cabinetmaker Eliphalet Chapin about 1780.

▶ This early nineteenth-century West Virginia parlor doubles as a schoolroom, where the lesson of the day appears to be geography and mathematics. At the circa 1800 mahogany desk, the private tutor has set his spectacles on a vintage pamphlet open to an article on "Sacred Geography," while at the table opposite, a student refers to the 1846 wood, brass, and paper globe. The setting in the West Virginia Period Room reflects the time when the state was still part of the Commonwealth of Virginia. The post-1801 watercolor over the mantel depicts a river view of Mount Vernon, while the pair of hand-colored engravings opposite capture sweeping scenes of both the Potomac and Shenandoah rivers. After school recessed, householders would roll out the remarkable barrel organ, made in London between 1790 and 1798, which would play dance music for reels, waltzes, minuets, and mazurkas.

members, and, while it would disband only six years later, in its short life, it would help to establish the Sitka Public Library.

The Julia Hancock Chapter, of Lewiston, Montana, is the caretaker of artifacts from the Tiegen School, the only DAR-owned building in Montana. This one-room rural schoolhouse was built in 1914 by Mons Tiegen and served the community until 1935, when the chapter acquired it as a gift from the Tiegen family. While the school itself was too fragile to survive a recent move required by the Lewiston Museum expansion, the chapter has placed in safe storage items rescued from the schoolhouse, including the contents, the original chalkboards and windows, and the small steeple bell tower that used to summon the children to school.

Two historic log cabins still stand in Nebraska, thanks to the efforts of two chapters there. In 1928, the Quivera Chapter in Fairbury accepted as a gift and paid to have moved the 1862 two-room log cabin built on the banks of the Blue River by

▲ By the early twentieth century, larger American homes could devote entire rooms to one purpose, like this library in the Michigan Room. The large, classical cylinder desk, made in Paris by Joseph Stockel around 1775 and decorated with gilt bronze or "ormolu" mounts, dominates the room. Educated gentlemen, in the quest to understand the physical world, often acquired scientific and navigational instruments, such as the globes and "orreries," mechanical models of the solar system. The terrestrial globe between the two orreries shows the then-recent voyages of Captain James Cook and Captain Jean-François de La Pérouse. Charles Delamarche of Paris made all three instruments in the late eighteenth and early nineteenth centuries. The large celestial globe next to the desk, made by John Cary of London in 1800, shows the position of the stars and planets. In 1819, Jacob Eichholtz painted the portraits of General George Porter and his wife, Sarah Hume Porter. Appointed by President Andrew Jackson in 1831, Porter served as the third governor of the Michigan Territory.

PHOTO BY MARK GULEZIAN

▲ Throughout the last half of the eighteenth century, the dining room became another specialized space, serving as a place for dining as well as an opportunity for the family to share the activities of the day. "Just desserts" are the fare in this late-eighteenth-century dining room sponsored by the Virginia Daughters, which displays an array of neoclassical decoration in the wallpaper and furniture. Wealthy Virginians could choose from a variety of specialized furnishings to enhance the dining room's importance, such as the inlayed sideboard and dining table, perfect stages for the impressive arrangements of expensive silver plate, ceramics, and glass.

▶ Frothy confections describe both the fare and the furnishings in the 1820s North Carolina dining room. The creamware dinner service setting the table and displayed about the room includes more than one hundred pieces, each piece decorated with a squirrel holding an acorn and made by John Turner in London around 1790. One of the most important pieces in the room is the circa 1800 silver and glass epergne made by Matthew Boulton in Birmingham, England. Like the table, the tiered mahogany dumbwaiter beside it is set for the dessert course. Five matching Chinese porcelain urns decorate the mantel, and beside the mantel is another piece for entertaining. A boldly carved and veneered sideboard holds a silver coffee urn and a pair of mahogany knife boxes.

PHOTO BY MARK GULEZIAN

◀ The New Jersey Room was the first period room installed in Memorial Continental Hall and has changed little since 1910. Designed to suggest a late seventeenth-century English council chamber, the paneling and furniture were carved from the oak timbers of the British ship *Augusta*, which sank during the Revolutionary Battle of Red Bank off the coast of New Jersey, October 23, 1777. The ship was raised and towed to Gloucester City, New Jersey, in 1869. Two New Jersey Daughters, Ellen Mecum and Ellen Matlock, devised the idea of salvaging the timbers for installing this room in Memorial Continental Hall, which was then being built. Even the anchor was reused to create the room's chandelier, crafted by Samuel Yellin, a Polish immigrant, who later became the most important ironworker of the twentieth century. The stained glass windows depict Revolutionary War battles in New Jersey and were made by D'Ascenzo Studios in Philadelphia around 1925. On the walls hang oil portraits of the five New Jersey Declaration of Independence signers. G. Gerald Evans, who also made the furniture, crafted the Bible box on the table from *Augusta* wood as well. The box and the eighteenth-century cannon ball add further interest to the eclectic array.

▶ In the Delaware Period Room, originally installed in 1956, an imagined wisp of steam rises from a small pot of tea and teacup sitting on the corner of a circa 1750s writing desk beside a clay pipe and writing quill in this gentleman's 1780s study. Sticks of beeswax lay ready to seal the document spread on the desk's surface, and in the pigeonholes facing the writer are numerous other papers, carefully folded and filed. Over the desk, an eighteenth-century looking glass enhances the light from the dim candle. An upright chair, covered in a green check slipcover, lies pushed away from the desk, awaiting the gentleman's imminent return. The slipcovers reflect a seasonal change: a looser, cooler feel covering the red wool "moreen" or heavy, embossed upholstery underneath. The two-piece desk, called a "desk-on-frame," offered more mobility and was more economical because it used much less wood.

◄ Filled with useful domestic and cooking accessories from north to south and from Maine to Oklahoma, the Oklahoma kitchen represents that colonial gathering place where so many activities centered on the great open hearth. Completed in 1931, the room incorporates a fireplace crane and brickbats purchased from an old house on Providence Road near Media, Pennsylvania. The objects in the room represent late-eighteenth-and nineteenth-century cooking, baking, candle making, textile production, food preservation, dairy production, and laundry items.

► The Wisconsin Period Room uses mannequins to help interpret the earliest period of all the rooms—late seventeenth-century New England. This multipurpose room or "hall" might be used as a kitchen, dining room, sitting room, bedroom, nursery, office, or schoolroom, depending on the time of day. Despite the humble atmosphere of the room, the variety, quality, and number of objects suggest a fairly well-to-do family. The carefully crafted seventeenth-century cradle exhibits the same rectangular joined construction as the carved oak chest of Connecticut origin, which held the family linens and other fine objects. A reproduction crimson silk quilt and bracket clock also speak of relative affluence. The little family wears elaborate clothing, copied from early New England portraits, that incorporates fine imported wool trimmed in ribbon and fine lace. The youngest child's dress has "leading strings" on the back that were used to keep her nearby and lift her if she fell. The "pudding cap" device around her head helped protect it from a fall.

▲ The Texas bedroom reflects the German immigrant movement to the West in the nineteenth century, but the flavor of the room is distinctly Texas. A copy of a room from a mid-nineteenth-century house in Alleyton, Texas, the walls are hand-stenciled with designs found in the Lone Star State farmhouse using green, blue, and white paints reproduced using samples from the original bedroom. The room is full of Texas-made furniture with a German influence, such as the large pine wardrobe or "kleiderschrank." The pine cradle closely resembles those made in seventeenth-century Germany and in early German-American settlements.

▼ Many of the objects in the simple but elegant 1810 South Carolina bedchamber have histories in that state. The mahogany bedstead hung with white silk "pavilions" (to safeguard sleepers against mosquito-plagued southern summers) features a rice motif on the carved foot posts. A gorgeous white quilt with lavish fringe made in South Carolina circa 1830 complements the bed hangings. A rare child's bedstead, made about 1800 in the Saluda Valley of South Carolina, and a walnut bookcase and chest, descended from the Huger family of South Carolina, further illustrate the region's artistry. Green silk lines the bookcase doors to protect the contents from light. A nineteenth-century walnut and mahogany veneer washstand and 1820s washbowls at left and a lone brass candlestick, right, complete the spartan bedchamber.

William Smith and his wife, with the help of a young boy named Edward Hawkes, later one of the most prominent early settlers along the Oregon Trail. The last available log structure in the county, it is now owned by the City of Fairbury and stands at the west end of Fifth Street in the City Park. Meantime, the last log cabin and first schoolhouse in North Platte, Nebraska, was about to be destroyed when the Sioux Lookout Chapter saved and restored the building in March 1923.

Liberty Park in Salt Lake City boasts the oldest monument erected by the Utah Daughters, a drinking fountain given to the city by the Spirit of Liberty Chapter in 1905. In 1923, Spirit of Liberty Chapter dedicated a stone monument to the memory of Spanish Franciscan friar Sylvestre Velez de Escalante and his party of eight, the first white men to visit what is now Spanish Fork. They came in search of a direct route from Santa

The Way They Were

Those familiar with the period rooms of the DAR Museum may find it hard to envision them as offices for the daily workings of the National Society. In fact, many of the state organizations donated funds to sponsor a room in Memorial Continental Hall to help finance this incredible edifice that would gleam like the White House. With the addition of the Administration Building in the 1920s, period settings replaced office furnishings, and "modern equipment" such as telephones and file cabinets were removed. Reserving the rooms for display also minimized any damage to donated artifacts from more frequent use.

As the rooms were refurbished, each state selected a theme. The DAR Chairman of the State Rooms and the DAR Art Critics Committee then approved the theme and any furnishings. One of the first to be converted was the Indiana Room (formerly the President General's office), which initially became a colonial library. The DAR Museum period rooms continue to evolve. Some have done so dramatically, while others have been "frozen" in their original décor, reflecting the Colonial Revival era in American cultural history.

PHOTO BY E. L. CRANDALL

▲ Some of the "state" or "period" rooms began to evolve even as they remained working office spaces, like the Office of the Recording Secretary General pictured here approximately 1910, where staff worked carefully amidst objects scattered throughout the room, such as the Jacobean-style chair in which the woman at right is seated. Note the architectural detail of the neoclassical fireplace, beside which hangs a painting of Ellen Hardin Walworth. This space is now part of the Museum as the New York Period Room.

▼ Before its conversion to the Tennessee Room, elegant Colonial Revival furnishings collided with the practicality of early twentieth-century necessities, such as the safe, radiator covers, and electric light in this circa 1910 photo of the Treasurer General's Office in Memorial Continental Hall.

◄ The Georgia tavern exudes the spirit of 1776 and the Revolutionary War. Based on the "Long Room" of Peter Tondee's Tavern in Savannah, Georgia, the room is set for one of the historic secret meetings of the "Sons of Liberty," a society created in protest of the British Stamp Act. At the larger table, the men are eating oysters and meat pies with beer or hard cider. On July 4, 1775, the first Georgia Provincial Congress met at the tavern, and it was here that the Declaration of Independence was first read in Georgia on August 10, 1776. Sadly, Peter Tondee did not live to witness that moment. Although chosen as a delegate to the Continental Congress, he died in October 1775. However, his widow, Lucy Mouse Tondee, kept the torch of liberty burning, operating the tavern until 1783. The Georgia Daughters chose objects for the room that match the items listed on Tondee's estate inventory, such as the Windsor chairs, pewter, brass and iron objects, as well as 108 pieces of creamware, china bowls, and a delft punch bowl.

PHOTO BY SCOTT BRAMAN

▶ Some of the period rooms are an eclectic blend of that state's culture, as is the California Period Room pictured here. The room re-creates an 1860s parlor in one of Monterey Bay's oldest adobe houses and melds three styles: the Mexican adobe architecture; Chinese imports, as evidenced by the lacquered tilt-top table and the mantel vases; and American furniture from the East Coast, such as the rush-seated armchair and work table. The room is modeled after the Old Whaling Station in Monterey. Whaling implements and pictures emphasize the importance of the industry to early Monterey, like the early nineteenth-century spyglass resting on the window sill and the set of four 1814 engraved aquatints showing a whaling chase sequence on the wall at right. Local touches also dot the room, including the portrait of the lovely "Minnie" painted approximately 1856 by San Francisco artist William Smith Jewett. One of the maps beside the mantel depicts *Mexico, California & Texas* printed circa 1850.

PHOTO BY MARK GULEZIAN

PHOTO BY MARK GULEZIAN

▲ Instead of building a room around one period or scene, the Louisiana Gallery displays art and objects in an exhibition that reflects the state's rich cultural history and provides glimpses of domestic life interpreted through the lives of Louisiana women. Large gallery labels chart women's roles as wives, mothers, household managers, educational and religious instructors, and occasionally, financial providers. French émigré craftsmen working in New Orleans likely crafted the neoclassical or Grecian-style sofa, and Louisiana artisans also made the large armoire and sewing table in the far alcove of the gallery. On the walls are paintings of various Louisiana views and engraved maps, including one of particular interest entitled *Plan of New Orleans the Capital of Louisiana*.

▶ The original Kansas Period Room re-created a scaled-down version of the Sargent Chapel in the Congregational Church in Topeka. Stained-glass windows, removed from the 1911 Carnegie Library in Wichita before it was razed, provided the focal point of the chapel. Adorned with the sunflower, which grows wild in Kansas and which was adopted as the state flower in 1903, the windows represent the agrarian economy and religious spirit of its citizens. Religion played an important role in the lives of many early pioneers. This was especially true of the settlers of Kansas, who quickly established churches and religious schools and strongly supported such moral issues as the abolition of slavery and Prohibition. In 2004, the Daughters moved the Kansas Chapel to the stone hall in Constitution Hall, where it is accessible to many more visitors and has even been the site of a number of small weddings. The simple space also provides a quiet place for meditation or reflection.

PHOTO BY BREN LANDON

▲ One of the most notable early achievements of the North Dakota State Society was the preservation of the cabin that Theodore Roosevelt ordered built following his first trip to the North Dakota Badlands in 1883. The one-and-one-half-story cabin, complete with a shingle roof and cellar, was almost a mansion in its day, with wooden floors and three separate rooms, including the kitchen, living room, and Roosevelt's bedroom. Like the adventurer who built it, the Roosevelt cabin went on quite a road trip, appearing at the Louisiana Purchase Exposition in 1904 and returning to the grounds of the North Dakota state capitol in Bismarck where it stood unprotected for twenty years. The Minishoshe (now Minishoshe-Mandan) Chapter of the DAR adopted it in 1919, moved it to the grounds of the Liberty Memorial Building in 1924, and maintained it for forty years as a historic site before the State Board of Administration and the Legislature decided in 1959 that it should be moved to a more appropriate setting. Today the cabin is part of Theodore Roosevelt National Park.

Fe, New Mexico, to Monterey, California, and hoped to become better acquainted with the Indians inhabiting the region. The following year, this same busy chapter placed a bronze tablet at the entrance to the *Salt Lake Tribune* Newspaper Building, the site of a Pony Express station in the 1860s.

Also in New Mexico, a marker placed by the Thomas Jefferson Chapter, in Carlsbad, commemorates the circa 1890 Old Stone House, the first substantial dwelling in the area, built by Charles Bishop Eddy and his brother John Arthur, which became part of the Eddys' extensive ranch. The Eddy brothers' vision for the area inspired the

Then and Now

While some of the period rooms remain almost frozen in time since they were first furnished, others have evolved to showcase different types of rooms or to highlight certain collections. Not long ago, the Illinois State Society added welcome diversity to the types of period rooms in Memorial Continental Hall by converting their Colonial Revival parlor (inset right) to a mid-1800s bedroom (right). The Illinois "best" bedroom is now a cornucopia of colors, patterns, fabrics, and furnishings common during the 1840s.

The increased wealth and accumulation of personal property allowed the luxury of separating the bedroom from the previous multifunctional rooms of the past to afford a level of privacy that, during the eighteenth century, was virtually nonexistent. Even so, the best bedchamber was not just a place for sleeping. Women spent much time there birthing, nursing, and caring for children, as well as reading, writing, and sewing. In the scene depicted here, a young mother tends to her sewing, her thimbles and needles spread on the table, her sewing basket set beside her. Meanwhile, her little daughter has fashioned a grand pavilion and set up her own tea party from her mother's tablecloth.

On June 26, 1928, the New Hampshire State Organization voted to furnish a room in Memorial Continental Hall. While certainly a departure at the time from the theme of other period rooms, the New Hampshire Children's Attic, shown as it was in 1932 (left inset), is an austere shadow of the fun-filled room that exists today, as pictured left. A collection of children's furnishings, toys, and games spanning almost 150 years fills this room designed in the 1930s by Wallace Nutting, a New England collector, antiquarian, writer, and cabinetmaker. Planning it around an 1830s overmantel painting of two young girls from a house in Piermont, New Hampshire, he decided that the room "be done in panel work of the period 1770." The room represents a dramatic change in attitudes toward childhood and play, from early colonists' views that childhood behavior should be restricted to the development of playtime into a way of teaching developmental and social skills. Among all the period rooms, the New Hampshire Attic remains unique, appealing to both the young and young-at-heart.

▲ From 1910 until 1998, the Minnesota DAR owned and preserved the Sibley House, built in Mendota in 1835 by Henry H. Sibley, an agent in the lucrative fur industry. When Alexander Ramsey arrived in May 1849 to assume his duties as the first governor of the Minnesota Territory, he and his family were guests at the Sibley House where, on June 1, Ramsey issued the proclamation declaring the territory officially opened. The first laws of Minnesota were passed in the Sibley House and the first territorial legislature met here as well as the first territorial court. Reported to be the first stone house built in the territory, it is now owned by the Minnesota Historical Society.

establishment of Carlsbad (originally christened the town of Eddy), early irrigation, and the ultimate arrival of the railroad. In Albuquerque, the Madonna of the Trail Monument, whose guardian is the Lew Wallace Chapter, was the first placed on the National Register of Historic Places.

The New York Daughters are undeniably passionate preservationists. Eighteen different chapters own and have restored and furnished historic buildings as their chapter houses, and open them to the public for tours and events. From a 1695 Dutch stone house to a Georgian Revival row house, these historic structures represent hundreds of thousands of dollars invested by the New York Daughters to capture and celebrate the state's rich history.

▲ The last log cabin and first schoolhouse in North Platte, Nebraska, pictured here in an early photo, was about to be destroyed when the Sioux Lookout Chapter saved the building in March 1923. Constructed in 1867 by the Rowland family, it was still occupied by their descendants until 1922 when it was sold to the chapter, who paid to have it moved and restored. It is now part of the Lincoln County Historical Museum, where some of the pioneer relics displayed there have included items from the home of W. F. "Buffalo Bill" Cody and mementos of General George Armstrong Custer.

Although some states have a relatively small DAR presence, these Daughters have big hearts when it comes to preservation.

◄ States without period rooms at NSDAR Headquarters take advantage of historic properties elsewhere to showcase Colonial history. One example is the late eighteenth-century parlor, shown here, furnished by the Arkansas State Society at the Old State House in Little Rock, Arkansas. In 1911, the Arkansas Daughters rallied to save the historic building when it was no longer being used as the state capitol building.

▼ One of the most ambitious projects ever undertaken by a DAR state society is the Rosalie Mansion in Natchez, Mississippi, now headquarters of the Mississippi State Society. The mansion, a magnificent example of the Federal style of architecture, remains one of the state's most prestigious antebellum mansions. The Mississippi State Society purchased the house in 1938 and has lovingly restored and maintained it ever since. It sits on a high bluff overlooking the Mississippi River, the site chosen by the French for the first settlement on the river in 1716, and was named "Fort Rosalie" in honor of the Duchess de Pontchartrain. Peter Little built the mansion circa 1820–1823, using the design of his brother-in-law, James S. Griffin. Rosalie is visited by thousands of tourists each year.

▲ In 1924, instead of a single period room such as those at DAR Headquarters, the Rainier Chapter, Washington, in a salute to the state's namesake, constructed a replica of George Washington's entire home, Mount Vernon. The Rainier Daughters furnished many of the rooms appropriate to the Colonial era and use it as their chapter house. The chapter also incorporated itself and rents Rainier House for public functions, including weddings, luncheons, and receptions. Located in downtown Seattle, it transports visitors for a brief moment from the west coast to the east.

▶ For its chapter home and library, in 1958, the Aloha Chapter, Hawaii, purchased the circa 1914 home (pictured here) of Ernest Kopke, a Swiss-German merchant and sugar industry businessman in the Makiki district of Honolulu. In addition to providing an ideal location for chapter and state meetings, the home also houses the chapter's genealogical library, an important collection of books and reference materials numbering in excess of four thousand volumes, which the chapter staffs and opens to the public during regular hours or by appointment.

The Daniel Newcomb Chapter of the South Dakota Daughters preserved the building used by the Council of the First Dakota Territorial Legislature in 1862, now owned by the city of Yankton. And some chapters leave legacies despite being dissolved, such as the Paha Wakan Chapter, South Dakota, which funded the construction of a replica of the first schoolhouse in the Dakota Territory; and the Lake Voorhees Chapter in Wyoming, which preserved the first cabin in Niobrara County for use as its chapter house before the chapter disbanded. A city park now surrounds the cabin, which is maintained by the Niobrara Historical Society.

There are many more examples of such initiatives too numerous to name. More than half of the fifty state societies or their chapters either lease or own historic properties that not only serve as chapter meeting houses but are also open to the public. Visitors to the NSDAR headquarters get a glimpse of history in thirty-one rooms created specifically to preserve the past and present it to the public in a forum that appeals to all ages. For those who cannot make it to the nation's capital, there are historic buildings or sites preserved by the DAR in every state and the District of Columbia.

PHOTO BY BEVERLY PRZYBYLSKI

PHOTO BY ELAINE OLSON

▲ Oregon may have been far removed from the intensity of the Revolutionary War, but the roots of the state's pioneer settlers were strong, and Oregon formed its first DAR chapter—Portland's Multnomah Chapter—in 1896. Today, thirty-six chapters with over 1,600 members comprise the state society with a major focus on historic preservation. The Oregon Daughters own, operate, and maintain four museums: the reconstructed 1852 Robert Newell House and the Pioneer Mother's Memorial Cabin, both in Champoeg State Park, near Portland; the Dalpheus Schminck Memorial Museum in Lakeview; and the 1870s Dr. Charles Green Caples House in Columbia, pictured here. Caples, the first doctor in Columbia County, built this two-story, wood-frame house on the site of his father's log cabin overlooking the Columbia River. Descendants of the Caples family donated the house to the Mount St. Helens Chapter in 1959. It opened as a museum in 1970, and today, virtually unaltered and still offering an impressive view of the river, the eight-room house and several outbuildings occupy a full city block.

◀ In 1919, the Maricopa Chapter, in Phoenix, Arizona, recognized the need to preserve Arizona's fast-disappearing historic treasures and began a movement to establish a museum in Phoenix. Thirty other civic organizations had joined their efforts by 1923, and in December 1927, the Arizona Museum of History opened its doors in the adobe structure pictured here, designed by Phoenix architects Fitzhugh and Byron. On January 20, 1996, Phoenix voters chose the old museum to occupy the city's new history museum, renamed the Phoenix Museum of History, a 20,000-square-foot facility at the heart of the city of Phoenix's Heritage and Science Park. The Maricopa Chapter continues to support the museum's mission to collect, preserve, interpret and exhibit materials incident to the development of Phoenix and the Salt River Valley. ▼

phoenix
museum *of*
history

▲ The Nevada Sagebrush Chapter in Reno ensured that some acres of Fort Churchill are now part of the Fort Churchill State Park maintained by the State of Nevada. The adobe fort was built in 1860 and provided protection for the emigrant trail to California, along with the Central Overland Mail Route and the Pony Express. The Nevada Sagebrush Chapter deeded the land to the State of Nevada in 1961.

▲ The De Soto Chapter, in Tampa, Florida, still owns and maintains Tampa's first schoolhouse. Built circa 1858 by General Jesse Carter for his young daughter, Josephine Carter, this one-room building is believed to be the city's oldest surviving structure. City officials gave the historic little schoolhouse to the De Soto Chapter on September 8, 1931. At that time, it was moved to its present site on the west side of the University of Tampa, close to McKay Auditorium. The schoolhouse was added to the National Register of Historic Places on August 28, 1975.

Whether in Washington, D.C., across the country, or even overseas, the evocative spaces created and preserved by the DAR allow visitors to fully realize what it means to walk through time and almost touch the past. "Period rooms hold a significant place in the consideration of a people's social history," wrote antiques expert Liza Montgomery in her review of *Period Rooms in the Metropolitan Museum of Art* by James Parker and Amelia Peck. Sally Anne Duncan of Plymouth State University, a member of the Association for Museum History, adds, "Their accessibility and theatrical appeal to diverse audiences spoke to the founding spirit of America's museums to entertain and enlighten." Scenes of such authenticity and location seem to summon ghostly players as if conjured up by some dimly remembered memento. These spaces, which use the power of imagination to help the visitor form an emotional connection to our nation's history, are DAR gifts to America.

CHAPTER THIRTEEN

DAR Headquarters
A Stage for World Events

THE DAUGHTERS' VISION FOR THEIR MEETING PLACE was always that of "A great hall for lectures, addresses and general conventions of the Society . . . .", as expressed by Vice President Presiding Mary Virginia Ellet Cabell at the first Continental Congress in 1892. But they likely never imagined just how popular a meeting place their house beautiful would become, that millions of guests would eventually stream through when they opened the doors to their first new home in Memorial Continental Hall and later Constitution Hall.

Each year, more than 600,000 people pass through the doors of Constitution Hall, the largest concert hall in Washington, D.C. A popular venue for concerts and live performances, the biggest names in entertainment perform at the hall year-round. From Jane Goodall to Whoopi Goldberg, from Placido Domingo to Alex Trebek, and from the Washington Symphony to the National Basketball Association TeamUp Celebration, thousands of nationally and internationally known celebrities have graced the Constitution Hall stage over the years. It has also been the backdrop for numerous television specials, including the Country Music Association Awards, the Horatio Alger Awards, and HBO specials with Eddie Murphy and Whitney Houston. Of course, for one week every summer, the Hall serves its original purpose of hosting over three thousand DAR members for their annual convention, Continental Congress.

But the NSDAR headquarters complex became a stage for world events long before the construction of Constitution Hall. When it was announced that President Warren G. Harding would host a Conference on the Limitation of Armaments, to convene in Washington in conjunction with Armistice Day, the Daughters offered assistance "by placing Memorial Continental Hall at its disposal," wrote President General Ann Rogers Minor in a message to the members of the Society. "Our offer has been accepted and thus our beautiful build-

▶ The DAR Memorial Portico is a regular star in movies, television series, special events, and private affairs. Adjacent to the O'Byrne Gallery, it is one of the favorite NSDAR facility sites for private and corporate events, and is the only venue in town with a partially covered outdoor area with a view of a major Washington monument.

ing is likely to go down in history linked with an event which may be epochal in its issues," her message concluded. How prescient she would prove to be.

On November 12, 1921, President Harding opened the conference, which brought together the major Allied naval powers in Great Britain, France, Italy, Japan, and the United States, as well as other nations with concerns about Pacific territories— Belgium, the Netherlands, Portugal, China, and the British colonies. In the opening session, considered one of the most dramatic moments in American diplomatic history, Secretary of State Charles Evans Hughes shocked the delegates by going beyond platitudes and offering a detailed plan for arms reduction. Hughes, who led the United States delegation and presided at the conference, proposed the scrapping of nearly two million tons of warships and a moratorium on the construction of new ships. Over the next three months, the major Allied naval powers would produce nine treaties, agreements, and pacts to reduce the size and armament of their navies and ensure security in the Pacific. In 1972, Memorial Continental Hall was designated a National Historic Landmark because of that historic event.

▲ Secretary of State Charles Evans Hughes, seated at the small table in the center, signs the first arms limitation treaty on February 5, 1922, while other members of the American delegation witness the dramatic moment. The Conference on the Limitation of Armament was perhaps the most historic event ever to take place in Memorial Continental Hall. The carnage of World War I and the hugely expensive naval construction rivalry between nations created the need for arms control. In the summer of 1921, President Warren G. Harding sent invitations to key world leaders to attend the "International Conference on Naval Limitation." The Hall would require major modifications, but, at the invitation of President General Anne R. Minor, on November 12, 1921, the five principal naval powers, as well as other nations concerned over issues in the Pacific and Far East, convened the conference in Memorial Continental Hall.

The parade of dignitaries and important events at the new auditorium, Constitution Hall, would begin just seven years after the 1921 Arms Limitation Conference when First Lady Grace Goodhue Coolidge laid the cornerstone on October 30, 1928. Lou Henry Hoover, wife of President Herbert Hoover, did the honors as guest speaker at the formal dedication on April 19, 1929. The *Evening Star* hosted the first public event at Constitution Hall on October 26, 1929: an international oratorical contest with seven entries. Just one week later, the first musical event held at the Hall was on November 2, 1929, and featured Anna Case, Efrem Zimbalist, Sophie Braslau, and Hans Barth. Every president beginning with Calvin Coolidge has attended events at DAR Constitution Hall.

In an insightful move, the Daughters also invited the Honorable Charles Moore, Chairman of the National Commission of Fine Arts, to the laying of the cornerstone for Constitution Hall. In his remarks, he predicted: "For the highest form of music, the symphony concert, this auditorium will make suitable and adequate provisions. It may lead to a permanent orchestra. You may make it a platform for the world's thinkers, as well as a place to honor men of achievements." It was no coincidence that three years after the cornerstone ceremony in 1928, the National Symphony was founded, a venture made possible

PHOTO BY PEGGY MARTZ

PHOTO BY HARRIS & EWING

▲ On May 10, 1917, President Woodrow Wilson, honorary chairman of the Red Cross, announced the creation of a War Council to direct the efforts of the Red Cross and to launch a $100 million fund drive. In this photo taken May 21, 1917, President Wilson (second from left) pauses with members of the newly appointed War Council on the steps of the portico at Memorial Continental Hall. Pictured are (front row, left to right) Robert W. deForest, Vice President of the Red Cross; President Wilson; former President William Howard Taft; and Eliot Wadsworth, Vice Chairman of the Executive Committee of the Red Cross; (back row) Henry P. Davison, Chairman of the War Council; Grayson M. P. Murphy; Charles D. Norton; and Edward N. Hurley.

▲ Portions of the DAR buildings, both exterior and interior, so closely resemble the White House that they make frequent appearances in any number of movies and television series. Nine episodes from the award-winning television series *The West Wing* featured scenes on the portico, in the Pennsylvania Foyer, the Library, the O'Byrne Gallery, and several hallways. The O'Byrne Gallery became the set for a birthday party for First Lady Abbey Bartlet (Stockard Channing), and in another episode, President Josiah Bartlet (Martin Sheen) watched the fireworks (filmed earlier on the Fourth of July) from the Truman balcony (actually the Banquet Hall balcony). Another episode in the series portrayed the President's college-aged daughter being welcomed to the DAR as a member. The producers also filmed an Emmy-winning documentary on the series at the DAR complex, featuring interviews with the real members of the White House staff, including Betty Curie, President Clinton's personal secretary, and Dee Dee Myers, the first woman and youngest person ever to serve as White House Press Secretary. In this May 2000 photo, *The West Wing* cast members pose on the portico of Memorial Continental Hall: (clockwise, left to right) Bradley Whitford, Dulé Hill, Richard Schiff, Allison Janney, Janel Moloney, John Spencer, Martin Sheen, and Rob Lowe.

▲ On November 8, 2002, the DAR President General's Assembly Room was transformed into the White House "Situation Room" for the British Broadcasting Corporation series of the same title, starring both real members of President Bill Clinton's Cabinet as well as actors.

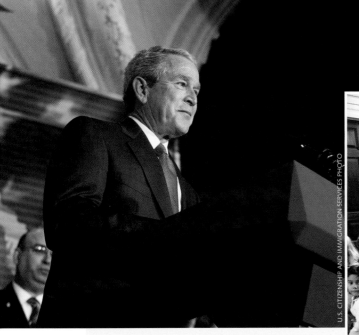

▲ ▶ Underscoring the Society's longstanding mission of nurturing good citizens, its headquarters often hosts naturalization ceremonies. On March 27, 2006, President George W. Bush delivered the keynote address in the DAR O'Byrne Gallery at a naturalization ceremony organized by the U.S. Citizenship and Immigration Services, where thirty new citizens took the Oath of Allegiance. In his remarks, President Bush thanked the Daughters of the American Revolution and DAR President General Presley Merritt Wagoner for hosting the event. Noting how fitting that the event was being held in the DAR building, the President stated, "I appreciate the work of patriotic organizations like the Daughters of the American Revolution. Some of the new Americans here today might have used *The DAR Manual for Citizenship* to prepare you for the citizenship test." He quipped to the new citizens that the manual "must be good because you passed." President General Wagoner, who greeted President Bush upon his arrival to DAR Headquarters, congratulated and visited with the new citizens at the close of the ceremony.

because it now had the spectacular Constitution Hall in which to perform. On January 31, 1930, the symphony performed its inaugural concert at the Hall, which would remain its home for forty years until 1971, when the symphony performed for the first time in its own concert hall, the new Kennedy Center for the Performing Arts.

The National Geographic Society also presented its popular lecture and film series at the Hall for over forty years, until modern technology and popular demand replaced the series with widely viewed television and cable television specials and lectures across the country. The lecture series included such notables as Hiram Bingham, a scholar, aviator, and explorer, as well as U.S. senator who, in 1911, with funding from the National Geographic Society, uncovered the fabulous Incan ruins of Machu Picchu and may have been the inspiration for the popular Indiana Jones character in contemporary books and movies. The series also featured aviator Amelia Earhart, who received a gold medal from the National Geographic Society presented by President Herbert Hoover at Constitution Hall for her solo flight across the Atlantic in 1932 and who would address the 1933 Continental Congress. In 1985, Constitution Hall, like its predecessor Memorial Continental Hall, was designated

▲ President John F. Kennedy, First Lady Jacqueline Kennedy beside him, shakes hands with Howard Mitchell, music director and conductor for the National Symphony Orchestra, prior to a concert at Constitution Hall circa 1962.

▼ Once again, NSDAR Headquarters became the backdrop for world affairs as participants at the G-7 Conference convened in the Banquet Hall, in Memorial Continental Hall, in April 2005. The forum of industrialized nations was established in 1975 to focus primarily on economic policy coordination. Chairman of the Federal Reserve Alan Greenspan is seated at the center on the left side of the table. To his left is Secretary of the Treasury John W. Snow. The term "G-7" refers to the "Group of Seven" nations represented at each forum. Originally a group of four—the United States, West Germany, France, and the United Kingdom—the group is now referred to as the G-8, expanded to include Japan, Italy, Canada, and, most recently, Russia. DAR Headquarters also hosted the signing of the U.S.-Oman Free Trade Agreement in January 2006.

▲ President Ronald Reagan quips with then–Vice President George H. W. Bush (far right) at an event in Constitution Hall in the 1980s. Secretary of Defense Caspar Weinberger is second from right.

a National Historic Landmark for its national significance in commemorating the history of the United States of America.

The array of luminaries who perform at Constitution Hall continues to grow, including such headliners as the British Royal Philharmonic and the Bolshoi Ballet, Tom Brokaw and Art Buchwald, Maria Callas and Van Cliburn, Leontyne Price and Lena Horn, and such old favorites as Bob Hope and Burl Ives. From highbrow to hard rock—from Frankie Avalon to Yo-Yo Ma, and from the B-52's, Jimmy Buffet, and Fleetwood Mac to Frank Zappa—the Hall has hosted them all. The two halls (one of which is now, of course, the DAR Library) are no longer the only popular sites at the DAR complex. Portions of it, both inside and out, so closely resemble the White House that it is a favorite location for filming movies and television specials and series, such as *Suspect*, starring Cher, and *The West Wing*. A popular Washington guidebook features the NSDAR in its chapter titled "Hollywood on the Potomac."

Although inconceivable now, initially the Daughters wrestled mightily with whether they should take on such an enormous project as the construction of Constitution Hall, having already invested so much in the construction of Memorial Continental Hall and the then-new Administration Building. Ultimately, of course, the Daughters voted to proceed. Their investment would

Marian Anderson's Legacy

On January 27, 2005, at the invitation of the U.S. Postal Service and the family of Marian Anderson, the National Society Daughters of the American Revolution co-hosted the unveiling of a commemorative United States postage stamp honoring the operatic and concert star at the Society's headquarters in Washington, D.C. There were so many in attendance for the event that cameras broadcast the ceremonies to the DAR Library to accommodate the overflow. Special guests included Deputy Postmaster General John M. Nolan, who dedicated the stamp; James DePriest, Anderson's nephew and Director of Conducting and Orchestral Studies at the Juilliard School; mezzo-soprano Denyce Graves; soprano Kathleen Battle; Dr. Allan R. Keiler, musicologist and Marian Anderson biographer; and performers from the Duke Ellington School of the Arts.

For many in the audience, the ceremony represented a touching time of healing and at last hopefully a happy ending to a painful chapter in history. As President General Presley Merritt Wagoner emphasized in her remarks:

> *Ms. Anderson's legendary concert on the steps of the Lincoln Memorial will always be remembered as a milestone in the Civil Rights movement. I stand before you today wishing that history could be re-written, knowing that it cannot, and assuring you that DAR has learned from the past. On this day we celebrate the life, the talent, and the legacy of Marian Anderson. America is a better place because of her dreams and her sacrifices. As a nation, we can be grateful that she opened so many doors for all those who follow; and, as an organization, the DAR is genuinely pleased to pay tribute to her memory.*

Although Marian Anderson would perform at Constitution Hall on numerous occasions from 1943 to 1969, including the first performance of her farewell American tour in 1964, in 1939 she was denied the opportunity to perform her Easter concert there. The years of outrage that would follow have often eclipsed not only the talents of Anderson but also the significant contributions of the DAR. In a February 2006 interview, Dr. Keiler, author of *Marian Anderson: A Singer's Journey* published in 2000, said, "The most important reason she and her family allowed me to have free access and were so open about documents is that I believed the same thing they did—that Miss Anderson's

▲ Honored guests applaud after the unveiling of the stamp commemorating Marian Anderson, one of the greatest classically trained singers of the twentieth century and an icon in the struggle of African Americans for racial equality. President General Wagoner emphasized in her welcoming remarks, "The beauty of Marian Anderson's voice, amplified by her courage and grace, brought attention to the eloquence of the many voices urging our nation to overcome prejudice and intolerance." Those pictured include (left to right) the Honorable Jukka Valtasaari, Ambassador of Finland, where Anderson enjoyed her first successes in Europe; civil rights pioneer Reverend Walter E. Fauntroy; soprano Kathleen Battle; Dr. Allan R. Keiler; James DePriest; Deputy Postmaster General John Nolan; DAR President General Presley Wagoner; ABC News reporter Angela Russell, ceremony emcee; mezzo-soprano Denyce Graves; and soprano Mattiwilda Dobbs.

connection to civil rights, to politics, overshadowed her greatness as a singer. That side, the artistic side, had grown dim compared to her symbolic status in life as part of civil rights. I wanted to restore balance and record her importance as a singer."

Keiler agrees that something similar happened to the DAR after the 1939 incident despite every effort they have made to right that wrong. He summed up the feelings of many of those at the stamp unveiling in 2005: "A lot of us, when we were invited, talked about the irony of it. It was exciting. We were very moved to be inside Constitution Hall. We didn't think of it as a place that was denied to her."

The President General's remarks were even more compelling to Keiler. "I was incredibly moved," he acknowledged. "It was very courageous. And they had gone to such effort to create this program for the stamp occasion, probably much more than most stamp dedications tend to be. My impression was that the DAR was very pleased to be able to do this, that the DAR is different now. The feeling I saw was pride. They wanted to do this for Marian Anderson."

▲ Marian Anderson performs at Constitution Hall on January 7, 1943, before a capacity audience of four thousand, "a third of them Negro," as reported in the January 25 Life magazine article published two weeks later. "Whites and Negroes sat side by side." Also filling the audience were Eleanor Roosevelt, Supreme Court justices, the Attorney General, ambassadors, senators, and cabinet members. Described the Life reporter, "When [Marian Anderson] walked out on the stage of Constitution Hall, as always, she sang simply and beautifully."

◀ "The National Geographic film lecture at Constitution Hall used to be *the* ticket in Washington, back in the '40s, '50s, and '60s," asserts Paul Guilderson, Constitution Hall Managing Director. "They had four or five presentations a week for 12 to 15 weeks every year. Each session was sold out." During one particularly exciting evening in the early 1930s, just outside the President General's Reception Room, Captain C.W.R. Knight (left), a well-known falconer, naturalist, author, actor, filmmaker, and showman, introduced his pet golden eagle to Dr. Gilbert Grosvenor (center), president of the National Geographic Society and editor of the magazine. Another of this majestic species would return to Constitution Hall on July 12, 2003, during the 112th Continental Congress when a golden eagle flew from the back of the seating area to the stage. The bird was a special guest of the Congress, along with Jonathan Wood (pictured in the more recent photo), who was honored that night with the NSDAR Conservation Medal for his organization, The Raptor Project, a wildlife education program employing rehabilitated birds of prey that cannot be returned to the wild.

▶ The NSDAR starred on the *National Geographic* "stage" in a 32-page feature article in the November 1951 issue. The lead article, by Lonnelle Aikman, featured twenty-nine photos, nineteen in "Natural Colors" by *National Geographic* photographers B. Anthony Stewart and John E. Fletcher. The National Geographic Society had close ties to the DAR beyond their use of Constitution Hall for more than forty years: Dr. Gilbert H. Grosvenor, long-time president and later chairman of the board of the National Geographic Society, was married to DAR member Elsie May Bell Grosvenor, daughter of Alexander Graham Bell. She belonged to both the Molly Pitcher and Chevy Chase Chapters.

▲ Soaring eagles projected on giant video screens set the stage for opening ceremonies at the April 2005 Horatio Alger Awards Dinner at Constitution Hall filmed for broadcast on PBS. Founded in 1947 by Dr. Norman Vincent Peale and Dr. Kenneth Beebe in honor of Unitarian minister and prolific author Horatio Alger Jr. (1832–1899), each year the awards honor ten community leaders whose remarkable achievements personify a deep-seated commitment to assisting those less fortunate than themselves. Honorees that year included astronaut Buzz Aldrin, Southwest Airlines president Colleen Barrett, and James W. Keyes, president and CEO of 7-Eleven, Inc. NSDAR President General Presley Merritt Wagoner stepped in to provide the invocation at the request of organizers when one of the dignitaries on the agenda could not attend.

succeed beyond their most modest projections, both for the Society and for the Capital City as well.

Constitution Hall and the many other facilities available at the DAR complex are such frequent destinations for sold-out performances and events that they are often assumed to be public buildings. While the Daughters built the DAR complex to accommodate their annual conventions and to carry out the work of the Society, they decided from the very beginning that, wherever possible, they would share their "house beautiful"— initially on a minimum "at cost" basis—with the people in the District of Columbia and surrounding areas as a service to the people. Today, the Daughters use the revenues realized from the use of all their various spaces to further their nonprofit mission to promote patriotism, preserve American history, and secure America's future through better education for young people.

The headquarters of the Society remains a stage for world events. Not long ago, the Dalai Lama lunched with Richard Gere in the O'Byrne Gallery. The Dalai Lama also spoke at Constitution Hall during the 2005 Mind and Life Conference held November 9, 2005, at the DAR complex. Kathie Lee Gifford was on hand for a recent Childhelp event, an organiza-

▲ President Bill Clinton arrives at DAR Headquarters for a meeting of the Democratic National Committee in 2001.

▲ With the hundreds of thousands of volumes of history and biography as backdrop, the DAR Library became the site of a taping January 19, 2001, to be broadcast in classrooms as part of the inaugural festivities for President George W. Bush. Students from New York and North Dakota questioned DAR member and First Lady Laura Bush, second from right, and Secretary of Education designate Dr. Roderick R. Paige regarding literacy and education initiatives proposed by the new administration. Dr. Paige would be confirmed as the seventh Secretary of Education just two days after the filming.

▶ First Lady Barbara Bush addresses students, faculty, and guests at a D.C. Public Schools graduation at Constitution Hall in 1990. The Hall, its marble columns and golden eagles lending an additional touch of ceremony, is a popular venue for graduations and hosts as many as three of them a day in June. School officials in Northern Virginia, Maryland, and D.C. have learned that the location in downtown Washington also draws more high-powered speakers than a gymnasium or football field. The back-to-back ceremonies fill the steps and street with guests and often lead to tense moments for DAR staff. With sometimes only half an hour to prepare the Hall for the next event, "We have no room for error," Paul Guilderson, Constitution Hall manager, said in a story in the *Washington Post* in June 2003. "Sometimes you might have a long-winded speaker up there, and it can get interesting."

tion whose mission to help abused children mirrors some of the DAR-supported schools. The O'Byrne Gallery has also welcomed various functions attended by such notables as Presidents George W. Bush and Bill Clinton, Maya Angelou, and Tommy G. Thompson, former U.S. Secretary of Health and Human Services. HBO filmed a portion of its 2006 special *Sometimes in April*, an account of the genocide in Rwanda, at the DAR complex.

In a fitting irony, for forty-eight hours in September 2003, the 17th Street exterior of Memorial Continental Hall was transformed to look like the White House, circa 1832, for a blockbuster movie starring Nicholas Cage, Jon Voight, Christopher Plummer, and Harvey Keitel released in 2004. In the opening scene, as a machine creates a pelting rain, a driver whips a horse-drawn buggy through the streets and then dashes into the circular driveway, reining the horses to a quick stop under the covered portico, a scene reminiscent of the early days of the hall itself. As the plot unfolds, America's most sacred and guarded document—the Declaration of Independence—is in jeopardy. While purely entertainment, much as art imitates life, the aptly named movie, *National Treasure*, mirrors the sentiment and the mission of the Society, to protect and preserve. Like the treasures housed in the DAR Library, Museum and Americana Collection, the historic landmark DAR Headquarters complex has also become a national treasure, preserved and shared by the Daughters to benefit the American public.

Washington Opera: Dramatic Transformation

One day in early 2003, Washington National Opera Director Placido Domingo arrived by limousine for a tour of DAR Constitution Hall. The opera company had been scouring Washington to find a suitable temporary home for their 2003–2004 season while the Opera House at the Kennedy Center was closed for renovation. Opera officials decided that Constitution Hall was the prime location, but presenting fully staged opera would require major modifications, including removal of 380 seats to accommodate an enlarged stage, installation of state-of-the-art cinematic projectors, and enhanced acoustics to help project the non-amplified voices and instruments. The arrangement meant that the Washington Opera would have a home for the season and Constitution Hall would receive extensive upgrading.

Because the Hall lacks an orchestra pit, the placement of the orchestra behind the stage provided the designers and directors the opportunity to stage the action closer to the patrons. In the absence of a traditional theater "fly" or rigging system normally used for quick changes in scenery and lighting, the use of cutting-edge projection created the dramatic sets.

Constitution Hall debuted as the Washington National Opera's temporary home on February 22, 2003, with the performance of *Aida*. In all, the Washington company performed six operas, including *Don Giovanni, Fidelio,* and *Die Fledermaus,* which starred June Anderson and Wolfgang Brendel and included cameo appearances by Supreme Court Justices Ruth Bader Ginsburg, Stephen G. Breyer, and Anthony M. Kennedy. The *Die Fledermaus* opening night performance was taped for broadcast on PBS; other performances aired on the National Public Radio network. The ambitious production of *Die Walküre*, starring Placido Domingo, signaled the opera's farewell to Constitution Hall and was hailed by the *Washington Post* as "the best production they have ever done."

Domingo gave the Hall glowing reviews as well, noting in the program for *Die Walküre* that the show "means saying goodbye to a venue which became dear to us because so many of the intrinsic challenges it presented became virtues." The lack of an orchestra pit separating the audience from the stage, "created a unique sense of intimacy and made the audience feel especially involved in the performance," he said.

▲ Opera greats June Anderson, left, and Wolfgang Brendel highlighted the cast of the lighthearted Washington National Opera production of *Die Fledermaus* performed at Constitution Hall, which served as the opera's temporary home from 2002 to 2003.

For Washington Opera, a Sound Decision

By TIM PAGE
Washington Post Staff Writer

DAR Constitution Hall, at 18th and D streets NW, was once the epicenter of classical music in Washington. It was not only home to the National Symphony Orchestra for that ensemble's first 40 years, but it has been the site of countless recitals by the great, the near-great and the long-forgotten, both before and after the Kennedy Center opened in 1971.

And now preparations are underway to make it the temporary home of the Washington Opera. On Feb. 22 the curtain will rise on a new production of Giuseppe Verdi's "Aida," conducted by Heinz Fricke, directed by Paolo Micciche, with Maria Guleghina in the title role. The opera company's move—roughly a mile to the east of its usual climes—is made necessary by the renovation of the Kennedy Center

See OPERA, C8, Col. 1

Placido Domingo and opera technical director Noel Uzemack check out the Constitution Hall changes.

BY ROBERT A. REEDER—THE WASHINGTON POST

▲ Washington National Opera star and artistic director Placido Domingo (left) and technical director Noel Uzemack are pictured discussing changes to DAR Constitution Hall in a February 2003 *Washington Post* article announcing the Hall as the opera's temporary venue during Kennedy Center renovations.

▲ Chris Matthews of *Hardball*, NBC's highly rated cable talk show, speaks at an MSNBC forum in the O'Byrne Gallery. The Beaux Arts design of many of the rooms at the DAR headquarters provides a perfect backdrop for Washingtonian events.

▲ ▶ Concert violinist, composer, and conductor Efrem Zimbalist (right) and contralto Sophie Braslau (above) performed at the first musical event held in Constitution Hall November 2, 1929. Hans Barth, renowned classical pianist, and Anna Case, the famous Finnish soprano, completed the talented quartet of artists that evening.

▲ On December 10, 1980, the Society opened the first major loan exhibition ever held at the DAR Museum Gallery. The three-month exhibit, The Jewish Community in Early America: 1654–1830, traced the origins and early history of Jewish individuals who played vital roles in the development of this nation. A standing-room-only crowd of over three thousand filled the DAR Library to hear former President Gerald Ford's dedication speech in which he observed, "It is fitting that the exhibition . . . be presented in this historic setting and before so distinguished a company. The work of Jews and the ideals of Judaism have enriched the American experience throughout our history. Almost to a man, the Jews supported the cause of independence." Pictured here with President Ford, Ambassador John L. Loeb Jr., New York investment banker and philanthropist, initiated the Jewish exhibit to honor his late grandmother, Adeline Moses Loeb, who was a DAR member and whose portrait, shown here, held a place of honor in the display. Ambassador Loeb (who served as ambassador to Denmark during the Reagan administration) approached several prominent organizations in Washington, including the Smithsonian, before finding a warm welcome for the exhibit at the DAR facilities. Stated Ambassador Loeb, "President General Patricia Shelby saw immediately the relevance of the exhibit to the DAR. It is thanks almost entirely to her insight and leadership that not only was the original exhibit brought to the DAR, it was broadened in concept and content." A smaller version of the exhibit originally opened at the historic Fraunces Tavern in New York City. It is interesting to note that almost forty years before, the DAR hosted another tribute to the Jewish community. Pictured is the program cover for the "Mass Memorial Dedicated to the Two Million Jewish Dead of Europe" held in Constitution Hall April 12, 1943.

◀ Academy Award–winning actress, singer, songwriter, and director Cher, seated at left, gets into character as cast and crew prepare to shoot a scene for the movie *Suspect*, filmed in the DAR Library and released in 1987.

Special Moments, Grand Affairs

An impressive complex between the White House and the World War II Memorial, the three adjoining NSDAR buildings present a significant presence in the downtown Washington community. Yet the popularity of Constitution Hall as a concert venue often overshadows the other two DAR buildings, leaving many visitors with the impression that the entire complex is Constitution Hall. Portions of the entire facility have always been available to the public, not only for period room and Museum tours, exhibitions, and Library research but also special events. Yet after a visit to the DAR complex, Washingtonians often comment, "I've lived here thirty years and didn't know this existed."

As part of its mission of education, under the administration of President General Dorla Dean Kemper, 1995–1998, DAR leaders endorsed a major initiative to properly introduce the public to all the Society has to offer, knowing that once the public saw what was inside, they would come back again and again. Since then, the demand on the facilities for private events has skyrocketed. The refined elegance and atmosphere of the historic buildings provide a rare, rich dimension to events for such national and international corporations as Sony, General Electric, Procter and Gamble, Booz Allen Hamilton, Toyota, Best Buy, Office Depot, Campbell's Soup, and several pharmaceutical companies and law firms, who often incorporate a docent-led tour of the thirty-one period rooms as part of a reception, banquet, or sit-down dinner. National real estate and lending corporations such as Akridge, Freddie Mac, and Sallie Mae find the DAR buildings the perfect setting for their functions.

The O'Byrne Gallery, with its barreled ceiling, herringbone hardwood floor, and original rams-head sconces and other rich furnishings, is requested most. Frequently engaged for large dinners and receptions, it also has been host to numerous government press conferences, filmings, weddings, and corporate meetings. The O'Byrne Gallery opens onto the partially covered, magnificent portico with its view of some of Washington's most notable monuments. Used together, the gallery and portico afford one of the most enviable locations in the Capital City.

Three assembly rooms offer meeting and conference space to accommodate from 75 to 180 people. The National Officers Club Assembly Room provides a quiet meeting space with rich architectural dimensions. High ceilings and a large skylight make it perfect for large lectures or corporate gatherings. The Connecticut Board Room, with gold-leaf moldings and crystal

▲ A special weddings edition of *InStyle* magazine featured the DAR complex as an elegant place for a wedding.

▲ A bride and groom share their first dance as husband and wife on the moonlit portico of the NSDAR. With the rich architecture and furnishings of the DAR as backdrop, weddings here become the stuff of fairy tales.

chandeliers, provides an impressive setting for small dinners or corporate meetings. Overlooking the White House Ellipse, with a splendid view of the National Christmas Tree and Menorah during the holidays, the Connecticut Board Room also offers lovely accommodations for small weddings. Tucked away on the second floor of the Administration Building, the President General's Assembly Room offers function as well as beauty for meetings, featuring not only a projection screen and Internet hookup, but also crystal chandeliers and items from the DAR archives.

The Banquet Hall on the third floor of Memorial Continental Hall, with its antique furniture, Oriental rugs, and Czechoslovakian crystal chandeliers, is the perfect stately setting for important meetings or intimate evening receptions. The Banquet Hall experience becomes even more unique with the doors opened to take advantage of the private balcony with its picturesque views of the Washington Monument and National Mall. The Daughters offered this space gratis for one event there in 1998. As Honorary President General Kemper remembers, "Senator Bob Dole asked if he could rent the Banquet Hall for a luncheon." The former senator, whose wife Elizabeth is a DAR member, had been appointed the volunteer co-chair of the World War II Memorial, and they planned to invite the presidents of the veterans organizations to a luncheon as the kickoff party to raise interest. "I told him we'd be delighted to

▲ The gilded Beaux Arts flavor and historic furnishings of the Pennsylvania Foyer evoke reverence and dignity at the most elegant occasion. At a stand-up reception, guests mingle in a surrounding of marble busts of Revolutionary War heroes and Martha Washington. Outside, the covered entrance to the elaborate foyer affords guests a most impressive first step into the O'Byrne Gallery and DAR Library.

have him as our guest," stated Kemper, who was then extended an invitation to the luncheon as well. "I left office suggesting to the next Executive Committee that DAR become very much involved," she recalls. President General Georgane Love, who succeeded her, asked Mrs. Kemper to chair the DAR World

Continued on next page

▲ Guests in black tie and evening gowns enjoy a formal candlelit dinner in the O'Byrne Gallery.

War II Memorial Committee, and ultimately the Daughters raised $500,000 to support the monument. During the dedication, as Senator Dole stepped off stage, he hugged Mrs. Kemper and whispered in her ear, "You know, Deanie, this all started at the DAR Banquet Hall."

As a nonprofit organization, the Society's home is a most attractive location for events sponsored by other philanthropic and humanitarian agencies, such as Ronald McDonald Charities, the American Red Cross (an NSDAR next-door neighbor), the Netherland-America Foundation, the Congressional Youth Leadership Council, and the National Endowment for the Humanities. Publishing and media interests like *USA Today*, *The New Yorker* magazine, and Harcourt Publishers often tie their special events to the educational, patriotic, and preservation themes of the Society where guests are surrounded by exquisite furnishings, art, and artifacts representing the richness of American history.

More and more brides choose the DAR facilities for their special day, be it a grand affair for hundreds or the most intimate ceremonies with only a handful of guests, where they can combine rooms for large receptions or divide spaces for smaller gatherings of family and friends. In addition to weddings and receptions, various rooms at the DAR buildings accommodate dinners, meetings, bar and bat mitzvahs, sweet sixteen parties, proms, graduations, and anniversary celebrations. At first glance, such gatherings seem contrary to the mission of preservation and exhibition that guide most museums and galleries. But the Daughters always intended that what they built and preserved would be shared, remembered, and celebrated. Just as the thirty-one period rooms tell the story of an earlier era, the DAR facilities continue to showcase the ever-evolving fabric of American culture, a living history of both everyday life and momentous occasions.

◀ The DAR Library becomes a stately setting for grand affairs for both heads of state and family gatherings, as well as diplomatic events and corporate functions. Its sparkling skylights, crystal chandeliers, lavish architecture, and graceful opera boxes that are ideal niches for musicians make the space perfect for the most elegant seated dinners and special occasions.

▲ Period furnishings and rich architecture, including those in the President General's Reception Room and DAR Library, became the perfect accessories for a fourteen-page photo spread in a 2001 issue of *Marie Claire* magazine featuring fashions in the "Capital style."

▼ As pictured in this *Washington Post* article in April 2002, National Security Adviser Condoleezza Rice realized a lifelong dream of being a classical pianist when she had the opportunity to perform a duet of Brahms' Violin Sonata in D Minor with renowned cellist Yo-Yo Ma at the National Medal of Arts awards ceremony at Constitution Hall.

▲ In addition to concerts, DAR Constitution Hall hosts many award ceremonies, speakers, and corporate functions. On the first year anniversary of 9/11, Muhammad Ali, pictured here, was one of the special guests at this 2002 event: "Washington, D.C., Honors America's Heroes of Freedom."

[The Washington Post]

The Arts
Television
Comics

Style

TUESDAY, APRIL 23, 2002

High-Powered Duet For Arts Medalists

Yo-Yo Ma Teams With Condoleezza Rice

By JACQUELINE TRESCOTT
Washington Post Staff Writer

On occasion, the annual presentation of the National Medal of Arts will have an impromptu performance moment. Bob Hope talked in 1995, and no one dared stop him. But usually the protocol at the official ceremony is a hug and handshake from the president and a gracious smile from the honoree.

Yesterday was a departure. Yo-Yo Ma, the celebrated cellist and one of this year's medalists, took the stage at Constitution Hall. That's not unusual

for him. But his musical partner this time was pianist Condoleezza Rice. Yes, that Condoleezza Rice—the one who is national security adviser. Even President Bush seemed amused by the combo. "Ma is performing with another world-renowned figure," said Bush, laughing slightly and looking toward the woman who is more familiar for staring down questioners on television news shows.

Without hesitation, Ma and Rice played a graceful movement from Brahms's Violin So-

See MEDALS, C2, Col. 1

Yo-Yo Ma, a co-producer of this year's Folklife Festival, performs with Condoleezza Rice at yesterday's arts and humanities medals ceremony at Constitution Hall.

BY MICHAEL DAME JR. FOR THE WASHINGTON POST

▲ ▶ Each Christmas, the DAR hosts its annual Open House, chosen by the *Washington Post Express* as one of the "top stops" for any holiday tour, where guests marvel at the beauty and size of the elegant DAR headquarters. Welcomed by the Daughters' warm hospitality, Open House guests often express awe at the extensive array of collections. Lavish lighting enhances the architecture outside while inside, early American decorations adorn the period rooms and other areas throughout the historic complex. Hundreds of guests take advantage of special docent tours and enjoy refreshments, often to the strains of musical ensembles performing carols from one of the opera boxes in the Library or in the Americana Room. The Pennsylvania Foyer, lavishly decorated and opened for this special time, affords visitors the breathtaking view of the National Christmas Tree and Pageant of Peace on the White House Ellipse.

▶ A popular Washington holiday tradition remains the flurry of free concerts at Constitution Hall. In addition to annual performances by the Army, Air Force, Navy, and occasionally the Marine Corps bands, other popular performers have included the Trans-Siberian Orchestra, Jim Brickman, Donny Osmond, Lorie Line, Dave Koz Smooth Jazz Christmas, and the Boston Pops Holiday Concert.

▶ The emblematic wheel on *Wheel of Fortune* took center stage, along with Pat Sajak and Vanna White, for three days in October 2000 when national audiences saw Constitution Hall for three weeks of the syndicated game show's series. It took fifteen tractor trailers of equipment and more than two hundred staff members to create the set—one of the largest staged in the Hall—which included a 50-foot-wide, 32-foot-high replica of the U.S. Capitol, a perfect fit between the columns of the stage. To show off the classic Constitution Hall dome and the gold eagles atop the columns, the designers set the lighting trusses at the height of the ceiling. Technical support included an extra 2,000 amps of power, 60-plus phone lines, and a 20-by-80-foot stage extension that required removal of the first few rows of seats. *Wheel of Fortune* executive producer Harry Friedman, who also produces *Jeopardy!*, declared it "the best location taping we have ever done." The Hall also hosted two engagements of *Jeopardy!*, in 1997 and again in 2004.

▲ Constitution Hall rocks with the performance of comedian Chris Rock during this HBO special that aired on April 17, 2004. At the DAR complex in 2003 while filming the movie *Head of State*, produced by and starring Rock, the comedian asked to see the Constitution Hall stage where his friend Eddie Murphy had performed previously.

In a sampling of recent performances at Constitution Hall, Dizzy Gillespie (right) is joined by David Amram (left) and Percy Heath at a Thelonious Monk Tribute; Dolly Parton charms as always; the R&B group the Whispers has the crowd on their feet during a recent performance; Grammy-winning Alicia Keys sings from her soul; rhythm and blues icon Bonnie Raitt demonstrates some of her well-known soul-stirring slide guitar techniques; and the U.S. Air Force Singing Sergeants stir hearts with their patriotic talents.

PHOTO BY MICHAEL WILDERMAN/JAZZ VISIONS

PHOTO COURTESY OF WASHINGTON POST

PHOTO BY MARK GULEZIAN

MICHAEL HOLZWORTH PHOTO COURTESY OF U.S. AIR FORCE BAND

PHOTO BY LAURA FAPR/AD MEDIA

Constitution Hall: Casts of Thousands

▲ Sheryl Crow performs at Constitution Hall as part of the National Basketball Association All-Star Weekend events sponsored by TNT and TBS in February 2001.

Performing Artists

Aerosmith	Quincy Jones
Alabama	The Judds
Tori Amos	R. Kelly
Marian Anderson	Kenny G
Frankie Avalon	Alicia Keys
Burt Bacharach	Chaka Khan
Joan Baez	B.B. King
Anita Baker	Gladys Knight
The Bangles	Lenny Kravitz
The Beach Boys	Patti Labelle
The Bee Gees	Barry Manilow
Harry Belafonte	Ricky Martin
The Black Crowes	Johnny Mathis
Mary J. Blige	Meatloaf
Toni Braxton	John Mellencamp
Brooks and Dunn	Van Morrison
Buena Vista Social Club	Willie Nelson
Jimmy Buffet	Wayne Newton
Johnny Cash	Ozzy Osbourne
Ray Charles	Dolly Parton
Natalie Cole	Peter, Paul and Mary
Elvis Costello	The Pointer Sisters
Crosby, Stills & Nash	Bonnie Raitt
Sheryl Crow	REM
Miles Davis	Smokey Robinson
Sammy Davis Jr.	Kenny Rogers
John Denver	Diana Ross
The Doobie Brothers	Santana
The Doors	Carly Simon
Bob Dylan	Paul Simon
The Eagles	Nina Simone
Earth, Wind and Fire	Frank Sinatra
Duke Ellington	Britney Spears
Melissa Etheridge	Bruce Springsteen
Roberta Flack	Steve Miller Band
Fleetwood Mac	Sting
Ella Fitzgerald	James Taylor
The Four Tops	The Temptations
Aretha Franklin	Jethro Tull
Jerry Garcia	Tina Turner
Dizzy Gillespie	U2
Josh Groban	Luther Vandross
Herbie Hancock	Dionne Warwick
Isaac Hayes	Barry White
Whitney Houston	Stevie Wonder
The Isley Brothers	Tammy Wynette
Billy Joel	Yo-Yo Ma
Elton John	Frank Zappa

Symphonies

Boston Symphony Orchestra
British Royal Philharmonic
French National Orchestra
Israeli Symphony
Japanese Symphony
London Philharmonic
Moscow Philharmonic
National Symphony Orchestra
New York Philharmonic
Philadelphia Symphony

Comedians

Tim Allen
Bad Boys of Comedy
George Carlin
Bill Cosby
Rodney Dangerfield
Steve Harvey
Bob Hope
Jay Leno
Eddie Murphy
Tyler Perry
Richard Pryor
Joan Rivers
Chris Rock
John Stewart
Robin Williams

Speakers

Muhammad Ali
Tom Brokaw
Walter Cronkite
Dalai Lama
Jane Goodall

Corporate Functions

America Online
FBI
Ford Motor Company
IBM
MasterCard
Microsoft
NBA
NEA
World Bank

Dance

Ballet Folklórico de México
Bolshoi Ballet

Opera

Placido Domingo
Irish Tenors
Luciano Pavarotti
Washington Opera

Choir

Vienna Boys Choir
Mormon Tabernacle Choir

Other

Jeopardy!
Wheel of Fortune
Horatio Alger Awards Ceremony
NAACP Awards Show

CHAPTER FOURTEEN

Continental Congress
An Affair to Remember

Once each year, the Daughters briefly close their doors to the public and reclaim their "house beautiful" for the purpose for which it was originally built. That is when Constitution Hall becomes a stage where the Daughters and their guests celebrate a year's worth of accomplishments and honor outstanding Americans. Some three thousand members flock to their home on 1776 D Street overlooking the Ellipse. The DAR Library churns with members hunting for new patriot ancestors and helping others become members. Some undertake historic research in general, perhaps for events, markers, and historic buildings that are projects of their local chapters. Officers and committee chairmen report on the business of the Society, and forums provide updates on ongoing initiatives. Daughters also take the place of tourists, visiting the period rooms and the latest exhibits in the Americana Room and DAR Museum Gallery.

Both a homecoming and a reunion, the halls bustle with members renewing old acquaintances and meeting new members of this extended family of Daughters of the American Revolution. "I ask members if they've been to the headquarters and, if they say 'no,' then I tell them that it's worth the trip at least once just to see this spectacular building," said Beth Pomponio of Ye Olde Newton-Nassau Chapter in New Jersey. "This building is a reminder of what women can do. Every corner has something to be explored. Every inch is pure beauty."

This formal gathering, the DAR Continental Congress, is the annual national meeting of the National Society Daughters of the American Revolution. The membership of the Society blossomed so quickly that the leadership realized immediately they needed a national assembly to communicate with the chapters, especially in the days when commu-

▶ Framed by the doors to the Constitution Hall auditorium, the DAR Chorus, led by Jennifer Woodrow, performs at the 2005 Congress. "The most memorable experience for me was singing in the All-American DAR Chorus," recalls member Paula-Jo Cahoon, a member of the Linares Chapter, in San Diego, California, of her first Continental Congress. "After days of practice, nothing surprised me more than standing in the tiers among 220 voices when the 'Star-Spangled Banner' was sung. Every voice was strong and filled with conviction. It was just beautiful. Right then and there I knew why I would always be a member of the DAR."

PHOTO BY CONVENTION PHOTOGRAPHY SERVICES

▲ The United States Navy Ceremonial Band entertains the Daughters and their guests filling the Hall during the 115th Continental Congress, June 30, 2006.

▲ The lovely Memorial Continental Hall was finally complete, and impressive paintings provided a historic backdrop when, during each year of his administration from 1909 to 1913, President William Howard Taft addressed Continental Congress. President General Julia G. Scott, third from left seated at the table at left, looks on.

nication wasn't so easy. Named after the original Continental Congress that governed the American colonies during the years of the American Revolution, it too is democracy in action. Just as the executive and legislative bodies of American government work together to govern the people, so too does the DAR Continental Congress bring together those delegates chosen by their chapters and states to elect DAR national leaders, discuss and enact bylaws, and set the course for the Society at large, as proposed by the National Board of Management. "It is a delegate body, each chapter having representation, and every State a regent entitled to a seat and vote in the D.A.R. Congress," wrote Emily Sherwood and Mary Lockwood in the 1906 *Story of the Records*.

Social, ceremonial, and substantive, Continental Congress brings the Daughters together to celebrate the year's accomplishments; honor renowned leaders, young scholars, and good citizens; and make plans for the upcoming year. It is a time when Daughters from around the world can report their progress, express their patriotism, and rejuvenate themselves for the service work they provide in their local communities.

Pageantry and patriotism set apart the evening sessions from the breakfasts, luncheons, teas, and business meetings. The daytime meetings allow the Daughters to roll up their sleeves for a cross-pollination of ideas for fundraising, school programs, special community events, and other initiatives that further the mission of the Society. "My favorite thing about Continental Congress turned out to be networking with other DAR members," revealed Ardmore, Oklahoma, Chapter member Diane Brannum Hamill of her first attendance at Continental Congress after being a member for twenty-five years.

"It wasn't the gala evenings, though they were truly splendid," reflected Jeanney Lu Scott Horn, a member of the Arapahoe Chapter, of Boulder, Colorado, after attending the 2005 Continental Congress. "Those of us in attendance were excited to share our triumphs and failures." Estrella Chapter Regent, Frances B. Rakestraw, of Arizona, echoes that sense: "It is Daughter-to-Daughter exchanges that bring information, hints, and enrichment to mind and body and soul. Hearing what some 170,000 women can accomplish is exalting and motivating. One realizes that DAR has an important role to play."

On opening night, in a pageant of patriotism, pages in white parade the flags of the fifty states and foreign countries and escort the President General and members of the National Board of Management to their seats on the stage. In a tradition begun with the laying of the cornerstone for Memorial Continental Hall, "The President's Own" United States Marine Corps Ceremonial Band performs on opening night at every

▲ Cokie Roberts, keynote speaker for the 114th Continental Congress, pauses with DAR member Shelby Ward in the President General's Reception Room prior to opening night ceremonies July 6, 2005. Roberts, senior news analyst for National Public Radio and political commentator for ABC News, shared reflections from her book, *Founding Mothers: The Women Who Raised Our Nation*. Roberts' mother, Congresswoman Corinne Claiborne ("Lindy") Boggs (a DAR member) was the first woman elected to the U.S. House of Representatives. Shelby Ward serves on the Marshall Committee, one of over thirty Congress Committees on which hundreds of members serve to manage the behind-the-scenes logistics of the annual convention.

◄ Winners of the 1992 National DAR Service for Veteran-Patient Awards presented at Continental Congress included George T. Gentry Jr., Outstanding Veteran-Patient and a paraplegic Vietnam veteran who helped establish accessibility for handicapped students at California State University and a computer learning center at the Long Beach Veterans Affairs Medical Center. Also pictured are Ida Cook Klages (left), recipient of the Outstanding DAR Veterans Affairs Voluntary Service Award for her work supporting hospitalized veterans; Rebecca Jo Knapp (center), Outstanding Youth Volunteer, also recognized for her efforts at a local VA Medical Center; and Billie Walters Ettling, National Chairman, DAR Service for Veteran-Patients Committee.

▲ By 1924, just fourteen years after completion of Memorial Continental Hall, the body politic of the NSDAR so filled the hall in this April 14, 1924, photo that one of the resolutions passed at the 33rd Congress that year was authorization of the President General, Lora H. Cook (pictured seated at the table at left), to proceed with tentative plans for building a bigger auditorium on the vacant land facing 18th Street. The following year, the Daughters were forced to split their meetings between the Washington Auditorium and their beloved Memorial Continental Hall. Even so, some four hundred delegates and all the alternates had to stand in the hall during sessions.

Continental Congress. For the next few nights, Daughters and their guests hear remarks from inspirational speakers, authors, and leaders; are entertained by world class musicians; and honor those selected as DAR Medal of Honor, scholarship, Good Citizen, and other award winners through various levels of competition. From presidents to pioneers, the list of appearances includes nearly every president since Benjamin Harrison, either in person or through a personal letter or videotaped greetings. Lynne Cheney, Senators Elizabeth and Robert Dole, actor and diplomat Shirley Temple Black, and aviatrix Amelia Earhart also top the list of notables.

Rituals at Continental Congress reinforce the Daughters' mission and bind them as one Society, energizing them for the coming year as they return home and share their Congress experiences with their fellow members. "When we arrived at Constitution Hall, we were awed by the beauty and the ele-

▼ Although the Daughters held their first Continental Congress in Memorial Continental Hall in 1905, it remained incomplete in 1906, as can be seen in this photo of the opening session of the 15th Congress.

An "Old Soldier" Visits

In a startling turn of events that kept the Daughters riveted during the unfolding of the 60th Continental Congress, one special guest would honor the Society with his appearance April 19, 1951. The Daughters were well aware that President General Marguerite C. Patton had invited General Douglas MacArthur to speak at the Continental Congress, but there had been no confirmation. Anticipation built over the opening days of Congress as they awaited word but dared not hope, since the General would be in Washington only one day, his first time in the continental United States in eleven years.

On Wednesday, April 18, at 1:30 p.m., the assembled Daughters erupted in a reverberating ovation when President General Patton announced that the General would speak the following day at 3:00 p.m. What they did not know was that the remarks he would deliver April 19 to the U.S. Congress and to the entire nation via radio would become one of the most famous speeches in U.S. history. It would be his farewell address, his "Old Soldier's Speech" following his removal as General of the Army by President Harry S. Truman. Daughter Dora Barhydt Hotaling of the Buekendaal Chapter, New York, attending her first DAR Continental Congress, would later recall:

> The Hall and corridor had been equipped with radio speakers so that all could hear General MacArthur's address at the Capitol. The corridors were quiet, very quiet, almost reverent, as we stood there with many others listening. [T]he General concluded his address with the words which will live in history . . . "like the old soldier of that ballad, I now close my military career and just fade away, an old soldier who tried to do his duty as God gave him the light to see that duty. Good-bye."

"There was not a dry eye in those corridors," wrote Hotaling, as Daughters slowly and somewhat mournfully made their way to their seats to await his visit to Continental Congress just two hours after his history-making speech.

The General, his wife Jean Marie Faircloth MacArthur, and their son Arthur were escorted to the stage where he delivered these remarks:

> When I heard from your President General that this distinguished group would be in session today, I determined to stop by to avail myself of an opportunity I have long

▲ Daughters surround General Douglas MacArthur, his wife Jean Marie Faircloth MacArthur, and their son Arthur during the General's visit to Constitution Hall to deliver his address to the 60th Continental Congress in 1951. Second from right is President General Marguerite Patton. General MacArthur had given his farewell address to the U.S. Congress just hours before.

> sought personally to pay you the tribute that is in my heart. Of all the great societies of the country during the past century, I know of none which has fought more diligently for the preservation of those great ideals which bulwarked our forefathers in their efforts to secure and preserve freedom. We have drifted far away and to a dangerous degree from the simple but immutable pattern etched by our forefathers. It behooves this distinguished society to assert a dynamic leadership in checking this drift and regaining the ground which we have lost. In this hour of crisis, all patriots look to you. Good-bye.

At the close of the 60th Continental Congress, the minutes recorded that General MacArthur's visit was probably the most important event ever to occur in the DAR Hall. Recorded Dora Hotaling, "At the closing banquet on Friday evening, a delegate arose to ask that the word 'probably' be struck from the minutes. This suggestion was applauded into action." Certainly, it was one of the events that would signify Constitution Hall as a historic landmark.

gance it gave to Opening Night, with ladies and gentlemen in evening dress, pages, and committee women hurrying about to see that everything was in place. National Defense Night and DAR Schools reports were so touching and memorable and filled us with joy to be a part of this great National Society," recalls Carole D. Gloger, of the New Orleans Chapter, after attending the 114th Congress.

"Something happens to everyone who goes [to Congress]" observed Char Edson, National Continental Congress Chairman. Edson tells the story of Tony Snow, White House Press Secretary, broadcaster, and newspaper columnist, who spoke at the 2003 Congress: "He was so impressed by the membership and their patriotism, he called home and said he wouldn't be home for dinner." At the President General's reception later that evening, Snow said, "'I've really enjoyed this,' and you could tell he had," Edson remembers. "It's just overwhelming and so much more than they pictured," she reasons.

At their own expense, the Daughters have come together every year but one since 1892. The first was held at the Universalist

▲ The dramatic unfolding of the American flag from the ceiling of Constitution Hall on the opening night of Congress, seen here circa 1958, thrills attendees to every Congress. The only resolution passed by the first Continental Congress concerned respect and honor for the flag, and the flag drop remains one of the highlights of the annual gathering. Whether the guest is eighteen or eighty, this moment never fails to inspire. As Chapter Regent Margaret Robinson, of the Major Nathaniel Mitchell Chapter, Georgetown, Delaware, recalls from the 2004 Congress. "I was seventy-five years old, and it was my first time at Continental Congress. I had heard about the flag coming down from the ceiling, but nothing could have prepared me for the thrill and awe I felt as it came down from above and floated over the Daughters as the President General walked down the aisle to mount the stage and take the podium. There were goose bumps all over my goose bumps!"

▶ Each year on the opening night of Congress, one of the armed forces bands plays a special piece of music written especially for the Daughters—the "Daughters of the American Revolution March," composed in 1904 by J. Bodewalt Lampe, whose wife was a member of the Society.

▲ Shirley Temple Black, one of the honored guests at the 1993 Continental Congress, describes the size of her Oscar following her introduction by President General Wayne G. Blair, right.

▲ Amelia Earhart was keynote speaker at the 42nd Continental Congress in 1933, one year after her successful solo flight across the Atlantic. She is pictured here in 1932, shortly after her flight, with Mayor James Walker of New York, where the city honored her with a ticker-tape parade. In her speech to the Continental Congress, she made a bold statement that is still being debated today: "I feel that equality with men is essential in all our activities. I, therefore, feel that women should be drafted in war, if such a thing should occur." She received a hearty round of applause from the Daughters.

► President Dwight D. Eisenhower would address sessions of the DAR Continental Congress on more than one occasion. On May 19, 1947, while serving as Chief of Staff of the U.S. Army, he addressed the Daughters on the first evening of Congress. In his remarks, Eisenhower cited a portion of the DAR National Bylaws, which state "To cherish, maintain and extend the institutions of American freedom, to foster true patriotism and love of country, and to aid in securing for mankind all the blessings of liberty." To this he added, "So long as this membership lives in that high purpose and so long as it devotes its efforts to interpret that purpose faithfully before the world, it will be an effective implement toward democracy's unity and the worldwide extension of its humanitarian principles. It will remain worthy of the great American traditions that you have been organized to perpetuate." Eisenhower would address the full assembly of the Continental Congress on April 22, 1954, his second year as president and the same year this picture was taken by the *New York Times*.

Church of Our Father, a small edifice at the corner of 13th and L streets. In 1905, they celebrated Congress in their new home at Memorial Continental Hall. Twenty-four years later, in 1929, the annual meeting of the Daughters moved to the newly completed Constitution Hall. In 1941, because of the press of people in Washington involved with the business of war, the Chicago Chapter welcomed the Daughters to their city for the 51st Continental Congress in 1942. The 52nd Congress met in Cincinnati, Ohio; the 53rd in New York City, in 1944. In 1945, in compliance with the United States government's request that all organizations call off their annual conventions, for the first and only time, the NSDAR cancelled its Continental Congress, what would have been the 54th. The National Board of Management also voted to cancel all state conferences that year. Both actions were taken for the "added comfort and convenience to our servicemen traveling to and from their line of duty," as thousands upon thousands of soldiers and sailors returned home from the war. The Daughters met in Atlantic City, New Jersey, for the 55th Congress in 1946 and returned to their Washington home in 1947.

Despite moves to no less than eight different venues, including a church, a movie theater, an opera house, Memorial Continental Hall, and finally Constitution Hall, the mission

▲ The DAR Chorus has become a fixture at Congress. In this 1941 photo, Alice Beck Haig, who would later become Vice President General and Treasurer General, leads the chorus in a rehearsal for the 50th Continental Congress.

▲ To commemorate its centennial of service in 1990, the NSDAR created Centennial Medallions to be awarded to only nine "Women Worthy of Honor." At the 1990 Continental Congress, the Society presented Medallion Number 1 to First Lady Barbara Bush to honor its long affiliation with the First Ladies of the White House. The other recipients honored that night included Sandra Day O'Connor (pictured at right), the first woman appointed to the Supreme Court; Admiral Grace Hopper, pioneer computer scientist; Jeane J. Kirkpatrick (second from left), the first woman to serve as the United States Representative to the United Nations; Marian Anderson, world-acclaimed singer and civil rights symbol; Elizabeth Pfohl Campbell (second from right), founder of WETA, greater Washington's educational public television and radio station; Shirley Temple Black, child movie star, international volunteer, and former ambassador to Ghana; Elizabeth Hoysington, the first woman Army Corps Officer; and Catherine Filene Shouse, who founded the Wolf Trap Foundation for the Performing Arts and was the first woman to receive a Masters of Education from Harvard as well as the first woman appointed to the Democratic National Committee.

American's Creed

In 1917, Henry Sterling Chapin of New York, Commissioner of Education of New York State, conceived the idea of promoting a contest to write an American creed, a brief summary of American political faith reflecting distinctly American history and tradition. Mayor James H. Preston of Baltimore, Maryland, offered a $1,000 prize since Maryland was the birthplace of the National Anthem.

Thousands of entries poured in, and the contest was in its final days when someone suggested to William Tyler Page that he consider entering. Page was serving as clerk of the House of Representatives in Washington. Incorporating passages and phrases from the Declaration of Independence, the Preamble to the Constitution, the Gettysburg Address, and the words of Daniel Webster, Page said of his 100-word entry: "It is a summary of the fundamental principles of American political faith as set forth in its greatest documents, its worthiest traditions and by its greatest leaders." In March 1918, the selection committee notified Page that, out of more than three thousand contestants, his was the winning entry.

Twenty-four years later, on Sunday evening, October 18, 1942, Page was a guest of the Daughters of the American Revolution at the fiftieth anniversary celebration of the Pledge of Allegiance. He led the recitation of the American's Creed. It was his last public act. He died the next day, and the House of Representatives adjourned in his honor. He had worked at the United States Capitol for sixty-one years. His creed, created for America, remains a solemn annual rite of the DAR Continental Congress and at DAR meetings around the globe. Jane Page Hibbits, a DAR member and granddaughter of William Tyler Page, has on occasion led the American's Creed at Continental Congress.

I believe in the United States of America as a government of the people, by the people, for the people; whose just powers are derived from the consent of the governed, a democracy in a republic, a sovereign nation of many sovereign states; a perfect union, one and inseparable, established upon those principles of freedom, equality, justice, and humanity for which American patriots sacrificed their lives and fortunes.

I therefore believe it is my duty to my country to love it; to support its Constitution; to obey its laws; to respect its flag; and to defend it against all enemies.

▶ More than one of the roots of the family tree of William Tyler Page (pictured in inset) went back to patriots of the Revolution, including John Page and Carter Braxton, one of the signers of the Declaration. On October 12, 1955, dignitaries and family members gather at the dedication ceremony of the memorial tablet erected by the NSDAR honoring the memory of William Tyler Page at Oak Hill Cemetery, Washington, D.C. Pictured are (left to right) the Honorable Edith Nourse Rogers, representative from Massachusetts and a DAR member; Katherine Glascock Cory, Historian General; President General Gertrude S. Carraway; and Page's descendants, Mary E. Page and Elizabeth Tyler Page.

of the organization remains the focus of every Daughter who attends Continental Congress. Next year, and the year after that and the year after that, the foyers and halls of the DAR Headquarters will buzz with the business of Continental Congress. Once again, first-time attendees will gasp at their first sight of Memorial Continental Hall, Constitution Hall, and the entire DAR complex: "We own all that?!" as one new Daughter exclaimed. More than three thousand members will come to "an ample auditorium, a hearthstone around which shall gather the Daughters from the North, the South, the East, and the West, even from the islands of the sea, where each shall find a greeting, a welcome home," predicted President Cornelia Fairbanks at the dedication of Memorial Continental Hall. Both newcomers and veterans of Continental Congress will "go home inspired and anxious to begin a new year of DAR action," as did Nancy Lynn Gum of the Massanutton Chapter, Harrisonburg, Virginia.

"Each annual meeting brings to the Congress many new members . . . concerned only with the interests of their own locali-

▲ Representatives from many national service, patriotic, and lineage organizations, such as the Sons of the American Revolution, bring greetings each year to the Daughters at Congress. But no tradition is more precious than the appearance by the two young ambassadors from the National Society Children of the American Revolution dressed in Colonial attire to represent the forefathers and mothers, like these pictured at the 1949 Continental Congress.

▶ Senator Robert J. Dole, shown here visiting with President General Dorla Dean Kemper, would address the Opening Night Ceremonies of the 108th Continental Congress on April 19, 1998. As National Chairman of the World War II Memorial Campaign, he spoke that night on the progress of a project with which the DAR would become a strong partner. The following year, he made another guest appearance at Congress, to accept the DAR donation to the World War II Memorial.

▲ In addition to the annual Continental Congress, Daughters gather each year at their respective state conferences, where they also honor individuals for their singular achievements. In this 1986 photo, President General Ann D. Fleck congratulates heavyweight boxing champion Larry Holmes after presenting him with the DAR Medal of Honor at the Pennsylvania Daughters' state conference.

▲ This lighthearted depiction by Polly Keener of President Georgane Ferguson Love and her executive officers accurately captures the challenge that awaits each new administration. The day after the election, the new executives take office.

▶ National Defense Chairman Helen D. Mitchler (left) and President General Presley Merritt Wagoner (center) present General Peter Pace, United States Marines, Chairman of the Joint Chiefs of Staff with the DAR Patriot Award during National Defense Night at the 115th Continental Congress in 2006. General Pace accepted the DAR Patriot Award on behalf of the nation's service members. Other military members honored that night included Lieutenant Thomas E. Ceremuga, who received the Dr. Anita Newcomb McGee Award for his service as an Army Nurse Corps officer and educator; and Sergeant Leigh Ann Hester, winner of the Margaret Cochran Corbin Award and the first woman soldier since World War II to receive the Silver Star Medal for valor. John S. Gonsalves, founder of "Homes for Our Troops," received the DAR Medal of Honor for his nonprofit efforts to provide specially equipped homes for wounded service members.

PENTAGON PHOTO BY D. MYLES CULLEN

Nights in White Satin

"Being a page means learning the DAR from the inside out," says Mary Kittell, Regent of the Boston Tea Party Chapter in Massachusetts. "Whether it is at the state level or at Continental Congress, the pages help to keep the meetings flowing," she explains. Much like the hand-picked U.S. Marines who stand as silent sentinels guarding the White House and its occupants, these courteous but resolute, well-trained young women ensure that both the Society's Hall and its traditions are respected.

The white "uniforms" of the pages set them apart and distinguish them as the doorkeepers and ushers of the annual assembly. Not only do they lend pageantry to the processions as they carry more than sixty flags in and out of the auditorium for the opening and closing sessions, these skilled hostesses of Congress run errands, help the thousands of attendees enter and exit Constitution Hall, provide directions, hail taxis, hand out programs and news releases, and deliver messages. Because they are literally on their feet from before sunup to long after sundown for the week of Congress, the lighthearted description of a page is "a Daughter with tired feet and helping hands."

The most coveted paging assignments may be as personal assistants to the President General and other key officers and Congressional committees, special roles requiring just the right amount of interaction and discretion. As Kittell emphasizes, "In order to stay one step ahead of the agenda, you have to know the inner workings of the meeting and the organization." But the extra steps as well as homework are worth it, according to Lisa Lents from

PHOTO BY CONVENTION PHOTOGRAPHY SERICES

▲ A signature event at Congress remains the parade of more than sixty flags from all the states and various nations into Constitution Hall. At this moment, pages become part of one of the largest color guards ever assembled. National Page Committee Co-Chairman Holly Lynne McKinley (left) and Tara Lampman Boulden, Vice Chairman, present the United States and NSDAR flags at Congress.

▲ Another Congress event remains the group photo of the President General with all the pages, such as this 2005 photo with President General Presley Wagoner.

the Lady Washington Chapter in Texas, who paged at the 2005 Continental Congress: "My position as personal page for the Congress Program Committee allowed me the great honor of viewing all Congress proceedings from a seat on the platform! I have learned that this is a rare and special treat for any DAR member."

▼ Since the early days of Congress, the NSDAR has hosted an excursion for the hardworking pages who, like all the other Daughters, receive no pay and travel to Washington at their own expense. In this 1925 photo, more than 125 pages at the 34th Continental Congress pause for a group photo in front of the White House as part of a reception held in their honor.

The invitation to serve as a page at Continental Congress comes in a letter from the President General, based on the recommendation of the state regents. Any member between the ages of eighteen and forty is eligible. While ushers were listed in the program for the first Continental Congress in 1892, they were not promoted to pages until the 1900 Congress. The 1906 DAR *Story of the Records* describes them in those early days as "the thirteen young Daughters, our pages, who are annually appointed by the Board, and represent the thirteen original states." Today, many Congress activities would not be able to function without the helping hands of as many as 250 to 300 pages who come from every state, the District of Columbia, and units overseas. Their roles at Continental Congress, state conferences, and special ceremonies throughout the year are also a training ground for developing DAR leaders.

The pages eagerly anticipate one tradition at Congress begun in 1963: the announcement of the Outstanding Junior Member. Chosen from outstanding juniors at the chapter and state levels, she exemplifies a member between the ages of eighteen and thirty-five who has promoted the historical, educational, and

Continued on next page

PHOTO BY CONVENTION PHOTOGRAPHY SERVICES

me something more than regalia. To really understand the DAR, one really needs to participate in Congress and there is no better introduction to Congress than paging."

Jamie Durham, a former C.A.R. member and now a Daughter in the Anthony Smith Chapter in Austin, Texas, emphasizes that her paging experience has played an important role in her life: "Not only did I meet amazing people across the country who have become my friends for life, but that experience has helped to lay the groundwork for the adult I am becoming. I think that if you can get a young woman excited about the DAR, she's hooked for life." A sisterhood within a sisterhood, where, as with their more senior mentors, duty and service remain paramount, they are the building blocks of leadership and commitment, the white-gloved backbone of the Society who will continue to ensure its success.

▼ Four of the approximately three hundred pages at Congress 2005 pause for a close-up. During Congress, pages form a special bond not only with one another but also with past generations of their own families. One of those pictured is Lisa Wood Shapiro (second from left), whose grandmother and great-great-aunt were also Daughters. "Being at Congress was a tangible connection to my ancestors, not just the ones who fought in the Revolution," she explained. Also pictured are (left-right) Cheryl Kaplan, Shapiro, Lisa Brown, and Sarah Layla Voll, all from the Peter Minuit Chapter, New York.

▲ At every Continental Congress, the pages are treated to a special tour or event scheduled especially for them in appreciation of all their long hours and hard work. In this photo from the 2005 Continental Congress, pages pause during a private tour of the United States Capitol.

patriotic objectives of the National Society, as well as participated in community activities. Although not required, the service of each year's Outstanding Junior almost always includes extensive time as a page.

While the pace is grueling, the experience offers unique rewards. Affirms Lisa Lents, who admits she is "nearing the end of 'page age,'" her two years as a page at Congress "have been exciting, fulfilling, fun, and educational." As for the all-white attire, says Lisa Wood Shapiro of the Peter Minuit Chapter in New York, "There was something novel about packing up my 'white wardrobe,' saying good-bye to my husband, my two little children, and heading off to Congress. We live in such casual times, so putting on pins and my page sash, along with my gloves, gave

PHOTO BY CONVENTION PHOTOGRAPHY SERVICES

▲ A longstanding DAR tradition begun at the 1st Continental Congress in 1892 remains the official photo of the members of the Executive Committee. Members of the Wagoner Administration assembled for this 2005 photo at the 114th Continental Congress. Seated (left-right) are Linda Gist Calvin, Recording Secretary General; Gale Jones Fixmer, First Vice President General; President General Presley Merritt Wagoner; Mary Lou Clutter James, Chaplain General; and Al'Louise Suthers Ramp, Corresponding Secretary General; standing (left-right), Linda Barron Wetzel, Curator General; Cindy Segraves Phillips, Historian General; Bea Worden Dalton, Treasurer General; Susan Adams Gonchar, Organizing Secretary General; Shirley Miller Wagers, Registrar General; Vicky Thresher Zuverink, Librarian General; and Eloise Rossiter Clark, Reporter General.

ties and [who] have hardly realized the scope of the society as a whole," noted that first report to Congress in 1899. "On reaching Washington they find a large building filled with earnest women equally interested in patriotic endeavor, but striving to advance the interest of the whole society . . . . The new members invariably go home with a broader outlook and enthusiasm aroused to produce a larger action in their chapters. They arouse public opinion in their localities . . . and almost before it is aware the quietest town is awake to the knowledge that its interests are interwoven with those of the whole body politic."

The solemn traditions of the DAR Continental Congress endure to remind the Daughters of the objectives of the NSDAR, the same ones laid forth at its founding and throughout more than one hundred years of service to the nation. As President Dwight D. Eisenhower stressed during his address of the 63rd Continental Congress on April, 22, 1954, this mission of historic preservation, education, and patriotic endeavor "increases, and keeps alive, and nurtures that dedication to the dignity of man, to the greatness of our country, and the right of every man to walk upright, fearlessly, among his own equals."

▲ Members representing what would become a decade of NSDAR leadership pose in 1984 with President General Sarah M. King, center, and other members of her administration. Ann D. Fleck, standing far left, would succeed King in 1986, followed in 1989 by President General Marie H. Yochim, seated at left.

Formality sets the tone for evening sessions of Congress, but breakfasts, luncheons, teas, committee meetings, and workshops allow the Daughters to roll up their sleeves to share ideas and renew friendships. *Photos by Convention Photography Services*

Meet the Presidents General

Caroline Scott Harrison (Indiana): 1890–1892
Mary Washington Monument in Fredericksburg, Maryland

Letitia Green Stevenson (Illinois): 1893–1895; 1896–1898
Funding for George Washington Monument in Paris, France

Mary Parke McFerson Foster (Indiana): 1895–1896
Jamestown embankments support; Prison Ship Martyrs Monument Fund

Mary Margaretta Fryer Manning (New York): 1898–1901
Memorial Continental Hall, USS *Missouri* steam launch; nurses monument, Arlington National Cemetery. Lafayette statue in Paris, France

Cornelia Cole Fairbanks (Indiana): 1901–1905
Memorial Continental Hall; Prison Ship Martyrs Monument

Emily Nelson Ritchie McLean (New York): 1905–1909
Memorial Continental Hall; DAR-approved schools

Julia Green Scott (Illinois): 1909–1913
Memorial Continental Hall; University of Washington George Washington statue

Daisy Allen Story (New York): 1913–1917
Memorial Continental Hall; Belgian relief

Sarah Elizabeth Mitchell Guernsey (Kansas): 1917–1920
Restoration of Tilloloy, France; war relief for French orphans

Anne Belle Rogers Minor (Connecticut): 1920–1923
Final land purchase for Headquarters complex; first Administration Building; patriotic education at DAR-approved schools.

Lora Haines Cook (Pennsylvania): 1923–1926
Constitution Hall; the war effort; patriotic education at DAR-approved schools

Grace Lincoln Brosseau (Connecticut): 1926–1929
Constitution Hall; Caroline Scott Harrison Memorial

Edith Irwin Hobart (Ohio): 1929–1932
Constitution Hall construction; patriotic education at DAR-approved schools

Edith Scott Magna (Massachusetts): 1932–1935
Retired Constitution Hall debt; patriotic education at DAR-approved schools; Archives Room

Florence Hague Becker (New Jersey): 1935–1938
Memorial Continental Hall elevators; patriotic education at DAR-approved schools

Sarah Corbin Robert (Maryland): 1938–1941
Archives Room; patriotic education at DAR-approved schools

Helena R. Pouch (New York): 1941–1944
National war projects; patriotic education at DAR-approved schools

Mary Erwin Talmadge (Georgia): 1944–1947
National war projects; DAR war bonds ($152,332,213 total)

Estella A. O'Byrne (Indiana): 1947–1950
Patriotic education at DAR-approved schools; expanded Administration Building groundbreaking

Marguerite Courtright Patton (Ohio): 1950–1953
Administration Building; the Memorial Bell Tower at Valley Forge

Gertrude Sprague Carraway (North Carolina): 1953–1956
Administration Building completion; Constitution Hall construction

Allene Wilson Groves (Missouri): 1956–1959
Allene Wilson Groves Cottage for Little Girls; Constitution Hall

Doris Pike White (Maine): 1959–1962
Restoration of the Founders' portraits; auditorium and gymnasium at Kate Duncan Smith DAR School

Marion Moncure Duncan (Virginia): 1962–1965
Expansion and furnishing of DAR Library

Adéle Woodhouse Erb Sullivan (New York): 1965–1968
Sullivan Building air conditioning at Tamassee School; air conditioning in Constitution Hall

Elizabeth J. "Betty" Newkirk Seimes (Delaware): 1968–1971
Constitution Hall air conditioning completion

Eleanor Washington Spicer (California): 1971–1974
Refurnishing Governor's Council Chamber and Assembly Committee Room in Independence Hall

Sara Roddis Jones (Wisconsin): 1974–1975
U.S. Capitol Murals in East Corridor

Jane Farwell Smith (Illinois): 1975–1977
U.S. Capitol Mural project completion

Jeannette Osborn Baylies (New York): 1977–1980
Administration Building expansion

Patricia Walton Shelby (Mississippi): 1980–1983
North portico and Founders Monument repairs

Sarah McKelley King (Tennessee): 1983–1986
Constitution Hall ramp restoration and climate control system; Statue of Liberty restoration

Ann Davidson Duffie Fleck (Massachusetts): 1986–1989
Modification of existing structural building equipment at Constitution Hall; New Immigrants Gallery at Ellis Island

Marie Hirst Yochim (Virginia): 1989–1992
Restoration of DAR Headquarters complex; funding of centennial programs; established NSDAR Second Century Endowment Fund

Wayne Garrison Blair (Ohio): 1992–1995
Constitution Hall restoration and renovation

Dorla Dean Eaton Kemper (California): 1995–1998
Constitution Hall restoration and renovation; Year 2000 technology upgrades; established Heritage Fund

Georgane Ferguson Love Easley (Mississippi): 1998–2001
Extensive remodeling and landscaping of DAR complex grounds; genealogical research seminars

Linda Tinker Watkins (Tennessee): 2001–2004
Digitization project of genealogical records; transformed DAR magazine into two publications

Presley Merritt Wagoner (West Virginia): 2004–2007
Continuation of digitization project; began making genealogical records more accessible through online research system

CHAPTER FIFTEEN

Relevance and Reality
The Legacy Continues

THE FORT CRAILO CHAPTER IN RENSSELAER, NEW YORK, maintains the Knox monument in their area, one of fifty-six markers in New York and Massachusetts that commemorate the 300-mile route followed by General Henry Knox to deliver artillery to General Washington in the winter of 1775–1776. One day, in the summer of 2006, Chapter Regent Kathy Keenan recalls, "Foregoing the usual hats and white gloves, we donned knee pads and gardening clothes to pull weeds, plant flowers, and landscape the monument." A driver passing by stopped and asked the members, "Who are you?" and they explained, "We're the Daughters of the American Revolution." The driver laughed and replied, "My grandmother was DAR, but I don't remember her ever doing anything like this." Replied the Fort Crailo Daughters, "This is the new DAR!"

Just who are the members of this "new DAR"? Molly Ker Hawn, National Chairman of the Public Relations/Motion Picture, Radio and Television Committee, has observed that prospective members who attend meetings "expect tea and crumpets and ladies with white hair." But "that is an outdated picture of our organization," she emphasized. "What they often see now is a young chapter regent with an MBA, someone with lots to do. They meet Daughters who are attorneys, writers, actresses, and architects." As the Utah State DAR Web site proclaims, "DAR members are educators, students, professionals, mothers, historians, genealogists, and homemakers who take an active role in their communities." Observed Daughter Terry Ward, who is also Director of the Registrar General's Department of the NSDAR: "We are every woman. We are every age and every religion. We are Democrats and Republicans and Independents."

▶ Helping to spread awareness and dispel misconceptions about the DAR before even becoming a member herself is Cece George, a fifth grader from Alpharetta, Georgia. Cece's award-winning entry for her social studies fair states, "If you think [the DAR] is a chatty tea party with grandmas, then you're wrong." Her research paper elaborated on the many different service projects DAR members participate in to further the mission of historic preservation, education, and patriotism and draws the conclusion, "The Daughters of the American Revolution is an organization full of active, hard-working women patriots of all ages." Cece may have known a little bit about the DAR prior to her project; she is a member of the C.A.R., and her grandmother, Sallie Mackey, is a member of the Mary Shirley McGuire Chapter in Texas.

▲ Organized in 2004, the Daughters at University of Tennessee Chapter, one of the newest DAR chapters, are also DAR champions. These active chapter members manage to meet their demanding university schedules, as well as promote NSDAR scholarships and ROTC medal awards to their fellow students, support the Kate Duncan Smith DAR School, advocate women's health programs and breast cancer awareness, participate in cancer walks, and support historic preservation of local historic sites, such as the Blount Mansion and John Sevier House.

The challenges of any national nonprofit organization are many, especially one such as the DAR where the members and their chapters are its bedrock. It must fund its mission, communicate effectively at all levels, attract and nurture effective leaders, protect and maintain its resources and properties, and keep up with technology while keeping administrative costs down. Most importantly, however, it must ensure a vital program that appeals to and meets the needs of a rapidly changing society. In 2001, NSDAR established two new committees—the Chapter Development Committee and the Chapter Revitalization Committee—to explore ways to bring the DAR to colleges, retirement communities, corporations, small towns, and subdivisions, and to appeal to working women through more flexible meeting times as well as locations, emphasized Carol S. Rilling, Chapter Development Committee National Chairman. Former Chapter Revitalization National Chairman Beverley G. Bills added, "One of the key messages promoted by this committee was to facilitate the needs and interests of today's busy woman," such as flexibility in programming, as well as meeting times and places. She echoed the sentiment, "This is not your grandmother's DAR!"

The fast-paced culture of the times demands an equally action-packed meeting formula for chapters. The "One Hour Way," the brainstorm of Missouri State Regent Sally Bueno, enforces a prompt start and divides meetings into three sections of no more than twenty minutes in each section to cover reports, program, and chapter business. "It's perfect for working women's chapters and for lunch or breakfast meeting time slots," explained Carol Rilling.

▶ Members of the Pentagon Chapter and others assemble care packages at the Fort Belvoir, Virginia, USO warehouse for troops stationed overseas. The Pentagon Chapter also organized "Project We Care" in conjunction with the Red Cross and nearby Walter Reed Army Medical Center to provide clothing, toiletries, and other items to patients who arrive at the Medical Center, often without even the most basic necessities. The Society organized the Pentagon Chapter of Virginia on July 3, 2003, following the terrorist attack at the Pentagon. The chapter normally holds its meetings at the Pentagon, making it easier for its approximately forty members to attend. Unique to the chapter is its very own coin (inset), a proud tradition of many military units.

◄ While the University of Tennessee Chapter is one of the newest on a college campus, it was not the first. Although no longer in existence, the University of Washington Chapter formed not long after the Society's founding. In this July 4, 1918, photo, Daughters of the University of Washington Chapter march in a "preparedness parade." Such parades were demonstrations against a policy of isolationism regarding U.S. entry into World War I and were a display of public sentiment that the nation must be "prepared" to play a role in the Great War.

▲ Members of the Fort Crailo Chapter in Rensselaer, New York, pause for a photo in the summer of 2006 while tending to the landscaping around the monument marking the route General Henry Knox took to deliver artillery to General Washington.

Marsha Bratton, who in 2002 helped to organize the Lydia Barnes Potter Chapter in Waterford, Michigan, is a "One Hour Way" champion. "We follow the One Hour Way format with great success," she explains. The chapter grew from twenty-five to thirty-eight members in a relatively short period. "After the meeting, one member leaves to go to work, several young mothers get back to their children, and the rest of us congregate around the refreshment table and get to know one another."

One of the newest chapters not only sets the example of the new DAR but is also its own living historic marker of sorts. In 2001, following the terrorist attack on the Pentagon, the Chapter Development Committee proposed the idea of a new chapter as a way for the Society to honor the building and the women who work there. The clear choice for the name was always the "Pentagon Chapter." The name also embraces and welcomes the DAR members, both uniformed and civilian, who work at the Pentagon or support the military in the National Capital Region. By the time it organized in ceremonies on July 3, 2003, forty-four members had signed up; thirty-

▲ Two of the Lady Washington Chapter Daughters in Houston, Texas, are veterans of World War II. Chapter members captured the veterans' memories of service as part of the Library of Congress Veterans History Project, of which the DAR is a founding member. Jeanette Eaton, standing, and Patricia Raymond pause for this 2005 photo following the interviews.

▶ In December 2004, DAR officials hold one of the boxes of original documents and records to be shipped off to Iron Mountain for safe storage, the first to leave the Society's headquarters in almost a century. Pictured are (back row, left to right) Technology Advisory Committee Members Tracy Robinson, Merry Ann Wright, Eric Grundset, Victor Kunze, Darryn Lickliter, Terry Ward, and Committee Chairman Jean Sutton; (front row, left to right) Registrar General Shirley Wagers, President General Presley Wagoner, and Librarian General Vicky Zuverink. The momentous event was the next step in a giant preservation project titled "Preserving our Patriotic Heritage" under the Wagoner Administration and was an extension of Linda Tinker Watkins's President General's Project, "Preserving Our Family Tree." DAR staff and member volunteers have digitized approximately one million member applications and nine million supporting documents so far, and their work on this initiative continues. Digitization now allows electronic access to the records so the increasingly fragile hard copies can be stored and protected in a climate-controlled environment.

▲ Far beyond their link to patriot ancestors, Daughters often pass down their commitment to the Society and its mission from generation to generation, from grandmothers and mothers to younger sisters, daughters, and granddaughters, such as the Gist family. Pictured in 1977 when they all served as pages at the Continental Congress are (left to right) sisters Linda Gist Calvin, Carol Gist Reeder, and Barbara Gist Jaggers. Calvin, Recording Secretary General and a third-generation DAR, was inspired by the dedication of her mother and sisters. Their involvement in DAR has definitely been a family affair. All four served as chapter regent and as California District V Director. The sisters "paged" at state as well as national levels, were California Outstanding Juniors, and served as National Chairmen of the Guest Hospitality Committee.

▶ The Turnbow sisters, all members or prospective members of the Monticello Chapter of the District of Columbia, are descendants of Aaron Grigsby, a colonial seaman and British captive in the Revolutionary War. They include (clockwise from left) Alfreda Turnbow, Acquanetta Anderson, Barbara Rogers, Percie Lee Hines, Rosemary McCray, Gwendolyn Turnbow-Wade, Charlotte Erskines, and Debra Turnbow. Some of their daughters—Levette Foundermire, June Relph Nixon, and Patrice Turnbow—have also joined, and, adds Acquanetta Anderson, "we are in the process of submitting applications for five other nieces." She emphasizes, "My sisters and I joined the Daughters because we are proud of our patriots and their roles and contributions in the founding of our Nation. We also joined because we wanted to join other Daughters in their commitment to preserve our Nation's history and promote patriotism for future generations."

Capturing the
American Spirit

Having grown to 1,306 members by the time it was just two years old, the National Society Daughters of the American Revolution quickly realized that, to keep pace with its rapid growth, some form of official communication between the National Board of Management, chapters, and individual members was critical. For a time, the NSDAR leadership used "Circular Letters" to disseminate information. There were also offers from other leading publications for a "DAR Department," but the National Board felt that such a fast-growing, visible organization needed its own publication.

In May 1892, a resolution was passed authorizing the Board of Management to produce a monthly publication. Only two months later, in July 1892, the Daughters published the first issue of *American Monthly Magazine*, with Ellen Hardin Walworth as its founding editor and manager. The first issue, a soft-cover magazine measuring 5½ by 9 inches, contained a staggering 108 pages, a major publishing feat considering the short time that had elapsed since its initial approval.

The magazine came out just in time for publication of the proceedings of the 1st Continental Congress. While the bulk—a full 88 pages—of that first issue contained the proceedings of both the Congress and the Board of Management, it also featured the biography and photo engraving of Caroline Scott Harrison, short articles on "the Principles of Organization" and the proposed national headquarters building. An editorial by Ellen Walworth explained why the board felt the new publication was necessary and urged member support. Her words must have been quite compelling, for the magazine would become one of the longest continually published periodicals in the United States.

Changing to meet the times, over the next century it would undergo at least fourteen redesigns and at least three name changes, including *Daughters of the American Revolution Magazine* and *National Historical Magazine*. Coverage would expand to include pictures of both Society events and people, articles of historical interest on history or ancestry, and reprints of major addresses given at Continental Congress as well as remarks by prominent leaders. In 1910, the 19th Congress voted to publish the Proceedings in a separate volume.

In 2001, the magazine underwent a transformation, a bold step to provide better service to both members and the public with a newly designed and formatted bimonthly magazine. The newer award-winning publication, with superb layout and design and a new name—*American Spirit*—to match its new look, features well-written and beautifully illustrated stories, from American history to the history of lace making, from well-known to previously unheralded patriots, from education to preservation, and even horticulture. The new format also split information of interest primarily to members into a separate publication, the *Daughters* newsletter.

"It is the best of both worlds, with committee updates, information on the Continental Congress, and state-sponsored ads in the newsletter, as well as a compelling magazine," says Denise Doring VanBuren, Magazine National Chairman and Editor in Chief of both publications. The magazine remains a quality product reflecting what DAR stands for in terms of genealogy, preservation, and an appreciation of the nation's past, she emphasizes, but still with DAR content, such as feature stories on the enormous efforts undertaken by chapters and state offices to preserve historic homes and other sites.

The magazine continues to spotlight today's Daughters, like Helen Eileen Johns, athlete and Daughter, who won a gold medal as part of the 1932 United States Women's Swimming and Diving Team, and who, in 1996, carried the Olympic torch in Columbia, South Carolina. Other Daughters in *American Spirit* headlines include the Honorable Mrs. Mary Claire Hogg, High Court Judge in the British legal system, a Dame of the British Empire, and a member of the Walter Hines Page Chapter in England; speed skating champion Catherine Raney, a member of the Milwaukee Chapter in Wisconsin and three-time member of the U.S. Olympic speed skating team; and Diana Pardue, a member of the Peter Minuit Chapter, New York, who is Director of Museum Services at Ellis Island and the Statue of Liberty National Monument for the National Park Service, and who helped plan and oversee the establishment of the Ellis Island Immigration Museum, which opened in 1990.

Four years in a row now, since 2003, *American Spirit* has taken a top prize in the Awards for Publishing Excellence, or the APEX awards, in feature writing, photography, or layout and design, including the front cover. Other organizations have singled it out for excellence in editorial content, outstanding columns,

▲ ▶ The magazine of the National Society Daughters of the American Revolution has been published continuously since 1892. With no less than fourteen redesigns, numerous name changes, and some seventeen editors in its 100-plus years of publication, the new *American Spirit* continues to evolve to meet the needs of the Society but with a public appeal. Under the guiding hand of the DAR Magazine Chairman and Editor in Chief Denise VanBuren, the magazine staff at NSDAR headquarters works closely with the publisher, Hammock Publishing in Nashville, Tennessee, to produce an award-winning magazine attractive to both readers and advertisers.

and personal profiles. In selecting it for the APEX "Grand Award for Magazines and Journals," judges described it as including "Spectacular photography and illustrations . . . each different than the last, yet all coming together into a coherent whole to showcase fascinating articles, each marvelously written and superbly researched." Says VanBuren proudly, "Clearly the DAR has a world-class historical magazine, much the same as it has a world-class genealogical library and museum." The magazine also appears more and more on library and school shelves.

A great archive of DAR and general history, the magazine's success and appeal endure because it also remains true to the DAR mission of patriotism, education, and preservation. But also like the Daughters, *American Spirit* continues to evolve, remaining an educational, informative publication for both the Daughters and the public, but with fresh new perspectives on history and the people who made and continue to make it.

▶ Pazetta Mallette and her daughter, Pazetta Ann, credit the DAR with opening new worlds for them. Urged to join the DAR by her family pediatrician's wife in 1996, Pazetta Mallette's research into her genealogy revealed to her the significant role Native Americans as well as African Americans played in the Revolution, something even as a retired educator Mallette had not found in the history books. Mallette notes that the DAR experience has "worked wonders" for her somewhat shy daughter, a librarian assistant at Vanderbilt. "She has paged at Congress for four years now, including as personal page for the President General. She loves going to Washington, loves paging. It's been a beautiful experience for both of us." Both joined through the Belle Meade Chapter, Nashville, Tennessee.

▲ During the annual Christmas Open House, a member of the DAR staff leads a bilingual tour highlighting some of America's treasures on display in the DAR building for a group of adult English-as-a-second-language students. Such tours make the DAR Museum, period rooms, and special displays more meaningful to a broader audience.

PHOTO COURTESY OF PATTY STRECKER

nine of those were new to the NSDAR. As a convenience to members, the Pentagon Chapter holds its monthly meetings in the building it honors.

Named for the river that sustained Arizona pioneers, the Agua Fria Chapter in Sun City, Arizona, took the Society in another "new" direction more than forty years ago. Organized in 1961, it became the first DAR chapter established in a retirement community. Its approximately ninety members include several with sixty or more years of service. In addition to traditional chapter projects, their monthly meetings include programs on history as well as topics of particular interest to their members, such as fraud and identity theft.

The Women's Issues Committee, established in 2001, provides support for members in other ways, offering program ideas for chapter meetings on such topics as stress management, women's heart health, benefits of exercise, starting a new career, using the Internet, and even coping with difficult people. The committee's yearly essay contest encourages members to share their experiences with challenges likely faced by all women. "The essays have been healing to the members who wrote them and other members as well, for so many have faced career and health issues, the loss of a child

▲ Although DAR members both in and out of uniform have served the military since the Society's founding, member Patty Strecker of Longmont, Colorado, jokes, "maybe I overdid it a bit with the patriotism." All three of her daughters, all of whom are also Daughters of the Society, have committed to careers in the U.S. Army. Pictured here, mom Patty Strecker pins Laura Strecker's second lieutenant bars at her commissioning ceremony in 2006. Laura is an Army nurse serving at Brooke Army Medical Hospital in San Antonio, Texas. Her sister, Captain Sarah Strecker, graduated from West Point and is currently stationed in Kuwait. The newest recruit, their younger sister Julie, received a full scholarship through the Reserve Officers' Training Corps at Marquette University, a program Laura completed in 2005 at St. John's University.

or loved one, or their lives have been affected by the war," explained Linda Gist Calvin, Recording Secretary General and Executive Liaison to the Long-Range Planning Commission that looks at such programs to ensure their member appeal. She pointed out that the various NSDAR committees are not devoted exclusively to the Society's service to the public. Some of them are specifically targeted to help the members, she explained.

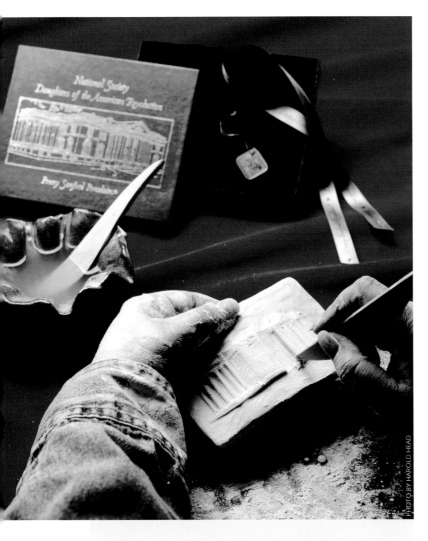

▲ The talented hands of sculptor and Daughter Penny Sanford Fikes, shown here, fashion a commemorative ornament capturing the architectural detail of Memorial Continental Hall. A member of the Thomas Rodney Chapter in Winona, Mississippi, Fikes is a nationally known porcelain artist whose company, Penny Sanford Porcelains, now trains other artisans. The former award-winning news director of a tri-states radio station, Fikes specializes in "portraits in porcelain" of historic buildings around the country for preservation fundraising, including Rosalie Mansion owned by the Mississippi Daughters. Her Nature's Angels series is prized by collectors in the United States and overseas. The National Museum of Women in the Arts in Washington, D.C., inducted her into their Archives of Women Artists from around the world in 2005.

Other innovations link Daughters like never before. The Internet allows almost instant communication between members at all levels and time zones, including overseas. It also expands the Continental Congress experience for Daughters who cannot attend in person. *Congress Live!* provides real-time viewing of Congress events via Webcams while the *Congress*

Herald, the daily newsletter of Continental Congress, is published online.

The Society also takes advantage of the latest technology to safeguard its priceless Museum, Library, and Americana collections with state-of-the-art, climate-controlled facilities. And technology is making these holdings more accessible than ever before, especially in the Library, where computerized databases allow both members and guests to browse various collections. The NSDAR Web site already features virtual tours of its thirty-one period rooms and the Yochim Gallery, while emerging technology such as digitized imagery will also one day provide increased access to electronic images of the Museum and Americana collections for researchers and for those who cannot view the various NSDAR exhibits and collections in person.

Not all "new" features at the NSDAR are electronic. Exciting new additions to the Museum, Library, and Americana collections constantly expand the range of artifacts as well as information available in all three of these priceless holdings. In January 2007, the Americana Collection acquired items pertaining to Revolutionary War General Henry Knox. They include thirty letters and an autobiographical manuscript written by Knox's daughter, Lucy Knox Thatcher. Letters between Knox and his wife Lucy, sister Hannah, brother William, and daughters Lucy and Caroline reveal intimate insights to this very public figure in America's independence. These and other documents in the collection will be featured in an exhibit planned by the Historian General's Office to highlight family correspondence written during the Revolutionary War era.

It is not only the pragmatic programs that are attracting new Daughters. Research by Workforce Management, which specializes in human resource trends, indicates that this generation's workers are "talented, educated, techno-savvy, open-minded, service-oriented young people" who are driven by a "chance to play meaningful roles in meaningful work that helps others." Honorary Missouri State Regent Carole Farmer, a retired educator who joined as a junior in 1959, firmly believes the DAR fills that niche for many women. What keeps her so involved is realizing the DAR is the only organization of its magnitude that supports all three goals of education, historic preservation, and patriotism. "I don't know of any other [organization] that does all three," she points out, "and it appeals to all different age groups." Cheryl Yearty, member of the Esther Reed Chapter in Spokane, Washington, echoes that belief. "I am a Daughter because I share these values and goals with capable, intelligent, dedicated women who are united in working to protect our heritage and to teach others to do the same," she wrote in an article for the July/August 2000 issue of *Daughters of the American Revolution Magazine.*

▲ Member Jan Zermeno, a former elementary school-teacher, gets a group hug from some of the children she tutors as part of Operation Hope, a nonprofit organization she founded with her husband, Jesse. More than a decade ago, Jesse Zermeno, himself a Mexican immigrant, began collecting old clothes, shoes, and furniture from customers in his carpet-cleaning business and distributing them to the needy. Their efforts spread, eventually becoming a full-fledged charitable organization. In addition to tutoring students of all ages in English, math, and computer skills, Operation Hope's four employees and thousands of volunteers each year provide more than ten thousand immigrant families in central Florida with food, clothing, furniture, and toys. In 2005, the organization received the Jefferson Award, one of the highest honors awarded by the American Institute of Public Service. Jan Zermeno, a member of the Abigail Wright Chamberlin Chapter in Melbourne, Florida, is the chief executive officer of Operation Hope.

Olympic speed skater Catherine Raney, age twenty-five, credits her love of country for inspiring her to do her best in international competitions. During one event, when her team had not done well, she remembers, "I wanted to quit, but then I realized that when you're racing as an American, you're not only there representing yourself, you're representing your country, too." Raney, a member of the Milwaukee Chapter in Wisconsin shared the importance of her DAR membership with Lena Basha, author of an article in the May/June 2006 *American Spirit*: "My membership is a very big deal to me and my family. I think it's important to remember our heritage and continue the tradition."

Women join the DAR to make a difference; they remain, in large measure, for the sense of community it provides. Lisa Lents, a Junior member of the Lady Washington Chapter in Houston, Texas, recently wrote, "When I joined the DAR just four years ago, I knew that I would enjoy the historical aspect of it and that I had a lot to offer to the charitable causes it supports. What I did not know was all that it would do for me in return. I have made countless numbers of girlfriends, 'moms,' 'aunts,' and even 'grandmas.'"

The DAR experience builds bridges of understanding between the members and the public. Pazetta Mallette, of both Native American and African American descent and a member of the Belle Meade Chapter, Nashville, Tennessee, relishes the opportunity to share the contributions of her ancestors at other DAR chapters and at local schools. "After other members learned about me, different chapters invited me to give programs on Native Americans, and I so much enjoy sharing," she noted with pride. Mallette also enjoyed dispelling myths in her role as Chapter Regent, such as when she visited a local high school to present a DAR Good Citizen Award. "When this African American person showed up representing the DAR, they were

▲ Waving the Stars and Stripes on a grand scale, a contingent of Daughters participates in Fourth of July celebrations in the nation's capital in 2005. The DAR has participated in the national event every year since the attacks on America in 2001. "We wanted to make a statement that this organization has the American spirit," said President General Watkins at the time. A similar picture from the 2002 event was featured in the week-long ABC television series *In Search of America* with Peter Jennings, as well as a companion book written by Peter Jennings and Todd Brewster.

▲ Some of the Daughters kick up their heels during the final reception at the close of Continental Congress.

stunned. And they didn't know Native Americans fought in the Revolutionary War. I realized that we need to educate the public, and I think DAR plays a big role in that."

There is an irony in a closer examination of this "new DAR," for the founders and early members were also career women—teachers, lawyers, political leaders, medical professionals, and pioneers in their fields—dedicated to making a difference in the world around them while raising families. Wrote Letitia G. Stevenson, founding member and second President General, in her *Brief History Daughters of the American Revolution* in 1911: "These women were of an unusual type and rarely gifted. Their patriotism was beyond question. They possessed in eminent degree the strong and sturdy characteristics of their forbears: courage, persistence, belief in themselves, and faith in whatever cause they espoused. Their services can not be computed by figures or in dollars or cents, but the monument of their works will be ever enduring."

The founders of the Society were products of the Progressive Era, a time of service when "throughout the country, Americans tried to figure out ways to make society work better for all," wrote historian Robert D. Johnston in *The Making of America*. But the pendulum swung sharply back to a more conservative icon of womanhood after they won the right to vote and the extremes of Prohibition were lifted. Femininity replaced feminism, and society as a whole became more conservative. The membership of the DAR reflected those times, but, as with society, it continues to evolve.

What continues to unite the Daughters is a shared commitment to the Society's mission, just as a shared credence in the rights of individuals to govern themselves united the patriots of the Revolution despite their different backgrounds, beliefs, and livelihoods. In her report in the 1893 issue of the DAR *American Monthly* magazine, Historian General Mary Lockwood wrote, "I was asked by a representative woman a few days since, 'What have you Daughters of the American Revolution accomplished, and what are you doing now, and what do you expect to do in the future?' My answer is: We are going to cherish, maintain, and extend the institutions of American freedom. We are going to foster patriotism and love of country. We are going to aid in securing for mankind all the blessings of liberty, and that, it seems to me, covers the law and the gospel."

At the unveiling of the Founders Memorial Monument, President General Grace Brosseau likened the beckoning arms of the figure to the appeal of the Society, an "appeal to carry on despite all obstacles and discouragements, to see no bitterness or pain in service but only its joy and beauty, and to work unitedly in the well-loved cause." Honorary President General Dorla Kemper emphasized in a recent interview, "education, preservation, and patriotism will last forever. These simple things—all about service—are the enduring focus of the DAR and are going to keep us strong through the years."

The attacks on America in 2001 spawned a wave of patriotism that knit the nation in a cause as clear as the fever of revolution in 1776. Denise Doring VanBuren, National Chairman of the DAR Magazine Committee, notes that there were "times when the popularity of the DAR waxed and waned, times when it wasn't the 'in' thing to be proud of patriotism, [yet] we have been there as a constant in American history," she continues, "reminding all American citizens of how special this country is, their rights and responsibilities as citizens, and reminding them to celebrate their history." In a letter to Daughters during her term as President General from 2001 to 2004, Linda Tinker Watkins said, "As a Society, we've been re-energized by the resurgence in American patriotism, and there's never been a more exciting time to be a member of our dynamic organization."

PHOTO BY DOUGLAS G. ASHLEY

▲ Christine Reiner (top) of Troy, Michigan, Registrar for the Piety Hill Chapter, picks up a few pointers from Ardis McLeod, State Registrar of Michigan and a member of the Sarah Ann Cochrane Chapter, as she does genealogy research in the DAR Library during the 2006 Continental Congress. During the annual DAR gathering, the Library is reserved for the use of the approximately three thousand who attend each year. Otherwise, it is open Monday through Saturday to the general public.

As Honorary President General Letitia G. Stevenson wrote in 1911, "The National Society was great in its inception, was great in its organization, has been great in its achievements, and its future is great in promise." The DAR continues to hold closely to the tenets captured in the minutes of the Society's first formal meeting:

Before the meeting was closed those present resolved to use their minds, their hearts, and their means to perpetuate the memory of the spirit of the men and women who achieved American Independence; to encourage patriotism, and engen-

◄ In the spring of 2007, more than thirty Daughters from various Texas DAR chapters came together for a naturalization ceremony in Houston to welcome new U.S. citizens. The Texas State Regent Lynn F. Young (second from right) led the Pledge of Allegiance at the ceremony of over one hundred new citizens. The DAR also hosted a reception to congratulate the families following the ceremony and handed out homemade treats, gift bags, and American flags. Also pictured are (left-right) Gina Bouchard, Leslie Powers, Pamela Marshall, (Young), and Jill Brooks.

der the spirit of Americanism; to teach patriotism by erecting monuments and protecting historical spots, by observing historical anniversaries, by promoting the cause of education, especially the study of history, the enlightenment of our foreign population, and all that makes for good citizenship—especially emphasizing education as the great National obligation, the Country's duty to the children who will some day be the rulers of the Nation; by the preservation of documents and relics, and of the records of the individual services of soldiers and patriots.

The nontraditional, strong-minded founders defied convention to build a framework for volunteerism that remains a legacy. The continued success of the Daughters of the American Revolution for well over a century speaks volumes for the vision of its founders and leaders and the commitment of the nearly one million members who have joined since 1890. As President General Presley Merritt Wagoner points out, "Our organization is simply lineage-based, without regard for race, religion, or political affiliation. Diversity gives us strength and helps us to achieve our mission to promote education, historic preservation, and patriotism."

The NSDAR, symbolized by the beckoning, outstretched arms of the Founders Memorial Monument, welcomes all eligible women to become Daughters, whose greatest legacy remains their continued commitment to preserve and perpetuate

▲ This potential new DAR recruit playfully points to the highlights of the proceedings of the 113th Continental Congress.

the American treasures embodied in the artifacts of its past, the blessings of education for its citizens, and the promise of freedom.

▲ These elegantly appointed bronze doors are one of three sets at the former main entrance to Memorial Continental Hall. After the construction of Constitution Hall and the Administration Building, the main entrance shifted to the side of the building. Made of both cast and sheet bronze, they feature cast eagle beaks holding massive door pulls. The central set was presented as a memorial to the founders and charter members; Connecticut and Massachusetts presented the north and south sets. Appropriately, Pennsylvania—the Keystone State—funded the keystone in each of the arches above the leaded glass fanlights. While no longer in frequent use, the doors have taken on their own historic significance and are carefully maintained by the Daughters, as are so many structures and sites important to American history. They stand as symbols of the enduring mission of the Society as it continues to evolve to meet the needs of members and the public. Regardless of their location, the doors to the NSDAR Headquarters welcome members and visitors to the Museum, Library, and Americana collections, just as the DAR welcomes all those eligible to join.

Selected Bibliography

This bibliography is by no means a complete record of all the works and sources consulted during research for this work. In addition to more than forty interviews, reference resources included scores of unpublished documents, letters, reports, and other imprints in the DAR archives as well as those listed below. In most cases, sources quoted have been cited throughout the text. Therefore, the works listed here are for the convenience of those who wish to pursue further research.

Books and pamphlets:

Anderson, Peggy. *The Daughters: An Unconventional Look at America's Fan Club—The DAR.* New York: St. Martin's Press, 1974.

Baker, Jean H. *Sisters: The Lives of America's Suffragists.* New York: Hill and Wang, 2005.

Brownstone, David M., Irene M. Franck, and Douglass Brownstone. *Island of Hope, Island of Tears.* United States: Barnes & Noble, 2000.

Carroll, Andrew, ed. *Letters of a Nation.* Foreword by Marian Wright Edelman. New York: Broadway Books, 1999. Originally published New York: Kodansha America, 1977.

Chenoweth, Lillian, Adella R. Kuhner, Cecil Norton Broy, and Catherine A. Newton. *D.A.R. Buildings in the Nation's Capital.* Washington: N.S.D.A.R., 1951.

Collins, Gail. *America's Women: Four Hundred Years of Dolls, Drudges, Helpmates, and Heroines.* New York: HarperCollins, 2003.

Darwin, Gertrude Bascom, Georgia Stockton Hatcher, Anita Newcomb McGee, and Susan Riviere Hetzel. *Report of the Daughters of the American Revolution: 1890 to 1897.* Washington: Government Printing Office, 1899.

Felder, Deborah G. *A Century of Women: The Most Influential Events in Twentieth-Century Women's History.* Secaucus: Carol Publishing Group, 1999.

Garrett, Elisabeth Donaghy, *The Arts of Independence.* Washington: N.S.D.A.R., 1985.

Hunter, Ann Arnold. *A Century of Service: The Story of the DAR.* Washington: N.S.D.A.R., 1991.

Johnston, Robert D. *The Making of America: The History of the United States from 1492 to the Present.* Foreword by Laura Bush. Washington: National Geographic Society, 2002.

Johnston, Robert D., Glenda Glimore, Matthew Jacobson, James Gregory, Paul Boyer, David Oshinsky, Clayborne Carson, Susan J. Douglas, Michael Kazin, and Gaddis Smith. *National Geographic Eyewitness to the 20th Century.* Washington: National Geographic Society, 2001.

Keiler, Allan. *Marian Anderson: A Singer's Journey.* Chicago: University of Illinois Press, 2002. Originally published New York: Scribner, 2000.

Lockwood, Mary Smith and Emily Lee Sherwood Ragan. *Story of the Records, D.A.R.* Washington: George E. Howard, 1906.

Millard, Candice. *The River of Doubt: Theodore Roosevelt's Darkest Journey.* New York: Doubleday, 2005.

Miller, James and John Thompson. *Almanac of American History.* Washington: National Geographic Society, 2006.

Nash, Gary B. *The Unknown American Revolution: The Unruly Birth of Democracy and the Struggle to Create America.* New York: Viking, 2005.

National Society Daughters of the American Revolution. *Preserving the American Spirit in the DAR Museum.* Virginia Beach, VA: Donning Co. Publishers, 2006.

National Society of the Daughters of the American Revolution and United States Capitol Historical Society. *The American Story in Art: The Murals of Allyn Cox in the U.S. Capitol.* Washington: N.S.D.A.R., 1986.

Roberts, Cokie. *Founding Mothers: The Women Who Raised Our Nation.* New York: HarperCollins, 2004.

Somerville, Mollie. *Historic and Memorial Buildings of the Daughters of the American Revolution*. Washington: N.S.D.A.R., 1979.

———. *In Washington: The National Society Daughters of the American Revolution*. Washington: N.S.D.A.R., 1965.

———. *Washington Historic Landmarks: Pillars of Patriotism*. Washington: N.S.D.A.R., 1985.

———. *Washington Landmark: A View of the DAR–The Headquarters, History and Activities*. Washington: N.S.D.A.R., 1976.

Stevenson, Mrs. Adlai E. *Brief History, Daughters of the American Revolution*. Washington: N.S.D.A.R., 1913. Reprinted by Elizabeth Stevenson Ives, Bloomington: 1991

Treese, Lorett. *Valley Forge: Making and Remaking a National Symbol*. University Park: Pennsylvania State University Press, 1995.

Washington, Eugenia. *History of the Origin of the Society*. Washington: N.S.D.A.R., 1895.

Young, Dwight, Ian Frazier, Thomas Mallon, Henry Petroski, Francine Prose, Ray Suarez, and Phyllis Theroux. *Saving America's Treasures*. Foreword by Hillary Rodham Clinton. Washington: National Geographic Society and National Trust for Historic Preservation, 2001.

Zieger, Susan. *In Uncle Sam's Service: Women Workers with the American Expeditionary Force, 1917–1919*. Philadelphia: Cornell University Press, 1999.

Periodicals:

Crews, Ed. "Hercules of the American Revolution: Peter Francisco." *Colonial Williamsburg* Vol. 28, No. 4 (Autumn 2006), 20–25.

Guilderson, Paul, ed. *DAR Constitution Hall News*. Various articles, 2000–2006.

Daughters of the American Revolution Magazine, *American Spirit* (previously published under other names) 1892–2007.

Daughters of the American Revolution Newsletter. Supplement to N.S.D.A.R. *American Spirit*, 2001–2007.

Dobyns, Lloyd. "Revolutionary City." *Colonial Williamsburg* Vol. 28, No. 4 (Autumn 2006), 26–35.

Web sites:

In addition to those sites listed below, much of the information used in this work was found at the thousands of individual Web sites maintained by DAR state organizations and chapters.

American Composers Orchestra. "How to Write an American Symphony: Amy Beach and the birth of 'Gaelic' Symphony." http://www.americancomposers.org/beach_article.htm (accessed March 20, 2006).

American Red Cross. "World War I Accomplishments of the American Red Cross." http://www.redcross.org/museum/history/ww1a.asp (accessed August 7, 2006).

American Revolution.com. Various articles. http://www.americanrevolution.com/ (accessed 2005, 2006, 2007).

American Revolution, The. "Continental Army." http://www.myrevolutionarywar.com/campaigns/continental%20army.htm (accessed November 19, 2006).

American Studies at the University of Virginia. "City Beautiful: The 1901 Plan for Washington D.C." http://xroads.virginia.edu/~CAP/CITYBEAUTIFUL/dchome.html (accessed May 5, 2005).

Ancestry.com. "Building Bridges: Recognition of a Pioneering Engineer." http://www.ancestry.com/learn/library/article.aspx?article=2820 (accessed March 16, 2006).

Ancient Burying Ground Association, The, Hartford. "The Ancient Burying Ground History." http://theancientburyingground.org/history.html (accessed August 29, 2006).

Architect of the Capitol. "Frances E. Willard." http://www.aoc.gov/cc/art/nsh/willard.cfm (accessed March 30, 2006).

Arkansas.gov. "The Journey Began in Arkansas." http://www.lapurchase.org/ (accessed June 22, 2006).

Arkansas State Parks. "Louisiana Purchase State Park." http://www.arkansasstateparks.com/parks/park.asp?id=37 (accessed July 2, 2006).

Arlington National Cemetery. "Anita Newcomb McGee." http://www.arlingtoncemetery.net/anitanew.htm (accessed March 18, 2006).

———. "Jane Arminda Delano." http://www.arlingtoncemetery.net/jadelano.htm (accessed March 25, 2006).

Berkshire Web. "Welcome to D.A.R. State Forest." http://www.berkshireweb.com/sports/parks/dar.html (accessed July 10, 2006).

Centennial Exposition. Answers.com. *The Reader's Companion to American History.* Eric Foner and John A. Garraty, ed., published by Houghton Mifflin Company. http://www.answers.com/topic/centennial-exposition (accessed January 12, 2006).

Coley, Jeannette Cabell. "A Biography of Charles Ellet, Jr." CivilWarStudies.org. Presented by The Smithsonian Associates. http://civilwarstudies.org/articles/Vol_5/charlesellet.htm (accessed March 16, 2006).

College of Staten Island City University of New York Program of Women's Studies. "Gertrude Vanderbilt Whitney." http://www.library.csi.cuny.edu/dept/history/lavender/386/gvanderb.html (accessed March 14, 2006).

Department of Conservation and Recreation, Massachusetts. "DAR State Forest." http://www.mass.gov/dcr/parks/western/darf.htm (accessed July 10, 2006).

Encyclopedia Britannica's Guide to Women's History. "300 Women Who Changed the World." http://search.eb.com/women (accessed throughout 2005, 2006).

Flag of the United States of America, The. "The American's Creed." http://www.usflag.org/americancreed.html (accessed August 27, 2006).

Georgetown University Libraries Special Collections. http://www.library.georgetown.edu/dept/speccoll/ (accessed May 11, 2006).

George Washington's Fredericksburg Foundation. "The Gordon Family Cemetery." http://www.kenmore.org/gordon_family/gordon_cemetery.html (accessed February 11, 2006).

———. "The Mary Washington Monument." http://www.kenmore.org/WashingtonFamilyInfo/monument.html (accessed February 9, 2006).

Ginger Rogers Official Site. "About Ginger Rogers." http://www.gingerrogers.com/about/bio.html (accessed March 19, 2006).

Harvard University Library Open Collections Program. "Women Working, 1800–1930: Catherine Filene Shouse." http://ocp.hul.harvard.edu/ww/people_shouse.html (accessed March 23, 2006).

Hindman Settlement School. "Mission & History." http://www.hindmansettlement.org/about_us/mission.html (accessed April 10, 2006).

Historic Opera. "American Sampler." http://www.historicopera.com/jseries_english_sampler1.htm (accessed September 14, 2006).

Horatio Alger Association. "The Horatio Alger Association of Distinguished Americans." http://www.horatioalger.com/members.cfm (accessed September 16, 2006).

Infoplease. "Edith Nourse Rogers." http://www.infoplease.com/ipa/A0878995.html (accessed March 22, 2006).

Kate Duncan Smith DAR School. Various articles. http://www.kdsdar.com/ (accessed April 12, 2006).

Library of Congress. Prints and Photographs Division. http://www.loc.gov/rr/print/ (accessed throughout 2005, 2006, 2007).

———. Veterans History Project. http://www.loc.gov/vets/about.html (accessed July 24, 2006).

Minnesota Historic Sites. "Sibley House Historic Site." http://www.mnhs.org/places/sites/shs/index.html (accessed June 28, 2006).

Montgomery, Liza, review of *Period Rooms in the Metropolitan Museum of Art,* by James Parker and Amelia Peck. http://www.antiquesandthearts.com/bookreview.asp?var=122 (accessed June 21, 2006).

Mountain Monthly. "Cloudcroft Founding Father Series: John Arthur Eddy." http://www.mountainmonthly.com/eddy.html (accessed October 10, 2006).

Natchez Trace Parkway. "Explore the Natchez Trace." http://www.scenictrace.com/ (accessed July 2, 2006).

National Coalition to Save Our Mall. "History of the Mall: The 19th Century and the McMillan Plan of 1901–1902." http://www.savethemall.org/mall/resource-hist03.html (accessed May 5, 2006).

National Park Service. "Cumberland Gap." http://www.nps.gov/cuga/ (accessed July 6, 2006).

———. "Natchez Trace." http://www.nps.gov/natr/ (accessed July 2, 2006).

————. "Theodore Roosevelt National Park: Maltese Cross Cabin."
http://www.nps.gov/archive/thro/tr_cabin.htm (accessed June 22, 2006).

————. "Valley Forge." http://www.nps.gov/vafo/ (accessed July 20, 2006).

National Society Daughters of the American Revolution. Various articles. http://www.dar.org/
(accessed throughout 2005, 2006, 2007).

National Symphony Orchestra's 75th Anniversary Website. "National Symphony Orchestra Anniversary Selected
Highlights." http://www.kennedy-center.org/nso/history/75th/feature/open_feature.html (accessed
September 2006).

National Women's Hall of Fame. Web site design, development and hosting provided by Choice One
Communications. Various articles. http://www.greatwomen.org/women.php (accessed February,
March 2006).

Naval Historical Center. "Rear Admiral Grace Murray Hopper, USNR."
http://www.history.navy.mil/photos/pers-us/uspers-h/g-hoppr.htm (accessed June 1, 2006).

New River Notes. "The Red Cross Magazine: The Red Cross War Council, July 1917."
http://www.newrivernotes.com//ww1/redcross.htm (accessed August 7, 2006).

Notable Women Ancestors. "Margaret Cochran Corbin." http://www.rootsweb.com/~nwa/corbin.html
(accessed February 1, 2006).

Office of Medical History, U.S. Army Nurse Corps. "The Army Nurse Corps in the War with Spain."
http://history.amedd.army.mil/ANCWebsite/anchhome.html (accessed July 29, 2006).

Official Virginia Mayo Site. "Biography." http://www.virginiamayo.com/index.htm (accessed March 20, 2006).

O'Maxfield, Karen. Studio O'Maxfield. "Center Church & Ancient Burying Ground."
http://hartford.omaxfield.com/ancient.html (accessed April 2, 2006).

Raptor Project, The. "About Jonathan Wood." http://www.raptorproject.com/johnbio.htm
(accessed August 29, 2006).

Revolutionary War. "Revolutionary War Casualties." http://www.revolutionary-war.info/casualties/
(accessed July 6, 2006).

River Bend. "About Carlsbad." http://www.lakeviewchristian.com/Riverbend/demo.htm (accessed
October 10, 2006).

Rocherolle.com. "Eugenie Ricau Rocherolle." http://www.rocherolle.com/bio.html (accessed March 22, 2006).

San Diego Unified School District. "The History of Fort Kearny."
http://www2.sandi.net/kearny/history/swk/fk.html (accessed September 5, 2006).

Santa Fe Trail Scenic and Historic Byway. "Sites of Trinidad on the Santa Fe Trail Mountain Branch: Largest DAR Marker."
http://www.santafetrailscenicandhistoricbyway.org/sitetrin.html (accessed July 1, 2006).

Stennis Center for Public Service. "Southern Women in Public Service: Corinne 'Lindy' Clairborne Boggs."
http://www.stennis.gov/boggs.htm (accessed February 17, 2006).

Travelers' Rest Preservation and Heritage Association. "Travelers' Rest." http://www.travelersrest.org/
(accessed July 3, 2006).

Trinklein, Mike, and Steve Boettcher. "The Oregon Trail: Introduction."
http://www.isu.edu/%7Etrinmich/Introduction.html (accessed July 3, 2006).

U-S-History.com. "Harding and Foreign Affairs: Washington Naval Conference, November 1921–February 1922."
http://www.u-s-history.com/pages/h1354.html (accessed June 17, 2006).

Ushistory.org. Created and hosted by Independence Hall Association. "Historic Valley Forge: Who Served Here?"
http://www.ushistory.org/valleyforge/served/index.html (accessed October 30, 2006).

Wikipedia. "American Revolutionary War: Casualties."
http://en.wikipedia.org/wiki/American_revolutionary_war#Casualties (accessed July 6, 2006).

————. "Centennial Exposition." http://en.wikipedia.org/wiki/Centennial_Exposition (accessed September 29, 2006).

Women In Military Service For America Memorial. "About the Memorial."
http://www.womensmemorial.org/About/welcome.html (accessed July 24, 2006).

WomenOf.com. "WomanOf the Month: Marsha J. Evans." http://www.womenof.com/Articles/wm_3_8_04.asp
(accessed March 22, 2006).

Index

About the Author

Editor of more than twenty books, author Diana L. Bailey has thirty years of experience as both a writer and editor. She retired with nearly thirty-eight years of federal service in the field of public relations. Her previous books include *The Mayflower: Washington's Second Best Address* and *My First Seventy Years in Golf*, the biography of golfing legend Chandler Harper. Her essays have been broadcast on public radio in Richmond, Virginia, and published in the *Virginian-Pilot*. She lives with her family in Virginia Beach, Virginia.